URBAN PUBLIC DEBTS

URBAN GOVERNMENT AND THE MARKET FOR ANNUITIES IN WESTERN EUROPE (14th-18th CENTURIES)

SEUH

III

Studies in European Urban History (1100-1800)

Series Editor

Marc BOONE

Urban Public Debts

Urban Government and the Market for Annuities in Western Europe (14th - 18th centuries)

M. Boone, K. Davids, P. Janssens (eds.)

BREPOLS

Under the auspices of the 'Interuniversity Attraction Poles Programme (Phase V nr. 10) - Belgian State - Federal Office for Scientific, Technical and Cultural Affairs' Programme

Illustration de couverture: Il Camarlingo si lave le mani, la Vergine protegge Siena Scuola di sano di pietro 1451 (Siena, Archivo di Stato, 29)

D/2003/0095/155

ISBN 2-503-51383-2

Printed in the E.U. on acid-free paper

Contents

Acknowledgements

The present volume is the direct result of a colloquium organised at the University of Ghent on November 23-24, 2001, in the context of a joint Flemish-Dutch research project funded by both the Dutch (NWO) and Flemish (FWO-Vlaanderen) organisations for scientific research in the context of a VNC (Vlaams-Nederlands comité) research project entitled *'Burgers, geld en stadsbesturen. Vergelijkende studies over de relatie tussen overheid, burgerij en stadsfinanciën in de Lage Landen tussen ca. 1400 en 1700'* (Burghers, money and city-governments. A comparative study of the relation among government, bourgeoisie and city-finances in the Low Countries between 1400 and 1700), conducted by research teams of the University of Ghent (M. Boone), the Catholic University of Brussels (P. Janssens) and the Free University of Amsterdam (K. Davids). Both administrations, NWO and FWO-Vlaanderen, the latter in the person of its secretary-general J. Traest, are to be thanked for the generous funding of both the project and the conference.

Several colleagues, who for different reasons do not appear in the ranks of the authors, actively participated however in the conference: as chairs of sessions or commentators like prof. dr. Wim Blockmans (University of Leiden, NIAS), prof. dr. Bruno Blondé (University of Antwerp), prof. dr. Stephan Epstein (London School of Economics), prof. dr. Maarten Prak (University of Utrecht), em. prof. dr. Walter Prevenier (University of Ghent). Others took active part in the discussions; their presence and the comments they made have helped to improve the texts presented in this book. Among them we would like to mention Karel Degryse, Bernd Fuhrmann, Joost Jonker and Peter Stabel.

While preparing the texts for publication the editors received very precious help from Susie Speakman Sutch (University of California, Berkeley) and Elodie Lecuppre-Desjardin (University of Ghent) who gave most welcome support with the correction of texts written by non-native speakers in English and French respectively. Claudine Colyn (University of Ghent, Department of Mediaeval History) and Jo De Groote (Centre for Public Finances, EHSAL, Brussels) gave valuable administrative support during the conference and during the preparation of the proceedings for publication.
Finally, the editors were happy to find the editors of the series '*Studies in European Urban History (1100-1800)*' (SEUH) willing to accept this collection of essays as part of a new series with the publisher Brepols (Turnhout, Belgium) started by the IAP (Interuniversity Attraction Poles-programme funded by the Federal office for Scientific, Technical and Cultural Affairs - OSTC of the Belgian government) Phase V nr. 10 directed by M. Boone (University of Ghent) in collaboration with the research teams of Leiden University, the ULB (Université Libre de Bruxelles), the University of Antwerp and the Royal Library Albert I in Brussels.

INTRODUCTION

URBAN PUBLIC DEBTS FROM THE 14TH TO THE 18TH CENTURY. A NEW APPROACH

Marc Boone, Karel Davids, Paul Janssens

The essays in this volume offer a state-of-the art analysis of a heretofore somewhat neglected part of financial history: the way in which during the late Middle Ages and Early Modern Times urban governments in Western Europe handled the public debts their cities were confronted with. The financial aspects of the sale of annuities (*renten, rentes*) may have already been abundantly studied, but the links with social and political history still needed to be tackled. Who bought these annuities and thus participated in sharing the burden and profits which were likely to arise from them? What were their motives? How did the obvious links with urban elites work? And, perhaps most significantly, how did these occasional sales evolve into a structural way of linking financially important private persons with public finances, in the context both of cities and of growing states, since often the cities needed the money on a short-term basis in order to accomplish their own financial obligations toward the 'state'?

The essays were first presented at a colloquium held in Ghent in November 2001[1]. They cover the urban strongholds of Europe in the period under scrutiny: all the cities are situated within a wide curve, which links the areas from the North Sea, via the Rhineland and the Alps, with the urbanised areas around the Mediterranean. An introductory chapter outlines the medieval annuities in Italy and Northern France. The further development in the late Middle Ages is discussed in contributions about Barcelona and the surrounding smaller urban centres, and in contributions about Basel and other Swiss and German cities with which she held financial ties in the 14th and 15th century. The influence of state formation on the urban interest policy clearly appears in 15th century Bruges, which shared the ups and downs of the Burgundian-Habsburger state complex. This influence is also apparent in smaller Zutphen, from which the interest policy is followed from the 14th till the 16th century. The chapters on Dordrecht and Amsterdam make for a good comparison between bigger and smaller Dutch cities in the 16th century. Amsterdam can also be put in contrast with London of which the special 17th century credit mechanism is explained, or else with Italian cities such as Venice and Rome whose development from the 14th century, the 16th century respectively, is outlined. In all these cities the pace of state formation is very different. The effect of this factor will come out well through the reading of the different chapters.

The colloquium in Ghent offered the opportunity to place the ongoing research in the social and political dimension of the urban debt policy in the Low Countries in a wide international perspective. With this initiative, the organisers wanted to encourage further research along the newly traced chalk marks. Additional results were already presented at the international conference on Urban History in Edinburgh in September 2002[2]. Hopefully studies on other regions will soon complete and

1 The conference *Urban Public Debt, Urban Government and the Market forAnnuities in Western Europe, 14th-18th centuries* was organised in Ghent on 23-24 November 2001 under the auspices of the Flemish *Fonds voor Wetenschappelijk Onderzoek (FWO)* and the *Nederlandse Organisatie voor Wetenschappelijk Onderzoek (NWO)*.

2 *Power, Knowledge and Society in the* City, Sixth International Conference on Urban History, Edinburgh, 4-7 September 2002. In the session *Citizens, Money and Urban Governments in Late Medieval and Early Modern Europe* the next papers were presented: M. Van der Burg, L. Derijcke and M. van der Heijden, "Annuity buyers and urban debt: A comparison between 15th century Bruges, 16th century Dordrecht and 17th century Rotterdam"; J. Miller, "Urban indebtness in the Habsburg monarchy: The case study of

refine the results to date. The assumptions at the basis of the conference in Ghent and Edinburgh are hereafter discussed in detail.

Annuity sales, urban development and state-formation

Urban fiscality has been at the centre of many considerations on the development of the 'modern' state: both the recent European Science Foundation-syntheses as well as general syntheses by Charles Tilly and others have paid attention to the way in which cities have acted first to finance their own policy, and later to collect fiscal revenues for the state they had become part of[3]. It is no wonder that Tilly counted the Dutch Republic, the Italian city states and the crown of Aragon to be the most typical examples of what he labelled a state-trajectory characterised by a high concentration of capital. These three regions of Europe are well represented in the following essays, not to confirm once more, nor to reject and adapt the Tilly hypothesis, but in an attempt to dig deeper into the social and political background of the financial movements which are at stake.

Indeed, the high concentration of capital available, offering a substantial basis for the making of an encompassing political construction is typical for a certain type of city. These cities are in general economically dominated by commerce or by a commercialised highly developed industry, and politically dominated by an urban elite, conscious of its economic and social interests and hence eager to negotiate the defence of the same interests and the 'protection' offered by state-institutions holding a firm grip on the tools of war-fare, the so-called bargaining metropoles labelled as such by W. Blockmans[4]. Nearly all of these cities are part of an urban network, another new field of interest of recent urban history, thus defining the often complex relationships between great cities of the 'metropolis' type and smaller, dependant cities, caught in the existing urban networks and linked by a multitude of ties, financial and other, to the big cities[5].

What is central in the inquiry tackled in the following essays, and most prominently presented as such by James Tracy, is the urban precocity in establishing financial techniques meant to bring together an important sum of money with which to handle certain expenditures or exceptional needs. The so-called 'financial revolution' may prove to be yet another urban invention, taken over at some moment by state-authorities to their own profit. In other fields – that of public legislation for instance – a similar urban precocity had already been noted. Tracy suggests a correlation between the political regime a city lives by and the way it handles its debts: a greater republican tradition leads to the establishment of long-term debts through consolidation of forced loans, while a city ruled by '*signori*' – a political rule modelled on the dynastic monarchy – prefers voluntary loans. Renewal in the field of financial techniques, therefore is related to both the size of the city and its incorporation in an urban network, on the one hand, but also to the political organisation within the city and outside the city, on

---

Moravian cities, 1560-1630"; I. Paquay, "Maires et échevins namurois face aux finances de leur ville: entre intérêts publics et intérêts privés (1362/1364-1500)"; J.-C. Zofio Llorente, "The social credit network in the leather working sector: *censos, obligaciones* and informal loans in Madrid, 1550-1650".

3 See the collection of essays regarding finances in the context of the ESF-project "The making of the modern state", R. Bonney (ed.), *Systèmes économiques et finances publiques*, Paris, 1996 (also in an English version), chapters on spending, revenues and public debt by M. Körner and R. Bonney. Among a series of preparatory colloquia, see: J.-Ph. Genet and M. Le Mené (eds.), *Genèse de l'Etat moderne. Prélèvement et redistribution. Actes du colloque de Fontevraud 1984*, Paris, 1987. Ch. Tilly, *Coercion, capital and European States, AD 990-1990*, Cambridge (Mass.), 1990.

4 W. Blockmans, "Voracious states and obstructing cities: an aspect of state formation in preindustrial Europe", in Ch. Tilly and W. Blockmans (eds.), *Cities and the rise of states in Europe, AD 1000 to 1800*, Boulder,1994, pp. 228-234.

5 See in general for the Southern Low Countries: *Le réseau urbain en Belgique dans une perspective historique (1350-1850). Une approche statistique et dynamique. Actes du 15e colloque international. Spa, 4-6 sept. 1990*, Brussels, Crédit communal collection histoire in 8°, n° 86, 1992 (passim). A case study for the eastern part of the county of Flanders: P. Stabel, *Dwarfs among giants. The Flemish urban network in the late Middle Ages*, Louvain/Apeldoorn, 1997.

the other hand. As Sánchez repeats however: one should be aware not to 'reinvent the Mediterranean' by which he means the fixation on the Mediterranean part of Europe as the region where all renewals in the field of finances had their start; many more analogies with the northern parts of Europe might emerge from a comparison as attempted in the following texts. Indeed, a recent survey of the existing literature brings A. Furio to stress the similarities between different parts of late medieval Europe, the consolidation of urban debts having played a decisive role in bringing about a permanent and regular fiscal system[6]. This fiscal system which benefited in the first place the members of the urban elites – in some cities at some moments the social profile of the buyers of annuities may have evolved, in general the percentage of members of the elite in power among them was and remained impressive. The '*image d'Epinal*' of the so-called Italian model has also been questioned and in some essential respects corrected: Maria Ginatempo made clear in a recent comparative study to what extent the forced loans, based on the '*estimo*' type tax, were exclusively characteristic of the big cities, with again – the argument joins the remarks by Tracy – a dominant republican organisation, leaving aside the '*contado*' and the subjugated smaller cities. Inside the city a social barrier was recognisable: only the elite benefited from the possibility of investing in the city's debt and thus of speculating with the titles it generated[7].

Yet the traditional frontier between rich and poor is not always recognisable as such. In this traditional view, the poor paid for the investments of the rich, who were able to finance and to participate in the funding of the debt by buying annuities, whereas the revenues from indirect taxation, the most indiscriminate of all and thus socially discriminating, were mobilised to pay back the annual income to the wealthy investors. The reason why this was not always the case belongs not necessarily to the field of economically rational behaviour, but touches upon the moral and ideological funding of the city(-state). In their study of the recovery of Amsterdam's credit in the last quarter of the 16th century, Martijn van der Burg and Marjolein 't Hart demonstrate how the richer Amsterdam burghers did predominantly pay the new 50th penny tax, destined to make the financial recovery of their city possible. The motives may have been economic and follow a clear rationale though one is entitled to wonder to what extent contemporary annuity-buyers were moved by the insight that much of the city's tax yields were thus pumped back in the city's own economy? A certain sense of civic responsibility was also present. The study of annuities links with other economically not always rational behaviour and with the study of the urban ideology. The burgher, whose role in buying annuities and financing urban collective debt was essential, got his ideological justification precisely in the daily practice of being part of a collective undertaking, bearing his individual part of the common burden, the taxes necessary to uphold the political construct of the 'polis'. As such he was also collectively responsible for the debts created in the name of the city, a share-holder in a collective undertaking, bearing a moral commitment to upholding the 'commonwealth' of his city[8].

The study of 'civic humanism' in the cities of Northern Europe is still not as well developed as it is for the classic case of the Italian city-states. Future research will however need to consider the role of financial commitment in the creation of a sense of belonging to a common republic of burghers, through the practice of the co-financing of the public debt (as yet another aspect among the judicial practices, the participation in the defence of the city and others). The scarce studies about

---

6 A. Furio, "La dette dans les dépenses municipales", in D. Menjot and M. Sánchez Mártinez, *La fiscalité des villes au Moyen Age (Occident médiéval). 3. La redistribution de l'impôt*, Toulouse, 2002, p. 345.

7 M. Ginatempo, *Prima del debito. Finanziamento della spesa pubblica e gestione del deficit nelle grandi città toscane (1200-1350 ca.)*, (Biblioteca Storica Toscana XXXVIII), Florence, 2000, pp. 13-31.

8 On these crucial notions of '*bonum commune*' or '*res publica*', both clearly linked to financial aspects of urban life, the literature is very abundant; see recently (with references to the older literature on urban ideology): U. Meier, "Gemeinnutz und Vaterlandsliebe. Kontroversen über die normativen Grundlagen des Bürgerbegriffs im späten Mittelalter", in R.C. Schwinges (ed.), Neubürger im späten Mittelalter. Migration und Austausch in der Städtelandschaft des alten Reiches (1250-1550), *Zeitschrift für Historische Forschung. Beiheft 30*, Berlin, 2002, pp. 53-81.

ideological manifestations of civic humanism in the Low Countries (the writings of 16th century Bruges-based humanist Franciscus Goethalsius for instance) make clear that the financial aspects of civic behaviour are an essential part of this political construct[9]. The contrast with what in the case of Italy has been labelled as princely urbanism and the need to spend tax-payers money without calculating the economic costs, but with the unique political gains as motivation, is striking[10]. As the case of London in the late 17th century, the focus of attention in the contribution of Vanessa Harding, makes clear, however, the presence of strong city with a booming economy, being the unquestioned centre of a national economy, does not necessarily lead to the adequate handling of public debt. Are the reasons for this to be looked for in inadequate accounting procedures alone, or is it more a question of the very absence of the moral commitments which allowed Amsterdam in the last decades of the 16th century to overcome a not less desperate situation?

The most revealing aspect of the study of the sale of annuities undoubtedly concerns the link between state making and the role of local elites and intermediary levels of decision. The tensions between cities, regional institutions (the so-called 'representative institutions') and princes allow the researcher to penetrate into the motives of individual burghers, the collective ambitions of families or clans and the '*raison d'état*'. As many of the following essays illustrate, a clear-cut distinction, a black and white opposition between these forces, is seldom present. In most cases, the strategies and interests can coincide temporarily, ready to be attenuated in a slightly different context. So the role of 'regional' intermediary forces may come to the foreground, as studied by Wantje Fritschy in the case of the United Provinces of the Netherlands. In her analysis of how provincial and urban debt evolved, the abandonment of a crucial part of local autonomy by the cities explains to a large extent the strength of the Republic: this is not the result of extreme decentralisation but of a centralisation on the provincial level. Is this the result of a centuries-old tradition and habitus of negotiating fiscal policy and a willingness to abandon principal strongholds, when 'higher' interests were at stake? Is this the outcome of the financial politics in place in the urban environments of the Burgundian and Habsburg Netherlands and successfully applied in the Republic of burghers? In comparison to the more 'coercion-intensive' paths some of the great, centralised nations of Europe followed in the same years, the urban experience in the preceding periods, but also the extent of information-exchange and the size of the territory seemed to have played an important if not decisive role.

Social implications of debt management

Why did cities in the Middle Ages and the Early Modern Times often resort to loans rather than increase taxes? A loan only meant a deferment of tax, not a cancellation. The borrowed sum had to be paid back anyway on top of which came the interest burden. In principal, it was clearly preferable to finance state expenditures by additional taxes. However, this wasn't always possible. When an exceptionally high amount was needed immediately, the increase of the current taxes was not a solution. In case of an empty treasury, one had to make an appeal to the savings of bankers (short-term credit) or of the public (war taxes, forced loans or long-term credit).

Forced loans can be found almost everywhere in the Middle Ages. Tracy mentions this form of credit loan in France during the 12th and 13th century. Such loans were just as common in medieval Venice (Luciano Pezzolo) as in Aragon. Apparently this remained a suitable credit tool as long as

9 K. Tilmans, "Republikeins burgerschap en het civic humanism in de Bourgondisch-Habsburgse Nederlanden (1477-1566)", in J. Kloek and K. Tilmans, "Burger. Een geschiedenis van het begrip 'burger' in de Nederlanden van de Middeleeuwen tot de 21ste eeuw", Amsterdam, 2002 (Nederlandse Begripsgeschiedenis IV), pp. 92-94: apart from moral corruption the greatest danger for a happy republic is a prince having at his disposal a well furnished treasury.

10 P. Boucheron, "Bien public et intérêts privés: la dépense édilitaire dans les villes de l'Italie centro-septentrionale (XIIIe-XVe siècle)", in Menjot and Sánchez Mártinez, *La fiscalité des villes au Moyen Age (3)*, p. 234.

warfare was not too capital-intensive and the money supplies were contained within a small group of prosperous citizens. It is in any case striking that annuities already existed between private citizens in Aragon before they were first used by the city council of Valencia in 1366 (Manuel Sánchez Martínez). Long-term loans were unknown in Italy before the 12th century. In the North of France they were first introduced during the 13th century and elsewhere in Europe only in the 14th century (Tracy). From then on the annuity slowly started to outstrip the forced loan. The role of the private banker in granting government credit also strongly diminished after the 14th century (Basel and elsewhere). The high share of taxes and forced loans in the United Provinces at the end of the 16th century was mainly due to the population's sense of public responsibility which they showed in the battle for independence against Phillip II (Van der Burg and 't Hart; Fritschy).

Government and annuity buyers could choose between two types of bonds: annuities and redeemable bonds. In principal, for the annuity there was no question of a loan. The buyer gave the government a sum of money in exchange for a regular payment of a fixed interest. This payment only subsided with the death of the subscriber. The city could not end the payment of its own accord by repayment of the capital sum[11]. Hereditary rent charges were in principal of a perpetual nature. Since the capital sum would never be repaid, the interest was, also in this case, not considered an interest on a loan but a partial repayment of the borrowed capital. The hereditary rent charge evolved into a redeemable bond when it was accepted that the government could end the payment of annuities by repaying the capital sum.

Bonds and annuities were very popular with the public. Even though buying a redeemable bond was a long-term investment, the buyer could at any time dispose of the loaned capital because the bond was negotiable. The overwhelming success of the annuity was due to the rare combination of security and high proceeds. Although nobody could estimate their own life span, every subscriber was guaranteed to dispose of a fixed income throughout his life. There were no real losers as whoever died prematurely could not cry over it. The heirs could. To provide for their interests, sometimes annuities were offered to cover two lives.

Bonds and annuities granted the government access to the capital market where one could borrow quickly and cheaply, with staggering of repayments in the long term. The higher interest rate on annuities meant a heavier burden on the budget. On the other hand, the debt burden diminished year after year. Issuing annuities wasn't always as loss-making as one thought. The image of the ancient annuity buyer who did a golden deal by subscribing as a young man was wide-spread. Hans-Jörg Gilomen gives the example of Anna Billung from Bern who enjoyed a high annuity for more than half a century[12]. Apparently the image of the bondholder who dies soon was not as popular. Mistakenly. The one scenario was as current as the other. Both scenarios were exceptional anyway. That's exactly what made the system so attractive to the government. The more subscribers, the lesser the importance of the predictability of their life spans. The annuity was a form of life insurance: those who had the misfortune to die soon actually paid for those who had the fortune to live longer. Until the 18th century one did not dispose of accurate death charts and of suitable calculation methods to accurately determine the interest rates upon issuing annuities[13]. During the 19th century, insurance companies would change this. At the time, they replaced the government who had acted as life insurer until then by selling annuities[14].

How heavy was the urban public debt? Some authors take the interest burden as their starting point and calculate the percentage of the annual budget. In Zutphen, the interests amounted to about

---

11 Gilomen mentions a few forced repayments by way of exception in Basel in the late 15th century.

12 The story shows some similarity with Jeanne Calment's (°1875), who sold her apartment for an annuity to a notary from Arles. His heirs had to pay the annuity until 1997, when she eventually died at the age of 122.

13 See G. Alter and J.-C. Riley, "How to bet on lives: a guide to life contingent contracts in Early Modern Europe", in *Research in Economic History*, 10 (1986), pp. 1-53.

14 P. Leroy-Beaulieu, *Traité de la science des finances*, Paris 1912, II, p. 326 e.v.

50% of the city expenditures in the second half of the 15th century; in 1479 they reached a record level of 85% (Remi van Schaïk). Other authors don't consider the yearly interest burden but the scale of the total debt. In 1283 Bruges, says Tracy, the loaned capitals were 6 times the amount of the annual urban revenues. The figures from Laurence Derycke point to a strong fluctuation of Bruges' debt in the 15th century: in peace time it constituted between one third and half of the annual income but in times of war, the debt got out of hand and in 1494-1496, reached a peak of two and a half times the annual urban revenues.

The development of debt cannot be seen separate from the population's development. Hence Fausto Piola Caselli's calculation of the Roman debt *per capita*. With a constant distribution of revenues and tax burdens, an increase in population could ease the debt burden on every tax payer provided that the debt burden would grow slower than the population. Moreover, one has to consider possible monetary devaluation and inflation[15]. Piola Caselli finds the Roman public debt quadrupled between the 16th and the 18th century, while prices only doubled to tripled during that period of time. When on top of this, one takes into account the increase in population from 1.5 to 2.5 million residents, one gets a very different view of the evolution of the Roman public debt. It is thus misleading to focus on the nominal increase of the public debt. The tax payer was only concerned with the much less important increase of the actual debt. The calculation of the debt per head of the population is also useful when the average income of certain sections of the population is known. Such data allow Fritschy to compare the tax burden in Amsterdam and Rome in the 16th-17th century. She estimates the interest burden in Amsterdam at the beginning of the 16th century at 4% of the income of an urban wage labourer which is twice the interest burden in the pontifical state.

The evolution of public debt was very different for each city. Often the international balance of power determined the urban debt. The unpredictable succession of war and peace was determining. Next to the consolidation of short term loans or a rearrangement of the debt, everywhere defence costs were the most important factor to issue bonds or annuities. In most cases, consolidation and debt conversions were related to previous military expenses. To a much lesser extent, public works were also financed by loans, like the expansion of the city of Amsterdam. The less space there was left to increase taxes, the sooner city council was forced to issue a new loan. In Zutphen, even the storm damage to the church tower was financed in the late 15th century by a public loan!

Just as the political climate determined the growth of debt, so was the economical climate decisive in the reduction of the debt burden. One should not, however, underestimate the financial policy. Pezzolo and others emphasize that commentators agreed in their dismissal of government loans and that most city councils took care to reduce debt as soon as possible. Until the 18th century, when economical thinking started to develop[16], public debt was considered a necessary evil. The spectre of insolvency urged the government to adopt a well-considered amortization policy by which expensive loans were repaid or at least replaced by new loans with a lower interest rate[17].

An important factor in debt management concerns the geographical scope of the debt. If part of the annuities ware sold outside the city itself, each burgher could be held responsible for claims in case of non-payment of the interests. Some burghers risked being taken hostage while others saw their goods being confiscated. It thus remains an open question why so many subscribers preferred bonds and annuities from their own city. It was obviously in the council's best interest to find as many subscribers as possible within the city itself. This was not only to avoid adverse legal consequences in case of non-payment. Issuing bonds in other cities was done through an agent who also took care of paying the interests locally. This generated extra costs. Payments in another city had an adverse effect

15 To protect annuity buyers against possible devaluation, they were sometimes offered the possibility to choose the currency in which the interest payments should be made.

16 A modernist as Jean-François Melon considered national debt as robbing Peter to pay Paul. According to him, tax payers and annuity buyers apparently shared the same interests.

17 S. Homer and R. Sylla, *A History of Interest Rates*, New Brunswick, 1996 (3th edition).

on the city's payment balance. When the interests were not or not regularly paid, this also had far-reaching consequences for the city's burghers. In this case the debt burden was passed on from the tax payers to the annuity buyers.

It remains difficult to determine which motives predominated the debt policy. To what extent did the interests of the treasury take precedence over the public interests of the annuity buyers? Was the urban policy aimed more at sparing the tax payer or at favouring the annuity buyers? Was the public debt a burden for some but a treat for others? To unravel the intertwinement of private interests with urban policy, it makes sense to sketch the social profile of the annuity buyers and to trace their involvement in the city council.

A profile of annuity buyers

Who were the buyers of annuities? If buyers' names – and preferably, other details – are recorded in urban accounts, it is possible by means of a prosopographic approach to build up a profile of the group of people who for some reason or another showed an interest in this kind of loan. Thus, the history of urban finances can be related to the broader context of social and political history. This issue is squarely addressed in the articles by Derycke, Van der Heijden and 't Hart and Van der Burg and it is also briefly touched upon in a number of other contributions to this volume, notably those by Gilomen, Pezzolo, Piola Caselli and Sánchez Martínez.

The first impression that emerges from these essays is that of a great variety in profiles. Or to put it more pointedly: the profile of the annuity buyers seems to have varied according to different circumstances. Whatever dimension one applies, variations leap to the eye. Consider the geographical origin of annuity buyers: whereas *renteniers* in Amsterdam between 1584 and 1604 were all inhabitants of that city, annuity buyers in Bruges at the end of the 15th century not only came from the ranks of its own citizens, but also hailed from a wide range of other towns in the county of Flanders and beyond. Venice between 1350 and 1650 or 15th-century Basel seem to have represented a kind of middle position: most annuities were sold to residents of these cities, but a small part was held by foreigners. The geographical distribution varied in the course of time, too. The share of non-residents among *renten*-buyers in Manresa in 1415 was more reduced than in the late 14th century and in Dordrecht in 1572 it was lower than in 1555, whereas the share of foreigners (mostly Genuese) among bondholders in Venice sharply increased since the 1620s.

The social origins of annuity buyers show a great diversity as well. Noblemen were strongly represented among the buyers of *censales* in Valencia in the 1360s, of *renten* in Bruges between 1472 and 1492 or of *luoghi di Monte* in Rome in the 1680s, but were almost absent among annuity buyers in Barcelona in the 1390s and did not figure among *renteniers* in Basel, Dordrecht or Amsterdam at all. Ecclesiastics and religious institutions carried much more weight among the *renten*-buying public in 15th-century Catalan cities or in 17th-century Rome than in late medieval Bruges or Basel. Merchants made up one-third of the known annuity buyers in Barcelona in the mid-14th century, constituted a sizable part of the *renteniers* in late 15th-century Bruges and almost two thirds of the individual buyers of annuities issued by the government of Amsterdam between 1584 and 1604. The liberal professions appear to have been better represented among annuity-buyers in Barcelona in the 1350s than in Amsterdam in the late 16th century. Derycke's and 't Hart and Van der Burg's detailed analyses of the social background of *renteniers* in Bruges and Amsterdam plainly demonstrate that at least in these cities annuities were bought by quite a number of craftsmen as well. In Rome, by contrast, Piola Caselli found that the vast majority of common artisans did not earn enough money on their own to buy even a small *luogo di Monte*. Like the geographical distribution, the share of various social strata could vary considerably in the course of time. Among annuity buyers in Rome, for instance, the share of noblemen at the end of the 17th century was twice as high as it was around 1600 or around 1800!

Turning to gender and marital status, the data in these studies do not reveal a fixed pattern either. Manon van der Heijden found that in Dordrecht women made up some 39% of the annuity buyers in 1555 and almost 34% in 1572. Among the female buyers, about 70% were widows, 7% unmarried women and 9% married wives. In Amsterdam between 1584 and 1604, about one-fifth of the annuity buyers were women, in Rome in 1585 about one-fourth. At other times and places the share of females could even be higher.

How can this variety in profiles be explained? The essays in this volume suggest that such differences partly stemmed from policy choices by urban governments and thus, that attention should be focused on the underlying continuities or dynamics of urban politics. Whereas the government of late 15th-century Bruges, for example, apparently did not mind if its *renten* came into the hands of foreigners in far-away places, magistrates in contemporary Basel or late 16th-century Amsterdam were eager to restrict the sale to non-residents as far as possible. Urban governments thus could leave their mark on the profile of annuity buyers by setting the conditions for the issue of *renten.* They could also affect the composition of the group in a more direct way by investing in urban annuities themselves. Although the role of political elites in the shoring up of municipal finances in Continental cities normally appears not to have been as crucial as in chartered towns in Tudor and Stuart England, where even magistrates were routinely 'expected to dig into their own pockets to provide bridging loans'[18], the three case-studies on Bruges, Dordrecht and Amsterdam nevertheless show that officeholders and their families in these cities were heavily involved in the purchase of *renten.* In late 15th-century Bruges, Derycke concludes, a small group of individuals holding 'important offices in the urban government' 'dominated the public annuity market and monopolised it at politically crucial moments'. In Dordrecht between 1549 and 1577, more than a third of the aldermen, councillors and burgomasters were active as buyers on the urban *renten* market. Together with their families, they formed almost half of the annuity buyers in 1555 and nearly two-thirds in 1572. In Amsterdam, the political elite between 1584 and 1604 furnished 38% of the total sum invested in annuities, with the burgomasters leading the way.

Structural factors were doubtless at play in the formation of the profiles of annuity buyers as well. A town's position in a regional urban hierarchy was clearly a relevant variable, as Sánchez Martínez's study on Aragon shows. The urban annuity market in smaller towns like Cullera, Cervera or Manresa was much more likely to be dominated by non-residents than the market in major cities like Valencia, Barcelona or Zaragossa. Variations in profiles of annuity buyers between cities moreover to some extent reflected differences in social structure and standard of living, although these differences are as yet hard to pin down in an exact way. Variations by gender or marital status may partly have been related with these structural factors, too, and partly with variables like the duration of the *renten* (short-term or long-term) or the nature of the issue (forced on heads of households or not) or with socio-cultural forces that are still imperfectly known.

In order to come to grips with the motives of annuity buyers, it might also be worthwhile to study this group from another angle, namely by looking into the relative attractiveness of annuities compared to other sorts of investments, such as investments in land, houses, bonds, stocks or shares. Decisions to buy (or to refrain from buying) annuities might be better understood if we had a complete picture of the investment pattern of different social groups or individual citizens and of the relative advantages and disadvantages of the alternatives that were available to potential buyers at any particular moment. This line of approach has not been followed in the contributions to this volume. It could be fruitfully explored by using, for instance, probate inventories and other corresponding sources. Made

18 I.A. Archer, "Politics and Government 1540-1700", in P. Clark (ed.), *The Cambridge Urban History of Britain*, II: *1540-1840*, Cambridge, 2000, p. 246.

up after their death, probate inventories after all often recorded not only movable goods of deceased persons, but also listed real estate and securities in their possession and gave an overview of their claims and debts.

Although most research of probate inventories has focused on their value as sources for the study of material culture, it is nevertheless manifest that they can yield relevant data on investment patterns as well. Luuc Kooijmans' work on the elite of the Dutch city of Hoorn between 1700 and 1780, for example, reveals that the share of annuities (including annuities issued by urban and provincial governments as well as by private firms or individuals) in the total wealth of the urban patricians decreased from 5% in the period 1700-1719 to 1.2% in the period 1760-1779. The bulk of their fortune was invested in land, shares of the Dutch East-India Company and (for more than 40%) bonds issued by the province of Holland. The only people among the Hoorn elite who after 1700 still invested a considerable share of their wealth in annuities were single persons and childless couples[19]. Thera Wijsenbeek's study on the property and life-style of Delft citizens in the 18th century confirms that the possession of annuities in all strata of the Delft population declined after 1700, but the least so among the richest people of the town. An increasing part of these annuities was bought from abroad. In contrast with Kooijmans' observation (and Van der Heijden's data on mid 16th-century Dordrecht), Wijsenbeek did *not* find that widows or unmarried people were more prone to buy annuities than married couples[20]. Both authors seek the explanation for the decreasing investment in annuities in the 18th century not only in a fall of demand, but also in a decline of supply. The provincial government of Holland issued far fewer annuities than before, because it had finally concluded that the benefits were too low[21].

Such findings on developments in the 18th century have also their uses for research on earlier times. They can not only provide a model for the kind of information that might be retrieved from similar sources from periods before 1700, but also inspire vital questions that may serve as guidelines for research. When did the share of annuities in total investments of urban citizens increase or decline? Did these changes take place in all cities simultaneously (was there a kind of secular trend?) or did they differ in timing and rate by region or type of city? Did they occur in all strata of the population and all types of family and household at the same time, or did significant variations emerge? And how can such changes be explained: by shifts in demand, or by developments on the side of supply, such as limitations on the issue of annuities or the rise of alternative investment opportunities? Clearly, there are still many issues concerning the profile of annuity buyers that need to be further explored.

19 L. Kooijmans, *Onder regenten. De elite in een Hollandse stad, Hoorn 1700-1780*, Amsterdam, 1985, pp. 101, 224.

20 Th. Wijsenbeek-Olthuis, *Achter de gevels van Delft . Bezit en bestaan van rijk en arm in een periode van achteruitgang (1700-1800)*, Hilversum, 1987, pp. 126-127.

21 Kooijmans, *Onder regenten,* p. 101, Wijsenbeek-Olthuis, *Achter de gevels van Delft*, p. 127.

ON THE DUAL ORIGINS OF LONG-TERM URBAN DEBT IN MEDIEVAL EUROPE

James D. Tracy
University of Minnesota

Introduction

This volume is part of an ongoing discussion of the public debt of pre-modern European governments[1]. Looking beyond Europe to financial arrangements in other parts of the pre-modern world[2], one could get the impression that public debt was an invention of medieval European cities and princes[3]. But it belies common sense to think that governments never had to exceed their current revenues. In Ming China, for example, merchants who provisioned troops posted along the northern frontier were paid, when they had made their deliveries, in salt contracts, permitting them to draw from the imperial salt granaries for sale to their customers. But since the expenses of frontier defense outstripped the supply of salt, merchants by the early 15th century might have to await as long as thirty years to redeem their contracts, and no doubt adjusted prices accordingly[4]. Wherever we can speak of a state, we may expect to find state debt.

But the mere fact that state debt may exist in one form or another does not imply that towns acted as intermediaries for the crown, as they did in parts of medieval Europe, by selling instruments of long-term debt on the open market. Any suggestion that medieval European urban institutions may have been historically singular in some particular calls to mind Max Weber, not to mention Henri Pirenne, both of whom assumed a sharper distinction between towns and villages than now seems reasonable[5]. Weber's essay on "The Nature of the City," published in 1921, says little about finance and nothing about public debt. But his forthright assertion of the historical singularity of the medieval

1 *Finances et comptabilité urbaines, XIIe-XIVe Siècles,* Brussels, 1964; B. Lyon and A. Verhulst, *Medieval Finance: a Comparison of Financial Institutions in Northwestern Europe*, Bruges, 1967; A. Guarducci (ed.), *Prodotto lordo e finanza pubblica, secoli XII-XIX,* Prato, 1976; A. de Maddalena and H. Kellenbenz (eds.), *Finanze e ragione di stato in Italia e Germania nella prima età moderna*, Bologna, 1984; C. Webber and A. Wildavsky, *A History of Taxation and Expenditure in the Western World*, New York, 1986; J.-P. Genet and H. Le Men (eds.), *Genèse de l'état moderne: prélèvement et distribution*, Paris, 1986; H. Dubois (ed.), *Local and International Credit in the Middle Ages and the Sixteenth Century*, Bern, 1986; H. Kellenbenz and P. Prodi (eds.), *Fisco, religione e stato nell' età confessionale,* Bologna, 1989; M. Veseth, *Mountains of Debt. Crisis and Change in Renaissance Florence, Victorian Britain, and Postwar America,* New York/Oxford, 1990; C. Tilly, *Coercion, Capital, and European States,* New York, 1990; P.T. Hoffman and K. Norberg (eds.), *Fiscal Crises and Liberty,* Stanford, 1995; M. Boone (ed.), *Finances Publiques,* Ghent, 1995. In September 2001, the Università Ca' Foscari Venezia and the Università di Trento organized a week-long seminar on "Credibility and Crisis in Financial History".

2 R.W. Goldsmith, *Premodern Financial Systems. A Historical Comparative Study,* Cambridge, 1987.

3 Goldsmith, *Premodern Financial Systems*, mentions "public debt" only in connection with Medici Florence and the United Provinces of the 17th century.

4 R. Huang, *Taxation and Governmental Finance in Sixteenth Century Ming China,* Cambridge, 1974, Chapter 5, especially p. 203: "Since the government had no regular means of obtaining credit, the disposal of official salt became a convenient device for receiving advance payments, though the fact of advance sale was never admitted".

5 E.g., S. Reynolds, *Kingdoms and Communities in Western Europe, 900-1300,* Oxford, 1984, p. 155: "Some of the distinctions usually drawn between urban and rural communities are false".

urban community (especially north of the Alps)[6] has, in the decades since World War II, inspired historians of urban life outside Europe to show where Weber was wrong. For example, if Weber dismissed Islamic cities as monolithic and undifferentiated, scholars have shown that leading families had considerable scope for initiative[7]. But since urban élites were not as differentiated among themselves as in European cities, the same scholars find that Islamic cities had a "public culture" rather than a "civic culture" in the European sense[8].

Might it be that European cities were unique also in their management of debt? Since the comparative study of pre-modern urban finance outside of Europe is altogether in its infancy, the point must be posed as a question, not asserted as a claim. Even so, this comparative dimension of the issue makes it worthwhile to re-visit the European origins of long-term urban debt. In what follows, I will first review the standard account, by historians of the German-legal school, and then offer two criticisms. First, the standard account says nothing about northern France, where towns began issuing the bonds or annuities known simply as "incomes" *(rentes)* during the 13th century, roughly a hundred years earlier than in Germany. Second, it excludes altogether the Italian towns that created different forms of long-term urban debt during the 12th century, roughly a hundred years earlier still.

1. Origins of Long-Term Urban Debt: the Standard Account

Early Modern jurists understood that the *rentes* issued by town governments had a precedent in similar *rentes* issued by ecclesiastical corporations. As Paulus Busius said in his *Tractatus de annuis redditibus* of 1601, it was by analogy with canon law that urban magistrates imposed *redditus* on the revenues of their city, with the permission of superior magistrates, unlike the latter, who could impose *redditus* on revenues subject to their control *pro arbitrio*[9]. The scholars who have worked out this connection in modern times have been German-language legal historians. Writing in 1904, Bruno Kuske traced the remote origin of life-term *rentes* or *rentes viagères*[10] to the Carolingian era, when a donor sometimes gave land to a monastery on condition that he received it back in *precaria*, to enjoy its fruits for the remainder of his life. In variant forms of precarial tenure, the donor could specify that his heirs would also enjoy the fruits of the land, or, instead of receiving the land back, he could accept the monastery's promise to provide him an income as long as he lived. With the transition to a monetary economy, donors could accept a lifetime income in cash rather than in kind, and it also became possible to make one's gift to the institution in cash rather than in land. By degrees, the gift became a purchase, and monasteries blazed a trail that cities would follow by seeking capital in this fashion. The

6 M. Weber, "Die Natur der Stadt", *Archiv für Sozialwissenschaft und Sozialpolitik,* 1921, p. 621ff., re-published in his *Wissenschaft und Gesellschaft,* 2 vols., Tübingen, 1956, II, p. 735; *The City,* translated and edited by D. Martindale and G. Neuwirth, New York, 1958, p. 80, "Neither the 'city' in the economic sense, nor the garrison, the inhabitants of which are accoutred with special political-administrative structures, necessarily constitute a 'community'. A 'community', in the full meaning of the word, appears as a general phenomenon only in the Occident", and p. 91, "The medieval occidental city presents striking contrasts to its Asiatic counterparts. This was particularly true for urban formations north of the Alps where the Western city developed in its purest form".

7 E.g., I. Lapidus, *Muslim Cities in the Later Middle Ages,* Cambridge, Massachusetts, 1967, pp. 185-191: in medieval Cairo and Aleppo, the urban élite had a good deal of freedom of action, but it was not differentiated, as in Europe, into separately-organized bodies of clerics, merchants, and town officials.

8 "Introduction: Was There an Ottoman City?" in E. Eldem, D. Goffman, and B. Masters, *The Ottoman City between East and West: Aleppo, Izmir, and Istanbul,* Cambridge, 1999, pp. 1-16.

9 Busius, *Tractatus de annuis redditibus,* Cologne, 1601, I, vi, pp. 42-43.

10 Life-term *rentes* were extinguished at the death of the named beneficiary, often a young child. Such *rentes* were also negotiable; in this case, the buyer had to make sure the name of the new beneficiary was entered in the records of the issuing body.

development of *rentes héritables* (or, as Kuske calls them, *Ewigrenten*)[11] followed a different trajectory. While *rentes viagères* could be assigned on urban excise taxes, or even "on the body of the city," *rentes héritables*, like the *Erbleihe* that in Kuske's view preceded them, had to be secured by real property. Thus the early *rentes héritables* issued by cities were funded by city property of one kind or another - houses, lands, or former seigneurial rights[12]. It may be noted that this point has been confirmed in subsequent research: *rentes viagères* and *rentes perpetuelles* did indeed have different origins, because in many cities the latter were, at least initially, funded by revenues from city property, as distinct from the newer excise taxes that usually supported *rentes viagères*[13].

Writing nearly sixty years later, Werner Ogris clarified the argument at a number of points. For example, the transition from a life-income in kind to a life-income in cash was facilitated by the fact that, as *census* and other dues on land became negotiable, the donor could present the monastery with the *census* on his land while keeping the land itself. Ogris also addresses the important question of security: why would the purchaser be willing to believe that he really would receive his life-income? In fact, despite the confidence in monasteries as institutions one may expect the faithful to have had, such contracts often included provisions for remedy in case of non-payment. In the case of urban *rentes viagères*, Ogris finds that investors, usually burghers of a neighboring city, were "astonishingly patient" in demanding their due. The ultimate sanction - causing burghers or merchants from the delinquent city to be distrained, along with their goods - was in his view based on the principle of *Gesamtbürgschaft* - that all burghers of a given city stood surety collectively for its debts. Finally, Orgis considers the circumstances in which bishoprics and monasteries in Germany, starting in the late 12th century, turned to the sale of *rentes viagères*. "Again and again." he finds, " there are references to a desperate financial situation, and to the pressure of debt that can only be relieved through the capital brought in" by the emission of these long-term instruments of credit. Orgis suggests that when cities began to issue *rentes viagères* it was for the same reason - to consolidate a heavy burden of short-term debt[14].

Finally, in light of the fact that ecclesiastical prohibitions on usurious loans were emphasized all the more strongly in the preaching of the new mendicant orders, one has to ask how monasteries (or towns) could justify the practice of selling *rentes*. One influential theologian, Henry of Ghent (d. 1293), contended that such transactions were indeed usurious, because they involved the sale of money. But as recent scholars have pointed out, canonists and theologians more commonly accepted the argument that the *rente* involved a licit purchase of the right to receive future income; since the buyer had no expectation of receiving his capital back, the *rente viagère* in particular was not a loan, and not usurious[15].

The idea that urban *rentes* depended on ecclesiastical precedents is widely accepted: towns could issue *rentes* because the town corporation, like an ecclesiastical institution, was an *unsterbliche Persönlichkeit*[16]. But surely it does not suffice to speak of town corporations in general, as if they were *per se* endowed with a potency for credit transactions of this kind. I am reminded in this connection of story told by my graduate school roommate, a biologist. At a marine biology conference where

---

11 *Rentes perpetuelles* were understood as payable in perpetuity to the buyer and his heirs; *rentes héritables* were extinguished when the issuing body repaid the capital sum to the buyer or his heirs. B. Schnapper, *Les Rentes au XVIe Siècle*, Paris, 1957, Chapter 4, shows how the former developed into the latter.

12 Kuske, *Das Schuldenwesen der deutschen Städten im Mittelalter, Vierteljahrschrift für Sozial- und Wirtschaftsgeschichte, Beihefte,* XII, Tübingen, 1904.

13 H. Pirenne, *Histoire de la Constitution de la Ville de Dinant au Moyen Âge,* Ghent, 1889, 60; G. Espinas, *Les Finances de la Commune de Douai des Origines au XVIe Siècle,* Paris, 1902, pp. 77-78; I. Eberhardt, *Van des stades wegene unde betalt. Städtischer Alltag im Spiegel der Rechnungen von Osnabrück, 1459-1519,* Osnabrück, 1996, p. 54.

14 Ogris, *Der mittelalterliche Leibrentenvertrag. Ein Beitrag zur Geschichte des deutschen Privatrechts,* Vienna, 1961 (the quote, pp. 246, 118).

15 I am grateful to Prof. John Munro (Department of Economics, University of Toronto) for sending me a copy of his paper on "The Late-Medieval Origins of the Modern Financial Revolution: Overcoming Impediments from Church and State".

16 H. van Werveke, *De Gentse Stadsfinanciën in de Middeleeuwen,* Brussels, 1934, p. 283; D. Houtzager, *Hollands Lijf- en Losrenten voor 1672,* Schiedam, 1950; E. Isenmann, *Die deutsche Stadt im Spätmittelalter,* Stuttgart, 1988, p. 384.

researchers presented for the first time fossil evidence for the existence of bi-valved molluscs, he met a group of German scientists who were not interested in queuing up to examine the new find because, they said, they had already thought of this possibility. Like the idea of biological evolution, the idea of historical or institutional development represents a logic of possibility. The biologist who accepts that organism B has evolved from organism A does not thereby postulate that the transition has occurred more than once[17]. Similarly, the historian who agrees that an urban institution develops from ecclesiastical precedents does not thereby say anything about when or where the development first occurred.

2. Thirteenth-Century Origins of Long-Term Urban Debt: Northern France

To the best of my knowledge, the earliest urban *rentes viagères* for which documentation survives were issued by the city of Rheims in 1218. But since the sale of *rentes* in the name of the commune was condemned as usurious by no less a personage than Guillaume de Joinville, who was Archbishop of Rheims from 1219 to 1226, this innovation, if indeed it was the first transaction of its kind, was not followed by further issues in Rheims[18]. By 1228, investors in both Arras and Saint-Quentin held *rentes viagères* issued by Tournai[19]. Six *titres de rente* for this issue are preserved in the town archives, apparently turned in after the death of the beneficiaries[20]. Four years later thirty-two bourgeois of Rheims agreed to purchase *rentes viagères* from Troyes for a total annual interest of 1,000 *livres de Paris*, somewhat more than the 870 *livres* the commune of Troyes owed at the same time to *rentiers* in Arras. Though Troyes was an important city, a center of the Fairs of Champagne, the issuance of long-term annuities by the commune was clearly a novelty, as is shown by the fact that Bishop Robert promised to constrain city officials to keep their oath to creditors by ecclesiastical sanctions if need be; for good measure, Count Thibaut IV of Champagne (1222 - 1253) also agreed to stand surety for his subjects in Troyes[21]. Other bourgeois of Reims concluded a similar agreement for the purchase of a smaller issue of *rentes* by Auxerre in 1235, and in 1247 Pope Innocent IV released Bar-sur-Aube, another of the Champagne Fair towns, from its obligation to pay 125 *livres* in annual interest to two *rentiers*[22]. Meanwhile, Arras, itself a major financial center, had a *rente* debt of 2,610 *livres* a year by 1241 if not earlier[23]. Bourgeois of Arras were the principal buyers for *rentes* issued by the cities of Roye in 1260, and Saint-Riquier in 1268[24]. In 1262, for which records are preserved of accounts rendered by cities to the king's officials, in keeping with Louis IX's ordinance of 1259, Amiens owed 1,900 *livres* for annual interest on *rentes* and Soissons 1,700 *livres*, while Compiègne, Noyon, and Saint-Quentin owed smaller amounts[25].

All of the cities thus far mentioned are found in the lands of the *Langue d'oil.* From the relatively few studies we have of urban finance in the lands of the *Langue d'oc*, one gets the impression that Southern France was impervious to this novelty; in Toulouse, as in smaller towns like Saint-Flour or Agde, magistrates met special needs more or less as ancient cities had done, with short-term loans,

17 S.J. Gould, *Wonderful Life: the Burgess Shale*, New York, 1989.
18 P. Desportes, *Reims et les Rémois au XIIIe Siècle*, Paris, 1979, p. 128.
19 P. Bougard and C. Wyffels, *Les Finances de Calais au XIIIe Siècle*, Brussels, 1966, p. 58.
20 H. Braun, *Geschichte der Lebensversicherung und der Lebensversicherungstechnik*, 2e Auflage, *Veröffentlichiungen des Deutschen Vereins für Versicherungswissenschaft*, 70, Berlin, 1963, p. 21.
21 Desportes, *Reims et les Rémois*, p. 128.
22 Desportes, *Reims et les Rémois*, p. 129.
23 Desportes, *Reims et les Rémois*, p. 127.
24 Van Werveke, *Gentse Stadsfinanciën*, p. 283.
25 Desportes, *Reims et les Rémois*, p. 128.

or by levying a second *taille* on tax-payers in general, or forced loans on a wealthy few[26]. But in the northern half of the kingdom, both French- and Netherlandish-speaking towns eagerly made use of this new means of credit. Calais first sold *rentes viagères* in 1263, and emissions multiplied over the next several years, apparently for the consolidation of short-term debt. An *état* of the city's debts for the year 1262/1263 shows 4,849 *livres* in outstanding loans; a similar document for 1271/1272 shows 3,194 in loans, and 537 *livres ad vitam.* Many of Calais' annuities were held by bourgeois of Arras[27]. Douai's first issue of *rentes viagères* dates from 1270 – though in this case *rentes héritables*, funded by incomes from city property, were carried on the books as early as 1250[28]. Saint-Omer sold *rentes viagéres* for the first time in 1271, perhaps inspired by the example of the abbey of Saint-Amand, whose earliest issue dates from the same year[29]. In 1275 Ghent placed its first issue with financiers of Arras[30]. By 1283, Brugge had a capital debt in *rentes viagères* amounting to more than six times the city's annual income[31].

In territories lying just beyond the northern borders of the kingdom of France, this form of urban long-term debt makes its appearance only in the next generation. In Brabant, Brussels issued *renten* for the first time in 1307, Leuven about a decade or so later[32]. In the prince-bishopric of Liège, Dinant issued its first *rentes* in 1324[33]. Dordrecht, the leading town in the county of Holland at this time, was selling *renten* not long after 1300. A bit farther north, Leiden's first issue dates from 1352[34]. But a few years earlier, in 1345, Leiden, Dordrecht and Delft – along with Middelburg and Zierikzee in Zeeland – had been dragooned into selling *rentes* for the benefit of Count Willem IV, against the surety of domain revenues that were in theory to be placed at their disposition[35]. By this time, many German towns had discovered the advantages of relatively cheap long-term credit. Hamburg and Lübeck, cities in close touch with the Low Countries, were marketing *Leibgedinge* or *rentes viagères* by about 1350[36]. The same can be said for south German towns like Konstanz, Speyer, and Esslingen[37]. Basel's early records perished in an earthquake of 1356, but as of 1360 the accounts show an established debt in *Leibgedinge*[38]. In the 1360s and 1370s, the small imperial city of Wetzlar financed a series of wars against the Counts of Solms by taking on a huge debt in *Leibgedinge* that was not extinguished until 1482[39]. Farther afield from imperial Germany's main commercial highways, Vienna did not begin issuing annuities until the 15th century[40]. Meanwhile, in the Iberian peninsula, Barcelona, followed by other towns in the crown of

26 P. Wolff, *Commerce et Marchands de Toulouse (vers 1350-vers 1450),* Paris, 1954, pp. 394-396; A. Rigaudière, *Saint-Flour, ville d'Auvergne au Bas Moyen Âge. Étude d'histoire administrative et financière,* 2 vols., Paris, 1982, II, pp. 903-905; A. Castaldo, *Le Consulat Mediéval d'Agde (XIIIe - XIVe Siècles),* Paris, 1974, pp. 383-390.

27 Bougard and Wyffels, *Les Finances de Calais,* pp.58, 161-162; Van Werveke, *Gentse Stadsfinanciën,* p. 283.

28 G. Espinas, *Les Finances de la Commune de Douai des Origines au Xve Siècles,* Paris, 1902, p. 313.

29 A. Derville, *Saint-Omer des Origines au Début du XVIe Siècle,* Lille, 1995, p. 231.

30 Van Werveke, *Gentse Stadsfinanciën,* p. 283.

31 A. Derville, "La finance arrageois: usure et banque", in M.-M. Castellani and J.-P. Martin (eds.), *Arras au Moyen Âge: Histoire et Littérature,* Arras, 1994, p. 41, citing C. Wyffels and J. de Smet, *De rekeningen van de stad Brugge, 1280-1319,* 2 vols., Brussels, 1965-1971.

32 C. Dickstein-Bernard, *La gestion financière d'une capitale: Bruxelles, 1334-1367,* Brussels, 1977, pp. 167-168; R. van Uytven, *Stadsfinanciën en Stadseconomie te Leuven*, pp. 203-204.

33 Pirenne, *Histoire de la Constitution de Dinant*, p. 60.

34 H.W. Dokkum and E.C. Dijkhof, "De oude Dordtse Lijfrenten", in L.M. Verloren van Themaat (ed.), *De Oudste Dordtse Lijfrenten,* Amsterdam, 1983, p. 37; J. W. Marsilje, *Het Financiële Beleid van Leiden in de Laat-Beierse en Bourgondische Perioden, +/- 1390-1477,* Hilversum, 1985, p. 284.

35 L.M.N. Verloren van Themaat, "De geschiedenis van de lijfrente", in Verloren van Themaat, *Oudste Dordtse Lijfrenten,* p. 9.

36 R. Sprandel, "Der städtische Rentenmarkt in Nordwestdeutschland im Spätmittelalter", in H. Kellenbenz (ed.), *Öffentliche Finanzen und Privates Kapital im Späten Mittelalter und in der ersten Hälfte des XVIen Jahrhunderts,* Stuttgart, 1971, pp. 14-23.

37 B. Kirchgässner, "Zur Frühgeschichte des modernen Haushalts, vor allem nach den Quellen der Reichsstädte Esslingen und Konstanz", in E. Maschke and J. Sydow, *Städtisches Haushalt- und Rechnungswesen,* 1973, pp. 10-15, 40.

38 J. Rosen, "Der Staatshaushalt Basels von 1360 bis 1535", in Kellenbenz, *Öffentliche Finanzen,* pp. 25-35.

39 G. Fouquet, "Die Finanzierung von Krieg und Verteidigung in Oberdeutschen Städten im Spätmittelalter", in B. Kirchgässner and G. Stolz (eds.), *Stadt und Krieg,* Sigmaringen, 1989, p. 70.

40 O. Brunner, *Die Finanzen der Stadt Wien von den Anfängen bis ins 16es Jahrhundert,* Vienna, 1929, pp. 414-417.

Aragon, led the way by issuing its first *censales al quitar* around 1340. In this case, however, the precedents cited were not French, but Italian[41].

This is but a fragmentary list of cities that entered the long-term debt market some time before about 1400. But it does suggest a pattern of diffusion, beginning in the first half of the 13th century in or near major financial centers of *Langue d'oil*, like Rheims and Arras, and spreading to the rest of northern France, then to surrounding countries. How might one account for the emergence of urban *rentes viagéres* in this region at this time? To start with, one may assume that some degree of currency stability was a prerequisite for investors to consider buying cash annuities. Concerns of this kind are evident from the fact that some contracts included clauses allowing the *rentier* to demand payment in a second currency if the primary currency were devalued[42]. But during the early years of Philip Augustus' reign, just prior to the beginning of the 13th century, the crown had issued "conservation of coinage" agreements in various towns of northern France, ushering in what Thomas Bisson has called a durable conception of monetary stability. Instead of making the unrealistic pledge not to issue any new coinage, the king now promised that he would allow old coins to continue circulating along with any new issue, meaning that money-changers would be the arbiters of relative value[43].

In fact, money-lenders domiciled in major financial centers were prominent among the investors in early urban *rentes viagères*. As noted above, various *bourgeois* of Rheims bought up the entire issue of *rentes* by Troyes in 1232 and by Auxerre in 1235, while burghers of Arras invested in issues by Tournai, Roye, Saint-Riquier, Calais, and Ghent. The latter were also the principal creditors of Brugge in 1283, both for the city's *lijfrenten* and for a somewhat larger short-term debt[44]. In the special case of Rheims, Pierre Desportes finds that men of wealth preferred investing in long-term rather than short-term debt because the city's ecclesiastical authorities, vigilant in the enforcement of usury laws, threatened a formal inquiry into their usurious practices in 1234[45]. In general, one would expect lenders to diversify their investments, blending relatively secure long-term loans with high-interest short-term credits. On the other side of the equation, as Ogris suggested, both cities and ecclesiastical institutions were heavily burdened with short-term debt, some of which both were now attempting to consolidate through the sale of *rentes viagères*[46]. In cases where bankers were already holders of a city's short-term obligations, as the Arrageois were at Ghent in the 1280s, they may have encouraged magistrates to think about consolidation, as a way of lessening their own risks.

But if cities were using long-term debt as a means to avoid default on short-term loans, one must also ask why lenders believed that towns would continue to honor their obligations on through the years. Could magistrates really and truly obligate for the long term not just the revenues of the town itself, but also the property of its citizens, which stood surety for these loans? To understand why it was believed that they could, one must consider the place of these towns both in the communal revolution that had swept across much of France during the12th century, and in the legal revolution of the 13th century. The mere fact of having a charter as a commune, granting security of property to its citizens and some degree of autonomy to its magistrates, did not in itself make a town worthy of credit on a long-term basis. Although the first urban *rentes viagères* were not issued until the early 13th century,

---

41 M.A. Ladero Quesada, "Formas de credito en los reinos españoles, siglos XII al XV", in H. Dubois (ed.), *Local Administration and International Credit in the Sixteenth Century,* Bern, 1986, pp. 29-35.
42 Desportes, *Reims et les Rémois,* p. 128.
43 Bisson, *Conservation of Coinage. Monetary exploitation and its restraint in France, Catalonia, and Aragon (c. 1000 A.D.-c. 1225),* Oxford, 1979, pp. 159-163.
44 Derville, "La Finance Arrageoise", p. 41.
45 Desportes, *Reims et les Rémois,* pp. 126, 131.
46 Derville, *Saint-Omer,* p. 231.

as we have seen, some towns had charters in the 11th century: Le Mans as early as 1039, Cambrai in 1076[47].

The crucial point seems to be that the French crown entered into a new relationship with the communes of the *Langue d'oil* during the reign of St. Louis. In a period when the king's council now included many graduates of university law faculties, royal initiatives tended not so much to overturn customary law as to confirm its principles through legislative enactments. Thus the communes experienced what Charles Petit-Dutaillis called the second stage of their development. The chartering of new communes by the king or by other princes was by now quite rare; indeed many communes had already been suppressed, often at the instance of local ecclesiastical lords. At the same time, however, many other communes came to be accepted by the king's jurists as privileged entities. The principle that collective entities could be "legal persons," capable of owning property and swearing oaths, had been widely recognized since the latter half of the 12th century, when, in Petit-Dutaillis' words, the status of legal personhood "sprang up at the slightest pretext" and with no legal authorization. Monasteries and bishoprics were legal persons in this sense, but so were institutions dependent on the Church, like hospitals and confraternities; communes were legal persons, but so were groups of townsmen, like "the poor of Chartres," who brought suit in the king's court in 1150. During the 13th century legal personhood was defined more clearly, and treated as a privilege that could be granted only by the king. To quote Petit-Dutaillis again, this "doctrine must have been elaborated at the *curia regis* in St. Louis' reign, because right from the start of his successor's reign the pleas and decrees of the Parlement of Paris show that it was applied as a matter of course"[48].

Meanwhile, the towns of the *Langue d'oil* were being called upon to make novel contributions to the crown, particularly for the king's ill-fated Crusade to Egypt; according to estimates by William Jordan, so-called gifts from the towns of northern and central France provided between 15% and 20% of the nearly 2,000,000 *livres tournois* the crown is thought to have expended for the Crusade[49]. Jordan estimates that the crown's cash outlay for the first two years of the Crusade (1248 - 1250) was 1,500,000 *livres parisis* or 1,875,000 *livres tournois*, of which about 950,000 l.p. came from clerical tenths, and about 270,000 from contributions by towns in northern and central France; the rest came mainly from the confiscated property of Albigensian heretics in the south, and from royal oppression of the Jews. Might some of the towns have raised the money they contributed through short-term loans that were then consolidated by sales of *rentes*?

This new relationship between the crown and northern and central communes may also help to explain why cities in southern France seemed impervious to the idea of issuing *rentes viagères*. According to Jordan, the towns of the *Langue d'oc*, where the king's rights as suzerain were not so clearly defined, made no contributions for the Crusade of 1248, though they did for the Tunis campaign of 1270[50]. Petit-Dutaillis divides the south of France into two zones as far as urban government is concerned. East of a line running from Aire-sur-Adour to Limoges, towns continued to have consuls and were not chartered as communes; towns west of this line are designated in the texts as communes, and were governed by a mayor and *jurats* rather than by consuls, as provided by the *Établissements de Rouen*, dating from the 1160s. But in this western zone, under English rule, communes were often divided by bitter internal strife during the first half of the 13th century. Thus while northern communes continued to enjoy such autonomy as the French king found useful, a stronger English crown forcibly subjected the southwestern communes to its control after about 1260[51].

---

47 C. Petit-Dutaillis, *Les Communes Françaises. Caractères et Évolution des Origines au XVIIIe Siècle,* Paris, 1947, p. 44; *The French communes in the Middle Ages,* tr. J. Vickers, Amsterdam, 1978, p. 21; J. Krynen, *L'empire du roi. Idées et croyances publiques en France, XIIIe-XVe Siècles,* "L'invasion du droit", pp. 69–84.

48 Petit-Dutaillis, *Les Communes Françaises,* pp. 126-140; *The French Communes,* pp. 77-86.

49 W.C. Jordan, *Louis IX and the Challenge of the Crusade,* 1979, pp. 78-98.

50 Jordan, *Louis IX and the Challenge of the Crusade,* p. 96.

51 Petit-Dutaillis, *Les Communes Françaises,* pp. 155-168; *The French communes*, pp. 95-103.

It seems, then, that the emergence of urban long-term debt in this form was made possible by a convergence of four distinct developments, two of which depended directly on the initiative of the French monarchy. First, from about the end of the 12th century, royal ordinances offered some assurances against erratic and unpredictable fluctuations in the value of currency. Second, urban communes, apparently in imitation of ecclesiastical corporations, contracted short-term debts at a level that many found difficult to manage. Third, investors concentrated in financial centers like Rheims and Arras proved willing to help their corporate customers roll over short-term debt into long-term obligations - possibly in connection with sums demanded by the crown for the king's Crusade. And last but not least, royal jurists established the principle that urban communes were one of the few forms of association privileged by the king to act as moral persons. At this point, and only at this point, the entity postulated by German legal historians - the town that takes its place alongside ecclesiastical corporations as an *unsterbliche Persönlichkeit* - emerges into view. And yet it was not the first time. If some cities in northern France created long-term debt in the early 13th century, some northern Italian cities had done so fifty or a hundred years earlier.

3. Twelfth-Century Origins of Long-Term Urban Debt: Northern Italy

As Philip Jones remarks, the long-term debt that holds our attention was only a part of what might be called an urban fiscal revolution in Italy:

> Starting in the mid-12th century the communes progressively multiplied and diversified, refined, and finally revolutionized the forms of public funding, in the process far surpassing ancient and contemporary Europe in fiscal ingenuity and sophistication, taxing resources for state purposes on a scale unequaled elsewhere[52].

Surely one of the great innovators was the commune of Genoa, the *campagna communis*, mentioned for the first time by the early 12th-century chronicler Caffaro, when he comes to recount how the republic's citizens distinguished themselves in the First Crusade, fighting under the banner of San Giorgio. Long-term debt is first mentioned by one of Caffaro's continuators, who describes how Genoa sent sixty-three galleys and 163 sailing ships to Spain to assist Count Berengar of Barcelona in the siege and conquest of Tortosa in 1148. To pay for this expedition, Genoa borrowed heavily from bankers in Piacenza, as much as 8,600 *lire*. Then, to reduce some of this debt to more manageable terms, in February 1149 the commune ceded control of certain direct taxes to creditors willing to accept the promise of annual payment. This was the first so-called *compera*, or consortium of lenders vested with public rights, but by no means the last. Later the same year the city created new taxes on ship construction and on certain types of merchandise; another *compera* was given control of all these revenues for a period of twenty-nine years, again in connection with debts from the Tortosa campaign. These loans became the basis for a permanent long-term debt[53]. Some *compere* were eventually retired, but others remained on the books for generations, with separate accounting for each loan and the revenues associated with it. The first consolidation occurred in 1340, when loans dating as far back as 1258 were capitalized at various rates. Further consolidations of more recent *compere* were made in 1368, 1381, and 1395. Finally, in 1407/1408, all *compere* whose shares were still outstanding were merged to form the *Banco di San Giorgi*[54].

52 Jones, *The Italian City State from Commune to Signoria,* Oxford, 1997, pp. 390-391.

53 H. Sieveking, *Studio sulle Finanze Genovesi nel Medioevo e in Particolare sulla Casi di San Giorgio, Atti della Società Ligure della Storia Patria,* XXXV, Parte Prima, Genoa, 1905, pp. 47-50; T.O. De Negri, *Storia di Genova,* Milan, 1968, pp. 232-235, 261-265.

54 J. Day, *Les Douanes de Gênes, 1376-1377,* 2 vols., Paris, 1963, I, pp. xxxi-xxxiii; on the Banco di San Giorgio, H. Sieveking, *Studio sulla Finanze Genovesi nel Medioevo e in Paricolare sulla Casa di San Giorgio, Atti della Società Ligure della Storia Patria,* XXXV, Parte Seconda, Genoa, 1907.

Many other Italian cities used the same method of raising capital, either for emergencies or to consolidate short-term debt. During the 1160s, similar emergency loan operations are recorded for Piacenza, Milan, and Pisa[55]. In 1164, in return for a loan of 1,150 marks of silver *in maxima necessitate* by twelve members of leading aristocratic families in Venice, the Doge ceded to their control for eleven years the city's rental income from the Rialto market. In 1187, those who provided 40,000 *lira* to finance a naval expedition against Zara received for a term of thirteen years the revenues from direct taxation, and from houses owned by the city[56]. In Verona, a 13th-century consortium that provided the city with 27,000 ducats formed itself into a society, the *unitas civium*, whose descendants continued for centuries to collect the revenues set aside for this purpose[57].

But as Gino Luzzatto argued in his pioneering study of Venice's public debt, the Doge and the Consiglio dei Savi did not wish to abandon fiscal sovereignty to the city's creditors: "This dangerous path was soon abandoned, in favor a system of forced loans" imposed on all citizens who met a certain threshold of wealth. The earliest such loan that can be documented occurred in 1172, when, to help mobilize a fleet against the Byzantine Emperor Immanuel Commenus, citizens agreed to lend against promises of repayment; to collect the declarations of wealth that served as a basis for assessment, the city was divided into six districts, and each of these into its component parishes. For greater assurance, Doge Sebastiano Ziano, "with the advice of the Savi," decreed that records of "the loans made thus far" were to be kept by the Procurators of San Marco, "until such time as the Republic can pay off its debt." For a second loan of the year 1187, the ninety citizens who contributed, seemingly according to their wealth, were promised that "we shall not burden you for two years hence with any further loan on behalf of our commune." The transition from one form of borrowing to the other seems to have been completed by 1207, when Doge Pietro Ziani made three pledges to "all those who have made loans to our commune at 4%, 2%, or 3%." First, all income from taxes levied on vendors' stalls, the Rialto market, and the weigh house was to be set aside "until your loans are repaid." Second, the names of all creditors were to be inscribed in the assessment books of the commune, kept by the Procurators of Saint Mark. And third, twice each year the Procurators or their agents would demand the said incomes from those who farmed them, in order to make distributions to creditors[58]. Some Venetian historians have suggested that these interest-bearing forced loans took the place of a tax that was levied in lieu of military service, but Luzzatto believes they grew out of the "good old custom" whereby citizens were expected to come to the aid of their city in time of need[59]. In any case, though interest continued to be paid, the loans were not retired as promised. Nonetheless, demands on the treasury rose dramatically in the 1260s, because of Venice's war with Genoa, and prospective lenders demanded further assurances. In 1262, the Grand Council decreed a so-called *ligatio pecuniae*. Payments on loans as well as collection of the revenues assigned to them was entrusted to a new board of officials, the *Ufficiali degli Prestiti*; the *Ufficiali* were required to swear a solemn oath that, after deducting 36,000 *lira* for the city's ordinary expenses, they would use the revenues under their control to pay interest on loans, and only then to meet the expenses of Venice's overseas territories, or to amortize the loans. In effect, all earlier loans that were still outstanding now lost their individuality, being consolidated into a single pool of debt. Creditors were not given certificates, but on the basis of entries in the public ledgers, still kept by the Procurators of Saint Mark, shares in Venice's debt had clearly become negotiable, for the Grand Council's decree specifies that purchasers of loan credits have the same rights as the original lenders[60].

55 Jones, *The Italian City State,* pp. 396-397.
56 G. Luzzatto, *I Prestiti della Repubblica di Venezia (secoli XIII-XV). Introduzione, Storia, e Documenti*, Padua, 1929, p. xii.
57 R.C. Mueller, *The Venetian Money Market, Banks, Panic, and the Public Debt (1200-1500),* Baltimore, 1997, p. 456.
58 Luzzatto, *I Prestiti,* iv, pp. x-xiv.
59 Luzzatto, *I Prestiti,* pp. xv-xix.
60 Luzzatto, *I Prestiti,* pp. xxv-xxvii; F.C. Lane, "Public debt and private wealth: particularly in 16th-century Venice", in *Histoire économique du monde Mediterranéen: Homage à Fernand Braudel,* 2 vols., Paris, 1973, II, pp. 317-326.

This too was a form of funded debt that some other Italian cities imitated, especially after the *ligatio pecuniae* of 1262. Even before this date, Genoa gave the principle of the consolidated forced loan a characteristic Ligurian twist. Starting in 1235, the commune financed some of its maritime campaigns by requiring the wealthy to lend according to their ability; to pay themselves back, lenders were formed into a society or *maona* vested with control of the enterprise; for example, the *maona* of Chios enjoyed for several generations the profits of Genoa's island dominion in the Aegean, including the lucrative alum trade[61]. In Siena, the earliest forced loan dates from 1291, when ninety citizens were asked to contribute 4,000 pounds, to be repaid six months later as a slightly higher sum, either in cash or in credits against what they owed in the annual levy of direct taxes. For a much larger loan of 20,000 gold florins in 1300, the commune's promise to repay lenders in six months at 15% interest was guaranteed by the General *Gabella*, the city's most important income, after deduction for the salaries of city employees[62]. In Florence, all still outstanding forced loans were consolidated in the 1340s in a *Monte Commune*, with interest initially set at 5%[63].

During most of the 14th century, Lucca was ruled either by native *signori*, like Castruccio Castracani (1316-1328), or by outsiders, notably Pisa, which ruled here from 1342 to 1369. In that year Emperor Charles IV granted the wish of the Lucchese by freeing them from Pisan control, but he also left behind and imperial vicar, the cardinal-bishop of Porto. Only in 1370, when the rights of the imperial vicariate were transferred to the *anziani* of the *popolo*, did the commune of Lucca regain its liberty. But the price was dear: 100,000 florins to the emperor and 40,000 for the bishop of Porto, a combined sum well in excess of the city's annual revenue of 60,000 to 70,000 florins. Neighboring states like the Republic of Florence, Pisa's great foe, came to Lucca's immediate aid, but to retire this debt to its friends Lucca turned, as in the past, to forced loans or *proventus* levied on its citizens. This time, however, it soon became clear that the principal could not be repaid from city revenues in a timely way. Accordingly, magistrates pooled citizen loans into a *Massa Creditorum*, to which an important revenue, the *douana salis*, was pledged as surety for annual interest at 10%[64]. By this time, the prestige of this new system of public credit had also radiated beyond Italy. In Catalonia, the city of Barcelona organized in 1340 a system of public debt based, it was said, on Italian models; as in the Venetian *ligatio pecuniae*, certain key revenues were solemnly set aside to fund the debt. But the debt that Barcelona's created looks more like an imitation of the northern French towns that had been issuing *rentes* for about a century: *censals morts*, considered to be perpetual, were offered for sale at 7.5% interest, and *censals vitalicios* at 14.24%[65].

From the standpoint of modern economics, it may seem that Barcelona's magistrates were confused about what they were doing. Towns that sold *rentes viagères* or *Leibgedinge* or *censals vitalicios* mainly to outsiders positioned themselves to take advantage of a growing market for life-annuities; the size of the long-term debt was limited only by the capacity of the city treasury to bear annual interest charges. Conversely, towns that relied on permanent forced loans levied on their own citizens missed out on this opportunity, save insofar as they accepted deposits from non-citizens. One might even take it as a sign of modernity that Italian states recognized the importance of market principles during the 16th century by switching from forced loans to life-annuities, starting in Venice, where the mint began in 1538 to accept deposits in gold or silver against a promise to pay 14% interest for the life-time of

61 Sieveking, *Studio sulle Finanze Genovesi*, 1905, pp. 52-53.

62 W. Bowsky, *The Finances of the Commune of Siena, 1287-1355,* Oxford, 1970, p. 172.

63 A. Molho, *Florentine Public Finance in the Early Renaissance, 1400-1433,* Cambridge, Massachusetts, 1971, p. 64.

64 C. Meek, *Lucca 1369-1400. Politics and Society in an Early Renaissance City-State,* Oxford, 1978, pp. 3-7, 53-60; according to the author, p. 56, "it does not seem that Lucca had a consolidated public debt earlier" than 1371.

65 M.-A. Ladero Quesada, "Formas de credito en los reinos Españoles, siglos XII al XV," in H. Dubois (ed.), *Local and International Credit,* Bern, 1986, pp. 29-35.

the depositor[66]. When I first looked at this question some years ago, it seemed to me the one form of long-term debt was modern, being based on market principles, while the other was not, even if I was not so crude as to say so explicitly[67].

On a closer inspection, however, the two forms of long-term debt have many points of contact. In both cases, there seems to be an inverse relation between taxing citizen wealth directly and calling on citizens for loans in one way or another. In Siena, where direct taxation disappeared toward the end of the 13th century, the practice of levying forced loans seems to have taken its place; in Ghent at about the same time, direct taxes, no longer so common as before, were to be levied on burghers who had not purchased *rentes viagères*[68]. In both cases too, creditors seem initially to have had most confidence in pledges of city property. Thus while northern cities often alienated domain revenue to satisfy holders of *rentes perpetuelles*, Italian cities placed revenues of the same kind into the hands of consortia of voluntary lenders. In addition, holders of shares in the consolidated debt of Italian cities, like *rentiers* north of the Alps, had to deal with scruples relating to Church sanctions against usury[69].

The most fundamental similarity is that the same developments that converged to make long-term urban debt a possibility in 13th-century France were present also in 12th-century Italy. If royal ordinances created the conditions for relative stability of currency struck at royal mints in France, in Italy it was the major towns themselves that provided some predictability, through the issue of a reliable silver currency that preceded the gold ducat and the gold florin by about a century. In 1138 a charter of Emperor Conrad II conceded to Genoa the right to coin money in perpetuity; in 1150 the commune promised 400 *lire* a year to a group of investors who undertook to operate at least eight banks or tables of exchange in the city[70]. In Venice during much of the 12th century, contracts were usually denominated in the silver *denarii* of the Imperial mint at nearby Verona, which had as much as twice the silver content of Venice's own *denarii*. By the 1170s however, during the reign of the above-mentioned Doge Sebastiano Ziano, contracts were more commonly denominated in Venetian *denarii*, which now had the same silver contact as those issued by the imperial mint[71]. By this time, both Genoa and Venice had contracted, in the course of their respective wars, large debts that had to be stabilized through consolidation in one way or another. Genoa's rich men were free to participate or not, as they chose, in the *compere* that took control of tax revenues to pay themselves back for their loans; for the *maone* that funded the city's overseas enterprises, they had to contribute whether they wanted to or not, like the citizens assessed for forced loans in Venice.

Finally, it was of great importance whether a city government could obligate, over the long term, the wealth of its citizens as well as the revenues of the town. This was not an issue in cities that followed the *compera* model, but it was for those that imitated the example of Venice, through consolidation of forced loans. Reinhold Mueller suggests that the systematic use of forced loans implies a city government of a certain type: thus while cities that came to be ruled by *signori* "seem to have continued an ad hoc system of voluntary loans, organized into a floating debt," cities that preserved a republican form of government, like Venice itself, "changed to a system of forced loans based on assessment of ability to pay"[72]. One might cite the example of Vicenza in support of this view. During the decades it was ruled by Ezzelino da Romano, famed tyrant of Verona (d. 1259),

66 L. Pezzolo, *Società, finanza e fisco nella Repubblica Veneta del Secondo '500,* Treviso, 1990, p. 175. Cf. Jones, *The Italian City-State,* p. 396, speaking of the period before 1500: "With the growing recurrence of extraordinary or emergency occasions the most regular resource, even pre-dating tax-reform, was credit finance in various forms (only the sale of rents seeming not to have spread in Italy)."

67 J.D. Tracy, *A Financial Revolution in the Habsburg Netherlands,* Berkeley/Los Angeles, 1985, Chapter 1.

68 Bowsky, *The Finances of the Commune of Siena,* Chapter 5; van Werveke, *Gentse Stadsfinanciën,* p. 33.

69 J. Kirchner, "Moral Theology and Public Finance", *Archivum Fratrum Praedicatorum*, 40 (1970) pp. 47-72.

70 G. Airaldi and G. Marcenaro (eds.), *Credito e banco dall'Italia all'Europa, secoli XII-XVIII,* Genoa, 1992, p. 18.

71 F.C. Lane and R. Mueller, *Money and Banking in Medieval Venice,* 2 vols., Baltimore, 1985, I, pp. 108-113.

72 *The Venetian Money Market,* pp. 455-456.

Vicenza met its credit needs by voluntary loans, guaranteed either by citizens acting on the city's behalf but in their own name, or by giving creditors control of domainal incomes. But for the next half-century, as Vicenza's restored communal independence was backed by the Republic of Padua, Ezzelino's great foe, the city switched over to forced loans based on an assessment of citizen wealth[73]. More broadly speaking, the cities that funded all or part of their long-term debt through a consolidation of forced loans – Venice, Genoa, Florence, Siena, and Lucca – were indeed cities with strong republican traditions.

But the old idea of a sharp contrast between freedom and despotism has been relativized, notably in the work of Philip Jones, who argues that all Italian communes, whether republics or *signorie,* suffered a "failure of sovereignty" because of shared "congenital defects," such as the pervasive influence of wealth and class, the refusal by many citizens to bear their fair share of the common burden, and, above all, bitter factional rivalries among the great clans. In communes where a new sworn association, the *popolo*, took over the reins of government and restricted the privileges of the great, one-party rule continued as before, under a different name[74]. The most that Jones will acknowledge is that by the early 14th century, "two regimes and two ideologies were coming to divide and dispute the territory of city-state Italy." Across the northern plain, from Piedmont to the borders of the Venetian Republic, *signori* were by this time in firm control of all the major towns. In Jones's view, these were regions where landed power remained predominant – Machiavelli's "castle-owning *gentiluomini.*" In port cities like Genoa and Pisa and Venice itself, and in practically all of Tuscany, republicanism prevailed. These were regions where "feudalism was feeble or as at Venice non-existent, [and] where business wealth was greater or more concentrated in the hands of merchant-banking dynasties"[75].

In other words, the cities that created long-term debt by consolidating forced loans were cities that claimed to have governments that ruled in the interests of all members of the commune. Though such claims may not stand up very well after an examination of the struggles for wealth and power within each city, they amount nonetheless to a kind of legitimacy – a moral construct that probably gave some degree of confidence to citizen-lenders in Italy. In northern France, it was legitimacy of a different kind – namely, that the commune was chartered by the king as a legal person – that helped give *rentiers* some degree of confidence in the promises of town governments. When cities both north and south of the Alps failed to meet their annual interest obligations, as they regularly did, creditors who chose to hold on to their investments – rather than getting something back through the secondary market – could take solace in the thought that because something ought to be done, sooner or later something would be done. But at this point, the discussion of urban finance merges into a larger discussion of the history of the cities themselves, a history that discloses important common themes underlying the differences between urban communities in Italy and beyond the Alps. As one might say in a slightly old-fashioned German, *so geht die kleine Frage des Schuldenwesens in die grosse Frage der geschichtlichen Bedeutung des mittelalterlichen Städtewesens auf.*

---

73 N. Carlotto, *La città custodita. Politica e finanza a Vicenza dalla caduta di Ezzelino al Vicariato imperiale (1259-1312),* Milan, 1993, pp. 152-159.
74 Jones, *The Italian City-State,* pp. 522-540, 594-607.
75 Jones, *The Italian City State,* pp. 645-646.

CITIES, PROVINCES, STATES AND PUBLIC DEBTS

DETTE PUBLIQUE, AUTORITES PRINCIERES ET VILLES DANS LES PAYS DE LA COURONNE D'ARAGON (14e-15e SIECLES)

Manuel Sánchez Martínez
Institución Milá y Fontanals (CSIC) Barcelone

Introduction

Au cours du premier tiers du 14e siècle, c'est-à-dire de manière relativement précoce, les cités et les villes (*ciudades* et *villas*) de la Couronne d'Aragon recoururent pour financer leur déficit à une modalité spécifique de crédit, la vente de rentes viagères et perpétuelles, toutes deux rachetables. Après des débuts modestes et circonscrits à quelques localités, l'émission de rentes prit à partir des années 1350 et 1360 des proportions extraordinaires sur tous les territoires de la Couronne (de Perpignan aux *villas* du sud valencien, de Tarragone et Valence jusqu'aux confins occidentaux, limitrophes de la Castille) et concerna tous les noyaux urbains, quelle que fût leur taille, aussi bien les cités de Barcelone, Valence ou Saragosse, que les plus petites communautés rurales, sans oublier les villes-marchés, grandes ou moyennes. L'importance de la dette à long terme apparaît nettement si l'on examine le poids qu'elle occupait dans les bilans financiers urbains: comme je le montrerai par la suite, un grand nombre de *municipios* consacraient entre 60% et 70% de leurs dépenses au service de la dette[1]. Autrement dit, une part considérable des ressources municipales n'était pas employée à la satisfaction des besoins de la communauté, mais allait remplir les caisses des créanciers, qu'ils fussent ou non originaires de la ville. Cet impressionnant transfert de ressources publiques à des particuliers s'accentua lorsqu'en 1365, soit quelques dix années après les municipalités, la *Diputación del General* de Catalogne commença elle aussi à vendre des rentes. Comme on l'imaginera sans peine, le rôle considérable tenu par la dette à long terme dans les finances locales eut de profondes répercussions sur la vie économique, sociale et politique des municipalités catalano-aragonaises. La gestion d'une dette qui absorbait presque les trois quarts des dépenses devint ainsi dès le dernier tiers du 14e siècle le problème fondamental de la majorité des *municipios*. Elle polarisait les débats des conseils urbains, des débats dont la teneur permet de distinguer les intérêts contradictoires des groupes qui prenaient part au gouvernement des villes. D'autre part, nous verrons aussi comment l'insolvabilité de certaines municipalités put avoir pour conséquence une réaction des créanciers qui en vinrent à contrôler plus ou moins étroitement les appareils fiscaux et financiers de la cité ou de la ville en difficulté. Le cas de Majorque, dont les finances tombèrent aux mains des créanciers (surtout barcelonais) dès le début du

1 Voir A. Furió, "La dette dans les dépenses municipales", in D. Menjot et M. Sánchez Martínez (éds.), *La fiscalité des villes au Moyen Age (Occident méditerranéen), 3. La redistribution de l'impôt*, Toulouse, 2002, pp. 321-350, qui comporte une bibliographie sur la dette dans la Couronne d'Aragon. Voir aussi, dans ce même ouvrage, les travaux de J. Morelló, "La signification des dépenses dans deux localités du Camp de Tarragone: Reus et Valls (XIVe-XVe siècles)", pp. 99-112; P. Verdés, "Evolution des dépenses de Cervera", pp. 113-126; P. Ortí Gost, "La estructura del gasto municipal en Barcelona (1360) y Sant Feliu de Guíxols (1361-62)", pp. 127-136; A. Furió, "Les dépenses de la métropole valencienne", pp. 193-202 et A. J. Mira Jódar, "Les dépenses municipales d'Alcoy (1390-1517)", pp. 203-210.

15e siècle, constitue l'un des exemples les plus spectaculaires, mais ce n'est pas le seul. Enfin et fort logiquement, la politique d'assainissement des finances, en s'efforçant de diminuer une dette volumineuse, se traduisit fréquemment par un redoublement de la pression fiscale pesant sur la communauté: établissement de *tallas* nouvelles, plus lourdes, augmentation des impôts indirects ou bien encore, comme nous le verrons dans le cas de la Catalogne, apparition de nouveautés fiscales. Ces rapides observations préliminaires doivent permettre d'appréhender d'emblée l'ampleur d'un phénomène qui toucha toute l'ossature politique de la Couronne – la monarchie, les États régionaux et même les plus petits noyaux ruraux de peuplement – et dans lequel furent impliqués pratiquement tous les secteurs de la société, la noblesse, l'Église et surtout les oligarchies urbaines, mais aussi les investisseurs les plus modestes, sans oublier les petits commerçants et les artisans.

Bien que l'existence de la dette à long terme fût connue depuis longtemps, son importance considérable dans la vie économique, sociale et politique des territoires catalano-aragonais commence seulement peu à peu à être révélée au grand jour, au rythme des études réalisées sur les finances royales et municipales depuis une dizaine d'années[2]. Cet intérêt demeure encore trop récent pour permettre une synthèse profonde et équilibrée sur la complexe évolution fiscale et financière de la monarchie, des États régionaux et des municipalités de la Couronne d'Aragon entre le 13e siècle et le 15e siècle. Malgré les progrès réalisés depuis 1990 dans l'exploration de problématiques qui avaient jusqu'alors fort peu retenu l'attention des historiens, nous en sommes encore, à l'aide d'une masse documentaire réellement impressionnante, à reconstruire élément par élément l'histoire fiscale et financière de la Couronne et des municipalités.

La quantité et la qualité des sources documentaires font en effet des territoires catalano-aragonais, en particulier de la Catalogne et du Pays Valencien, les plus étudiés de ce point de vue, un excellent laboratoire pour l'analyse de la fiscalité et des finances centrales et locales aux 14e et 15e siècles. L'extraordinaire richesse des fonds conservés à l'*Archivo de la Corona de Aragón* (Barcelone), en particulier des registres de la Chancellerie royale et des séries du Patrimoine royal, se combine à merveille avec la documentation tout aussi abondante qui est abritée dans de nombreuses archives locales: livres d'actes municipaux, livres des comptes du *clavari* ou trésorier municipal, comptabilités diverses, fonds notariés, etc. L'ensemble de ce matériel documentaire rend possible sans difficultés particulières l'analyse du processus de construction du système fiscal municipal, mis en place pour répondre aux exigences de la Couronne, ainsi que celle de l'évolution des structures fiscales et financières de la monarchie et des municipalités tout au long des deux derniers siècles du Moyen Age. Quelques unes des sources locales déjà étudiées démontrent le niveau de maturité et de complexité, voire parfois de sophistication, qui avait été atteint dans l'utilisation des méthodes fiscales et financières, non seulement par les grandes cités, mais aussi, ce qui est beaucoup plus significatif, par des villes de taille petite ou moyenne[3].

Les difficultés qui s'opposent actuellement, comme je l'ai souligné, à l'élaboration d'une synthèse relativement complète sur la fiscalité et les finances à l'échelle de l'ensemble de la Couronne, se retrouvent évidemment aussi lorsque l'on aborde le thème de la dette publique. Nous manquons

---

2 Pour des synthèses générales rapides et assorties de bibliographies, voir J.-A. Sesma Muñoz, "Las transformaciones de la fiscalidad real en la baja Edad Media", in *XV Congreso de Historia de la Corona de Aragón*, Saragosse, 1994, I, vol. 1, pp. 233-291; M. Sánchez Martínez, *El naixement de la fiscalitat d'Estat a Catalunya (segles XII-XIV)*, Vic-Gérone, 1995; M. Sánchez Martínez, "Fiscalidad y finanzas municipales en las ciudades y villas reales de Cataluña", in *V Congreso de Estudios Medievales*, León, 1997, pp. 207-238; A. Furió, "Deuda pública e intereses privados. Finanzas y fiscalidad municipales en la Corona de Aragón", in *Edad Media. Revista de Historia*, II (1999), pp. 35-79; ainsi que la bibliographie rapportée dans l'annexe de D. Menjot et M. Sánchez Martínez, *La fiscalité des villes au Moyen Âge (Occident méditerranéen). 2. Les systèmes fiscaux*, Toulouse, 1999, pp. 506-516.

3 Sur quelques unes de ces sources, voir les articles de Ch. Guilleré, J. Morelló, P. Ortí Gost, M. Sánchez Martínez, M. Turull et P. Verdés in D. Menjot et M. Sánchez Martínez, *La fiscalité des villes au Moyen Âge (France méridionale, Catalogne et Castille). 1. Étude des sources*, Toulouse, 1996. Pour un exemple éloquent de la richesse et de la diversité des sources conservées, qui permettent d'étudier des bourgades aussi petites que Valls et Reus (respectivement 401 et 356 feux en 1378), voir J. Morelló, *Fiscalitat i deute públic en dues viles del Camp de Tarragona: Reus i Valls, segles XIV-XV*, Barcelone, 2002, pp. 33-55.

encore d'études approfondies qui, allant au-delà de simples allusions (aussi importantes soient-elles) au rôle joué par la dette dans le cadre des finances urbaines, fassent du thème de l'endettement public l'objectif même de la recherche, dans le but d'observer minutieusement ses modalités, sa chronologie, les causes de l'émission des rentes, la gestion de la dette, le monde des créanciers, etc. D'autre part, les travaux déjà réalisés ont conduit à des avancées quelque peu inégales selon les territoires. Ainsi, tandis que nous ne savons encore que très peu de choses sur l'apparition et le développement de la dette à long terme dans les *ciudades* et les *villas* aragonaises, les municipalités valenciennes et catalanes ont pour leur part constitué un champ d'études plus privilégié. Cependant, comme nous le verrons, alors que la genèse et le premier développement de la dette au 14e siècle ont été les mieux analysés pour la Catalogne, en lien étroit avec la fiscalité royale, les historiens qui travaillent sur le cas valencien ont plutôt étudié le *background* social de la dette, en particulier au cours du 15e siècle. Enfin, pour ce qui concerne Majorque, les recherches sur la dette ont été effectuées dans le cadre du contexte spécifique de la profonde crise économique, sociale et politique subie par la cité et l'île au 15e siècle.

Dans ces conditions, je me limiterai ici à la présentation d'un tableau très sommaire et général sur l'apparition, la perpétuation et la gestion de la dette publique dans quelques noyaux urbains catalans et valenciens, ainsi que de manière secondaire dans les Etats régionaux, en précisant d'emblée qu'en raison des carences et des déséquilibres auxquels je viens de faire allusion, il existe encore en ce domaine de nombreuses zones d'ombre et de grands vides qui restent à combler. J'espère malgré tout que ces pages contribueront à ce que le thème de la dette dans la Couronne d'Aragon soit désormais mieux pris en considération dans l'historiographie et cesse d'être absent des grandes études sur les finances et l'endettement public au bas Moyen Age.

L'apparition et la perpétuation de la dette publique dans les *municipios*...

Afin d'observer les débuts de l'émission de rentes par les cités et les villes, je commencerai par le cas de la Catalogne, où la question a été plus souvent et mieux étudiée, bien que le processus ne dût pas être foncièrement différent dans les autres noyaux urbains de la Couronne.

En Catalogne, comme dans d'autres régions d'Occident, la fiscalité municipale a été progressivement mise en place à partir du début du 14e siècle pour répondre aux besoins croissants de la Couronne, qui s'était ici engagée dans une expansion méditerranéenne particulièrement coûteuse. La monarchie a ainsi doté les villes des instruments fiscaux nécessaires pour faire face aux tributs et aux dons exigés par la Couronne elle même. Les *municipios* devinrent par conséquent des intermédiaires de la fiscalité royale et des rouages efficaces dans le processus de recouvrement des sommes demandées par le monarque. Nous avons montré ailleurs comment l'établissement de *tallas* proportionnelles (c'est-à-dire du premier pilier des finances locales du point de vue chronologique) au cours du 13e siècle s'expliquait principalement par la nécessité de payer au roi les contributions ordinaires de la *questia* (Catalogne), de la *pecha* (Aragon), de la *peyta* (Valence), de la *cena* (droit de gîte) ou bien les rachats épisodiques du service d'ost[4]. Par la suite, à partir des années 1320, et plus précisément entre 1320 et 1340, le monarque concéda aux pouvoirs municipaux l'autorisation d'établir des *imposicions* (impôts indirects sur la consommation et les transactions, appelés *sisas* en Pays Valencien), afin qu'ils puissent réunir les dons octroyés au roi pour financer la conquête de la Sardaigne (1323), les campagnes contre Grenade et les guerres contre Gênes (1330-1335) ou bien encore pour faire face aux menaces des Banu

4 M. Sánchez Martínez et P. Ortí Gost, "La Corona en la génesis del sistema fiscal municipal en Cataluña (1300-1360)", in M. Sánchez Martínez et A. Furió (éds.), *Corona, municipis i fiscalitat a la baixa Edat Mitjana*, Lérida, 1997, pp. 236-242; et M. Sánchez Martínez, "Le système fiscal des villes catalanes et valenciennes du domaine royal au bas Moyen Age", in Menjot et Sánchez Martínez , *La fiscalité des villes (2)*, pp. 18-21.

Marin du Maghreb (1340). Au seuil des années 1340, les pouvoirs municipaux disposaient donc déjà des deux principaux instruments fiscaux – impôt direct de la *talla* et impôts indirects (*imposicions*) – nécessaires pour payer au roi aussi bien les contributions ordinaires que les dons extraordinaires concédés dans les assemblées des *Cortes*. Ce n'est que de manière secondaire que les communautés pouvaient faire usage de ces recettes pour satisfaire leurs propres besoins. Le caractère irrégulier des dons ne permet cependant pas encore de parler de l'existence d'un véritable système fiscal municipal pour cette période. En d'autres termes, les *imposicions* étaient concédées exclusivement dans le but de rassembler les sommes consenties au roi et n'étaient effectives que pour la durée de la concession (deux ou trois ans): une fois satisfaits les dons, les *imposicions* étaient supprimées et l'appareil administratif qui avait été mis en place pour leur recouvrement était démantelé[5].

Or, il était clair que le caractère urgent des opérations militaires pour lesquelles le roi sollicitait les subsides ne pouvait guère s'accommoder de la lenteur propre au recouvrement d'une *talla* ou du long délai d'encaissement trisannuel des affermages des *imposicions*. Dès 1333, les dons concédés à la Couronne par les cités et les villes du domaine royal relevaient d'un principe de répartition: chaque assemblée procédait au vote d'une somme déterminée, qui était ensuite répartie entre les communautés, avant que ces dernières ne recouvrent chacune leur contribution grâce aux impôts concédés par le roi. Les avantages pour la Couronne étaient évidents: la perception du don était assurée dans les délais établis et, surtout, les coûts financiers de l'opération incombaient désormais aux pouvoirs municipaux. En d'autres termes, la Couronne exigeait que les dons fussent payés par avance ou dans des délais définis de manière très précise, et elle obligeait ainsi les *municipios* à s'endetter et à prendre en charge les coûts financiers que cette dette pouvait engendrer[6]. Tant que les dons demeurèrent relativement sporadiques, il semble que les prêts contractés ne posèrent pas de problèmes particuliers aux finances urbaines: les édiles municipaux (*regidores*) imposaient des prêts forcés ou bien recouraient au crédit auprès des juifs, des marchands-banquiers ou des membres les plus importants du patriciat local, puis le remboursement des prêts était effectué sur le produit de la *talla* qui s'ensuivait ou bien sur celui des *imposicions*. Il s'agissait toujours de prêts à court terme et à des taux d'intérêt élevés[7].

Le problème se posa de manière plus préoccupante à partir de 1340, comme le montre l'exemple de la Catalogne, une fois encore le mieux connu. Entre 1340 et 1344, les cités et les villes du domaine royal furent confrontées pour la première fois de leur histoire au paiement à la Couronne de trois dons importants qui se chevauchaient[8]. Les pouvoirs municipaux catalans recoururent alors au crédit plus que jamais auparavant, et ce fut à cette même occasion qu'apparurent de manière criante les inconvénients d'une dette flottante – à court terme et au taux d'intérêt élevé – qui ne faisait qu'aggraver

5 Sánchez Martínez et Ortí Gost, "La Corona en la génesis", pp. 242-260. Pour le cas de Barcelone, voir P. Ortí Gost, "La construcció del sistema fiscal municipal a Barcelona, segles XIII-XIV", in *Barcelona. Quaderns d'Història*, 2/3 (1996), pp. 17-34.

6 P. Ortí Gost, "La distribución de la carga fiscal entre las ciudades y villas de realengo en la Cataluña del s. XIV", in D. Menjot et M. Sánchez Martínez, *Fiscalidad de Estado y fiscalidad municipal en los reinos hispánicos bajomedievales*, Madrid (sous presse).

7 L'un des cas les mieux connus est celui de la cité de Valence. Les *regidores* durent dès les premières décennies du 14e siècle s'appuyer sur l'infrastructure bancaire de la ville: depuis 1320, un changeur municipal canalisait le crédit de petits prêteurs, à des taux d'intérêt qui oscillaient entre 10% et 30%, avec des délais de remboursement compris entre 9 et 12 mois; voir J.-V. García Marsilla, "La génesis de la fiscalidad municipal en la ciudad de Valencia (1238-1366)", in *Revista d'Història Medieval*, VII (1996), pp. 165-167; et surtout J.-V. García Marsilla, *La formación de un mercado del crédito. Orígenes y difusión del censal en la sociedad valenciana (siglos XIII-XIV)*, thèse de doctorat, Universidad de Valencia, 1999 (je remercie l'auteur de m'avoir permis d'utiliser ce travail, encore inédit au moment où j'écris ces lignes).

8 Un don de 40.000 livres fut consenti pour conjurer le péril d'une invasion des Banu Marin (1340), mais, avant que fussent écoulées les trois années prévues pour le recouvrement, un autre don de 50.000 livres (1342) fut concédé pour le financement de l'expédition qui allait conduire à l'incorporation définitive du royaume de Majorque à la Couronne d'Aragon. De plus, un nouveau subside de 70.000 livres fut offert en 1344 afin de payer la guerre en Roussillon, c'est-à-dire dans la partie continentale du royaume majorquin; voir M. Sánchez Martínez et P. Ortí Gost, *Corts, Parlaments i fiscalitat a Catalunya. Els capítols del donatiu (1288-1384)*, Barcelone, 1997, docts VII, VIII et IX, pp. 63-87.

les difficultés des finances[9]. Comme l'écrivait Y. Roustit, *charge ruineuse des intérêts, délais d'amortissement trop courts, ces deux raisons poussaient à un changement de méthode*[10]. La nouvelle méthode adoptée allait alors précisément être celle qu'utilisaient depuis longtemps les particuliers: le recours à la vente de rentes, d'abord viagères (*violarios*), puis perpétuelles (*censales*), aux taux d'intérêt respectifs de 14,28% et 7,14%. Il est presque inutile de souligner les avantages de cette nouvelle modalité de crédit pour les pouvoirs municipaux: ils pouvaient notamment rassembler un capital sur lequel pesait un intérêt beaucoup plus bas que s'il était provenu des circuits de crédit à court terme et, surtout, ils avaient dorénavant la possibilité de différer fortement l'amortissement. Même si nous connaissons quelques cas isolés de ventes de pensions effectuées dans les années précédentes, les premiers exemples significatifs et clairement documentés de vente de rentes par les pouvoirs municipaux catalans remontent aux années 1340[11].

Il faut cependant attendre 1344 pour assister à la première émission générale de rentes qui soit mise en œuvre par toutes les cités et villes royales en Catalogne – de Barcelone jusqu'au plus petit noyau rural –, une émission très clairement organisée par la Couronne elle même. À l'occasion du don déjà mentionné de 1344, le roi Pierre le Cérémonieux ordonna en effet que tous les noyaux urbains du domaine royal vendissent des rentes pour la valeur d'une partie de la somme qu'ils devaient fournir d'après la répartition du subside, des rentes qui devaient être assignées sur les impôts indirects concédés par le roi[12]. Il faut insister sur le fait que la Couronne, probablement en accord avec les procureurs urbains (*síndics*) présents au Parlement, fut l'organisatrice de cette grande émission, car elle décida de la part du don que chaque communauté devait vendre sous forme de rentes et chercha aussi les acheteurs parmi les citoyens de Barcelone. En suivant M. Boone, on pourrait donc dire que les trois acteurs de la pièce qui devait être jouée étaient déjà montés sur scène: le monarque, les dirigeants municipaux qui allaient vendre les rentes et les futurs acheteurs[13]. Le jeu à trois fonctionna: le roi reçut dans un délai extrêmement bref l'argent des deux premières années du don; bon nombre de citoyens de Barcelone, pour la plupart des marchands, furent invités à prendre part à cette vente générale de rentes; enfin, les *ciudades* et les *villas* concernées (c'est-à-dire toutes celles du domaine royal) assumèrent le coût financier de l'opération en vendant les rentes correspondantes et en prenant à leur charge la gestion de la dette contractée. On peut ajouter que cette émission générale de rentes fut aussi pour la monarchie l'occasion de faire œuvre de pédagogie, car elle mit en exergue les avantages d'un produit financier relativement neuf et le diffusa jusqu'aux endroits les plus reculés de Catalogne où il était encore inconnu. Tout ceci démontre le rôle de la monarchie non seulement dans la genèse de la fiscalité municipale, une facette déjà connue de son action, mais aussi dans l'adoption décisive de la dette à long

---

9 Nous sommes ainsi renseignés sur les difficultés financières de Barcelone entre 1342 et 1345, de même que sur le recours massif au crédit à des taux de 20% ou de 25% procuré par des juifs, qui agissaient parfois comme simples intermédiaires de prêteurs chrétiens; voir Y. Roustit, "La consolidation de la dette publique à Barcelone au milieu du XIVe siècle", in *Estudios de Historia Moderna*, IV (1954), pp. 31-39; ainsi que J. Sobrequés, "Contribució econòmica del municipi de Barcelona a l'empresa de recuperació del regne de Mallorca", in *VIII Congreso de Historia de la Corona de Aragón*, II, Valence, 1973, pp. 291-302. Sur la crise financière de la ville de Gérone entre 1339 et 1341, voir C. Guilleré, *Girona al segle XIV*, Gérone, 1993, I, pp. 247-261. L'étude du cas de la cité de Valence a aussi révélé les difficultés croissantes du pouvoir municipal à partir du début des années 1340, lorsqu'il devint nécessaire de contracter de nouveaux prêts pour pouvoir payer les intérêts des emprunts déjà effectués; voir García Marsilla, *La formación de un mercado del crédito*, pp. 380-382.

10 Roustit, "La consolidation", p. 38.

11 Par exemple, la ville de Cervera vendit un *violario* en 1332 et un *censal* en 1334 (M. Turull, *La configuració jurídica del municipi baix-medieval. Règim municipal i fiscalitat a Cervera*, Barcelone, 1990, p. 459), alors que les cités de Gérone et Manresa vendirent leurs premiers *violarios* respectivement en 1342 et en 1343 (Guilleré, *Girona al segle XIV*, pp. 253 et 261 et M. Torras, "El deute públic a la ciutat de Manresa a la baixa Edat Mitjana" in M. Sánchez Martínez (éd.), *Fiscalidad real y finanzas urbanas en la Cataluña medieval*, Barcelone, 1999, pp. 158-160).

12 M. Sánchez Martínez, "La Corona en los orígenes del endeudamiento censal de los municipios catalanes (1343-1344)", in Menjot et Sánchez Martínez, *Fiscalidad de Estado*. La cité de Barcelone, sur laquelle nous sommes bien documentés, payait en 1344-1345 les pensions de 48 *violarios* et en 1348-1350 celles de 33 *censales* (Roustit, "La consolidation", p. 75).

13 M. Boone, "'*Plus deuil que joie*.' Les ventes de rentes par la ville de Gand pendant la période bourguignonne: entre intérêts privés et finances publiques", in *Bulletin trimestriel du Crédit Communal de Belgique*, 176 (1991-92), pp. 3-4.

terme par les cités et les villes de la Couronne. L'idée selon laquelle les activités fiscales et financières des municipalités du domaine royal étaient jusqu'au milieu des années 1350 profondément imbriquées dans la politique financière de la Couronne en ressort encore un peu plus confortée.

Un nouveau pas décisif fut franchi quelques années plus tard, lorsque les cités et les villes de Catalogne durent payer entre 1353 et 1359 de nombreux dons pour financer les guerres méditerranéennes (Sardaigne et Gênes) et le début du conflit contre la Castille (1356-1365)[14]. Si, comme nous venons de le voir, la première émission générale de rentes fut directement organisée par la Couronne, l'initiative passa à partir de 1353 aux pouvoirs municipaux eux-mêmes. En effet, toute cité ou ville dut à partir de ce moment déposer dans les *taules de canvi* de différents banquiers la part du don qui lui correspondait. Afin d'obtenir dans de brefs délais la somme en question, le monarque octroya aux municipalités une autorisation générale pour vendre des rentes. De ce fait, les édiles eurent dès lors toute latitude pour décider de la quantité de *censales* ou de *violarios* qui devait être vendue et pour choisir les acheteurs de la rente parmi leurs propres concitoyens ou parmi des personnes étrangères à la localité[15]. A titre d'exemples, entre 1351 et 1359, la cité de Barcelone vendit 117 *censales* et 329 *violarios*; la ville de Manresa, 4 *censales* et 8 *violarios* au cours des seules années 1356-1357 et la ville de Cervera 11 *censales* et 6 *violarios* entre 1353 et 1356[16].

Les années comprises entre 1350 et 1360 furent donc décisives dans la mise en place de l'endettement galopant que connurent dans les années qui suivirent les *municipios* de Catalogne. Néanmoins, en dépit du jugement négatif avec lequel une certaine historiographie a appréhendé la dette publique, il semble clair que l'endettement à long terme constitua dans les moments d'urgence un puissant pourvoyeur de revenus pour les villes, et qu'il contribua aussi de manière déterminante au développement d'institutions proprement urbaines[17]. On peut ainsi affirmer que la dette à long terme fut la cause de la cristallisation du système fiscal municipal. Elle contribua d'une part à perpétuer de fait les impôts indirects alloués pour le paiement de la dette, puisque le roi avait autorisé le maintien des *imposicions* jusqu'au rachat de l'intégralité des rentes qui avaient été vendues pour payer les dons consentis. Mettre des impôts au service d'une dette difficilement amortissable à court terme, c'était d'évidence les rendre permanents et faire d'eux la clef de voûte du système fiscal municipal. D'autre part, les administrations financières municipales perdirent leur caractère épisodique à partir du moment où leur existence ne dépendit plus du versement sporadique de dons à la Couronne, elles étaient dorénavant au service d'une dette qui exigeait le maintien d'un appareil bureaucratique de plus en plus complexe ne pouvant plus comme auparavant souffrir de suppressions temporaires. À partir des années 1360, pour le formuler autrement, le système fiscal et financier des municipalités commença à couper le cordon ombilical qui l'avait jusqu'alors uni aux dons de la Couronne, il abandonnait progressivement son statut de simple instrument de la fiscalité royale.

A l'instar de ce qui s'était produit en Catalogne, les dons exigés par le roi pour financer les conflits méditerranéens des années 1350 eurent pour conséquence en 1355 la première émission de *censales* et de *violarios* par l'*universitas* de Majorque; les pensions furent probablement vendues avec un taux d'intérêt de 8% et acquises par les habitants de l'île. En 1356, le paiement d'un autre don au monarque suscita une deuxième émission de rentes, pour l'essentiel des *violarios* au taux moyen de 12,2% qui furent cette fois-ci achetés par des citoyens de Barcelone[18]. Ainsi commença à s'établir la

---

14 Sánchez Martínez, "*Corts*, *Parlaments* y fiscalidad en Cataluña: las *proferetes* para las guerras mediterráneas (1350-1356)", in *XV Congreso de Historia de la Corona de Aragón*, I, 4, Saragosse, 1996, p. 253-272.

15 Un bon exemple de cette méthode est présenté par P. Verdés, "La consolidació del sistema fiscal i financer municipal a mitjan segle XIV: el cas de Cervera", in Sánchez Martínez (éd.), *Fiscalidad real y finanzas urbanas*, pp. 185-217.

16 Roustit, "La consolidation", pp. 100-107; Torras, "El deute públic", pp. 163-164; et Verdés, "La consolidació del sistema fiscal", pp. 201-206.

17 Furió, "La dette", pp. 321-322.

18 P. Cateura, *La trentena esgarrifadora. Guerra i fiscalitat. El regne de Mallorca (1330-1357)*, Palma de Majorque, 2000, pp. 81-103 et 115-117. Le contrôle exercé par la Couronne sur l'émission de 1356, située dans la cité de Barcelone, rappelle un peu ce que nous avons observé pour la Catalogne en 1344.

forte présence des créanciers barcelonais sur le marché majorquin de la dette, une présence qui devait avoir des conséquences considérables à la fin du 14e siècle et au début du 15e siècle.

Dans le royaume de Valence, il est assuré que des *violarios* furent vendus dans les années 1340 et au début des années 1350 par certaines villes, telles Onda (1340), Peñiscola (1342) et Alzira (1351)[19]. Néanmoins, l'adoption de cette modalité de crédit par la cité même de Valence eut lieu un peu plus tardivement et se déroula de façon plus complexe. Comme nous l'avons vu précédemment, les finances valenciennes se trouvaient depuis le début des années 1340 dans une situation critique, qui s'aggrava encore au milieu des années 1350 en raison des pressions exercées par la Couronne pour subvenir aux dépenses engendrées par les guerres en Méditerranée. La vente de rentes paraissait dans ces conditions la solution la plus appropriée et la cité vendit de fait en 1356 un *censal* au taux d'intérêt de 7,14%. L'événement demeura cependant isolé. Une hypothèse a dès lors été avancée: les édiles eux-mêmes (ou bien le groupe social dont ils étaient les représentants) préféraient maintenir les procédures traditionnelles de crédit à court terme et au taux d'intérêt élevé, car elles les favorisaient de manière évidente, puisqu'ils étaient les principaux prêteurs d'argent à la municipalité. Le concept de dette flottante a donc pour cette raison persisté dans la cité de Valence encore une dizaine d'années après 1356. Or, les dépenses nouvelles et importantes engendrées par la guerre de Castille, tout particulièrement les dons concédés au monarque, laissèrent la voie libre à l'endettement à long terme: en 1366, la municipalité valencienne, incapable de rembourser les prêts contractés antérieurement, reconvertit par décret l'intégralité de la dette en pensions de *censales* à 8,33%, ouvrant ainsi une étape nouvelle et décisive dans l'histoire des finances municipales[20].

Le cas des cités et des villes aragonaises est beaucoup moins bien connu pour le 14e siècle. La ville de Fraga vendit, semble-t-il, deux *censales* dès 1309, tandis que les hasards de la documentation ont permis de savoir que des enclaves aussi petites qu'Almudévar ou Fuentespalda vendirent aussi des rentes, respectivement en 1324 et en 1340. De toute façon, les informations les plus consistantes à ce sujet concernent les cités de Huesca, Daroca ou Saragosse au 15e siècle[21].

Il est donc permis de conclure qu'au cours des années 1350 et 1360 la nouvelle modalité de crédit, utilisée de manière sporadique par quelques cités et villes dans les années 1320 et 1330, devint monnaie courante pour les autorités municipales catalanes et valenciennes ainsi que pour l'*universitas* de Majorque. Elle n'allait guère tarder à être adoptée aussi par les gestionnaires de la nouvelle fiscalité d'Etat.

... et dans les *Diputaciones* des États régionaux

Le financement de la guerre très dure qui mit aux prises les deux grandes Couronnes péninsulaires (Castille et Aragon) entre 1356 et 1365 conduisit à l'établissement d'une nouvelle fiscalité d'Etat dans la Couronne catalano-aragonaise et se traduisit par un redoublement de la pression fiscale

19 García Marsilla, *La formación de un mercado del crédito*, p. 313 et A. Furió, "Crédito y endeudamiento: el censal en la sociedad rural valenciana (ss. XIV-XV)", in E. Sarasa et E. Serrano (éds.), *Señorío y feudalismo en la Península Ibérica (ss. XII-XIX)*, I, Saragosse, 1993, p. 515.

20 L'ensemble de ce processus est parfaitement expliqué par García Marsilla, *La formación de un mercado del crédito*, pp. 385-404; sur les prêts forcés de la cité de Valence dans ces années, voir aussi A. Rubio et M. Rodrigo, *Antroponimia valenciana del segle XIV. Nómines de la ciutat de València (1368-69 i 1373)*, Valence/Barcelone, 1997, pp. 13-21. En dépit de contextes évidemment différents, on ne peut que souligner les similitudes entre la consolidation par décret de la dette à Valence et ce qui se produisit à Florence en 1345.

21 A. Berenguer Galindo, *Censal mort. Historia de la deuda pública del concejo de Fraga (siglos XIV-XVIII)*, Fraga, 1998, p. 38 et I. Falcón, "Finanzas y fiscalidad de ciudades, villas y comunidades de aldeas aragonesas", in *V Congreso de Estudios Medievales*, pp. 239-273 (en particulier pp. 267-270). Quelques indications sur l'émission de *censales* par Calatayud à la fin du 14e siècle se trouvent dans M. Diago Hernando, "Haciendas municipales en el reino de Aragón durante el s. XIV: el caso de Calatayud y su comunidad de aldeas", in Menjot et Sánchez Martínez, *Fiscalidad de Estado* (sous presse).

sur le territoire. En Catalogne par exemple, la pression fiscale exercée par la Couronne sur le Principat atteignit son maximum pour le 14e siècle dans les mois compris entre mai 1364 et mai 1367. Les pouvoirs municipaux continuèrent par conséquent à vendre des rentes de façon massive, afin de contenter rapidement la voracité fiscale de la monarchie[22].

La composante principale de la nouvelle fiscalité d'Etat est formée de l'ensemble d'impôts désignés sous le nom commun de *generalidades* qui pesaient d'une part sur la production et la commercialisation des textiles et d'autre part sur l'entrée et la sortie de marchandises à travers un réseau de ports établis sur les frontières des trois territoires composant la Couronne d'Aragon. En outre, respectant en cela les règles particulières du jeu politique en vigueur dans la Couronne depuis la fin du 13e siècle, la nouvelle fiscalité fut gérée non par le roi, mais par des commissions émanées des *Cortes*: les *Diputaciones del General* d'Aragon, de Catalogne (avec Majorque) et de Valence, qui percevaient et géraient les *generalidades* et d'autres impôts dans leurs territoires respectifs et au sein de leurs propres frontières, le monarque et ses officiers demeurant toujours expressément exclus[23].

Ces nouveaux organismes, créés en principe pour administrer les dons importants concédés par les *Cortes* au cours des années 1360, ne tardèrent cependant guère à financer les aides en question au moyen de l'émission de dette assignée sur l'impôt des *generalidades* et sur d'autres recettes des différentes *Diputaciones*. Dans le cas précis de la Catalogne où, comme nous le verrons, les premières émissions de dette par la *Diputación* datent de 1365, il est sans doute possible d'appliquer le même raisonnement que celui adopté précédemment pour la dette municipale. En effet, si la vente par les pouvoirs municipaux de rentes constituées sur les *imposicions* fut déterminante dans la consolidation de ces impôts et contribua à donner une certaine continuité à l'administration municipale elle-même, le même processus devait se produire *mutadis mutandis* à l'échelle de la *Diputación*. La nécessité de faire face à une dette croissante (dorénavant à l'échelle de l'ensemble du Principat de Catalogne) assignée sur les *generalidades*, conféra de fait à ces impôts un caractère permanent et transforma la *Diputación*, jusqu'alors simple organisme gestionnaire des dons, en une institution durable. Ses compétences allaient à partir du début du 15e siècle dépasser les domaines strictement fiscaux et financiers pour en faire un organisme politique puissant qui put dans certains cas s'opposer au monarque lui-même, par exemple lors de la guerre civile catalane dans les années 1460.

Nous connaissons encore mal la chronologie et les modalités de l'émission de dette publique par les trois Etats régionaux de la Couronne. En Catalogne, la première vente de rentes par la *Diputación* eut lieu en 1365. Afin de régler une partie du don élevé qui avait été concédé au roi par les *Cortes*, les députés durent vendre des rentes pour un montant de 50.000 livres, assignées sur les *generalidades*. Le taux d'intérêt proposé était de 10% et l'émission de *violarios* (au taux de 14,28%) demeurait prohibée, bien qu'il fût permis de vendre des rentes mixtes – ½ *censal* et ½ *violario* – au taux

22 M. Torras a par exemple observé l'émission croissante de *censales* par la cité de Manresa entre 1354 et 1367, qui atteignit son point culminant dans les années 1364-1367, c'est-à-dire durant ces véritables "trois années noires" (Torras, "El deute públic", pp. 165-169). De façon plus générale, sur la pression fiscale durant les années 1360, voir P. Ortí Gost, "Una primera aproximació als fogatges catalans de la dècada de 1360", in *Anuario de Estudios Medievales*, 29 (1999), pp. 747-773 et M. Sánchez Martínez et M. Hébert, "La 'part du prince': contributions et transfert au roi dans les dépenses des villes des pays de la Couronne d'Aragon et de Provence", in Menjot et Sánchez Martínez, *La fiscalité des villes (3)*, pp. 302-306. Sur la place occupée par la dette dans les recettes de quelques municipalités durant cette période, voir Furió, "Deuda pública e intereses privados", p. 61.

23 Voir de manière générale Sesma Muñoz, "Las transformaciones", pp. 281-290; et Sánchez Martínez, *El naixement*, pp. 129-134. Sur les *Cortes* déterminantes du milieu du 14e siècle, à l'occasion desquelles naquit la nouvelle fiscalité, voir notamment : J.-L. Martín Rodríguez, "Nacionalización de la sal y aranceles extraordinarios en Cataluña (1365-1367)", in *Anuario de Estudios Medievales,* 3 (1966), pp. 515-524; et les travaux suivants de J.-A. Sesma Muñoz, "La fijación de fronteras económicas entre los estados de la Corona de Aragón", in *Aragón en la Edad Media*, V (1983), pp. 141-165; "Estado y nacionalismo en la baja Edad Media. La formación del sentimiento nacionalista aragonés", in *Aragón en la Edad Media*, VII (1987), pp. 245-273; et "Fiscalidad y poder. La fiscalidad centralizada como instrumento de poder en la Corona de Aragón (siglo XIV)", in *Espacio, Tiempo y Forma. Revista de la Facultad de Geografía e Historia*, IV (1989), pp. 447-463. Le système fiscal élaboré durant la deuxième moitié du 14e siècle, le fait mérite d'être rappelé, restera en vigueur jusqu'au début du 18e siècle, lorsqu'il fut supprimé par la nouvelle dynastie des Bourbons.

moyen de 10,71%. Il faut souligner qu'au cours de cette première émission (et la même chose devait se produire en 1376), tant que ne fut pas atteint le montant évoqué de 50.000 livres du don, personne ne put acheter de rentes en Catalogne, si ce n'est aux députés. La *Diputación* surgit ainsi dans le marché de la dette en nette position de monopole, elle offrait un taux d'intérêt attractif, exemptait les rentes qu'elle vendait du paiement des impôts indirects et des dépenses administratives, tout en interdisant l'achat de rentes à des personnes ou à des entités autres que les députés. Il semble que l'échec de cette émission centralisée conduisit la *Diputación* à se diriger là où le marché de la dette était le plus actif et où il fonctionnait depuis presque une décennie, c'est-à-dire dans les cités et dans les villes. Cette même année 1365 (et la même chose devait se reproduire en 1375 et 1378), il fut décidé que les villes seraient chargées de vendre les rentes au nom de la *Diputación*. Naturellement, les pensions ne seraient dans ce cas pas payées sur les ressources propres des municipalités, mais avec les impôts de cette institution, c'est-à-dire avec les *generalidades*. Les *municipios* apparaissent donc ainsi comme des intermédiaires de la fiscalité d'Etat au même titre qu'ils l'étaient pour la fiscalité royale. Les importantes implications économiques, sociales et politiques de ce lien spécifique que les cités entretiennent avec la *Diputación* par le biais de la dette publique demandent encore à être étudiées. Quoi qu'il en soit, il est d'ores et déjà certain que la dette à long terme s'installa durablement dans la *Diputación* de Catalogne et que, dès 1371, des mesures commencèrent à être prises afin de réduire le volume de l'endettement et d'assainir les finances de l'institution[24]. Quelques sondages dans la maigre documentation comptable de cet organisme permettent d'affirmer que dans les dernières années du 14e siècle et les vingt premières années du 15e siècle, une moyenne de 66% des dépenses de la *Diputación* catalane était consacrée au service de la dette[25].

Pour ce qui concerne la *Diputación* du royaume de Valence, il semble qu'elle recourut pour la première fois à l'émission de rentes en 1390. L'étude réalisée sur les finances de cette institution pour les vingt premières années du 15e siècle a permis d'attester l'existence d'émissions nouvelles en 1401, 1402, 1403 et, surtout, en 1404, lorsque furent vendues 97 rentes à 7,14% qui constituèrent 69% des recettes annuelles de la *Diputación*. D'autre part, entre 1404 et 1417, les intérêts et l'amortissement de la dette absorbaient environ 45% des dépenses[26].

Enfin, les premières émissions de *censales* par la *Diputación* du royaume d'Aragon paraissent aussi dater des dernières décennies du 14e siècle, et l'on considère que le plus ancien de tous les *censales* fut vendu en 1397 au taux d'intérêt de 5,5%. Une étude des finances de la *Diputación* aragonaise à la fin du 15e siècle indique par ailleurs que 56% des dépenses entre 1481 et 1490 étaient consacrées au service de la dette[27].

Vers 1370, la dette publique était donc solidement installée dans la quasi-totalité des *municipios* catalans et valenciens, de même que dans les finances de la *Diputació* catalane, un exemple que n'allaient pas tarder à suivre une vingtaine d'années plus tard les *Diputaciones* de Valence et d'Aragon.

---

24 Toutes les données relatives aux premières émissions de dette par la *Diputación* de Catalogne sont issues des chapitres des dons concédés aux *Cortes*: Sánchez Martínez et Ortí Gost, *Corts, Parlaments i fiscalitat*, docts. XX (2) et XXI (Cortes de Tortosa et Barcelone, 1365), doc. XXIV (Cortes de Tortosa, 1371), doc. XXVI (Cortes de Lérida, 1375), doc. XXVII (Cortes de Monzón, 1376) et doc. XXVIII (Cortes de Barcelone, 1378).

25 M. Berthe, *Les finances de la "Generalitat" de Catalogne (1382-1479)*, Diplôme d'Études Supérieures d'Histoire, 1958 (je remercie l'auteur de m'avoir permis la consultation de ce travail inédit).

26 Rosa Muñoz Pomer, *Orígenes de la Generalidad valenciana*, Valence, 1987, pp. 315-333, 343-348 et 352.

27 J.-A. Sesma Muñoz, *La Diputación del reino de Aragón en la época de Fernando II (1479-1516)*, Saragosse, 1977, pp. 125-137 et 151-163.

Les types de rentes: *censales* et *violarios*

Quittons un instant le chemin de l'endettement emprunté par les cités et les villes pour examiner, ne serait-ce que rapidement, la nature des rentes et les procédures suivies pour leur émission.

Nous avons déjà vu que pouvaient être distingués par leur nature deux types de rente: les *violarios* (en catalan *violaris*), limités à la vie du créancier, même s'ils sont généralement allongés à deux vies, et les *censales* (en catalan *censals*) ou rentes perpétuelles[28]. L'expression *censal mort*, par laquelle on a coutume de désigner la rente perpétuelle, indique clairement que, dans ce cas, seul était vendu le droit de percevoir une pension, explicitement détachée de la propriété du bien qui garantissait l'opération. Le théologien franciscain Francesc Eiximenis le formulait très bien à la fin du 14e siècle: [les *censals morts*] *són dits morts car lo comprant no ha nengun dret en les coses que compra lo dit censal, sinó solament dret de percebra la quantitat que compra*...("les *censales morts* sont dits morts parce que l'acheteur ne possède aucun droit sur les choses [sur lesquelles] il achète le *censal* en question, si ce n'est le droit de percevoir la quantité qu'il achète")[29]. Pour cette raison, comme il s'agissait de la perception d'une pension qui n'était pas rattachée à un bien concret et déterminé, le pouvoir municipal avait pour habitude de garantir la vente d'un *censal* non pas sur son propre patrimoine (d'ailleurs inexistant ou d'une importance négligeable dans les cités valenciennes et catalanes) mais sur les biens de toute la communauté comprise sous le concept juridique d'*universitas*. Il convient à ce sujet de distinguer clairement deux phénomènes dont la confusion conduit parfois à commettre des erreurs: l'assignation des pensions sur une recette fiscale concrète – ici, les impôts indirects – n'est pas identique à la garantie du contrat-vente, garantie qui n'était autre que la communauté elle-même. Tous les habitants étaient de la sorte rendus responsables en leur personne et en leurs biens de l'accomplissement de l'intégralité des clauses pénales et financières du contrat. De ce point de vue, la vente de rentes à partir du premier tiers du 14e siècle peut être considérée comme un signe de la maturité politique et institutionnelle de nombreuses communautés, déjà qualifiées d'*universitates* dans le langage juridique du 13e siècle. La vente d'une rente impliquait en effet que l'on possédât la capacité juridique de la garantir avec tous les biens de la communauté et de l'assurer devant la *cort* du *veguer* ou bien d'un officier ecclésiastique. Cela supposait aussi que l'on disposât des recettes fiscales suffisantes pour payer la pension et que l'on fût capable d'organiser un appareil administratif, aussi rudimentaire fût-il, susceptible de gérer la dette à long terme.

---

28 Voir A. García, "El violari", in *Homenatge al Dr. Sebastià García Martínez*, Valence, 1988, I, pp. 179-187 et, du même auteur, "El censal", in *Boletín de la Sociedad Castellonense de Cultura*, XXXVII (1961), pp. 281-310. Sur les deux types de rentes, voir notamment D. Rubio, "L'estructura diplomàtica dels censals morts i els violaris", in J. Serrano Daura (éd.), *El territori i les seves institucions històriques*, Barcelone, 1999, II, pp. 843-863; et les travaux de Furió, "Crédito y endeudamiento", pp. 509-515 et "Deuda pública e intereses privados", pp. 58-59. La documentation conservée relative aux ventes de *violarios* pour deux vies est susceptible d'apporter des indications de valeur sur les relations familiales de l'acheteur, sur des liens précis de caractère économique et/ou professionnel ou bien encore sur certaines relations de patronage. En ce sens, dans le cas de la cité de Barcelone des années 1340 par exemple, ces informations constituent des données de premier ordre pour la connaissance des élites urbaines, voir Sánchez Martínez, "La Corona en los orígenes del endeudamiento censal..."

29 Voir J. Hernando Delgado, *El "Tractat d'usura" de Francesc Eiximenis*, Barcelone, 1985, p. 78. C'est pour cette raison que lors de la vente d'un *censal mort*, il était spécifié que la transaction était effectuée *absque fatica et laudimio*, c'est-à-dire sans les contraintes caractéristiques de la vente d'un cens emphytéotique ou de la constitution d'une rente sur un bien immeuble concret. Sur les différences entre ces divers types de rente (parfois appelées de manière indistincte *censal*, d'où des confusions fréquentes), voir García, *La formación de un mercado del crédito*, pp. 277-314 et Rubio, "L'estructura diplomàtica", pp. 848-853. Tandis qu'en Catalogne, depuis le début du 14e siècle, le droit de percevoir la rente était constitué sur la personne même de celui qui la vendait, à Valence et dans ces mêmes années, le *censal* était encore garanti sur un bien immeuble déterminé; voir respectivement J. Hernando Delgado, "*Questio disputata de licitudine contractus emptionis et venditionis censualis cum conditione revenditionis*". Tratado sobre la licitud del contrato de compraventa de rentas personales y redimibles. Bernat de Puigcercós, O.P., s. XIV", in *Acta Historica et Archaeologica Mediaevalia*, X (1989), pp. 23-25; et García, *La formación de un mercado del crédito*, pp. 306-308. Dans le domaine privé cependant, la garantie de paiement de la rente était au 15e siècle constituée par un bien meuble ou immeuble; J. Hernando Delgado, "Crédit i llibres a Barcelona, segle XV. Els contractes de venda de rendes (censals morts i violaris) garantits amb vendes simulades de llibres. El llibre, instrument económic i objecte de cultura", in *Estudis Històrics i Documents dels Arxius de Protocols*, XVIII (2000), p. 50.

Vers 1344, c'est-à-dire quand eut lieu en Catalogne la première émission généralisée de rentes, des cités telles que Barcelone, Lérida, Gérone, Manresa ou bien des villes comme Cervera réunissaient à l'évidence toutes ces caractéristiques. Néanmoins, soulignons-le, des rentes furent aussi vendues par des communautés aussi minuscules que Tagamanent, Mura ou Ódena, qui comportaient quelques dizaines de feux à peine et durent pour cette émission se doter d'une organisation fiscale et administrative sommaire afin de payer les pensions et de gérer leur petite dette. Pour la communauté, l'émission de rentes dut alors contribuer au renforcement de sa propre cohésion sociale. En somme, la vente de rentes non seulement refléta la maturité institutionnelle de nombreuses villes et cités, mais elle contribua aussi à créer dans d'autres noyaux urbains les conditions requises pour atteindre cette même maturité[30].

Les *violarios* comme les *censales* étaient rachetables, c'est-à-dire qu'ils étaient vendus *a carta de gracia* (acte de réméré). L'existence de la *carta de gracia* (c'est-à-dire de la possibilité de racheter le *censal* au même prix qu'il avait été acheté sans que les pensions annuelles diminuent le capital) constitua précisément l'un des motifs qui déchaînèrent la polémique sur le caractère licite de ces contrats. La place nous manquant ici pour développer cet aspect important, il suffira donc de rappeler que les discussions sur le caractère licite ou illicite des *censales* et des *violarios* se déroulèrent dans la Couronne d'Aragon de manière plus précoce que dans d'autres régions d'Europe. En effet, la première polémique importante – entre le dominicain Bernat de Puigcercós et Ramon Saera – eut lieu en Catalogne vers 1342 et il n'est pas anodin qu'elle coïncidât avec le moment où les deux types de rentes commençaient à être utilisés par les pouvoirs municipaux comme instrument de crédit[31].

Quant au taux d'intérêt (*for*), mentionné dans la documentation sous la forme "tant pour mille" (par exemple, 7.000 x 1.000: 14,28%; 12.000 x 1.000: 8,33%; 20.000 x 1.000: 5%, etc.), celui des *violarios* fut presque toujours de 14,28%. Puisque son extinction n'impliquait pas la restitution du capital, le *for* comportait aussi une quote-part d'amortissement[32]. Les premiers *censales* publics, au contraire, furent vendus au taux de 8,33% ou plus généralement de 7,14% en Catalogne. Par la suite, comme dans le reste de l'Europe, le taux d'intérêt baissa pour se situer à la fin du 14e siècle et au cours du 15e siècle à 6,66%, 5%, 4%, 3,33%, voire moins encore[33]. Comme nous le verrons par la suite, quelques-unes de ces réductions drastiques des taux d'intérêt résultèrent d'accords passés ponctuellement par certaines cités et villes avec les créanciers lors du processus de renégociation de la dette.

Même si manquent encore les études nécessaires qui permettraient d'établir des conclusions certaines sur la diffusion de l'un ou de l'autre type de rente, il semble que les premières ventes effectuées par les pouvoirs municipaux furent presque toujours des *violarios*, encore proches des prêts à

30 Sur ces questions, voir M. Turull et J. Ribalta, "*De voluntate universitatis.* La formació i l'expressió de la voluntat del municipi (Tàrrega, 1214-1520)", *Anuario de Estudios Medievales*, 21 (1991), pp. 143-231; et M. Turull, "*Universitas, commune, consilium*: sur le rôle de la fiscalité dans la naissance et le développement du Conseil (Catalogne, XIIe-XIVe siècles)", in B. Durand et L. Mayali (éds.), *"Excerptiones iuris": Studies in honor of André Gouron*, Berkeley, 2000, pp. 637-677. En ce qui concerne le caractère 'public' très marqué des rentes émises par les pouvoirs municipaux et les *Diputaciones*, voir P. Ortí Gost, "Fiscalité (municipale et d'État) et finances publiques dans la Couronne d'Aragon", in *L'impôt dans les villes de l'Occident Méditerranéen (XIIIe-XVe siècles)* (sous presse).

31 On peut renvoyer ici à quelques uns des travaux de Hernando Delgado, "*Questio disputata*", pp. 9-87; "Ramon Saera. *Allegationes iure factae super venditionibus violariorum cum instrumento gratiae.* Un tratado sobre la licitud del contrato de compraventa de rentas vitalicias y redimibles (violaris)", in *Acta Historica et Archaeologica Mediaevalia*, XI-XII (1990-1991), pp. 9-74; "El contracte de venda de rendes perpètues i vitalicies (censals morts i violaris) personals i redimibles (amb carta de gràcia). El tractat d'autor anònim *Pulchriores allegationes super contractibus censualium* (segle XIV)", in *Arxiu de Textos Catalans Antics*, Barcelone, XI (1992), pp. 137-179; et *El "Tractat d'usura" de Francesc Eiximenis.* Voir aussi le résumé suggestif sur ces questions fourni par R.J. Puchades Bataller, *Als ulls de Déu, als ulls dels homes. Estereotips morals i percepció social d'algunes figures professionals en la societat medieval valenciana*, Valence, 1999, pp. 101-116.

32 García, "El violari", pp. 180-181.

33 Cependant, entre particuliers, l'intérêt des *censales* oscillait au 15e siècle à Barcelone entre 5% et 10%; Voir Hernando Delgado, "Crédit i llibres", p. 40.

court terme du fait de leur taux d'intérêt relativement élevé[34]. Très vite cependant, et de manière générale en Catalogne à partir du milieu des années 1350, le *censal mort* occupa une place prépondérante et finit par éclipser presque complètement le *violario*. La *Diputación* de Catalogne, comme nous l'avons remarqué précédemment, interdit formellement la vente exclusive de *violarios* lorsqu'elle commença à émettre des rentes en 1365[35]. D'autre part, nous verrons par la suite que, dans le contexte de la politique d'assainissement financier entreprise dans le dernier tiers du 14e siècle, l'un des objectifs prioritaires des pouvoirs municipaux consista à vendre des *censales* afin de racheter les *violarios* qu'ils devaient encore payer. Il semble donc que le *censal* finit par devenir la rente par excellence des *municipios* et des *Diputaciones* de la Couronne d'Aragon[36].

L'émission de rentes était en principe soumise à l'autorisation du seigneur, c'est-à-dire du roi dans le domaine royal et des seigneurs laïques ou ecclésiastiques dans leurs territoires respectifs[37]. Nous avons déjà pu observer comment la Couronne elle même, à l'occasion du Parlement de 1344, avait organisé les premières ventes généralisées de *censales* et de *violarios* dans chacune des villes et cités du domaine royal afin de financer rapidement le don voté dans cette même assemblée. Néanmoins, à partir du milieu des années 1350, les nombreuses émissions de rentes, sans doute un peu incontrôlées, durent compliquer de nombreuses finances urbaines au point de mettre en péril leur efficacité comme instruments fiscaux et financiers de la Couronne. Afin d'éviter la 'destruction' – c'est le terme même du document ici utilisé – de beaucoup de noyaux urbains, soumis pour le paiement des pensions de la dette à une fiscalité écrasante, le roi Pierre le Cérémonieux promulgua une pragmatique sanction en 1363, par laquelle il était rigoureusement interdit de vendre des rentes qui ne fussent pas destinées au rachat d'autres rentes dont les taux d'intérêt étaient plus élevés[38]. Il est clair que la pragmatique sanction interdisait en fait toute augmentation de la dette dépourvue d'une autorisation expresse du roi, mais, puisqu'il rendait possible (et d'une certaine façon stimulait) l'émission de rentes pour le rachat d'autres rentes plus coûteuses, l'ordre royal ne constitua pas un frein à la dynamique du marché de la dette. En outre, la pragmatique sanction ne forma pas non plus un obstacle insurmontable à la poursuite de la vente de nouveaux *censales*: soit de manière collective aux *Cortes* dans la seconde moitié du 14e siècle, soit sur l'initiative individuelle d'une municipalité, les édiles urbains sollicitèrent maintes fois du roi la suspension momentanée de la pragmatique et la permission de continuer à vendre des rentes.

Une fois obtenue l'autorisation du roi ou du seigneur, l'assemblée générale (ou restreinte) des habitants nommait les procureurs chargés de négocier la vente de la rente et leur délivrait la procuration adéquate, qui leur conférait notamment la capacité de s'engager au nom de tous les habitants (*...obligandi vos et dictam universitatem et eius singulares...in personis et bonis cum iuramento, homagio et hostagio, scripturis terciorum et alias...*). La procuration, un document généralement assez long, indiquait aussi les mobiles qui poussaient la communauté à émettre une rente ainsi que le type d'intérêt préférable au moment où l'on devrait procéder à la vente. Après que l'acheteur eut été trouvé, le contrat était formalisé devant notaire: on y spécifiait le montant de la pension, le *for* (taux d'intérêt) à laquelle elle serait vendue et sa qualité, par exemple "x sous de *censuale mortuum*". Afin de bien marquer

34 Furió, "La dette ", p. 328.

35 En effet, tandis que les acheteurs avaient la possibilité d'acquérir *mig censal e mig violari ensemps* (c'est-à-dire une rente mixte au taux d'intérêt moyen de 10,71%), personne ne pouvait acheter de *violari tan solament*; Voir Sánchez Martínez et Ortí Gost, *Corts, Parlaments i fiscalitat a Catalunya*, doc. XX (2), cap. 7, p. 299.

36 Un travail récent consacré au crédit privé dans la cité de Barcelone au 15e siècle a néanmoins démontré comment le *violario* avait eu le dessus sur le *censal* au cours de ce siècle; voir Hernando Delgado, "Crédit i llibres ", p. 15. Ce résultat, si l'on y ajoute d'autres éléments déjà mentionnés précédemment (par exemple sur la garantie réelle et non personnelle des *censales* privés ou sur leur taux d'intérêt relativement élevé) plaide en faveur d'une nette différenciation entre la vente de rentes dans le domaine privé et l'émission de rentes par les organismes publics, d'où la nécessité d'étudier en détails la coexistence des deux circuits – le privé et le public – sur un même marché monétaire et d'élucider leurs logiques respectives. Sur ce point, voir Boone, "*Plus deuil*", p. 9.

37 Par exemple, le roi prit en compte aux *Cortes* valenciennes de 1403 une demande de la noblesse et interdit la vente des rentes qui ne bénéficieraient pas de l'approbation des seigneurs; Furió, "La dette", p. 329.

38 Archivo de la Corona de Aragón, Cancillería real, reg. 908, f. 137v.-138r.

la différence avec les pratiques du cens emphytéotique, il était spécifié que la vente s'effectuait *in franco alodio absque fatica tamen et laudimio et in nuda perceptione*, ce qui revenait à souligner, rappelons-le, que seul était vendu le droit à percevoir la pension. On indiquait ensuite que le *censal* était garanti sur les *bonis mobilibus et inmobilibus dicte universitatis*, c'est-à-dire sur les biens de tous les habitants, avant de préciser la date et le lieu du paiement de la pension annuelle. La *carta de gracia* (ou acte de réméré) pouvait apparaître sous la forme d'une clausule insérée directement dans le contrat ou bien constituer un document à part. En vertu de l'acte de réméré, l'acheteur pouvait considérer le contrat comme arrivé à son terme si le prix d'origine du *censal* lui était remis avec ses arrérages jusqu'au moment de l'expiration. Enfin, on inscrivait aussi d'ordinaire les garanties exigées par les acheteurs, parmi lesquelles se trouvait parfois la nécessité d'enregistrer la vente à la *cort* d'un officier royal, qui pourrait imposer une peine proportionnée dans le cas où le contrat ne serait pas exécuté. La vente était aussi parfois enregistrée à la *cort* d'un officier ecclésiastique afin d'ajouter aux peines civiles les peines ecclésiastiques (l'excommunication) si la pension n'était pas payée dans le délai convenu. Les garanties s'achevaient d'habitude par l'exigence d'otages, généralement six *prohoms* du lieu, qui devaient être détenus jusqu'à ce que les pensions fussent entièrement réglées[39].

L'endettement à long terme depuis le dernier tiers du 14e siècle et ses conséquences

Reprenons le fil de la chronologie là où nous l'avions laissé, c'est-à-dire un peu avant 1370. Une fois passées les années 1355-1365 qui virent se mettre en place un nombre considérable de nouveautés fiscales et financières (consolidation du système fiscal municipal et des impôts indirects qui en constituent la colonne vertébrale, établissement de la nouvelle fiscalité d'État, émissions massives de *censales* et de *violarios*...) et qui se caractérisèrent par une pression fiscale particulièrement forte de la Couronne sur le territoire, les pouvoirs municipaux ainsi que la *Diputación* de Catalogne continuèrent à vendre des rentes à un bon rythme. Puisque dans la seconde moitié du 14e siècle les chapitres mêmes des dons qu'elle consentait à la Couronne au travers des *Cortes* ordonnaient que les subsides fussent obtenus immédiatement au moyen de l'émission de dette assignée sur les *generalidades*, la *Diputación* catalane continua à vendre des *censales*. La *Diputación* valencienne fit de même en 1390, sans dépasser pour le moment le stade de la péripétie[40].

Portons maintenant notre attention vers les cités et les villes. Tout d'abord, les pouvoirs municipaux continuèrent à vendre des rentes pour la même raison qui avait provoqué l'accélération de leur endettement au milieu du siècle: les exigences de la Couronne. Même si ces dernières diminuèrent considérablement par rapport aux terribles années de la guerre contre la Castille, leur poids se fit encore fortement sentir à plusieurs moments, lorsqu'il s'agit de réprimer l'état de révolte endémique de la Sardaigne, de défendre la Catalogne des menaces des Grandes Compagnies (par exemple en 1369, 1374 ou 1385) ou bien encore de satisfaire les demandes suscitées par les couronnements ou les mariages de membres de la famille royale[41]. Les *municipios* obtinrent par conséquent l'autorisation de continuer à vendre des rentes dans le but d'assurer le financement immédiat de ces aides à la Couronne.

39 Sur tout ceci, voir Rubio, "L'estructura diplomàtica", pp. 859-863 et Furió, "La dette ", pp. 329-330; sur les garanties exigées par les acheteurs de rente, F. Sabaté, "La insolvència municipal a la segona meitat del segle XIV", in Sánchez Martínez, *Fiscalidad real y finanzas urbanas*, pp. 264-270.

40 Les *Cortes* catalanes de 1371 et de 1379-1380 concédèrent par exemple toutes deux des dons qui devaient être recueillis au moyen de la vente de *censales* (voir Sánchez Martínez et Ortí Gost, *Corts, Parlaments i fiscalitat*, docts. XXIV et XXIX (1), pp. 423-438 et 543-560. Sur les *censales* émis par le *General* de Valence en 1390, voir García Marsilla, *La formación de un mercado del crédito*, pp. 462-467.

41 Sur ce point, voir Sánchez Martínez et Hébert, "La 'part du prince'", pp. 306-311.

Mais de nouvelles exigences vinrent s'ajouter aux anciennes. La construction et la réparation des défenses urbaines, rendues particulièrement nécessaires en Catalogne en raison des incursions des Grandes Compagnies, absorbèrent une partie non négligeable des dépenses des municipalités et obligèrent les dirigeants municipaux à s'endetter[42]. L'émission de rentes devint plus importante encore lorsqu'il fallut garantir l'approvisionnement en céréales des cités et des villes de la Couronne, notamment à la suite de la grande crise de subsistance de 1374-1375. Ainsi les pouvoirs municipaux financèrent-ils en grande partie par la vente de nouveaux *censales* l'achat direct de céréales ou le paiement de primes aux marchands qui les amenaient en ville[43]. Afin de relever rapidement ces défis anciens et nouveaux, les pouvoirs municipaux durent donc encore recourir au crédit des *censales*, mais ce fut à de nombreuses reprises la dette accumulée elle même qui les obligea à vendre plus de rentes pour pouvoir payer les pensions de celles qui avaient été vendues auparavant[44]. Par conséquent, que ce fût pour verser de l'argent à la Couronne, pour défendre la communauté, pour l'approvisionner en céréales ou bien pour s'acquitter du règlement de leur dette, le résultat fut pour les pouvoirs municipaux le même: ils continuèrent à émettre des rentes et à augmenter ainsi leur niveau d'endettement. D'autre part, dès le dernier tiers du 14e siècle et dans le cadre des premières tentatives de réduction de la charge des *censales*, les pouvoirs municipaux intervinrent très activement sur le marché de la dette, car ils y mirent en circulation des *censales* à un taux d'intérêt déterminé afin de racheter ceux qui avaient été vendus à un taux supérieur et, surtout, afin de racheter les *violarios*, dont le taux était, faut-il le rappeler, supérieur à celui des *censales*[45].

Au vu de ce qui précède, il n'est guère surprenant que dans pratiquement la totalité des cas étudiés, le service de la dette ait constitué le poste de dépenses le plus important: il dépassait de manière générale le seuil des 50% et des 60% et atteignit parfois les 80%[46].

---

42 Les livres de *clavaria* de Valls de 1374-1375 montrent par exemple que plus des ¾ des dépenses en services étaient affectées aux travaux de la muraille; la ville de Reus vendit aussi à certains moments des *censales* pour pouvoir réparer les murs ou se fournir en armes; voir Morelló, "La signification des dépenses", in Menjot et Sánchez Martínez, *La fiscalité des villes (3)*, p. 105; et, du même auteur, *Fiscalitat i deute públic*, p. 766.

43 La ville catalane de Cervera vendit par exemple 15 *censales* pour 60.000 sous dans la seule période 1374-1375 afin de subvenir à l'approvisionnement en céréales de la ville dans une année de disette; P. Verdés, "La carestia de blat de 1374-1376 a Cervera", *Miscel·lània Cerverina*, XII (1998), pp. 12-14. Sur cette question, voir J. Morelló (avec la collaboration de C. Guilleré), "Approvisionnement et finances municipales en Méditerranée occidentale: l'exemple de la Couronne d'Aragon", in Menjot et Sánchez Martínez, *La fiscalité des villes (3)*, pp. 267-294 (avec de nombreuses références bibliographiques). Sur l'impact de cette charge sur les finances de Reus, Valls, Cervera, Barcelone, Sant Feliu et Valence, voir les travaux cités note 1. Pour Valence, voir aussi R. Narbona, "Finanzas municipales y patriciado urbano. Valencia a finales del Trescientos", *Anuario de Estudios Medievales*, XXII (1992), pp. 496-502. D'autre part, à Vila-Real, à Gandía et dans d'autres villes plus petites du Pays Valencien, il semble que le ravitaillement ait constitué un des postes principaux des dépenses municipales et l'une des causes les plus fréquentes d'émission de *censales*; voir Furió, "Deuda pública ", p. 70; et pour le cas de Sueca dans la première moitié du 15Ie siècle, voir A.J. Mira Jódar, *Las finanzas del municipio. Gestión económica y poder local. Sueca (s. XV-XVI)*, Valence, 1997, pp. 157-161.

44 Pour citer un exemple parmi des centaines d'autres, les édiles de la ville de Reus vendirent pour 9.200 sous deux *censales* qui permirent de régler jusqu'à 13 pensions; voir Morelló, *Fiscalitat i deute públic*, p. 767.

45 Cervera vendit par exemple en 1372 et 1393 des *censales* à 6% pour en racheter d'autres qui avaient été émis à 7,14%; voir Turull, *La configuració jurídica del municipi baix-medieval*, p. 461; la cité de Tarragone émit pour sa part en 1375 des censales à 7,14% afin de racheter ceux qui avaient été vendus jusqu'alors au taux de 8,33%; voir F. Cortiella, *Una ciutat catalana a les darreries de la baixa Edat Mitjana: Tarragona*, Tarragone, p. 218; voir d'autres exemples relatifs à Valls et Reus dans Morelló, *Fiscalitat i deute públic*, pp. 771-772. La *Diputación* de Catalogne poursuivait le même objectif lorsqu'elle ordonna en 1371 d'émettre des rentes à un taux inférieur afin de racheter celles qui avaient été vendues en 1365; voir Sánchez Martínez et Ortí Gost, *Corts, Parlaments i fiscalitat a Catalunya*, doc. XXIV, cap. 28, p. 437. Mira Jódar, *Las finanzas del municipio*, pp. 50-65, fournit un bon cadre général pour Valence et les villes du royaume.

46 Sur le rôle et l'évolution de la dette dans les finances municipales de Valls, Reus, Cervera, Barcelone, Sant Feliu de Guíxols, Valence et Alcoy, voir les travaux cités note 1. Il existe d'autres exemples: le service de la dette représentait 81% des dépenses à Majorque (1378), 61% à Barcelone (1403), 54% à Tarragone (1393), 71% dans la ville valencienne d'Alzira (1380), 82% à Castellón (1450), 74% à Borriana (1449-1456), mais seulement 32,8% et 35% dans les cités aragonaises de Saragosse et Daroca (en 1442 et 1473 respectivement); sur ces exemples et d'autres encore, voir Furió, "Deuda pública e intereses privados", pp. 64-74 (particulièrement le tableau de la p. 69) qui fournit les indications bibliographiques nécessaires et, du même auteur, "La dette dans les dépenses municipales", pp. 337-342. D'autre part, dans la cité de Barcelone, le capital en dette publique passa de 228.000

La gestion d'une dette qui absorbait entre la moitié et les trois quarts des dépenses suscita d'emblée des changements importants dans la comptabilité municipale. Les émissions de rentes se reflétaient initialement dans les livres engendrés par l'administration du *clavari* (trésorier municipal)[47]: le capital obtenu par la vente de rentes figurait dans la partie des recettes et les sommes employées pour le paiement des pensions ou pour les amortissements réalisés étaient inscrites au chapitre des dépenses. Cependant, l'augmentation de la dette et son assignation sur les impôts indirects obligea à séparer une partie des informations auparavant contenues dans les livres de *clavaria* et à créer une autre administration consacrée exclusivement à la gestion de la dette. Désignée généralement sous le nom de *clavaria dels censals*, cette administration inscrivait ainsi dans les recettes le produit de chacun des impôts indirects affectés à la dette, de même que les sommes qui pouvaient provenir du rachat éventuel d'une rente, tandis que les sommes employées au paiement des pensions et aux amortissements figuraient au chapitre des dépenses. La *clavaria comuna* n'enregistrait plus dorénavant que les recettes et les dépenses de caractère général, d'ordinaire peu importantes par rapport à la dette. Dans la cité de Valence, aux deux *clavaries* qui précèdent vint s'adjoindre une troisième, appelée *clavaria del quitament*, consacrée exclusivement à la gestion de l'amortissement de la dette[48]. Comme on le devine aisément, cette diversification d'administrations qui possédaient leurs propres registres peut rendre plus difficile l'étude des finances d'une municipalité, notamment lorsque la documentation de la *clavaria dels censals* a disparu et que le chercheur doit se limiter à la *clavaria comuna*, perdant ainsi de vue le principal revenu de la ville (les impôts indirects) et le poste de dépenses le plus important: la dette municipale.

* * *

Dans de nombreux *municipios*, la gravité de l'endettement fut telle qu'elle provoqua de sérieuses difficultés financières, caractérisées notamment par une insolvabilité croissante, de dramatiques suspensions des paiements et des banqueroutes retentissantes. Les hasards de la recherche – encore balbutiante, rappelons-le – font que nous connaissons un peu mieux les cas des cités et des villes qui eurent à subir des désastres financiers fracassants et dont les édiles, confrontés à l'offensive des créanciers, finirent par perdre une part importante du contrôle des recettes fiscales et financières. Ces mêmes exemples sont d'ordinaire mis en avant afin de démontrer les effets pervers de l'endettement à long terme, en oubliant trop souvent que de nombreux autres noyaux urbains (peut-être la majorité) gérèrent certes indubitablement leur dette avec des difficultés temporaires, mais n'en arrivèrent pas pour autant aux situations extrêmes que nous allons maintenant examiner. Tel fut par exemple le cas de Barcelone, en dépit de l'énormité de sa dette. Plus encore, les besoins financiers des autorités municipales suscitèrent dans ce cas l'adoption de solutions novatrices dont la portée devait s'avérer considérable, comme par exemple l'ouverture en 1401 de la première banque publique européenne, la *Taula de Canvi*[49].

De manière générale, les mesures adoptées par les dirigeants municipaux pour assainir les finances et faire face aux difficultés engendrées par l'endettement furent presque toujours les mêmes:

---

livres en 1371 à 380.000 en 1398, des chiffres réellement spectaculaires (P. Ortí Gost, *Renda i fiscalitat en una ciutat medieval: Barcelona, segles XII-XIV*, Barcelone, 2000, p. 567).

47 Il faut ici préciser qu'il ne s'agit pas d'authentiques livres de comptabilité, mais de registres qui reflètent le bilan de l'administration financière effectuée par le *clavari*, qui devait ensuite être révisée par les auditeurs des comptes ou par le rational.

48 Pour une analyse de ces questions, voir M. Sánchez Martínez, "Fiscalidad y finanzas de una villa señorial catalana: Castelló d'Empúries, 1381-1382", in Sánchez Martínez, *Fiscalidad real y finanzas urbanas*, pp. 309-328 et, pour le cas valencien, Narbona, "Finanzas municipales", pp. 488-496 et Furió, "Les dépenses de la métropole valencienne", pp. 193-194. Dans un contexte bien sûr très différent, R.W.M. van Schaïk expose un cas semblable pour la ville de Zutphen depuis la fin du 14e siècle (voir chapitre 8).

49 Voir notamment A.P. Usher, *The Early History of Deposit Banking in Mediterranean Europe*, New York, 1967; A.M. Adroer et G. Feliu, *Història de la Taula de Canvi de Barcelona, seu fundacional de la Caixa de Barcelona*, Barcelone, 1989; et J. Mª Passola, *Els orígens de la Banca Pública: les taules de canvi municipals*, Sabadell, 1999.

comme nous l'avons déjà indiqué, ils réduisirent la dette au moyen du rachat des rentes les plus lourdes à supporter, procédèrent lorsque cela était possible à leur amortissement partiel en consacrant à cette fin une part importante des recettes de la municipalité et, pour finir, s'efforcèrent de renégocier la dette avec les créanciers, ce qui leur permit d'abaisser les taux d'intérêt à 5%, 4% et même à 3%. Examinons à présent quelques exemples.

Entre 1386 et 1404, les conseillers de la ville catalane de Cervera procédèrent à l'amortissement des *violarios* en émettant des *censales* à 6,6%, 7,14% ou 8,33%, tout en s'efforçant par ailleurs de liquider les *censales* les plus coûteux grâce à la vente d'autres *censales* au taux de 5%. Comme le *consell* éprouvait de sérieuses difficultés pour trouver des capitaux à un taux d'intérêt aussi bas, il s'aventura avec des marchands de Barcelone dans une opération financière risquée et complexe: en échange d'une somme préalablement fixée, les marchands s'engagèrent à payer les pensions et à procéder à l'amortissement des *censales* dont les taux d'intérêt étaient les plus élevés. L'échec de cette mesure eut en 1411 pour conséquence la suspension des paiements par la municipalité, qui tenta dès lors de renégocier la dette avec les créanciers. Ces derniers acceptèrent finalement deux années plus tard de réduire le taux d'intérêt à 3,3%. En échange, les impôts indirects furent alloués aux créanciers (en particulier des Barcelonais), et les autorités municipales perdirent de la sorte le contrôle de la principale recette fiscale de la ville. L'opération fut malgré tout un succès et son impact sur la diminution de la dette peut être observé à partir de 1420. Il faudra en fait attendre le déclenchement de la guerre civile catalane en 1462 et la suspension des paiements qui en résulta pour assister à une nouvelle dégradation de la situation[50].

Dans la cité catalane de Tarragone, après avoir essayé d'assainir la dette en recourant à des méthodes similaires à celles employées à Cervera, les autorités municipales suspendirent les paiements en 1462, là aussi au début de la guerre civile. Des accords furent ensuite passés en 1465 avec les créanciers barcelonais afin de mettre un terme à la banqueroute. Ils se traduisirent pas la création d'une commission qui devait prendre en charge la gestion des dépenses et des recettes municipales: à l'exception d'une petite somme destinée aux salaires et à d'autres menues dépenses, les revenus de Tarragone furent alloués au paiement des pensions, au rachat des rentes et au paiement des arrérages. Les accords de 1465 signifièrent donc pour le *municipio* la perte du contrôle de ses revenus et la remise aux créanciers de la direction de l'économie de la cité[51].

Le cas de Majorque est sans doute le plus spectaculaire de tous. Les problèmes financiers des autorités municipales s'accrurent dans les dernières années du 14e siècle, quand les impôts indirects ne suffirent plus au paiement des pensions. Pour cette raison, le *consell* de Majorque signa avec les créanciers de Barcelone le *Contrato santo*, un accord aux termes duquel fut créée l'*Universal Consignació*, une institution qui devait perdurer jusqu'au 19e siècle. En substance, tous les revenus fiscaux de Majorque étaient placés sous le contrôle des créanciers: un représentant de ces derniers devait percevoir les impôts indirects et payer les pensions, d'abord aux créanciers de Barcelone, puis en second lieu aux Majorquins. Comme l'importance considérable de l'*Universal Consignació* ne peut être résumée en quelques lignes, qu'il suffise donc ici de rappeler que cette institution joua un rôle déterminant dans la plupart des vicissitudes économiques, sociales et politiques du territoire majorquin

---

50 Verdés, "Évolution des dépenses", pp. 113-115. Sur les retards de paiement pour les pensions, voir Sabaté, "La insolvència municipal", pp. 255-280.

51 Voir J. Mª Recasens, *La ciutat de Tarragona*, Barcelone, 1975, pp. 242-258 et Cortiella, *Una ciutat catalana*, pp. 165-183 et 216-238. La ville voisine de Valls connut une situation semblable au début du 15e siècle. Après la suspension des paiements, les biens meubles et immeubles de la communauté et d'un nombre important de *prohoms* furent en 1406 cédés à un curateur qui, au nom des créanciers, devait payer les pensions et contrôler tous les revenus fiscaux de la municipalité. L'assainissement consécutif à la crise se traduisit à la fois par la création d'une *clavaria de censals* contrôlée par les créanciers et par la diminution des taux d'intérêt, qui furent abaissés à 2,5%, 2% et même 1,6%. En outre, mise en oeuvre à partir de 1425, une politique résolue à obtenir l'amortissement des rentes parvint à réduire sensiblement le poids de la dette dans les années centrales du 15e siècle; voir J. Morelló, "La crisi financera en una vila del Camp de Tarragona: Valls a principis del s. XV", in Sánchez Martínez, *Fiscalidad real y finanzas municipales*, pp. 219-254; et, Morelló, *Fiscalitat i deute públic*, pp. 873-892.

au 15e siècle et durant toute l'époque moderne, en particulier lors de la Révolte Foraine (1450-1453) et à l'occasion des *Germanies* de Majorque (1521-1523)[52].

Examinons pour terminer le cas de deux villes valenciennes. Burriana, comme de très nombreuses municipalités, consacrait 75% de ses dépenses au service de la dette dans les années centrales du 15e siècle et le spectre de l'insolvabilité commençait vers 1440 à planer sur les autorités municipales. La réduction du taux d'intérêt à 5% ne parvint pas à résoudre le problème et la Couronne elle même dut finalement intervenir: la municipalité reçut du *batlle general* de Valence (gestionnaire du patrimoine royal dans le royaume) un prêt pour assurer le financement de l'amortissement des rentes. Borriana parvint à assainir ses finances et à réduire de 40% le poids de sa dette, la mesure fut donc un succès, mais le coût en fut élevé: la Couronne avait dorénavant les coudées franches pour intervenir politiquement et les officiers royaux pour superviser les finances de la ville[53]. Les conséquences de l'endettement furent plus graves encore dans la ville de Gandía. Les difficultés rencontrées pour recouvrir les impôts qui garantissaient le paiement d'une dette élevée et les arriérés dans le paiement des pensions mirent les finances de la ville dans une situation critique vers 1485, lorsque la dette en question atteignit 66,3% des dépenses municipales. La Couronne intervint ici aussi et décida de vendre le duché de Gandía à la puissante famille des Borja, à charge pour cette dernière d'affronter la dette des *censales* et de réorganiser tout le système fiscal et financier de la ville, dont l'assainissement allait tarder encore quelque temps avant d'être obtenu[54].

L'endettement à long terme considérable de certaines villes et cités, difficile à gérer, conduisit donc les autorités municipales, à des degrés divers et pour des durées variables, à perdre le contrôle d'une partie importante de leurs ressources fiscales et financières, qui passèrent sous la tutelle des créanciers eux-mêmes ou bien sous celle des officiers royaux. Il ne faudrait cependant pas oublier une autre conséquence importante de la politique d'assainissement des finances, à savoir son coût social élevé. Le rassemblement du capital nécessaire pour pouvoir procéder à l'amortissement de la dette se traduisit en effet par une recrudescence de la pression fiscale qui eut de profondes répercussions sur le tissu social des cités ou des villes concernées. Même si elles ne résultent pas de cette seule cause, la diminution de la population et la crise économique que subirent certaines cités et villes catalano-aragonaises peuvent aussi être imputées à l'endettement à long terme et aux politiques de rigueur qui furent mises en œuvre pour pouvoir en alléger le poids[55]. En effet, pour payer les pensions ou pour

52 Voir notamment A. Santamaría, "La deuda pública en la parte forana al finalizar el s. XV", *Anuario de Estudios Medievales*, VIII (1972-73), pp. 257-304; L. Muntaner, "Dependència econòmica i reproducció estructural de l'endeutament públic a l'illa de Mallorca (segles XIV-XIX)", *Randa*, XII (1981), pp. 5-18; R. Urgell, "Dinàmica del deute públic a la Universitat de Mallorca en el segle XV", in M. Sánchez et A. Furió (éds.), *Col·loqui sobre Corona, municipis i fiscalitat*, pp. 675-701; et, R. Urgell, *El regne de Mallorca a l'època de Joan II: la guerra civil catalana i les seves repercusions*, Palma de Majorque, 1997.

53 P. Viciano, "Fiscalitat local i deute públic al País Valencià. L'administració de la vila de Borriana a mitjan segle XV", in *Anuario de Estudios Medievales*, XXII (1992), pp. 513-534; la situation financière de la ville voisine de Castelló est analysée aussi par P. Viciano, "Ingrés i despesa d'una vila valenciana del Quatrecents: les finances municipals de Castelló de la Plana (1426-1472)", in *Boletín de la Sociedad Castellonense de Cultura*, LXVI (1990), pp. 635-664.

54 V. Olaso, "L'endeutament censal a la vila de Gandia durant la baixa Edat Mitjana", in *Ullal. Revista d'Història i Cultura*, XI (1987), pp. 51-64.

55 *...cum dolore, tristitia et amaritudine cordis dicunt et proponunt quod universitas et singulares dicte ville et locorum termini sui... sunt tot et tantis debitis et creditoribus...obligati in tantum quod, propter mortalitates que in ipsis viguerent et annorum sterilitates ac propter debita censualium mortuorum, ipsa villa et loci termini sui sunt quasi ad nichilum deducta et deducti ac singulares ipsius et ipsorum... venerunt ad paupertatem maximam et nequerint satisfacere ipsis creditoribus...* Adressé en 1406 par les *síndics* de Valls au nom de la communauté à l'officier de l'archevêque de Tarragone, ce discours est semblable à beaucoup d'autres de la même période, qui peuvent sans difficulté être retrouvés dans la documentation municipale de nombreuses villes et cités de la Couronne. Certains chercheurs sont parvenus à montrer qu'en dépit d'une rhétorique qui frôlait parfois le lieu commun, ces discours dramatiques pouvaient être très proches de la réalité. Par exemple, la ville de Valls, à laquelle fait référence le texte cité ci-dessus, obtint du roi la diminution de moitié (!) du nombre de feux qui étaient comptabilisés pour ce noyau urbain dans le recensement de 1378; voir Morelló, *Fiscalitat i deute public*, p. 879. Et tandis que le *batlle* de Castelló voyait *aquesta vila totalment perduda e carregada de diverses censals, de què ja aquesta vila no pot bastar a més, ans tota se despobla* (cette ville totalement perdue et grevée de divers *censales*, auxquels elle ne peut plus donner satisfaction, car elle se dépeuple complètement), Viciano a montré que la ville avait perdu presque 20% de sa population entre 1415 et 1427 et que la

amortir les rentes, on accrut le nombre des impôts indirects ou l'on augmenta les tarifs de ceux qui existaient déjà, des *tallas* plus lourdes furent établies ou bien de nouvelles formes d'imposition créées, comme cela advint en Catalogne avec les impôts dits sur la rente (*onzè*), mis en place dans le seul but d'amortir avec leur produit la dette accumulée[56].

C'est pourquoi, alors qu'avec la vente massive de *censales* et de *violarios* au milieu du 14e siècle, les édiles urbains avaient souhaité atténuer les effets qu'auraient pu avoir sur la population les lourdes exigences de la Couronne, les conséquences fiscales de ces dernières éclatèrent au grand jour une cinquantaine d'années plus tard. On retrouve ici un phénomène bien connu: l'émission de rentes peut être considéré comme un simple report de la pression fiscale[57].

Le monde des créanciers

Il semble relever de l'évidence que le fonctionnement d'un système de dette semblable à celui que nous venons de décrire suppose l'existence d'une autre composante fondamentale: des groupes sociaux disposés à investir leurs capitaux dans l'acquisition de rentes. La création même de la dette publique au milieu du 14e siècle et, surtout, sa perpétuation durant le reste du Moyen Age et à l'époque moderne attestent de l'existence d'une clientèle nombreuse et variée avide d'acheter des *censales* et de participer activement au marché de la dette. Il s'agit en premier lieu des élites locales elles mêmes, mais pas uniquement. Les études encore trop peu nombreuses dont nous disposons démontrent que le marché de la dette vit s'impliquer pratiquement tout le spectre social, même si les modes d'intervention varièrent selon les époques: des nobles, des marchands, des changeurs, des membres des professions libérales et des établissements ecclésiastiques y participèrent, et même les groupes sociaux les moins favorisés, tels les petits artisans, les paysans, les veuves ou les orphelins appauvris y jouèrent un rôle. Les membres illustres de l'oligarchie locale, dont les noms étaient déjà présents sur les listes des édiles municipaux et sur celles des fermiers des impôts indirects, se retrouvaient naturellement aussi au premier rang des bénéficiaires de la dette, en raison notamment du volume des capitaux investis. Cette situation fournit un élément supplémentaire susceptible d'expliquer la perpétuation de la dette publique et, au-delà, le maintien d'un système fiscal et financier qui favorisait ouvertement le groupe social dominant.

L'état de la recherche – de petits aperçus qui concernent des moments et des lieux très différents – ne permet pas encore d'effectuer une synthèse sur cet aspect essentiel de la dette qui soit valable pour l'ensemble de la Couronne d'Aragon aux 14e et 15e siècles[58]. Il faudrait en outre pour

---

pression fiscale engendrée par l'endettement dû aux *censales* ne fut pas étrangère à cette baisse démographique; voir Viciano, "Ingrès i despesa d'una vila valenciana", pp. 657-658.

56 Évoquons quelques exemples parmi d'autres. A Majorque, après l'établissement de l'*Universal Consignación*, de nouveaux impôts indirects furent instaurés et les impôts déjà existants furent alourdis par les redoutables *afitons* (ajouts). Dans le même temps, l'impôt de la *molitja* (qui pesait sur la consommation de pain et de farine) subissait une augmentation, une gabelle sur le sel était créée et les tailles étaient augmentées (Urgell, "Dinámica del deute públic", pp. 679, 682). A Manresa, de nombreuses tailles spécifiques furent mises en place afin d'amortir la dette (Torras, "El deute públic ", pp. 169, 173-174, 176). Une taille spéciale, qui devait rester en vigueur huit années, fut établie en 1419 à Reus pour racheter des *censales* (Morelló, *Fiscalitat i deute públic*, p. 358). Pareillement, la redevance de la *peita* (impôt direct) fut augmentée à Castelló et un droit particulier sur les terres et les possessions fut imposé à Gandía, là aussi dans le but d'amortir la dette (Viciano, "Ingrès i despesa", p. 659; Olaso, "L'endeutament censal", p. 61 et, de manière plus générale, Furió, "Deuda pública e intereses privados", pp. 71-73). Sur les "impôts sur la rente" (*onzens*) et sur les *milanars* ou tailles en espèce, voir Morelló, *Fiscalitat i deute públic*, pp. 681-741.

57 Comme le dit bien D. Morsa: *emprunter offrait l'avantage de ménager le présent en reportant la facture vers les générations futures* (chapitre 10). D'autre part, H.-J. Gilomen affirme avec raison que les dirigeants municipaux empruntèrent le chemin de l'endettement plutôt comme une voie alternative à une pression fiscale susceptible d'engendrer des troubles sociaux que dans le but d'offrir des investissements rentables pour les capitaux bourgeois (chapitre 9).

58 Pour une approche générale, voir Furió, "Deuda pública e intereses privados" pp. 74-76 et "La dette dans les dépenses municipales", in *La fiscalité des villes (3)*, pp. 342-344.

pouvoir tirer toutes les conséquences de l'analyse du monde des créanciers disposer d'études prosopographiques solides, encore peu nombreuses en ce domaine. Pour répondre à de multiples questions relatives à la nature même de la dette à long terme ainsi qu'aux motifs qui poussèrent les dirigeants urbains à procéder à son émission et à choisir comme clients leurs propres concitoyens ou bien des personnes étrangères à la municipalité, il serait évidemment nécessaire de connaître avec la plus grande précision possible le *background* socio-économique et politique des investisseurs[59]. Il faut donc pour l'heure se limiter à la présentation de simples exemples, sans ambition autre que celle de mettre en évidence quelques tendances générales pouvant caractériser la condition sociale et l'origine géographique des acheteurs de rentes dans quelques cités et villes de la Couronne catalano-aragonaise.

A Barcelone, plus de la moitié des 415 acheteurs documentés entre 1344 et 1362 appartenaient au patriciat urbain et il se trouvait parmi eux bon nombre d'officiers royaux et de membres de professions libérales, surtout des juristes et des notaires. Un tiers des créanciers étaient marchands et changeurs; on ne trouve en revanche que sept nobles et neuf personnes possédant l'état de clerc[60]. Par contre, dans la cité de Valence, en 1367-1368, la noblesse constituait le groupe social le plus représenté parmi les acheteurs, suivi de près par ceux qui sont qualifiés de *ciutadans*. Une trentaine d'années plus tard, en 1399-1400, la présence de membres de la noblesse continuait à être forte, mais la majorité des créanciers était dorénavant formée par les *ciutadans*[61]. Dans la ville de Fraga, dont la dette a été analysée entre 1309 et 1406, 77% des créanciers appartenaient au monde laïque, il s'agissait en majorité de citoyens, avec une présence non négligeable de la noblesse[62]. Enfin, dans la cité catalane de Manresa, tandis qu'en 1365 les membres des oligarchies de Barcelone et de Manresa prédominaient parmi les acheteurs de rentes et que le pourcentage d'ecclésiastiques était encore très faible, la situation s'était quasiment inversée en 1415 et plus de la moitié des pensions étaient versées à des personnes et à des institutions religieuses (couvents, bénéfices ecclésiastiques, confréries, etc.)[63].

L'examen de la dette publique de la *Diputación* de Catalogne, étudiée pour la période allant de la fin du 14e siècle au milieu du 15e siècle, révèle aussi des changements significatifs au sein du groupe des bénéficiaires de la dette: alors qu'en 1398 les ecclésiastiques représentaient seulement 8,3%, leur participation atteint jusqu'à 16% en 1444, le rôle essentiel des couvents féminins de Barcelone méritant ici d'être souligné. Pour leur part, les membres de la noblesse, qui ne représentaient que 2,6% en 1398, atteignirent 20% en 1444. M. Berthe suggère que les guerres paysannes ont pu conduire les membres de la noblesse à rechercher une certaine sécurité dans la cité de Barcelone et sur le marché de la dette. La réduction drastique de la part des marchands dans le groupe des investisseurs paraît tout aussi significative: le pourcentage de 36,7% enregistré en 1398 se voit réduit à 12% en 1444, ce qui M. Berthe met en relation avec les difficultés du commerce barcelonais au cours des premières années du 15e siècle[64].

Cependant, pour en revenir aux cités et aux villes, l'origine géographique des acheteurs de rentes est tout aussi significative que leur appartenance sociale. Le rôle particulièrement remarquable des capitales des trois territoires (Barcelone, Valence, Saragosse) et d'autres centres urbains de moindre importance montre clairement une hiérarchisation régionale du marché de la dette et témoigne du flux continu de capitaux du monde rural vers les centres urbains de grande taille ou de taille moyenne[65]. Les créanciers de la cité de Valence contrôlaient ainsi 90% de la dette de Cullera, d'Alcoy et d'autres villes

59 Quelques unes de ces questions sont évoquées par M. van der Heijden (chapitre 12).
60 Roustit, "La consolidation", pp. 113-133.
61 García Marsilla, *La formación de un mercado del crédito*, pp. 405-438.
62 Berenguer Galindo, *Censal mort*, p. 234.
63 Torras, "El deute públic", pp. 178-182.
64 Berthe, *Les finances de la "Generalitat"*, pp. 173-197.
65 La configuration spatiale du marché de la dette constitue ainsi un indicateur fort de la hiérarchie des cités et des villes (grandes, moyennes et petites) dans le dense réseau urbain de la Catalogne et du Pays Valencien. L. Derycke effectue (chapitre 11) un constat similaire au sujet des investisseurs de la dette à Bruges au 15e siècle.

moyennes; même dans des noyaux urbains plus importants comme Alzira ou Castelló, la participation des investisseurs de la capitale ne descendait pas en dessous de 60% ou de 70%[66]. La même remarque peut être effectuée au sujet de la Catalogne: dans ce cas, les citoyens de Barcelone pénétrèrent grâce au marché de la dette jusque dans les localités les plus reculées du Principat. A Cervera par exemple, 70% des créanciers ne provenaient pas de la ville, mais un tiers des pensions les plus élevées furent acquises par des citoyens de Barcelone[67]. Dans la cité de Manresa, jusqu'à une période très avancée de la deuxième moitié du 14e siècle, les investisseurs les plus importants provenaient aussi de Barcelone. Ce n'est qu'à partir de ce moment que des pensions commencèrent à être vendues dans la cité elle même afin de racheter celles qui avaient été acquises par des hommes étrangers à la cité, en particulier par des Barcelonais. Le profil des créanciers de Manresa avait de la sorte radicalement changé en 1415: 82% étaient de la cité même, contre seulement 2% qui provenaient de Barcelone[68]. Afin d'expliquer ce changement, il faudrait aussi prendre en compte la baisse des taux d'intérêt (3,3% pour presque 84% des pensions de Manresa en 1418) qui rendait l'investissement peu attractif pour la lointaine bourgeoisie barcelonaise et ouvrait la porte à des acheteurs de la cité même, en fait surtout des établissements ecclésiastiques et de petits investisseurs. Bien que ces données concernent la cité de Manresa, je crois qu'elles sont susceptibles d'être appliquées avec les précautions de rigueur à de nombreuses autres villes et cités.

Le poids de Barcelone se fit néanmoins sentir aussi hors de Catalogne. Nous avons déjà vu comment la majeure partie de la dette publique de Majorque était au pouvoir des Barcelonais, mais le même phénomène peut être observé dans certaines cités valenciennes et aragonaises, dans la *Diputación* d'Aragon elle même, car une partie des *censales* de cette institution étaient à la fin du 15e siècle aux mains de citoyens de Barcelone[69]. Pour cette raison et ainsi que nous l'avons vu précédemment, quand eurent lieu des suspensions de paiements ou surgirent d'autres difficultés, les investisseurs de Barcelone prirent en main les commandes fiscales et financières de Majorque ou de cités et de villes comme Tarragone ou Valls.

De tout ce qui précède, il ressort que la majeure partie du produit de la ponction fiscale effectuée sur les cités et les villes, même si les exigences de la Couronne servaient toujours de justification, ne bénéficiait pas directement au monarque, mais était absorbée par les grandes capitales et, de manière secondaire, par les centres régionaux les plus importants afin de remplir dans un cas comme dans l'autre les caisses des oligarchies urbaines. La Couronne agissait dans ce processus presque toujours comme un simple intermédiaire. En Catalogne par exemple, lorsqu'il fallut en 1344 décider des pensions que chaque cité et chaque ville devait vendre et sélectionner les acheteurs parmi les membres de l'élite barcelonaise, le roi Pierre le Cérémonieux mit en contact les deux parties et limita son intervention à l'organisation du transfert des recettes publiques à des particuliers. Evidemment, il obtint en contrepartie les fonds nécessaires pour mener à bien sa politique dynastique[70].

66 Furió, "Deuda pública e intereses privados', pp. 76-77.

67 Turull, *La configuració jurídica del municipi baixmedieval*, pp. 484-487.

68 Il est bien connu que les dirigeants municipaux eurent au bout d'un certain temps la volonté de conserver les pensions dans la cité elle même. La dette était alors plus facilement négociable et, de plus, les autorités municipales s'épargnaient ainsi les dépenses non négligeables que supposait le paiement de l'annuité hors de la cité; voir Torras, "El deute públic", pp. 181-182; voir aussi les cas de Bruges, Berne ou Bâle dans Derycke (chapitre 11) et dans Gilomen (chapitre 9).

69 Sesma Muñoz, *La Diputación del reino de Aragón*, pp. 125-138 et 209-230 étudie en détails la gestion de la dette de cette institution et les problèmes posés par les créanciers catalans à la suite du début de la guerre civile dans le Principat en 1462. Sur la présence de Barcelonais parmi les acheteurs de rentes dans la cité aragonaise de Teruel et dans les villes valenciennes de Morella et de Segorbe, voir Furió, "Deuda pública e intereses privados", p. 77.

70 Sánchez Martínez, "La Corona en los orígenes del endeudamiento censal" (sous presse).

Conclusion

Même si la dette publique n'a pas cessé d'être présente dans les études consacrées aux finances urbaines et si elle en constitue avec les impôts directs et indirects l'une des composantes essentielles, nous manquons encore – à de très rares exceptions près – de recherches systématiques qui placent la dette au cœur même de l'analyse. Une telle recherche devrait notamment commencer par une plongée consciencieuse dans la documentation abondante et variée qui est conservée, afin de connaître avec la plus grande précision possible la nature exacte des rentes vendues par les municipalités et les États régionaux, en affinant au maximum la chronologie des émissions, en enquêtant sur leurs causes et en mettant à jour les circonstances qui conduisirent les dirigeants urbains à opter le moment venu pour un type déterminé de rente. Il faudrait ensuite étudier en profondeur la gestion de la dette dans certains *municipios* méticuleusement sélectionnés sur des critères significatifs, afin d'enrichir l'assortiment d'études de cas dont nous disposons pour l'heure et de pouvoir estimer en meilleure connaissance de cause les différentes répercussions de la dette – au-delà du pourcentage qui lui correspond dans les chapitres des recettes et des dépenses – dans la vie économique, sociale et politique des villes. Corrélativement, il serait nécessaire d'étudier en détails les politiques d'assainissement mises en pratique par le gouvernement municipal, ainsi que leurs effets à deux niveaux, fiscal, puis politique pour ce qui a trait aux négociations avec les investisseurs et à leurs conséquences. Il faudrait aussi, *last but not least*, connaître grâce à des études prosopographiques soigneusement préparées la composition sociale et la provenance géographique des acheteurs de rentes et, surtout, l'évolution de l'une et de l'autre au 14e et au 15e siècles.

Cependant, aussi nécessaire que puisse apparaître l'étude systématique de ces différentes questions relatives à la dette, il me semble dès à présent indispensable d'effectuer des comparaisons de fond avec les autres formes d'endettement public que connut l'Europe médiévale et moderne. Il s'agit ce faisant de conjurer deux périls opposés: nous risquons d'abord de 'découvrir la Méditerranée' en attribuant ingénument à l'endettement de nos cités et de nos villes des traits prétendument spécifiques, alors que leur singularité s'estompe dans le contexte de l'Occident européen; inversement, nous encourons le risque de passer sous silence ou de ne pas mettre suffisamment en exergue d'autres caractéristiques qui peuvent réellement conférer une originalité certaine à la dette publique catalano-aragonaise. Seul un dialogue profond et continu avec l'historiographie sur la dette dans les villes italiennes, françaises, suisses, allemandes et des Pays-Bas permettra de situer le cas de la Couronne d'Aragon à sa juste place; de surcroît, la compréhension exacte de certains processus encore obscurs dans l'évolution de l'endettement de nos cités et de nos villes en sera rendue plus aisée.

Ceci étant dit, l'état actuel de nos connaissances sur la dette publique dans les *municipios* et les Etats de la Couronne inciterait plutôt à cesser de nous regarder dans le miroir italien et suggère qu'il serait plus profitable de diriger notre attention vers d'autres régions de l'Occident européen[71]. En effet, comme on le sait, le modèle 'italien' par excellence est celui de l'endettement basé non sur l'acquisition de titres sur le marché libre, mais sur l'imposition de prêts forcés qui ne peuvent être rachetés, sont rétribués avec des intérêts, transmissibles, négociables et fondamentalement (mais pas exclusivement) garantis sur les impôts indirects (*gabelle*). Ce système permettait par conséquent de créer des liquidités pour la cité, mais de manière coercitive, par le recours à des prêts forcés – répartis selon l'*estimo*, c'est-à-

71 Je ne souhaite naturellement pas dire que certains aspects de l'endettement public catalano-aragonais ne rappellent pas des épisodes observés dans des cités de l'Italie centrale et du Nord. Lorsque je parle du miroir italien, je me réfère précisément à la dette publique consolidée (de type florentin par exemple) qui était considérée encore très récemment comme le modèle typique de l'endettement public dans les cités italiennes. Pour tout ce qui suit, j'ai utilisé les travaux de synthèse, pourvus de riches bibliographies, de M. Ginatempo, *Prima del debito. Finanziamento della spesa pubblica e gestione del deficit nelle grandi città toscane (1200-1350 ca.)*, Florence, 2000; "Spunti comparativi sulle trasformazioni della fiscalità nell'Italia post-comunale", in P. Mainoni (éd.), *Politiche finanziarie e fiscali nell'Italia settentrionale (secoli XIII-XV)*, Milan, 2001, pp. 125-216; et "Les transformations de la fiscalité dans l'Italie post-comunale", in *L'impôt dans les villes de l'Occident Méditerranéen (XIIIe-XVe siècles)* (sous presse).

dire avec les méthodes de l'impôt direct – qui équivalaient pour une grande partie des habitants à une imposition directe très fréquente et pesante[72]. Or, comme l'a démontré M. Ginatempo, ce soi-disant modèle, dont on croyait qu'il était caractéristique de toutes les cités-Etats et des Etats régionaux d'Italie, est en fait circonscrit à Gênes et à Venise (depuis 1407 et 1363 respectivement), aux Cités Dominantes ou à celles qui aspiraient à le devenir (comme Florence, Sienne, Pise) et aux centres qui demeurèrent indépendants ou bénéficièrent d'une certaine autonomie (comme Lucques, Bologne et peut-être Ancône). La dette publique conçue sous cette forme ne concernait ni les cités soumises aux Dominantes ni les habitants du *contado*[73]. De plus, même là où elle existait, le corps social touché par cette forme de dette publique ne comprenait pas tous les habitants: pour beaucoup et surtout pour les couches inférieures, les prêts forcés n'étaient pas autre chose qu'un impôt direct à fond perdu, ce n'est que pour l'élite marchande qu'ils offraient une opportunité de participation aux finances de l'État, en même temps qu'une bonne occasion de spéculer sur les titres[74].

Il semble dès lors évident que cet endettement coercitif et si fortement limité dans l'espace comme dans la société n'a que peu de choses en commun avec celui qui prévalait dans la Couronne d'Aragon. Les principales différences, qui constituent aussi les traits essentiels de la dette publique catalano-aragonaise, sont les suivantes:

- En premier lieu, le caractère libre du marché de la dette. En ce qui concerne la Catalogne, nous avons vu qu'à l'exception de la première émission générale de 1344 (réalisée par les autorités municipales mais sous le contrôle de la Couronne, qui décida de la quantité de rentes que chaque communauté devait vendre et chercha les acheteurs), à partir des années 1350, le pouvoir municipal avait les mains libres pour décider de la quantité de rentes à vendre et rechercher les acheteurs là où bon lui semblait. Dans le cas de la cité de Valence, nous avons aussi pu observer comment, en 1366, les édiles reconvertirent par décret en titres rétribués à 8,33% les prêts forcés et les dettes accumulées, mais, par la suite, les nouvelles émissions de rentes furent dénuées de tout lien avec les prêts forcés et vendues sur le marché libre.
- Deuxièmement, l'extraordinaire diffusion sociale et spatiale de l'endettement public catalano-aragonais face au caractère doublement restreint du modèle italien. Nous avons vu que des rentes étaient émises par tous, par les grandes cités aussi bien que par les plus petits noyaux ruraux, en passant par les villes grandes ou moyennes[75]. Bien que les membres des oligarchies urbaines, de l'Église ou de la petite noblesse (surtout en Pays Valencien) fussent prédominants parmi les acheteurs, nous avons déjà fait remarquer que le marché de la rente permit aussi l'implication d'un spectre social extraordinairement large.
- En troisième lieu, et c'est ce qui sans doute importe le plus: le caractère nettement public de la dette, assignée sur les impôts indirects, mais garantie sur les biens de l'ensemble des habitants de la communauté. Cette responsabilité collective, associée à l'existence de recettes fiscales capables de financer la dette et à la maturité institutionnelle des *municipios* eux mêmes, suscita la confiance des

72 L. Pezzolo (chapitre 5)s'interroge sur la pertinence du concept de 'dette publique' dans le cas du système de prêts forcés, alors que l'acquisition de titres y était coercitive et que de nombreux citoyens – en ce cas, vénitiens – *were increasingly regarding themselves more as taxpayers rather than investors*.

73 Ginatempo, *Prima del debito*, p. 13-31 (chapitre intitulé de manière significative *il debito che non c'è*); et "Les transformations de la fiscalité" (sous presse).

74 Ginatempo, *Prima del debito*, pp. 15-16.

75 A ce sujet, je crois que la comparaison à première vue excessive entre les structures fiscales et financières de la métropole de Barcelone (avec 6.568 feux) et celles de la petite cité de Sant Feliu de Guíxols (avec 224 feux) s'avère très significative. P. Ortí Gost a démontré que malgré les différences évidentes entre ces noyaux urbains situés aux deux extrémités de l'échelle du réseau urbain catalan, les pourcentages de leurs différents postes de dépenses étaient très semblables – la dette publique exerçant un rôle de premier plan – et que Sant Feliu finissait par développer un système fiscal dont les composantes étaient très proches de celui de Barcelone (Ortí Gost, "La estructura", pp. 127-136).

investisseurs. Sans la prise en compte de ce dernier facteur, qui n'est certes pas le seul, le succès des différentes émissions demeurerait inexplicable[76].

Si l'examen des caractéristiques du cas catalano-aragonais nous éloigne des traits de la dette consolidée d'un certain nombre de cités italiennes, la lecture de quelques travaux consacrés à l'endettement public dans d'autres cités européennes nous fournit en revanche des éléments de comparaison plus adaptés et plus fructueux. Prenons seulement deux exemples. Il suffit de lire les quelques pages de l'introduction de M. Boone à son étude sur les rentes vendues par la cité de Gand pour pressentir la fécondité de comparaisons éventuelles avec la Couronne catalano-aragonaise[77]. D'autre part, le chercheur qui s'intéresse à la dette publique catalano-aragonaise pourra aussi trouver des points communs avec la situation des cités du nord de la France, en particulier pour ce qui a trait aux facteurs qui aboutirent à l'émergence de l'endettement à long terme. J. D. Tracy les énonce dans ce même volume[78]: une certaine stabilité monétaire, la pratique très développée du crédit à court terme jusqu'à un niveau tel qu'il devienne difficile de gouverner, comme nous l'avons vu dans les cités de Catalogne et du Pays Valencien vers 1340, l'adoption consécutive de la dette à long terme sous l'impulsion des exigences de la Couronne motivées par la guerre et, enfin, la capacité des *municipios* à garantir l'endettement en question non seulement sur les recettes de la cité ou de la ville mais aussi sur les biens de l'ensemble ou de la majeure partie des habitants.

Cependant, si l'endettement à long terme des villes est un phénomène qui, sans être général, peut se rencontrer dans diverses régions de l'Occident européen au bas Moyen Age – et dans ce contexte, le cas catalano-aragonais peut présenter quelques particularités dans la forme ou la chronologie des émissions, je crois que nous devons considérer comme l'un des traits les plus originaux de la Couronne d'Aragon l'apparition et le développement de la dette publique dans les États régionaux à partir de la seconde moitié du 14e siècle. J'ai auparavant fait allusion au caractère profondément public conféré aux rentes émises par les autorités municipales en raison du fait qu'elles sont garanties sur les biens de l'ensemble de la communauté. On observe cette même dimension publique dans le cas des *censales* vendus par les *Diputaciones* de Catalogne, de Valence et d'Aragon durant la seconde moitié du 14e siècle: comme je l'ai montré, le paiement des pensions était assigné sur l'impôt des *generalidades*, mais les ventes étaient garanties sur les biens de toute la communauté politique comprise sous le concept de *General*[79]. C'est donc très précocement (rappelons que les premières rentes émises par la *Diputació del General* de Catalogne datent de 1365) que nous pouvons observer des organismes de nature

---

76 Comme le fait remarquer M. Ginatempo, la confiscation par les seigneurs ou les Cités Dominantes des recettes fiscales et du pouvoir de décision sur ces mêmes recettes avait dépourvu les cités de l'Italie post-communale (à l'exception de Venise) de la capacité de susciter la confiance dans la continuité institutionnelle: *des villes les plus riches, les plus puissantes et les plus indépendantes de l'Europe, elles devinrent peut-être les moins autonomes*; c'est pourquoi l'absence de dette publique est le symptôme le plus net de ces carences (Ginatempo, *Prima del debito*, p. 107 et, surtout, "Les transformations de la fiscalité" (sous presse).

77 Boone, "*Plus deuil que joie*", pp. 3-24. On retrouve par exemple le même jeu triangulaire entre le prince, l'élite gouvernante et les acheteurs de rentes, une même logique de boule de neige dans l'augmentation incessante de la vente de rentes, en raison du caractère permanent en soi des émissions (*si l'on n'avait jamais émis de rentes, on n'aurait jamais eu besoin de le faire*, dit R. van Uytven). On discerne là aussi l'intérêt des oligarchies à maintenir un financement du déficit par cette méthode plutôt que par un impôt direct sur le patrimoine et la même coexistence entre deux circuits de vente des rentes, l'un privé, l'autre public, avec des logiques différentes et, par conséquent, des effets distincts sur le domaine productif. Les similitudes apparaissent même à une plus petite échelle : comme dans le cas de Tournai opposée à Charles le Téméraire étudié par M. Boone, les *censales* des cités et des villes de Catalogne rebelles au roi Jean II durant la guerre civile catalane en 1462 furent confisqués par le monarque, ce qui provoqua un véritable tremblement de terre financier non seulement dans le Principat mais aussi à Majorque et à la *Diputación* d'Aragon où, comme nous l'avons vu, de nombreuses rentes étaient en possession de Catalans.

78 J.D. Tracy (chapitre 2).

79 Par exemple, un *censal* vendu par les députés de Catalogne en 1383 était garanti sur *dictum Generale Cathalonie et omnes universitates, corpora, collegia et personas et quoscumque deputatos et administratores ac officiales et universa et singula bona ipsius Generalis presentes pariter et futuros* (Archivo de la Corona de Aragón, Generalitat, G 11 n° 1, f. 16r.), et un *censal* émis par les députés de Valence en 1404 était garanti par *omnia bona et iura Generalis dicti regni [Valentie] et omnium et singulorum brachiorum tam ecclesiastici, militaris quam regalis predictorum et quorumvis singularium brachiorum ipsorum simul et cuiusvis ipsorum in solidum mobilia et inmobilia ubique habita et habenda...* (Rosa Muñoz Pomer, *Orígenes de la Generalitat valenciana*, doc. n° 16, p. 481).

étatique émettre une dette publique, assignée sur leurs propres impôts – les *generalidades* – perçus dans leurs propres frontières et garantie sur les biens de l'ensemble des habitants. Avec toute la prudence que requiert l'analyse d'une question encore peu étudiée, il me semble que nous sommes donc bien ici, du fait de sa précocité, en présence de l'une des caractéristiques les plus originales de la dette publique catalano-aragonaise.

THE CROWN, THE CITY, AND THE ORPHANS: THE CITY OF LONDON AND ITS FINANCES, 1400-1700

Vanessa Harding
Birkbeck, University of London

In any discussion of the ways in which medieval and Early Modern cities financed their activities and managed the problem of indebtedness, the case of London seems to stand out as an anomaly, a paradox. London was by far the largest urban entity in medieval and Early Modern Britain, containing an enormous concentration of mercantile and commercial wealth. The city's fortunes did not slump in the late Middle Ages, and despite the breakdown of established patterns of international trade in the mid-16th century, London retained its dominant position and increased its lead over other British cities and ports. At the end of the 17th century, it was the largest city in western Europe, with a population of over 500,000 (one-tenth of the total population of England and Wales). London accounted for nearly 80% of the value of England's import trade, and over 70% of the value of its exports[1], and was the source of a high proportion of all the direct and indirect tax revenues of the nation. Nevertheless, in the late 17th century, the municipality came to the brink of bankruptcy, owing an enormous debt of over £700,000 which it had no means of repaying. The resulting inquiry revealed the inadequacies of the City's accounting procedures and its surprisingly unsophisticated attitude to sustaining long-term borrowing. The debt had accumulated, not as a result of annuity schemes or selling rents on the City's credit, but through the Corporation's failure to review and control its own spending, and its readiness to draw on a capital fund that should have been held in trust, rather than funding expenditure at its current levels through taxation or secured loans. In the last years before the crisis there were several schemes to improve the Corporation's revenues, including one based on the sale of annuities, but none of these could effectively deal with a problem on this scale[2]. Recent events may have contributed to the coming of crisis at that moment, but there were also much more long-lasting structures and assumptions which helped to make it virtually inevitable at some time.

CLRO: Corporation of London Records Office, Guildhall, London.

1 B. Dietz, "Overseas trade and metropolitan growth", in A.L. Beier and R. Finlay (ed.), *London 1500-1700, the making of the metropolis*, London, 1986, pp. 115-140.

2 J.R. Kellett, "Some late seventeenth-century schemes for the improvement of the Corporation of London's revenues", *Guildhall Miscellany*, 1.9 (1958), pp. 27-34; J.R. Kellett, "The financial crisis of the Corporation of London and the Orphans Act of 1694", *Guildhall Miscellany*, 2.5 (1963), pp. 220-227; I. Doolittle, "The City of London's debt to its orphans", *Bulletin of the Institute of Historical Research*, 56 (1983), pp. 46-59.

Events

The crisis of the 1680s was certainly tied to three relatively recent events or developments: the period of civil war (1642-9) and republican government (1649-60), which London had been very heavily taxed to support; the Fire of 1666, which burnt 4/5ths of the city centre, including many public buildings owned by the Corporation, and which also involved the Corporation in major expenditure on surveying, dispute resolution, and street and public works improvements; and the rupture in the Corporation's relationship with the Crown which led to the suspension of the City's charter of privileges in 1681 and cast serious doubts on the survival of the municipality as an autonomous and privileged body and therefore as a reliable security. Connected with the latter was the Crown's own financial crisis of the Stop of the Exchequer – suspending repayment of the Crown's financial obligations – in 1672[3].

All of these were important, but none of them, in fact, caused the Corporation's indebtedness or the crisis of 1682, though they certainly limited the resources of moral and financial credit on which it might have drawn. The Corporation's debt was actually lower in 1660 (c. £116,000) than it had been in 1642 (£160,000)[4], despite the high taxation of the Commonwealth period. However, many individuals and institutions had suffered, and the City's Parliamentarian stance in those years meant that it had to buy its way back into the confidence and sympathy of the restored monarchy, and was always regarded with some suspicion. The Fire was certainly a major loss for the Corporation, which had to rebuild its Guildhall, the cloth market of Blackwell Hall, and the Royal Exchange, and also embarked on a scheme of land purchase and building to set out a series of new marketplaces within the City, but much of this was charged to a new resource, the duty on coal imports to London, rather than being made up from the Corporation's ordinary revenues. The crisis in the City's relationship with the Crown involved it in an expensive legal contest, and broke its monopoly of market provision in the capital, but it was probably the crisis of confidence in the Corporation's future that mattered most.

Structures and attitudes

If the situation in the 1680s was not rendered critical by immediate events, we must look at underlying structures to see what was wrong, and also to gain a longer picture of London's finances. The obvious prosperity of individuals and of London as a commercial centre obscures the relative poverty of the municipality. Very large sums were raised in London, usually in response to demands from central government, but perhaps because so much of this task was done by delegation – relying on individuals or the City's guilds to find the sums required – the municipality did not develop sophisticated or robust means of raising revenue on its own account. Historians of the 16th century and earlier have pointed to elements in the City's financial and accounting practices that 'laid the foundation of the more serious problems which [the City] was to experience in the 17th century'[5].

The systemic problem was that London's governors had for centuries no real incentive to reform its financial affairs or to innovate ways of raising money. London was a rich commercial centre, seemingly able to yield substantial sums in revenue without excessive difficulty, so maximising fiscal efficiency was not a priority. London's oligarchic rulers were individually wealthy, and for many years were prepared to subsidise the City government's liabilities, rather than embark on more inclusive

3 R.R. Sharpe, *London and the Kingdom*, 3 vol., London, 1894; T.F. Reddaway, *The rebuilding of London after the Great Fire* , London, 1940; J. Levin, *The charter controversy in the City of London, 1660-1688, and its consequences*, London, 1969; H. Roseveare, *The financial revolution, 1660-1760*, 1991.

4 Kellett, "Financial crisis", pp. 221-222.

5 B. Masters (ed.), *Chamber Accounts of the 16th century*, London, 1984, p. xxxviii.

schemes of revenue collection that would have necessitated a wider distribution of power. For the most part, too, they were raising money to lend or give to the Crown, rather than for the expenditure of the municipality itself, and this must have influenced their choice of fiscal expedient. And fourthly, almost by chance the City came to accumulate a substantial reserve of capital, in the shape of the Orphans' fund, the inheritances of the children of deceased citizens. Given a *laissez-faire* attitude to City finances, it was not inevitable, but it was perhaps a likely risk, that the Corporation should slide from using this fund as a reserve, to exploiting it as an ordinary part of municipal expenditure.

The oligarchic structure and ethos of London's government was one factor in the problem, though London was less patrician than many other European cities[6]. Medieval and Early Modern London was ruled by a council or court of 25 (later 26) Aldermen, serving for life, who formed a cohesive elite, with a strong tendency to minimise faction among themselves and present a united front to the City and the outside world. The Aldermen were largely merchants, in inland and overseas trade; wealth, status, and public service were closely connected and mutually reinforcing, and the ethos of personal contribution and charitable munificence was strong. The Court of Common Council, with 2-300 members (its numbers increased over time), formed a more representative or democratic element in the structure of city government, but the Court of Aldermen made almost all the important decisions, in terms of policy, administrative initiative, and the exercise of authority. Common Council advised and proposed matters to the Aldermen, and passed local legislation.

Relations between Aldermen and Common Council were for the most part good, but Common Council obviously represented a wider and sometimes divergent range of interests and opinions, both political and economic. The oligarchic and conservative nature of the Court of Aldermen was apparent, and they were not prepared to concede much in the way of oversight or veto of their activities as a governing body to Common Council. Their reluctance to share authority more widely must have contributed to the financial problems that the municipality developed. In particular, although Common Council had to approve grants of taxation on the City and had a say in major expenditure projects, the day-to-day finances of the City were in the hands of the City's Chamberlain who took his orders largely from the Aldermen. The Aldermen had considerable discretion in negotiating with the Crown over taxes, loans, and benevolences, and when courting royal favour by means of gifts and entertainments, but the financial implications of their actions were universal.

London and the Crown

The city of London was known as 'the king's chamber' in the Middle Ages, and it certainly acted as a kind or treasury or reserve for funding central government. London bore a heavy burden in the form of direct taxation, the subsidy assessed on wealth which formed the mainstay of medieval, Tudor and Stuart finance, but it also paid heavily in indirect taxation, since so much of the customs-bearing overseas trade passed through its port[7]. However, it was London's contribution of exceptional sums in loans and gifts that gave it a unique status in national finance. Its ability to promise and find large sums within a short period was crucial to the success of competing dynastic claimants in the 15th

6 See V. Pearl, *London and the outbreak of the Puritan Revolution*, Oxford, 1960; F.F. Foster, *The politics of stability, a portrait of the rulers in Elizabethan London*, London, 1977; I.W. Archer, *The pursuit of stability: social relations in Elizabethan London* , Cambridge, 1991; A.B. Beaven, *The aldermen of the City of London,* 2 vol., London, 1908, 1913; R.M. Wunderli, "Evasion of the office of Alderman in London, 1523-1672, *London Journal*, 15.1 (1990), pp. 3-18.

7 A. Dyer, *Decline and growth in English towns, 1400-1640* , London, 1991; J.C. Cornwall, *Wealth and society in 16th-century England*, London, 1988; I.W. Archer, "The burden of taxation on sixteenth-century London", *The Historical Journal*, 44.3 (2001), pp. 599-627. The taxes of the Civil War years also fell heavily on London: S. Porter, "The economic and social impact of the Civil War upon London", in S. Porter (ed.), *London and the Civil War*, London, 1996, pp. 175-204; Sharpe, *London and the Kingdom*, II.

century[8]. Under Henry VIII (1509-47) London contributed an unprecedented amount both to Parliamentary taxation and to royal prerogative taxation (often in the form of loans that were retrospectively converted into taxes)[9]. Later in the 16th century, other opportunities for government finance through continental money markets may have relieved the City for a time, but by the later Elizabethan period, and through the 17th century, raising loans in London was central to the rule of both monarch and parliament[10].

There were several ways in which money could be raised from London, and the choice between them reflects both the origin of the demand and the political choices of the City's rulers. From the 1520s, Parliamentary direct taxation was assessed by commissioners on the citizens, taking the ward as the intermediate constituency. Only the wealthier inhabitants paid[11]. The Corporation also at times imposed a wealth tax, the 15th, on its citizens, assigning a sum to be raised by each ward but leaving the assessment of individuals to the ward assembly. Assessment on a ward basis had to be approved by Common Council, but it was fairly obviously regressive and liable to be resented[12]. It thus appears that the Aldermen often chose to distribute the burden of raising money in other ways.

The City's guilds or livery companies – all citizens belonged to one – offered an alternative, for both civic enterprises and the demands of national government. Numerous loans and gifts for the Crown were in fact raised by assessing the companies, sometimes without the formal sanction of Common Council. This could and did provoke complaint, both from Common Council and from some of the companymen[13], but it remained an attractive option, and one that was often used. The companies already had the machinery for assessing and if need be disciplining their own members; they were also perhaps, as collectivities, more susceptible to pressure or coercion from the collective authority of the City, than the more informal meetings of wards. Thus, between 1575 and 1598, the City raised five separate loans for the Crown, totalling £120,000, from the companies[14]. In the 17th century, as the Crown's necessities increased, a flow of demands for loans was passed on the companies. In the first surviving municipal account for 1632-3, for example, the City was collecting money from the companies both for an assessment of £4,300 granted by authority of Common Council for the so-called Royal Contract in 1628, and for a new loan of £1000 granted in 1633[15]. The distribution of assessment by company was graded according to notions of their relative wealth, and within the companies the leading members paid quite a large share[16]. The system thus offered a show of fairness, with the rich appearing to shoulder a significant part of the burden. Even though this may have been more apparent than real, since disparities in actual wealth were so great, it was perhaps a useful fiction for the City's elite.

A very significant element in London's lending and giving to the Crown, however, was the role of private individuals. This was not new. Loans by groups of individual Londoners, as well as corporate City loans, featured in the financial dealings of the 15th and indeed 14th centuries. The quasi-legendary mayor Richard Whittington lent to the Crown in the early 15th century; consortia of London

---

8 C.M. Barron, "London and the Crown, 1451-61", in J.R.L. Highfield and R. Jeffs (eds.), *The Crown and local communities in England and France in the fifteenth century*, Gloucester, 1981; V. Harding, "The king and the City in fifteenth-century England", in S. Gensini (ed.), *Principi e città alla fine del medioevo*, Centro di Studi sulla Civiltà del Tardo Medioevo, San Miniato: Collana di Studi e Ricerche 6, 1996, pp. 295-314.
9 Archer, "The burden of taxation", pp. 607-609.
10 See especially R. Ashton, *The Crown and the money market, 1603-40*, Cambridge, 1960.
11 R.G. Lang (ed.), *Two Tudor London Subsidy rolls*, London, 1992, *passim*. See J.P. Boulton, *Neighbourhood and Society, a London suburb in the seventeenth century*, Cambridge, 1987, for an appreciation of 'subsidymen' as a relatively select segment of society.
12 Archer, *The pursuit of stability*, pp. 19, 53.
13 Archer, *The pursuit of stability*, pp. 20, 142; Lang, *Two Tudor London Subsidy rolls.*
14 Foster, *The politics of stability*, p. 138.
15 CLRO, *City Cash Accounts* 1/1; Sharpe, *London and the Kingdom*, II, p. 104-105.
16 See e.g. L. Lyell and F. Watney (ed.), *Acts of Court of the Mercers' Company, 1453-1527*, Cambridge, 1936, pp. 187-189, 752-755.

merchants did so later[17]. Although, as noted above, the City lent £120,000 to the Crown in the later 16th century, raising that from the companies, in the same period at least £60,000 was lent by smaller groups of leading Londoners. A group of fifteen Merchant Adventurers, of whom ten were Aldermen, lent £16,000 in 1569; 128 merchants lent another £15,000 in 1589[18]. The Aldermen personally advanced £20,000 to the Crown in 1626, on the security of the customs, when a much larger corporate loan was refused on the grounds that it could not be raised; a similar sum was advanced by the Aldermen in 1628, in response to an urgent request[19]. Compared with corporate City loans, personal lending placed these individuals in a different relation with the Crown, as creditors with an obvious need for a personal payback. In the Middle Ages, London's lending to the crown helped to secure its privileges against other towns and against the Crown's own tendency to revoke and restrict its grants, but it is arguable that the major beneficiaries of this were London's rulers, whose authority was thereby bolstered. In the 16th and 17th centuries, it appears that members of the City's elite were willing to lend or give to the crown themselves (given adequate security), rather than, or in supplement to, raising money from the citizens, and they must have perceived some benefit in doing so. 'Willingness' and 'adequate security' were both relative, of course, and the element of coercion was never absent even from so-called 'benevolences' and 'gifts', but the City's elite perhaps regarded personal lending as both the price and the guarantee of their autonomy in policymaking.

In the case of personal lending, however, in addition to the motives of private economic and political advantage that may have existed, it is probably pertinent to point to a reluctance on the part of the elite to be seen to tax the citizens too heavily. In Lord Chancellor Burghley's words, 'the English people be most inclineable to sedition when oppressed with extraordinary payments'[20]. Much later, the charge was made that the Mayor and Aldermen had consciously chosen not to assess contributions on the citizens, who would 'willingly' have paid 'according to their oaths', but had funded expenditure by raiding the Orphans' inheritances instead[21]. The situation was actually more complicated than this appears, since, in fact, the wealthy elite were themselves paying tax at a far lower rate by the end of the 16th century than in the 1540s. Heavy taxation under Henry VIII's firm government had probably gone the furthest toward accessing the real wealth of London, and the decaying efficacy of the tax, as avoidance increased, meant that Elizabeth's government was getting far less than her father's, and at a greater cost of resentment and criticism. Whether consciously or not, the wealthy had succeeded to a great extent in 'shuffling off their tax burden' on to the middling ranks of Londoners by the later 16th century, and their sense that increasing taxation on the citizens could be dangerous was probably justified[22]. In an interesting parallel with the contemporary Stuart monarchy, the oligarchic rulers of the City may have preferred not to expose themselves and their rule to criticism from below by making continual financial demands through a relatively democratic forum. The situation was obviously different, in that the origin of their predicament, the pressure to raise money for the Crown, was beyond their control, and they could not avoid reliance on both Common Council and the Companies, but they may have seen advantages of various kinds in minimising the occasions for dissent.

The fact that London's elite never, it seems, considered floating a long-term municipal loan, as a way of raising large sums for any purpose, as several other European cities did in the later Middle Ages and the Early Modern period, requires some consideration. London was prosperous, politically cohesive, relatively stable and free from factional strife, at least in the 15th and 16th centuries; its credit was good; it almost certainly could have raised loans with success. Several explanations are possible,

17 Barron, "London and the Crown"; C.M. Barron, "Richard Whittington: the man behind the myth", in A.J. Hollaender and W. Kellaway (eds.), *Studies in London History presented to P. E.Jones*, London, 1969.
18 Foster, *The politics of stability*, p. 138.
19 Sharpe, *London and the Kingdom*, II, pp. 98, 105.
20 Quoted in Archer, *The pursuit of stability,* p. 33.
21 British Library, MS Cup. 645 b 11 (27), quoted by Kellett, "Financial crisis", p. 223.
22 Archer, "Burden of taxation", p. 626.

though none seems conclusive on its own. The Aldermen were notably sensitive to accusations of usury in the late 14th century[23], and might have been concerned that a civic annuity scheme could be interpreted in this way. Though there was plenty of wealth in London, the ordinary revenues of the Corporation were limited; it did not directly own a large landed estate, on which a loan might be guaranteed, and property rents were slack in the 15th and early 16th centuries[24]. Although corporate city funds were used for building Guildhall in the 15th century and market buildings and conduits in the 16th, there was also strong tradition of personal, voluntary contribution to civic projects[25]. The building of the Royal Exchange in the 1560s was financed by individual subscriptions and forced loans from the Companies[26]. There was certainly conservatism in the financial management of the City, as well as a cautious, minimally interventionist style of civic government. Overall, it must be that there were never compelling advantages or attractions to floating a debt, and plenty of adequate alternatives.

Crucial to the success of the Corporation's somewhat *ad hoc* response to the Crown's demands, of course, was the continuing health of London's economy and the affluence of its leaders, and the assumption that the financial demands on them would remain within reasonable limits. In the long run, though the first assumption was justified, the second proved mistaken. The Stuart monarchy's demands on the City continued to escalate, and its unpaid debts to mount. One debt was rolled over to the next, and a variety of unsatisfactory schemes for repayment were floated. The City did not comply with every demand, but the Crown's exactions played a large part in the City's increasing financial difficulties. There is no doubt that the Crown leaned very heavily on London, and that its demands severely strained economic and political relations within the City, as well as between City and Crown, in the 17th century. This question has been thoroughly analysed by Ashton[27]. However, the City's rulers may be said to have failed to face up to the situation, partly through their preference for alternative ways of meeting the demands. In 1614, for instance, the City countered the Crown's request for a loan of £100,000 – the assessment for which would have had to be widely distributed – by offering instead a free gift of £10,000, which was paid, half by the Chamber (the City's treasury) and half by an assessment on the companies[28]. And though the City elite supplemented the collective contributions from their own wealth, they did not shoulder the whole burden. The Aldermen voted a gift of £2,000 in gold to the King in 1633, on his departure for Scotland, 'as a pledge of this City's love loyalty and obedience to his Majesty'; they also gave a basin and ewer of gold to the Queen, worth nearly £800. These gifts were paid for by the Chamber, and it is not clear that any special reserve was earmarked to support the cost[29]. The annual deficit in the City's accounts seems to have grown steadily.

The sustained financial pressure on the City to lend to the Crown, and the latter's failure to honour all its obligations, played a major part (among many other factors) in the alienation of support from the monarchy in the 1630s. Ironically, although the Parliamentary regime that replaced the monarchy in mid-century taxed London heavily, the municipality emerged from those years with a reduced burden of debt. In this period, London was effectively ruled by Common Council, rather than

23 R.R. Sharpe (ed.), *Calendar of letter-books preserved among the archives of the City of London at the Guildhall. Letter-book H, c. 1375-1399*, London, 1907, pp. 206-207, 261-262, 365.

24 D. Keene, *Cheapside before the Great Fire*, London, Economic and Social Research Council, 1987, pp. 19-20.

25 C.M. Barron, *The medieval Guildhall of London*, London, Corporation of London, 1974; I.W. Archer, C.M. Barron, and V. Harding, *Hugh Alley's caveat. The markets of London in 1598*, London, London Topographical Society, 1988, pp. 92-93, 95-97; W.K. Jordan, *The Charities of London, 1480-1660*, London, 1960, pp. 196-206; J. Stow, *A survey of London*, London, 1603; C.L. Kingsford (ed.), Oxford, 1908, I, pp. 104-117.

26 A. Saunders (ed.), *The Royal Exchange*, London, 1997, pp. 31-33.

27 Ashton, *The Crown and the money market*; R. Ashton, "Conflicts of concessionary interest in Early Stuart England", in D.C. Coleman and A.H. John (eds.), *Trade, Government and economy in pre-industrial England*, London, 1976, pp. 113-131; R. Ashton, *The City and the court, 1603-43* , Cambridge, 1979.

28 Sharpe, *London and the Kingdom*, II, p. 63.

29 Sharpe, *London and the Kingdom*, II, p. 111; CLRO, *City Cash Accounts* 1/1.

the Court of Aldermen, and it may be that the city could bear heavier direct taxation because the distribution of the tax burden was of necessity more equitable and transparent than the partly self-serving expedients of the Aldermen[30]. In the later 17th century, the Restoration Court of Aldermen were still it seems unwilling to lay a realistic tax burden on the citizens. Perhaps partly unnerved by the possibility of political faction and strife, and reluctant to alienate their constituents, they also feared literally alienating them to the less-governed and less heavily taxed suburbs[31].

This does not, however, fully answer the question why the City's financial situation seems to have been ignored for so long, or why it deteriorated so rapidly after the Restoration. For this we need to look at the shortcomings of the City's financial records and procedures.

Municipal revenues and accounting procedures

Compared with other aspects of its activities, the City's finances are not well documented for most of this period. The surviving series of City Cash Account books starts in 1632, earlier records having mostly been lost in a fire in the 18th century. Two 16th-century accounts have been reconstructed, however, and some indications of medieval practice survive[32].

All these combine to show that the municipality of London was relatively poor, with few valuable estates and limited regular sources of income. In 1584-5, for example, the City's income from its regular sources came to just over £3,500, of which just under £900 came from its estates. The City's lands were few and scattered; the revenues from certain markets and other tolls had long been assigned to other accounts. The Chamber's main sources of income were fees for apprenticeship and freedom enrolments, fines for various offences, fines for refusing office, and payments for holding certain offices of profit. The City's obligations included the cost of running the administration, legal fees, building works on the City's properties and public buildings, and various pensions and liveries. In 1584-5 these came to £4,200. Part of this overspend was due to the fact that some of the building works carried out this year were in due course paid for by an assessment on the citizens received in subsequent years, but in general it seems clear that the City ran its affairs on a narrow margin and that expenditure was not governed by any realistic projection of income.

What is more alarming is that the City's accounting systems were incapable of giving a clear state of its liabilities. The accounts took the traditional form of a defensive record of moneys in and out, 'charge' versus 'discharge', and included a range of other sums of income and expenditure from various sources. The sums mentioned, representing core income and expenditure, were almost lost within a much larger total movement of money in and out, capital and current, notional and real. The total charge for the year 1584-5 was £6,244; the total discharge, £6,189. But the charge included nearly £500 of arrears and old debts owed to the City, of which less than half was in fact paid in; the City also collected money from assessments and donations for ransoming foreign captives and for mustering soldiers, not all of which it paid out this year.

The same accounting structure (charge/discharge, conflating capital and current income and expenditure) continued through the 17th century, though the sums being handled increased enormously. In 1632-3 the City's core income was around £6,500, of which £2,500 came from the estates; expenditure on fees, public works, gifts to the Crown, etc.., came to around £13,000. Nevertheless, the overall account appeared to be in healthy surplus, with £98,000 in and £70,500 out. However, a large part of the charge was effectively a fiction, or at best misleading: £35,000 in arrears,

30 Sharpe, *London and the Kingdom*, II.
31 Doolittle, "City of London's debt".
32 Masters, *Chamber Accounts*, is the source for the following.

and £35,000 of debts now paid from previous accounting years. The discharge likewise included some £27,000 in repayments of interest and principal money lent to the City[33]. In 1661-2, the core of the account was similar: some £8,500 in current income, including £5,500 in rents and leases, and about £8,500 in ordinary expenditure. Again, though, the total charge (£69,000) and discharge (£51,000) gave a wholly spurious idea of the City's solvency, since they subsumed arrears, capital receipts and capital borrowings in the charge, and some capital repayments in the discharge[34].

It is hard to understand how London's rulers, who must have used much more sophisticated and informative accounting procedures for their own businesses, could have accepted this as an accurate picture of the City's financial situation. The City's accounts were audited every year, but the sorts of issues that this highlighted tended to be the allowability of certain expenditures, or the possibility of malfeasance, rather than the underlying financial state of the City[35]. Some anxiety was expressed from time to time: in 1599 auditors were appointed to examine the accounts and 'understand what and how much is owing by this City, what in right is due to be paid to the same, what sums remain elsewhere, and in whose hands the same is'[36]. But this flurry of activity probably sprang from a general sense of financial and political crisis in the 1590s, rather than a longer-running dissatisfaction with the operation of the City's accounts. Later attempts to increase revenue included imposing more fines for being excused office, and the value of the City's estate increased as land values rose across the metropolis, but neither of these could make much headway against the rising level of debt[37]. The City's rulers' apparent lack of interest suggests that utility and transparency in accounting procedures were not high priorities; and that both underlying and arising from this was a general sense of complacency about the City's financial health. The increasing indebtedness of the City seems to have passed them by, at least until the later 17th century, when real panic set in[38].

The Orphans

The most serious problem obscuring the real financial situation, both in accounting terms and, I would argue, in the psychology of the City's rulers, was the City's failure to separate its own business from its activity as trustee and guarantor of the estates of deceased citizens. London had a long tradition of overseeing the inheritances of the orphaned children of citizens. The custom dated from at least the 13th century, and until the 16th century it was mostly limited to approving guardians for the children, acting as their protector against financial or personal exploitation, and taking security from the executors or guardians for the repayment of their portions when they came of age or married. By the later 16th century, some executors and guardians preferred to deposit the inheritance in the City's chamber for the whole period of the children's minority, in return for the regular payment of 'finding money' – essentially an interest payment – for the children's maintenance. In the 17th century, this practice grew in popularity, and there was an increasing propensity for orphans to leave their money in the Chamber after they came of age and could have claimed it, simply because it represented an apparently secure investment with a reasonable return on capital – at compound interest, if the whole of the interest due was not taken – at a time when there were few other opportunities for investment[39].

33 CLRO, *City Cash Accounts* 1/1.
34 CLRO, *City Cash Accounts* 1/11.
35 Masters, *Chamber Accounts*, pp. xxxv-xxxvi.
36 CLRO, *Repertory* 24, f. 465, quoted by Masters, *Chamber Accounts*, p. xxxviii.
37 Sharpe, *London and the Kingdom*, II, p. 63.
38 Kellett, "Some late seventeenth-century schemes".
39 C. Carlton, "The administration of London's Court of Orphans", *Guildhall Miscellany*, 4 (1971), pp. 22-35; C. Carlton, *The court of Orphans* , Leicester, 1974; Kellett, "Financial crisis".

Capital sums thus came in every year, with a date for repayment some years into the future, so that annual income and expenditure never tallied; and as fewer estates were reclaimed on maturity, and the overall size of estates increased, the City's debt to its orphans mounted. It stood at about £5,500 in 1585, but it increased rapidly in the first half of the 17th century, reaching £191,000 in 1634. Some fluctuation was natural, as large estates were paid back, and this and retrenchment reduced it to £160,000 in 1642, and to £115,500 in 1660. After the Restoration, however, it rose exponentially, reaching £249,000 in 1669 and £559,000 in 1680. The practice of crediting compound interest contributed to the total, but it is clear that the City's credit was evidently high, right up to this point, and executors and orphans were ready to commit large sums to the Chamber's keeping[40].

As a way of guaranteeing the inheritances of fatherless children against fraud or misapplication, handing their money over to the City had obvious attractions. However, the long-term reliability of the arrangement depended on the Chamber's treating the inheritances as trust funds and not as part of its own resources. Given that the City acted as trustee for several pious and charitable endowments, accounting separately and scrupulously for their income and expenditure, this does not seem an impossible expectation[41]. In practice, however, as the earliest surviving accounts show, the Orphans' liabilities were merged with the total accountability of the Chamber. The Chamberlain listed the capital paid into the Chamber from the estates of newly-deceased citizens in the current income of the Chamber, and the repayments of capital sums to orphans coming of age, in its current expenditure. The City did attempt to identify the extent of its current indebtedness to the Orphans in the annual Chamber or City Cash accounts, and kept a separate Journal and Ledger for the orphanage accounts, but in practice these were mostly paper credits and debits, and it is impossible to see where the money actually was, or whether the City really had the money at all.

In fact, as ultimately became clear, it did not. It had spent it. By the late 17th century, the Orphans' capital had been used up in subsidising the running costs and other liabilities of the administration. It was not always so; the accounts and other records of the City show that at times the Corporation was lending Orphans' money at interest, as a trustee should, thus guaranteeing the annual interest or 'finding money' payable to the Orphans themselves[42]. If the matter had always been managed in this way, the mounting total of the Orphans' deposits with the City would have been an asset rather than a dangerous liability. But, as discussed already, the City's rulers were both reluctant to lay the full burden of the City's liabilities on the citizens as taxpayers, and perhaps in any case ignorant of the true state of affairs. The City's real annual expenditure normally exceeded its income, sometimes by a long way; the deficit on the current account seems to have been unthinkingly made up from the Orphans' capital. This had the double result that the capital itself – all of which was always technically due for repayment in a few years' time – was depleted, and at the same time the City's ability to generate 'finding money' in future was compromised. As long as new generations of orphans deposited their inheritances in the Chamber, the latter could afford to pay off the old, where required, and to sustain the interest payments on the whole notional sum. The tendency to leave inheritances in the Chamber longer than was legally required also deferred the day of reckoning, but meanwhile the interest liability continued to mount. One unrecognised feature of this tendency was that it transformed term annuities – with a maximum repayment term of 21 years - into indefinite ones, on which a lower rate of interest should have been paid.

40 Figures from Masters, *Chamber Accounts*; Kellett, "Financial crisis".

41 The chamber accounts reported separately on the income and expenditure from the charitable endowments of the Philpot, Carpenter, Reynewell, and later Costen estates: Masters, *Chamber Accounts*, pp. xxv-xxviii; CLRO, *City Cash Accounts*. The accounts of the Bridge House, the body responsible for administering a large estate dedicated to the upkeep of London Bridge, were kept entirely separate: CLRO, Bridge House Rentals; V. Harding and L. Wright (eds.), *London Bridge: selected accounts and rentals, 1381-1547*, London, 1995.

42 CLRO, *City Cash Accounts* 1/1.

In 1584-5, 'finding money' was only £245; in 1632-3 it was over £8,000. In 1670 it was nearly £13,000 (at around 5%), and the annual average payment in the years 1674-81 was £19,500. By the 1670s, the burden on the City was enormous. In 1682 the City announced that it would no longer accept the deposit of inheritances, and in 1684 it reduced the rate of interest on deposits from 4% to 2.5%[43]. In 1694 an Act of Parliament was necessary to resolve the issue, and consolidated the Corporation's debt into a fund paying 4% interest[44].

Conclusion

The story of the Orphans' debt and the City's near-bankruptcy is the most dramatic episode of the City's financial history. In its long-running structural causes, however, it vividly illustrates the practices of the municipal bureaucracy and the attitudes of London's elite rulers to its financial affairs. Historians are usually at pains to stress the exceptional character of London in Early Modern England, many times larger, richer, and more influential than any other town or city. Several aspects of this story are indeed unique, especially the scale both of the City's financial obligations and of the Orphans' fund. Whether there is anything specifically English in the situation and the way it developed is harder to assess. However, the direction taken by English government in the 16th century – towards a heavier reliance on taxation and direct levy, rather than the sale of offices and exemptions, the exploitation of feudal resources, or an excise on commodities – is certainly also an important factor. In due course, this narrowed the range of politically acceptable fiscal expedients for the Crown, and caused it to lean more heavily on London. But it may also have limited the horizons of London's rulers, when it came to the practicalities of raising money in the City to meet the Crown's demands, and contributed to the difficulties in which they found themselves.

43 Kellett, "Financial crisis".

44 Kellett, "Financial crisis"; Doolittle, "City of London's debt".

THE VENETIAN GOVERNMENT DEBT 1350-1650

Luciano Pezzolo
University of Venice, Ca' Foscari

Venetian government debt between the late Middle Ages and the Renaissance has been studied in particular detail by two scholars, both of whom explained the workings of the system and provided a great deal of data. Gino Luzzatto published a book of documents with a detailed introduction in which he examined Venetian debt from the 12th to the 15th centuries[1]. Recently, Reinhold Mueller has written a fundamental book on private and public finance in Renaissance Venice. While the former focused specifically on institutional aspects, the latter has put finance into a broader political and economic context[2]. Lane could also be set alongside these two historians. Although he did not analyse Venetian finance in depth, he nevertheless provided very important material on the subject[3]. The great tradition of Italian financial history, going as far back as between the end of the 19th century and the early 20th century, has thus moved hand in hand with the more recent American social and economic history. The result is that Venetian Medieval and Renaissance debt is most likely one of the best-known subjects in European financial history[4].

My task, therefore, is rather an easy one: relying mostly on published works I will provide a picture of the Venetian debt between the later Middle Ages and Early Modern times (Figure I)[5]. I will focus mostly on long-term debt, just touching upon the floating debt, which would deserve a further paper. The role of floating debt, however, was rather limited considering the amount of money raised through it in comparison with the volume of loans provided by the funded debt. My aim is to point to some peculiar features of the long-term debt mechanism and to set such elements in a comparative perspective by briefly considering the Florentine case, in order to highlight some differences between the two regimes and financial implications.

---

1 G. Luzzatto (ed.), *I prestiti pubblici della Repubblica di Venezia (sec. XIII-XV)*, Padua, 1929 (*Introduction* reprinted as *Il debito pubblico della Repubblica di Venezia*, Varese 1963).
2 R.C. Mueller, *The Venetian money market. Banks, panics, and the public debt, 1200-1500*, Baltimore/London, 1997.
3 F.C. Lane, "Public debt and private wealth: particularly in sixteenth-century Venice", in *Mélanges en l'honneur de Fernand Braudel*, Toulouse, 1973, I, pp. 317-325, reprinted in F.C. Lane, *Profits from power. Readings in protection rent and violence-controlling enterprises*, Albany (N.Y.), 1979; F.C. Lane, "The funded debt of the Venetian republic", Appendix to Luzzatto (ed.), *Il debito pubblico*, reprinted in *Venice and history. The collected papers of Frederic C. Lane*, Baltimore, 1966, pp. 87-98.
4 M. Knapton, "La finanza pubblica", in *Storia di Venezia*, Rome, 1995, II, pp. 371-407; M. Knapton, "La dinamica delle finanze pubbliche", in *Storia di Venezia*, Rome. 1997, III, pp. 475-528; L. Pezzolo, *L'oro dello Stato. Società, finanza e fisco nella Repubblica veneta del secondo '500*, Venice, 1990; L. Pezzolo, *Il fisco dei veneziani. Finanza pubblica ed economia tra XV e XVII secolo*, Verona, 2003; J-C. Hocquet, "Venice", in R. Bonney (ed.), *The rise of the fiscal state in Europe 1200-1815*, Oxford, 1999.
5 The figure, updated by myself, was kindly provided by Reinhold Mueller.

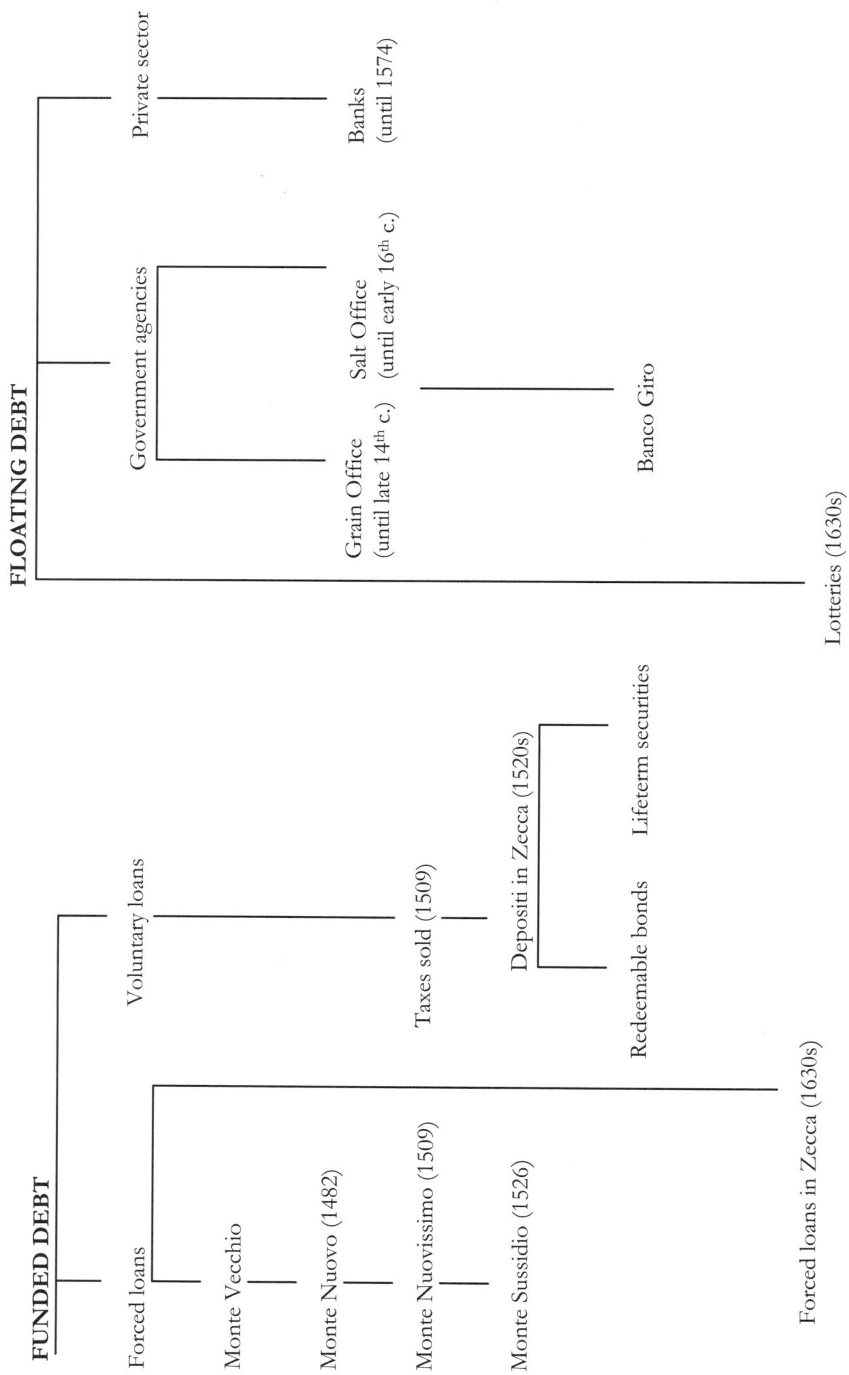

FIG I. **The structure of the Venetian debt (1350-1650)**

The floating debt

By the late 13th century the Venetian government had an agency – the *Camera del frumento* (Grain Office) – that actually managed the short-term debt. As the office collected deposits from clients and provided loans both to the government and individuals, it can be regarded as a sort of state bank[6]. Initially the return on state loans ranged between 8 and 12%, while in the second half of the 14th century, when long-term deposits were accepted, it varied between 3 and 5%. The severe crisis of the war of Chioggia against Genoa (1378-81) caused a heavy indebtedness and a worsening of the relations between depositors and office, so that its financial function declined as a result.

Throughout the 15th century the role of providers of short-term loans was played mainly by private bankers, the so-called *banchieri di scritta*. Bankers *di scritta* collected deposits and allowed giro operations among their clients[7]. Theoretically deposit banks were not permitted to grant loans, because the currency base had to match the volume of deposits exactly; in reality, however, the history of banks is studded of crisis provoked by lack of liquidity. Financial relations between bankers and government were characterized by reciprocity: the former could count on support in case of need, the latter resorted to their services to get loans both in cash and bank money. The amount of loans granted by banks do not seem huge. It has been estimated that the senate had borrowed from bankers about 230,000 ducats in 1465 and 297,500 ducats between 1473 and 1475[8]. It is a considerable figure, indeed, that allowed to rig 50 galleys for one year, but not to be considered enormous, since at that time the annual state income was about one million ducats, and one year of war cost 1.2 million ducats[9]. The role of the banks *di scritta* as state lenders seems to have declined after the first quarter of the 16th century.

In periods of military crisis, the government required loans also from private citizens. Those who were considered as the wealthiest, especially the patricians, were requested to either provide cash or precious metals against a return that was not always specified. In 1474 the money for a military expedition came from forty patricians chosen by the doge; and in 1483 60,000 ducats were called for from "gentlemen citizens and others" of Venice. Because in 1499 the richest city dwellers paid 20,000 ducats, revenues of the Salt Office were obliged to pay back both principal and interests[10]. The patriotic feeling was not always widespread among Venetian patricians. Thus, for example, in 1509 the government examined the possibility of asking for 300,000 ducats from more than 500 Venetians considered as very rich, but it seems that few were willing to give money because, as a chronicler states, "they have as example the principals do nothing"[11].

At any rate, the resort to short-term loans does not seem to characterize the relations between Venetians and state finance. It would, however, be wrong to argue that the Republic did not have a floating debt. After the banks *di scritta* disappeared in the early 1580s, the role of institute of deposit and giro was taken up in 1587 by a state bank, the *Banco della piazza di Rialto*, which nevertheless did not provide the government with clients' money[12].

---

6 Mueller, *The Venetian money market*, p. 359 ff.; Luzzatto, *Il debito pubblico*, pp. 37, 52-55.

7 Mueller, *The Venetian money market*, p. 425 ff.

8 J.-C. Hocquet, "Guerre et finance dans l'état de la Renaissance (la Chambre du Sel et la dette publique à Venise", in *Actes du 102e Congrès national des Sociétés Savantes*, Paris, 1979, p. 112; Mueller, *The Venetian money market*, pp. 431-432.

9 The cost of rigging galleys (30,000 ducats for 10 galleys in service for six months) in M. Sanudo, *Le vite dei Dogi (1474-1494)*, A. Caracciolo Aricò (ed.), Padua, 1989, I, pp. 11-12, 15; for military expenses, D. Malipiero, *Annali veneti dall'anno 1457 al 1500*, A. Sagredo (ed.), in *Archivio storico italiano*, 7 (1843-44), p. 66.

10 Malipiero, *Annali veneti*, p. 94; M. Sanudo, *Le vite dei Dogi (1474-1494)*, A. Caracciolo Aricò (ed.), Padua, 2001, II, p. 355; G. Priuli, *I diarii*, A. Segre (ed.), Città di Castello, 1921, I, pp. 120-121.

11 M. Sanudo, *Diarii*, Venice, 1883, X, col. 14-15 (3 Aug. 1509). See also Priuli, *I diarii*, p. 303.

12 U. Tucci, "Il Banco della Piazza di Rialto prima banca pubblica veneziana", in U. Tucci, *Mercanti, navi, monete nel Cinquecento veneziano*, Bologna, 1981, pp. 231-250.

The practice of assigning credits in some government agencies to suppliers spread by the early 17th century; credits recognized by government could be transferred from the holder to others. The part of this floating debt was managed, starting from 1619, by the *Banco Giro*, which within twenty years would take up also the functions of the *Banco della piazza di Rialto*[13]. As long as the political and financial frame was quiet, the debt managed by the *Banco* turned out to be quite limited, but as soon as the military involvements of Venice became urgent the government was forced to expand the volume of debt, which nevertheless did not reach enormous levels. The highest indebtedness of the *Banco* between 1619 and 1666, in fact, did not exceed 2.6 million ducats, an amount that can not be seen as dramatic, considering that in that period the state budget recorded incomes around 3.5 million ducats.

In short, as far as we know, the burden of short-term debt for the Venetian finance was not as onerous as elsewhere. No doubt the path the patricians chose was that of the long-term debt, which characterizes the history of the Republic since the late 12th century.

The forced loans system: a 'public' debt?

From the late 12th century, along with voluntary loans, loans were forced on the citizens whose wealth was assessed in the tax records (the so-called *estimo*). Venetians had to pay a sum according to their assessed income; in exchange they would receive a return of 5% as long as the principal was paid back. This system proved to be very profitable and effective both for lenders, who could count on a moderate but safe return, and state finance, hungry for money. The mechanism, however, entered a crisis during the fourth war against Genoa. The war caused a dramatic increase of indebtedness but, above all, started a spiral worsening the very structure of state finance. Because of the heavy requests, between 1378 and 1381 citizens were forced to pay 41% of their assessed wealth. The government had difficulties in paying the interest to lenders regularly, so much that it was forced to take the decision to stop paying it in the years 1379-81 (Figure II). The secondary market of government bonds, whose price dropped as low as 18 at par, collapsed (Figure III). War and tax pressure caused a redistribution of wealth within the city, and tax officers were unable to find new patrimonies. All these elements were at the roots of the first true financial crisis of the Venetian state; a crisis with severe consequences in the years to come. The 15th-century wars, in fact, put Venetian public finance under endless pressure and, despite some short periods of peace, the picture progressively worsened. The amount of arrears to be paid increased over the 15th century: the delay of payments to creditors was as high as 20 years during the Turkish war in 1463-79, and no interest at all was paid in 1480. Bonds were traded well below par and in the early 1480s the total amount of the state debt in terms of market prices can be estimated at one tenth of the nominal value. One has to bear in mind this spread when looking at Table I: from the late 14th century until the mid-16th century the amounts raised through the *Monti* underwent a severe devaluation on the secondary market. The total indebtedness, thus, has to be discounted considering that the capitals collected were later paid back at prices well below nominal value.

In order to regain the taxpayers-lenders' trust, in 1482 the government issued a new series of annuities to finance the war against Ferrara (1482-84). The new series was named Monte *Nuovo*, to distinguish it from the bonds issued until then, whose amount had reached a nominal value of 8,269,000 ducats. The Monte *Nuovo* succeeded in renewing the Venetians' interest, but only for a short time. The difficulties of war and increased fiscal pressure both revived citizens' uncertainty regarding their government's creditworthiness. It is, thus, not surprising that the government was compelled to sell – maybe on the open market – Monte *Nuovo* bonds well below par, but assuring the interest rate

13 U. Tucci, "Convertibilità e copertura metallica della moneta del Banco Giro veneziano", in *Studi veneziani*, 15 (1973), pp. 349-448.

FIG II. **Interest rates of the Venetian funded debt**

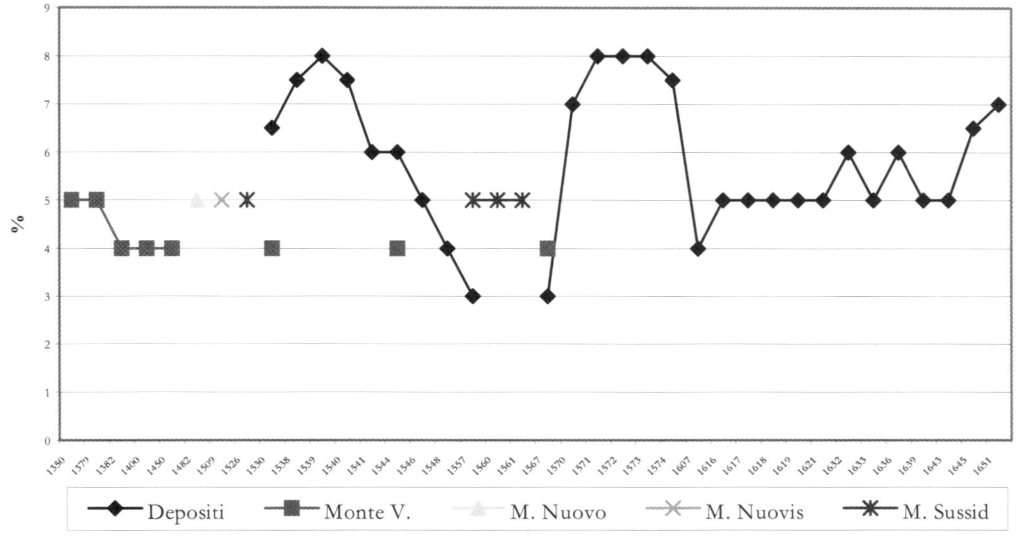

FIG III. **Market prices of government credits (Monte *Vecchio* and Monte *Nuovo*)**

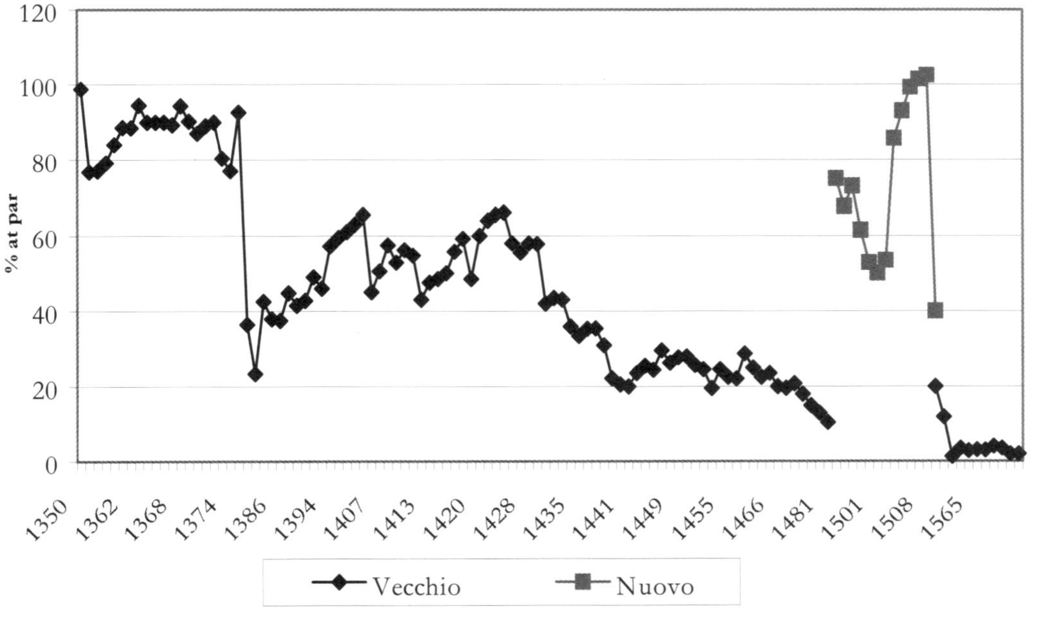

TABLE I. **Venetian debt and state finance**

(in ducats of account)

1	2 revenue	3 expenditure	4 service on debt	5 nominal capital	6 % 4/5	7 % 4/2	8 % 4/3
1343	250,000	257,000	79,000	423,000	18.7	31.6	30.7
1344	260,000	285,000	19,000			7.3	6.7
1349				385,000			
1353				1,192,000			
1363				1,423,000			
1372-73				2,308,000			
1378			150,000	3,269,000	4.6		
1380-81				4,731,000			
1386			246,690	4,923,000	5.0		
1387			239,830				
1388			228,180				
1389			220,870				
1390			211,480				
1391			236,230				
1392			218,000				
1393			241,190				
1394			193,589				
1395			217,660	3,846,000	5.7		
1396			197,310				
1397			188,950				
1398			195,500				
1402				3,654,000			
1404-08				5,385,000			
1413			224,000	8,850,000	2.5		
1422			300,000				
1423-27				6,000,000			
1432			320,000	9,300,000	3.4		
1439			225,000				
1464	1,120,000		150,000			13.4	
1469	1,120,000		154,000			13.8	
1490			211,000				
1500	1,150,000		211,000			18.3	
1508			230,000				
1550	1,601,000	1,735,000	575,000			35.9	33.1
1554	1,443,000	1,717,000	584,000	10,181,000	5.7	40.5	34.0
1559			445,120				
1609	2,550,000		19,000	611,000	3.1	0.7	
1641	2,960,000	2,770,000	492,000	8,435,000	5.8	16.6	17.8

Sources: M. Ginatempo, *Prima del debito*, Florence, 2001, p. 146-47; R. Mueller, *The Venetian money market*, pp. 478-79; F. Besta (ed.), *Bilanci generali*, I, p. 85; L. Pezzolo, "La finanza pubblica veneziana" (forthcoming).

on the nominal value: in 1503 out of 2.8 million ducats of nominal capital only one million proved to have been sold at par, while prices of the remaining had ranged from even 48 to 90[14]. This means that purchasers at 50 enjoyed an actual return of 10%, and so on. When the Council of Ten, the most important political-judicial body of the Republic, ordered the sale of bonds at 75%, buyers brought money – as Marin Sanudo writes in 1497 – "with great hurry"[15]. News of peace was received with sincere relief and, accordingly, the market prices of the new series increased. Moreover, the events concerning the Monte *Nuovo* were connected to the military involvement of the republic; political troubles made market prices decrease, while rumours of peace were sufficient to increase prices. Thus, for example, Monte *Nuovo* bonds were traded over par in 1505-6. It was, nevertheless, a brief period of euphoria, that was soon to vanish when war appeared again. The crisis of the League of Cambrai (1509-16) brought the Monte *Nuovo* to its knees; hence the Monte *Nuovissimo*, founded with the same task as the former series, which took it over in 1509. By the mid-1520s the health of the public debt did not look at all good. Interest was paid late, the securities of the Monte *Vecchio* were valued at 3%, those of the Monte *Nuovo* at 10%, and those of the *Nuovissimo* at 25%. The system of forced loans proved to be inadequate both for rapid financing of war and for the Venetians too, who were becoming taxpayers rather than lenders to the state. According to Lane, however, wealthy groups managed to profit from the debt mechanism, because through interest and capital they received more than they had been paying for direct taxes[16]. But this mechanism is profitable only in periods of light tax demand, otherwise the burden is heavy also for the rich, as the case of early 15th-century Florence shows[17].

It is worth examining whether the term 'public' debt looks appropriate as far as the forced loans system is concerned. On the one hand, if we consider that the guarantees offered by the government (state revenues) were regarded as a 'public' good, then the term appears to be adequate; on the other hand, the relation between government and lender was not clear. It is likely that Venetian citizens were increasingly regarding themselves more as taxpayers rather than investors. The coercive nature of the system dramatically emerged in the late 14th century and did not disappear as long as the government continued to launch securities on the open market[18]. If the term 'public' debt implies to a certain extent a primary market, the investors' free choice, then we should reconsider the use of such a concept with regard to Medieval urban debt. The supply side was actually missing and, if at all, played a modest active role. I argue that a true 'public' debt emerged in the early 16th century, when the Venetian government introduced some innovations concerning the means of deficit financing.

A market-oriented debt: the Depositi in Zecca

The response to the financial crisis emerged between the 1520s and 1530s, and was completed by the mid-century. After the establishment of the Monte *del Sussidio* in 1526, the mechanism of the forced loans, by that time worn-out and inefficient because of restless warfare, was progressively substituted by another system relying on loans directly raised on the open market. There had been some attempts in 1452[19], and especially in the 1520s to collect money among Venetians willing to invest: in 1528, for example, the government allowed citizens to deposit precious metals and

14 Priuli, *I diarii*, II, p. 272; and Sanudo, *Diari*, XX, col. 7-10.
15 Sanudo, *Diari*, I, col. 575.
16 Lane, "Public debt and private wealth", p. 322.
17 L. Martines, "Forced loans: political and social strain in Quattrocento Florence", in *Journal of modern history*, 60 (1988), pp. 307-308.
18 In 1496 Sanudo wrote that until then Venetians had been paying 14 loans to the Monte *Nuovo* and 'donating' an other 6 to the Monte *Vecchio*: Sanudo, *Diari*, I, col. 269-270.
19 F. Besta (ed.), *Bilanci generali della Repubblica di Venezia*, Venice, 1912, I, pp. 114-115.

money in the Mint against an attractive return[20]. Also after the end of the war the Mint kept receiving loans for a quite moderate interest rate and at short time[21]. The new loans enjoyed a great success: the loan of 50,000 ducats at 6% launched on 27 November 1532 was fulfilled even the day after; and two months later another 100,000 ducats were raised in less than twelve days[22]. Thus, through the Mint, the Venetians were called on to invest voluntarily in the state debt more systematically than before. The new series of voluntary loans was named *Depositi in Zecca*, and represented the most important and powerful tool for state financing. Lenders were reassured by assigning the yield of a tax to pay interest; the interest rate, usually moderate, was not subject to taxation, unlike the Monte bonds; the terms for paying back the principal were not pre-established; the bond was marketable and transferable to heirs. These were features that allowed the claim that the Venetian *Depositi in Zecca* represented a sophisticated means of deficit financing, and an advanced feature of 'modernity' usually ascribed to other state debts. It is worth stressing, however, that these kinds of annuities were not, as usual, bearer bonds: thus, every exchange had to be recorded in the *Officio degli imprestiti* (Loans Office) or in the Mint.

The range of loans varied according to the length of time and the rate of interest. In 1538, during the Turkish war, the government issued a series of life annuities (*Depositi sopra la vita*) at a rate of 14%, while at that time redeemable *Depositi* provided interest as high as 8%. It is worth noting that life annuities represented a certain novelty for the Venetian debt, although they were well known in the cities of southern Germany, Switzerland, northern France as well as Flanders[23]. In Italy the first life annuities issued by the major governments had spread by the mid-16th century: in 1550 the Papal Apostolic Chamber launched a vacable (lifeterm) Monte at 12%; and at the same time the Neapolitan government was paying an interest on life annuities at 20%, to be reduced to 12% in the early 1580s. In Holland, engaged in war in 1553, a life annuity yielded 16.66%[24]. It is very likely that the level of the interest rate was the result of observations and calculations, albeit not very sophisticated, on life expectancy. Thus, for example, the use of an ancient life expectancy table in Renaissance Florence could be connected with the Monte *delle doti* (Monte of dowries), which raised capital among parents who had daughters to be married, at an interest rate very close to the one provided by a life annuity[25]. Venice, however, in the second half of the 16th century did not resort significantly to life annuities. While in the war of 1537-40 against the Turks at least 20.4% of the total amount of money raised through the *Depositi in Zecca* came from life annuities, only 50,000 of 3.5 million ducats were collected

---

20 Sanudo, *Diari*, XLVII, col. 308-310; XLIX, col. 308-10, 312 ff., 320 ff., for the names of lenders. Earlier cases in Malipiero, *Annali veneti*, pp. 289, 344; Priuli, *I diarii*, I, p. 138.

21 Sanudo, *Diari*, LII, col. 330, 338; LIV, col. 144, 183, 443; LV, col. 28, 629; LVI, col. 545, 918.

22 Sanudo, *Diari*, LVII, col. 272, 378-379, 415, 447, 458.

23 E.B. Fryde and M.M. Fryde, "Il credito pubblico, con particolare riferimento all'Europa nordoccidentale", in M.M. Postan, E.E. Rich and E. Miller (eds.), *Storia economica Cambridge*, Turin, 1977, III, pp. 497-638; and the contribution of J.D. Tracy (see chapter 2.

24 See, for Rome, F. Piola Caselli, "La diffusione dei luoghi di Monte della Camera Apostolica alla fine del XVI secolo. Capitali investiti e rendimenti", in *Credito e sviluppo in Italia dal Medio Evo all'Età Contemporanea*, Verona, 1988, p. 198. It is worth pointing out that some vacable offices of third category (*i.e.* real state bonds) were being sold since 1486 by the papal government: F. Piola Caselli, "Aspetti del debito pubblico nello Stato pontificio: gli uffici vacabili", *Annali della Facoltà di Scienze Politiche*, 11 (1970-72), pp. 15-16. For the Neapolitan lifeterm securities, A. Calabria, *The cost of empire. The finances of the kingdom of Naples in the time of the Spanish rule*, Cambridge, 1991, p. 143. The high interest rate of the *lijfrenten* is in J.D. Tracy, *A financial revolution in the Habsburg Netherlands. Renten and Renteniers in the County of Holland, 1515-1565*, Berkeley/Los Angeles, 1985, p. 133. Further data on interest rates in some provinces of the Netherlands are provided by L. Van Der Ent, W. Fritschy, E. Horlings and R. Liesker, "Public finance in the United Provinces of the Netherlands in the seventeenth and eighteenth centuries", in W.M. Ormrod, M. Bonney and R. Bonney (eds.), *Crises, revolutions and self-sustained growth. Essays in European fiscal history, 1130-1830*, Stamford, 1999, p. 267.

25 A. Molho, *Marriage alliance in late medieval Florence*, Cambridge (Mass.), 1994, pp. 31-33, 41, 43, on returns; R. Trexler, "Une table florentine d'espérance de vie", in *Annales ESC*, 26 (1971), pp. 137-139; and the remarks by J. Dupâquier, "Sur une table (prétendument) florentine d'espérance de vie", *Annales ESC*, 28 (1973), pp. 1066-1070. An excellent essay on the matter concerning life annuities is G. Alter and J.C. Riley, "How to bet on lives: a guide to life contingent contracts in Early Modern Europe", in *Research in economic history*, 10 (1986), pp. 1-53.

during the war of 1570-73[26]. To Venetians the *Depositi* turned out to be profitable investments, with a return of 7-8% during wartime, and drew large amounts of money thanks to both the growth of economy and the attractive terms offered by the *Zecca.*

After the storm of the Turkish war and a severe plague, and despite a certain opposition within the patriciate, the government started paying back the whole state debt within about twenty years. First the *Depositi in Zecca* were paid off at their face value and then the old *Monti*, which were paid at market value. It was a huge operation that strengthened both the Republic's reputation and finance. The amortization required the payment of ten million ducats; about four times the annual ordinary state income. It was, therefore, a considerable undertaking that transferred a great deal of money to the Venetian citizens that was probably invested in purchases of land and private loans on the mainland[27]. Every Venetian received on average over 66 ducats, as much as a building worker could expect to earn in one year. The liquidation of the debt was allowed both by a political decision and financial factors. Since the money of account decreased in terms of gold by 10.3% between 1572 and 1584 the operation was eased, to a certain extent, by such a devaluation with respect to gold. A relative high level of taxation, moreover, was maintained even after the end of the war – a phenomenon which economists label as displacement effect – thus making resources available for 'freeing' the debt.

The military and political involvements of the early 17th century led the Venetian government to call on investors for money: between 1609 and 1641 the annual average of capitals raised through the *Depositi in Zecca* was 244,500 ducats, with peaks during the war of Gradisca (900,000 ducats in 1616). The state finances, however, were not burdened by debt: in 1619, for example, to fulfil the investors' pressing demand the government issued a series of redeemable bonds at 5% and life annuities at 10%. These terms were rather favourable to the Republic and pointed to quite a balanced relation between credit supply and state demand. It is to be considered that in the same period in Holland, maybe the most provided area with capitals throughout the whole 17th-century Europe, redeemable government loans (*losrenten)* yielded 6.25% and life annuities (*lijfrenten*) between 11 and 14%[28]. That means that the degree of trust the Venetian government enjoyed as debtor was rather high and, moreover, the government was able to draw capitals although the interest rate was not very attractive. The return of 5%, in fact, turned out to be slightly below the interest in the private capital market. In the 1620s and 1630s the average interest rate in Venice and on the central mainland was about 6%, while on northern and eastern mainland the usual interest was 7%. It is, nonetheless, worth considering that the chances of good investments in sea trade had dropped, hence the base of investors searching for sound rents secured by the state expanded.

Besides the *Depositi in Zecca* the government exploited other means to meet war needs. Although the forced loans were replaced by voluntary loans, they did not disappear entirely. When necessary, in fact, forced loans on the Venetian taxpayers were issued in the 1630s, after the great plague, and later on during the war of Crete (1645-1669). Moreover, by the mid-17th century, guilds, social institutions and subject cities were requested to give money as forced loans. Lotteries, life annuities and similar devices were established in order to raise as much money as possible. Thus, in the second half of the 17th century the range of financial tools at the disposal of the Venetian government was much broader than two centuries earlier: while the later-Medieval Venetian finances relied almost completely on forced loans, in the Early Modern age new means of deficit financing emerged, such as the *Depositi in Zecca*, life annuities, and lotteries. These proved to be relatively cheap means in terms of the interest rates paid by the State finance.

---

26 Figures based on State Archives, Venice, *Senato Terra*, regg. 30-31; *Consiglio dei Dieci*, *Comuni*, regg. 12-13; *Consiglio dei Dieci*, *Zecca*, reg. 1; Biblioteca del Museo Correr, Venice, *Donà delle Rose*, 26.

27 Pezzolo, *L'oro*, pp. 200-207.

28 Van Der Ent, Fritschy, Horlings and Liesker, "Public finance", p. 267.

The bondholders

On the whole, Venetian inhabitants held by far the largest part of government obligations. In the later Middle Ages foreigners were allowed to invest in the Monte, in some cases for conspicuous amounts, but it is likely that the percentage of credits in the hands of non-Venetians was very small. Throughout the 16th and 17th centuries, however, the structure of bondholders witnessed some change. The number of Venetian investors undoubtedly was the majority, but both inhabitants of the subject mainland and Genoese financiers joined them to a certain extent.

Between the 1610s and the 1620s the credit supply was enlarged by the arrival of the Genoese, who at that time were moving their investments from the territories of the Spanish monarchy to Italian state debts, particularly the Venetian and Papal ones. It seems that the Genoese first appeared in the lagoon as investors in the state debt in 1617, at the time of the war of Gradisca, and from then on the Genoese financiers played a significant role until the middle of the 18th century. They preferred life annuities both for the good yield they provided and, maybe, for the difficulties the Venetian authorities faced in getting information on the exact moment of a Genoese nominee's death. In 1641 Genoese citizens held 1,000,648 ducats out of a total amount of 2,177,795 ducats of life annuities. That means that 46.3% of the funds at 10, 12, and 14% was provided by Genoese lenders[29].

The enlargement of state bondholders is worth some comment. One might argue that the institutionalisation of the foreign debt was a sign of difficulty of capital supply in the Venetian market, not being as huge as it had formerly been. Yet evidence that money was in short supply among Venetians is not convincing. The demand for investors coming from subject cities might be considered as an indicator that the Venetian ruling group was willing to involve potential lenders until then not yet contacted. In the early 17th century the Venetian patriciate was particularly concerned with attempting to weave a kind of network binding different state realities, namely the city capital and the subject urban centres. The formalisation by decree of investing in the Venetian debt might be regarded in such a sense: an attempt to create, by means of a powerful tool such as the state debt, a kind of sharing of the state destiny. As far as foreign lenders were concerned, the flow of their capitals was undoubtedly proof that the *Depositi in Zecca* enjoyed wide and often merited confidence. Such a trust had to be met; it was no chance that the Venetian government showed itself very concerned with fulfilling its financial engagements first of all with Genoese investors.

Thus, by the mid-17th century, the area of investors in the Venetian debt looked much wider than a couple of centuries earlier. The emergence of a real primary market in the middle of the 16th century implied that some legal constraints had dropped: state bonds could now be bought without licence and, furthermore, the link between taxpayers and lenders was eliminated.

Reassuring lenders

One of the most important tasks of a government is reassuring its own lenders. The Venetian debt relied on both material and immaterial features to make state bonds an attractive investment. The yield of important taxes was assigned by law to the payment of debt charges. From the late 14th century, for instance, the income of eight valuable duties was devoted to paying interest on the Monte loans. As far as the *Depositi in Zecca* were concerned, when launching a new series the government was usually careful to assign a certain income to interest charges. It is worth wondering who, in actual fact, paid state creditors. It is generally argued that the mechanism of the public debt moved resources from

29 Besta (ed.), *Bilanci generali*, pp. 550-553.

the lower social groups to the upper ones. Taxation on consumption, in fact, provided the money needed to pay creditors, and the latter belonged mostly to the urban élite. Let us take the Venetian case and attempt to verify the model.

In the later Middle Ages the bulk of the financial resources to pay interest on loans came from duties on both trade and consumption (Table II). The duties on wine and wheat provided most of the amount required, while when necessary the receipts of the salt tax could be exploited. It looks, therefore, as if a great deal of people (consumers) paid in order to secure a rent for a relatively small group. Yet, this picture is not always adequate. First of all, we have to take into account that for a long period Venice was able to download a part of the debt charges on foreign merchants, that is on foreign consumers. Duties on international trade, in fact, to a certain extent provided resources to be devoted to the Venetian bondholders. Secondly, the financial relations between Venice and her dominion on the Italian mainland became closer by the second half of the 15th century and proved fundamental over the next century: accordingly, the taxpayers of the dominions shared the burden of the Venetian debt. A part of the proceeds of the salt tax, mostly collected throughout the mainland, represented an important source to fulfil the Venetian creditors[30]. Again, the subsidy established on the mainland in 1526 was conceived as a fiscal resource assigned to the new series of the Monte *Nuovissimo*. In short, the Venetian citizens received much more money through the financial rent provided by the state debt than they paid for interest.

TABLE II. **Financial funds devoted to payment of interests on state debt**

	1490	%	1559	%
VENICE				
taxes on consumption	126,810	48	199,283	45
taxes on trade	88,200	33	100,357	23
direct taxes	27,200	10		
other	6,500	2	13,965	3
MAINLAND	16,000	6	131,515	30
	264,710	100	445,120	100

Source: F. Besta (éd.), *Bilanci generali*, I.

It is worth stressing, moreover, that the tax system helped to make the state debt sound. The state revenue witnessed a fourfold growth in real terms between the mid-14th and the mid-15th centuries, but only doubled from the early 16th century to the early 17th century (Table I). Certainly, the Venetian government had to cope with the typical troubles concerning taxation (difficulties in tax collection, dealings and bargains with the subjects, problems of assessing taxable wealth, and so forth), but its right to tax and fiscal sovereignty were never questioned. It would not be too bold to claim that the relative peaceful fiscal atmosphere in the Venetian state reassured potential lenders about the fiscal capacity of the state.

Another important element strengthening the credibility of the Venetian state as debtor was the fact that many important bondholders most probably belonged to the patriciate, that is the ruling class. Thus, it was supposed that the rulers would avoid any means that would endanger creditors' interests. Moreover, the Republic was regarded as an immortal body, and so commitment toward creditors did not end with the death of the doge.

30 Hocquet, "Guerre et finance", pp. 109-131.

An efficient management of debt can be considered as a further feature of good credibility. In actual fact, interest payment was stopped during severe political and financial crises; the yield of the Monte *Vecchio* securities gradually declined (Figure II); and the return of the *Depositi in Zecca* was also sometimes reduced in order to alleviate the burden of debt charge on the state budget. Nevertheless, it is remarkable that as late as 1538 the Loans Office was paying interest on Monte *Vecchio* claims going back more than fifty years, meaning that, at least in principle, the government showed itself a reliable debtor in meeting its commitments toward creditors.

The reputation of the Venetian debt improved greatly in the later 16th century, when it undertook a significant reimbursement of the state debt. At first the *Depositi in Zecca*, the most onerous securities, were purchased from private holders at face value, and later on the *Monti* bonds were liquidated considering the market prices over the previous decades. So, the early 17th-century Venetian republic represented an almost unique case in Europe of a state without debt[31]. Since state securities accounted for a considerable part of citizens' assets, it is surprising that a ruling group decided to get rid of an important financial resource for the city. By the late 16th century the Genoese government, for example, attempted to reduce the size of debt consistently, but opposition within the patriciate prevented it from completing the task[32]. One can argue, therefore, that public interest prevailed in Venice over private interest: despite some complaints, the ruling group managed to reduce the debt drastically and to save half a million ducats every year. Such an accumulation of money enabled Venice to finance the war against the Austrian archduke in 1615-17 without resorting to costly indebtedness. The restless need for money, however, prevented the republic from undertaking an analogous operation during its following history.

The needs for debt

War, of course, was the first and foremost reason why loans had to be raised. Indebtedness has usually been considered as an evil to be avoided at all costs, a sort of cancer destroying the souls of citizens and the economy of the country. War and the related indebtedness, at any rate, cannot be avoided by any state, particularly in the ancien régime. The issue to deal with, however, is whether the huge amounts of money raised through debt (Table III) improved the economy of the country or not. In short: was that money well used? It is certainly not easy to find a satisfactory answer: we would need a huge set of data that is not yet available, and that may not be at our disposal even in the future. At any rate, I will try to put forward some hypotheses.

It is worth noting that, until the middle of the 15th century, the wars undertaken by Venice showed an aggressive character. The navy, above all, and the army proved to be powerful tools with which to build up both an economic space and a political dominion, which made the lagoon city one of the prominent powers in the Mediterranean Sea. The hegemony achieved by Venice brought about control over commercial routes and exploitation of a wide market with Venice as the fundamental pillar. An inflow of resources, therefore, enriched the city and her inhabitants. By controlling routes, information, and markets, the Venetians succeeded in lowering transaction costs and that made commercial investments more profitable to Venetian merchants. Forced loans called on from taxpayers could therefore be regarded as a social investment to increase the wealth of the city.

---

31 The Swiss city of Lucerne had no debt charge since the early 16th century, and that of Freiburg was very small: M. Körner, *Solidarités financièrs suisses au XVIe siècle*, Lausanne, 1980, pp. 271, 330.

32 H. Sieveking, *Studio sulle finanze genovesi nel Medioevo*, Genoa, 1907, p. 225 ("Atti della Società ligure di storia patria", 35); R. Savelli, "Tra Machiavelli e S. Giorgio. Cultura giuspolitica e dibattito istituzionale a Genova nel Cinque-Seicento", in A. De Maddalena and H. Kellenbenz (eds.), *Finanze e ragion di Stato in Italia e in Germania nella prima Età moderna*, Bologna, 1984, pp. 315-316. See for Florence, G. Brucker, *Dal Comune alla Signoria. La vita pubblica a Firenze nel primo Rinascimento*, Bologna, 1981, p. 467.

TABLE III. **Amount of funded debt of some Italian states**
(nominal value in kg of silver)

	Venice	Florence	Genoa	index (1400=100) Venice	Florence	Genoa
c1350	14,300	19,500		10	19	
c1400	146,700	102,300	108,000	100	100	100
c1425	234,300				146	
c1500	362,000	145,000*	191,600	247	142*	177
c1550	325,000		349,500	222		324
c1600	0		355,300	0		329
c1640	169,500	380,800	555,900	116	372	515

* Estimated figure.

Source: L. Pezzolo, *Il punto di Archimede* (forthcoming).

By the middle of the 15th century, however, Venice was forced to defend her territories from the Turkish threat and, later, also from enemies within Italy. At the same time, the system of forced loans turned out to be inadequate to provide the necessary money to cope with warfare. The shrinking of the territorial and economic area under Venetian control brought about difficulties in international trade and the emergence of tough competitors. In this context, the resources made available by the public debt proved to be crucial for defensive wars; the debt system was enlarged on the one hand by involving subject and foreign investors and, on the other hand, by collecting much more money through taxation on the mainland in order to pay interest.

Rents distributed by the government debt took on a particular meaning over the 17th century: the share of securities belonging to social and charitable institutions grew, and through them a redistribution of money occurred in favour of the poor classes in Venice. During the difficulties of the Venetian economy, the state debt, therefore, helped to keep social order and probably preserved the purchasing power of many Venetians. Moreover, the conspicuous consumption of the élite was made possible to a certain extent also by the financial rent; accordingly, such a kind of consumption supported the urban economy. Since a good deal of the required financial resources came from the mainland, we can argue that fiscal flows from the dominion enabled Venice to maintain her standard of living despite the economic decline.

Venice and Florence: two different solutions

By the mid-14th century, Florence and Venice were great powers which relied on an impressive financial capacity in comparison with other early Renaissance states. Until the middle of the 15th century, the systems of borrowing were quite similar: both cities raised money by means of forced loans on their citizens' assessed wealth[33]. Some evidence shows, however, that sometimes the Florentine government borrowed at higher cost than did the Venetian republic. By 1358, for example, Florentine bondholders were given a return of 10-15%[34], while in Venice at the same time government

33 The standard works are A. Molho, *Florentine public finances in the early Renaissance, 1400-1433*, Cambridge (Mass.), 1971; and E. Conti, *L'imposta diretta a Firenze nel Quattrocento (1427-1494)*, Rome, 1984. See also A. Molho, "L'amministrazione del debito pubblico a Firenze nel quindicesimo secolo", in *I ceti dirigenti nella Toscana del Quattrocento*, Florence, 1987, pp. 191-207.

34 M. Becker, "La trasformazione della finanza e l'emergere dello stato territoriale a Firenze nel Trecento", in G. Chittolini (ed.), *La crisi degli ordinamenti comunali e le origini dello stato del Rinascimento*, Bologna, 1979, pp. 174, 176.

credits were providing 5%. After the early 15th century, nevertheless, some marked differences emerged. The Florentine Medici régime resorted mostly to government intermediaries (officers of the Monte) to collect short-term loans among prominent citizens[35]. Officers borrowed from investors usually at 8-9% and received a return of 12-14% from the government. Thus, lending to the government turned out to be a profitable business for a rather narrow group of friends and relatives of the rulers. In the 1480s, the government was paying up to 16% interest on loans: a rather high return for lenders, considering that a passive investment in a firm could yield about 8-10%. Under the Medici régime, therefore, borrowing became a powerful device to construct and consolidate the patronage system. Later on, during the rule of Cosimo I in the mid-16th century, the Florentine duke preferred to rely on foreign bankers' expensive services than to call for the money of his subjects[36], maybe not to bind himself too closely to local lenders. It has to be pointed out, at any rate, that forced loans raised from well-being Florentines provided an appreciable return of 8-10%[37]. The two different ways of borrowing, thus, mirror the different institutional structures of late-Renaissance Venice and Florence. The former continued – and even implemented – the system of borrowing from a great deal of potential lenders on the open market; the latter, after the rise of the Medici, saw the emergence of the typical system of borrowing associated to a personal rule: short-term loans provided at high cost by a relative narrow circle of financiers and wealthy people close to the prince. This system did not deal with an open market of credit, but rather relied on personal relations between borrower and lenders; and the chance the latter had to be paid back might depend on the duke's benevolence. In Venice, on the other hand, an impersonal market emerged over the 16th century and allowed the government to exploit resources at a relatively low cost. The institutional structure of the two states should explain the divergence their debt systems underwent between the later Middle Ages and the Early Modern age. In the early 16th century the republican structure of Venice allowed the establishment of crucial financial innovations, which allowed both government to enlarge its indebtedness at moderate costs and also led to the emergence of a true 'public' debt connected to a primary market of state securities.

35 L.F. Marks, "The financial oligarchy in Florence under Lorenzo", in E.F. Jacob (ed.), *Italian Renaissance Studies*, London, 1960; A. Molho, "Lo Stato e la finanza pubblica. Un'ipotesi basata sulla storia tardomedievale di Firenze", in G. Chittolini, A. Molho and P. Schiera (eds.) *Origini dello Stato. Processi di formazione statale in Italia fra medioevo ed età moderna*, Bologna, 1994; S. Tognetti, *Il banco Cambini. Affari e mercati di una compagnia mercantile-bancaria nella Firenze del XV secolo*, Florence, 1999, pp. 259-264; R. Goldthwaite, "Lorenzo Morelli, Ufficiale del Monte, 1484-88: interessi privati e cariche pubbliche nella Firenze laurenziana", in *Archivio Storico Italiano*, 154 (1996), pp. 613, 630.

36 A. Teicher, "Politics and finance in the age of Cosimo I: the public and private face of credit", in *Firenze e la Toscana dei Medici nell'Europa del '500*, I, *Strumenti e veicoli della cultura. Relazioni politiche ed economiche*, Florence, 1983, pp. 217-227; G. Parigino, *Il tesoro del principe. Funzione pubblica e privata del patrimonio della famiglia Medici nel Cinquecento*, Florence, 1999, p. 56 ff.

37 G. Spini, *Cosimo I e l'indipendenza del principato mediceo*, Florence, 1980^2, pp. 67, 97.

THREE CENTURIES OF URBAN AND PROVINCIAL PUBLIC DEBT: AMSTERDAM AND HOLLAND

Wantje Fritschy
Free University Amsterdam

Introduction

The ability of cities to sustain a public debt was a major factor in the process of 'state-formation' in many European states. Where cities were abundant a 'capital-intensive' road to state-formation was a possibility as an attractive alternative for a 'coercion-intensive' road[1]. Cities meant the availability of a concentration of people whose wealth consisted in money rather than in land. This implied a demand for investment opportunities with a steady and safe return requiring as few additional chores as possible to secure old age and the livelihood of widows and children. Moreover cities with their highly monetised economies implied abundant possibilities for indirect taxation to service interest payments on public debt. This combination of facts made it relatively easy, not only to finance the building of city-walls or the improvement of urban infrastructure by way of loans, but also for princes to persuade city-governments to lend them the sums necessary for wars, guaranteeing their safety and that of their trade.

Tracy has described a 'financial revolution' in the highly urbanised Habsburg Netherlands that resulted from successful attempts of the Habsburg rulers in persuading the main cities in the county of Holland to strengthen their credit by selling annuities (*'renten'*) no longer on their individual, but on their *common* credit[2]. Since the 1540s the six cities with voting rights in the States of Holland all took part in the issues of these *common renten*, even Amsterdam which had stayed apart until then. Moreover since the 1540s the *'renten'* to be sold on this common credit were hypothecated on *common* excises as well. The States of Holland had agreed to these *'renten'*-sales. Their condition had been that the receipt of the new common taxes, as well as the payment of the interest to the holders of the new debt, would become the responsibility of the *provincial* tax receiver and no longer that of the emperor's receiver[3].

Tracy's main focus was on the consequences for the relation between *central* and provincial government of this 'financial revolution'. He pointed out that as a result not only Holland's credit was strengthened. Besides this the receipts of the emperor's receiver in Holland had dwindled to next to nothing in comparison to those of the provincial receiver. Formerly the receipts of the provincial

ARA = Algemeen Rijks Archief (General State's Archives)
FH = Financie van Holland (Finance Office of Holland)
GAA = Gemeente Archief Amsterdam (Municipal Archives Amsterdam)

1 Ch. Tilly, *Coercion, capital and European states, AD 900-1990*, Oxford, 1990.
2 J. Tracy, *A financial revolution in the Habsburg Netherlands,* Renten *and* renteniers *in the county of Holland, 1515-1565*, Berkeley, 1985; in 1514 about half the population in Holland lived in cities; see J. de Vries, *The Dutch rural economy in the Golden Age, 1500-1700,* New Haven/London, 1974, p. 81.
3 Tracy, *A financial revolution,* pp. 87-88.

receiver had been negligible in comparison to those of the emperor's receiver. It can be said that the failure of the centralising ambitions of the Habsburg state in the northern Netherlands found an acute expression in this reversal. It can be said to have been a decisive step in the victory of provincial 'particularism'.

This paper's main focus will be on the other end of the same process: the provincial and the *urban* government level, and more specifically Amsterdam's debt and Holland's debt. In accounts of political characteristics of the Dutch Republic 'local particularism' is often as much emphasised as a paralysing element harming the efficiency of the Dutch Republic as provincial particularism harming the efficiency of the central Habsburg state[4]. Provincial government had thwarted the centralising ambitions of the central state by the condition that its own receiver should encash the excises necessary for the payments on the interest of the provincial debt. It seems reasonable to expect that the cities were inclined to foster the same ambitions to counteract centralising tendencies on the provincial level[5].

The aim of this paper is twofold. It firstly draws attention to the simple fact how small Amsterdam's public debt was in debt-ridden Holland during the *18th* century, whereas Holland's debt had been still very small in the *16th* century compared to Amsterdam. Secondly, urban control over the taxation system that allowed the sustenance of the public debt will be examined. Tracy described how the emperor's receiver became less significant as the amounts of revenue and expenditure in the coffers of the provincial receiver grew. Did the same apply to urban tax receivers in comparison to provincial receivers? What tax streams flowed through which coffers?

Observations on the relative magnitude of Holland's and Amsterdam's debt, and of the tax streams controlled on the provincial and the urban level, are of importance for our understanding of the Dutch process of state formation. This paper will argue that developments in public finance question the emphasis on local particularism in characterisations of the Dutch Republic in the 17th century. As to public finance local autonomy seems to have been much more important in state formation *before* the Revolt than *after* it.

1. Amsterdam's and Holland's debt

In this first section some figures on Amsterdam's and Holland's debt and interest burden between 1500 and 1800 will be presented and discussed (see Table I). I will start with the last period, then turn to the 16th century and end with a discussion of the scarce data on the 17th century.

4 P. Blaas, "Stedelijke naijver. Een inleidende verkenning", in P.B.M. Blaas and J. van Herwaarden (eds.), *Stedelijke naijver. De betekenis van interstedelijke conflicten in de geschiedenis. Enige beschouwingen en case studies,* The Hague, 1986, pp. 11-27.

5 The theme is also mentioned by F. Piola Caselli, "Public debt, state revenues and town consumption in Rome (16.-18. centuries)", see chapter 7; for an in-depth analysis of the relation between urban public finance and state formation at the end of the Middle Ages see M. Boone, *Geld en macht de Gentse stadsfinanciën en de Bourgondische staatsvorming (1384-1453),* Ghent, 1990 (Verhandelingen der Maatschappij voor Geschiedenis en Oudheidkunde te Gent 15).

TABLE I. **Interest burden of Amsterdam and of Holland, 1514-1794**
(rough amounts in guilders [=Dutch pounds])

	Amsterdam	*Holland*
1514	25,000	
1540s	50,000	50,000
1560s	60,000	60,000-120,000
1600	90,000	400,000
1609	90,000 à 100,000	1,400,000
1648	33,000?	6,900,000
1680	450,000	7,000,000
1700	320,000	8,000,000
1750	300,000	14,500,000
1790	185,000	16,400,000
1794	390,000	17,000,000

Sources: GAA, arch.nr. 5014 City Accounts, inv.nrs. 76, 126-132; Ordinary Treasurers arch.nr. 5039, inv.nr. 294; Extraordinary Treasurers, arch.no. 5044, inv.nr. 102; M. 't Hart and M. van der Burg, 'Renteniers and the recovery of Amsterdam's Credit (1578-1605)', p. @ elsewhere in this book; J. Tracy, *A financial revolution,* passim; database Holland under construction by W. Fritschy and R. Liesker (to be published in 2003). I owe thank to M. 't Hart for her willingness to discuss parts of this table with me and for providing information.

1.1 The eighteenth century

It is well known that Holland's provincial debt burden was extreme during the 18th century. At the end of the century it was three times as large as the sum of the debts of the other provinces and twenty five times as large as the debt of the 'Generality', the central government level of the Dutch state. Holland's debt rose with some fluctuations from already about 200 million guilders in 1700 to about 400 million guilders in the first half of the 1790s, due to its participation in international warfaring. At the end of the 18th century it was about equal to total national income per year at the time[6].

The interest burden was about 8 million in 1700 being about 40% of provincial tax revenue. Elsewhere in this book one will notice that also in for instance the papal state the interest burden around 1700 was as much as about 50% of public expenditure. The interest payment per year per head, however, was here only about 0.7 roman *scudi*, and this was less than 2% of the year income of about 50 *scudi* of an urban wage labourer. In Holland interest payment per head per year was about 10 guilders around 1700, which was nearly 4% of the year income of about 260 guilders of an urban wage labourer in Amsterdam. At the end of the 18th century this had risen in Holland to about 8%. Moreover in the papal state the interest burden had remained about the same during the 18th century and population had increased, which means that here the relative burden had even decreased[7]. In Holland it had risen to about 17 million in the last years before the end of the Republic and then required no less than 74% of revenue[8].

One would expect that the easy way in which Holland was able to raise huge sums on the capital market to finance war expenditure would find its reflection in urban public finance. If Holland's credit was strong because of the fact that the cities in the States of Holland could supervise the priority

6 J.P. Smits, E. Horlings and J.L.van Zanden, *Dutch GNP and its components, 1800-1913,* Groningen, 2000, p. 172, estimates GNP in 1807, when prices were relatively high, at 495 million guilders.
7 Piola Caselli, "Public debt", see chapter 7, tables I and II.
8 Even after deduction of the receipt of a tax on bonds which reduced the nominal interest on Dutch obligations of 4% to 2.5%, the remaining burden was still 67% of the remaining revenue.

of interest payments, one would expect urban credit to have been even stronger, decidedly so in the wealthy city of Amsterdam. Besides this it seemed reasonable to assume that this credit would have been exploited whenever possible. Are not the rich in the Dutch Republic often blamed for having loathed tax paying, preferring loans, the interest payments on which had to be financed by excises burdening the common man? Is it not reasonable therefore to expect the cities to have been overburdened with debt as well? [9]

This, however, seems not to have been the case, at least not in Amsterdam. A figure of about 13.5 million guilders is mentioned for Amsterdam's debt at the end of the old Republic[10]. This figure is to be found in a – rare – study on Amsterdam's public finance at the period of the old Dutch Republic by H.J. Koenen dating from 1855[11]. Koenen's source was a report dated 21. February 1795 of the 'Financial Committee of the Provisional Representatives of the People of Amsterdam', erected after the Batavian Revolution. As the revolutionaries of this period were especially keen on pointing out the irresponsibility of the financial behaviour of the old government, there is little chance that this figure was too low.

Consultation of the original report learned that it contained in fact many items, which should be yet deducted to get the 'normal' amount of long-term debt[12]. Table II shows the composition of Amsterdam's debt in 1795. It was divided into five 'classes'. Only about 8.3 million (items 3 and 4) turn out to have consisted in long term debt. Nearly 6 million of this amount was the result of a very recent loan in 1791.

9 This is suggested for instance in the still much used study of F.N. Sickenga, *Bijdrage tot de geschiedenis der belastingen in Nederland,* Leiden, 1864, p. 455.
10 Sickenga, *Bijdrage*, p. 455.
11 H.J. Koenen, *Voorlezingen over de geschiedenis der finantiën van Amsterdam*, Amsterdam, 1855, p. 53.
12 The report was printed; a copy is preserved in ARA, Gogel, inv.nr. 168.

TABLE II. **Amsterdam's Public debt – February 1795**

1)	to be paid immediately			
	- provisional certificates bearing 3.5 or 4% interest		968,730	
	- one year interest not yet paid (long and short term debt)		388,148	
	- unpaid bills		77,985	
				1,434,863
	arrears in subsidies to almshouses and churches			724,800
2)	more or less urgent debts			
	- provisional receipts of monthly credit paper, which may be cancelled by the holders		3,699,447	
	- remaining part of a loan of 2 million in 1787		224,000	
				3,923,447
3)	old debts (not pressing) to almshouses and churches			1,994,790
4)	debts which cannot be redeemed			
	- 3%-obligations	99,124		
	- 3%-annuities (*'renten'*)	225,255		
	- old 3%-*'renten'*	81,693		
			406,072	
	- 6 million loan of 1791 at 3.5%		5,875,000	
				6,281,072

				14,358,972
5)	debts to be balanced with credits			
	- due to Holland for the extraordinary *'verponding'* or 1.5% on the value of houses (100. and 200. penningen) consented for 1792 and 1793		1,370,201	
	- idem for a consent of 1794		300,000	
				1,670,201

	TOTAL			16,029,173
	- item 5) was balanced against Holland's debt to Amsterdam on old obligations		2,459,824	
	- p. 74 of the report mentioned a debt of the E.I.C. to Amsterdam		95,463	
	Koenen's figure results when the last two items are deducted from the total in the report			13,473,886

Source: ARA, Gogel, inv.nr. 168

It should be noted that the report of 1795 states explicitly that the financial plight of the city at that moment was mainly due to significant rises in subsidies to almshouses and churches since about 1780. They had risen from an average of about 170,000 guilders per year – about 12% of ordinary revenue – between 1774 and 1781, to on average about 350,000 guilders per year – about 20% of ordinary revenue – between 1786 and 1793. In the report the remark was added that for the next years the charity institutions had estimated their needs even at nearly 450,000 guilders per year. The report also offers an overview of extraordinary public expenditure from 1774 to 1793 amounting to nearly 11 million guilders in total, out of which 5.2 million in total had been spent on subsidies to almshouses and churches during these years.

The remarkable fact is, however, that it had been possible to finance no less than nearly 6.7 million of this 11 million so called *extraordinary* expenditure out of *ordinary* revenue. So *despite* the rise in subsidies for the poor, still 1.5 million was left for other extraordinary expenditure during this period without having to take resort to loan financing. The 'other' extraordinary expenditure items mentioned were:

(1) the building of the new Workhouse	1,216,610
(2) the new Theatre	280,469
(3) the paving of the Amsteldijk	115,323
(4) cisterns	85,000
(5) the deepening of the IJ (total 1778-1793)	1,598,229
(6) several items related to the invasion of Prussian troops in 1787 not paid by Holland	1,124,583
(7) a subsidy to the Suriname Company (*Sociëteit van Suriname*) necessary due to the Fourth English Naval War	1,098,988
(8) barracks, fortifications, maintenance of troops	291,443
	5,810,645

With the exception of perhaps (3), (5) and (8) these seem to have been items for which loans would have been quite normal in modern public finance, because of either their investment character or their relation to actual warfaring.

I have given these figures in some detail because they show not only the situation in 1795 and its characteristics, but also important changes in local public finance in the biggest and most important of the cities of the Dutch Republic during the last decades of the 18th century. Only since the 1780s deficits had gradually led to payment arrears, and only since then a huge interest bearing short term debt had come into existence and long-term loans had re-emerged. Before that time surpluses instead of deficits must have been quite common.

The details of the report of 1795 show that still about 1790 Amsterdam's interest burden can not have been much higher than about 185,000 guilders, as the nearly 390,000 guilders for interest payments in 1795 included about 205,000 guilders on the big loan of 1791[13]. An overview for the years 1700 and 1701 of all the revenue and expenditure items of the city of Amsterdam showed that the total interest burden on old and new obligations, redeemable and life-annuities[14] at that time was about

13 As Amsterdam's population was about 220,000 at that time, this was about 1.2 guilder per head, which is less than 0.5% of the yearly income of a wage labourer: much less not only than in Holland, but also than in the papal state at that time.

14 In this article the Dutch word '*losrenten*' is translated by 'redeemable annuities'. Like '*lijfrenten*' (life-annuities) '*losrenten*' were long term debt paper. The difference with life-annuities was (1) that a '*losrente*' could be redeemed at will by the government and (2) that a '*losrente*' could be transferred by the holder, as well by sale, as to a heir. The name on the document had to be changed officially on such an occasion and a transfer-tax had to be paid to ensure legal property rights. A life-annuity was sold on the life

320,000 guilders[15]. The two contemporary overviews together, one from the end and the other from the beginning of the 18th century, suggest therefore that since about 1700 until 1791 long term loans cannot have occurred very often any more. Redemption of debts seems to have prevailed.

This conclusion was confirmed by closer research in the Amsterdam city accounts[16]. Graph I shows that during the years of the War of Spanish Succession (1702-1713) and the War of Austrian Succession (1740-1748), periods when Holland's debt increased hugely, Amsterdam's interest burden hardly rose, and after 1730 even continuously decreased. City accounts should be used carefully as one can never be sure what they contained and what was left out[17]. However the interest amounts in the accounts match those in the two contemporary reports. The conclusion seems justified, therefore, that an amount of 1,378,009 guilders sold in life annuities in 1723 was probably the only important exception to the rule that Amsterdam hardly practised long term debt financing any more during the 18th century until 1791[18].

GRAPH. I. **Interest Paytments and Revenue 'Big Exicse' in Amsterdam, 1700-1792**
(guilders)

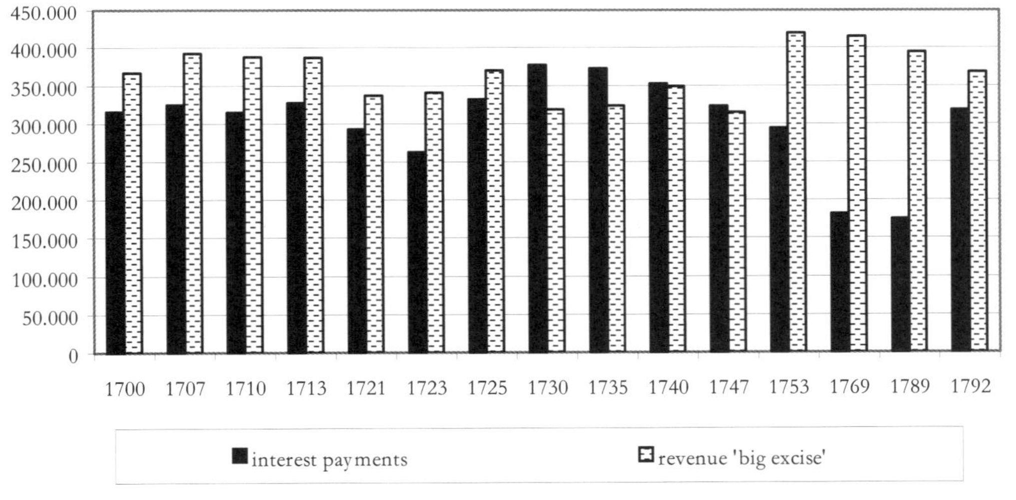

Source: GAA 5014, City Accounts.

of a specified person and could therefore not be transferred to someone else. Government on the one hand could not redeem a '*lijfrente*' against the will of the holder during his or her lifetime, but on the other hand the debt as well as the ensuing interest payments disappeared automatically on the death of the holder. '*Obligaties*' (obligations) were originally short term debt paper which was often prolonged endlessly in fact, however, as the holders were often more interested in interest payments than in redemption. Transfer of obligations did not require the payment of the transfer tax.

15 GAA, Thesaurieren ordinaris, inv.nr. 115 "Stadts Inkomen en Lasten volgens de Staetlijsten van de onderstaande Jaren" (1700, 1701 and 1664-1678).

16 GAA 5014 "Stadsrekeningen"; they have not been preserved completely, esp. after 1753 many accounts are missing.

17 M. v.d. Heijden, "Stadsrekeningen, stedelijke financiën en historisch onderzoek", in *NEHA-Bulletin voor de economische geschiedenis* 14, 2 (1999), p. 134.

18 I did not research the reasons for this huge sale in 1723.

1.2 The sixteenth century

'In former times, and even at the time of Charles V and Philip II, Holland was not significantly burdened by debts'. This observation is to be found in a manuscript overview of Dutch public finance in the period from 1544 to 1755 probably written by the 18th century state-pensionary of Holland P. Steyn, known as a financial specialist[19]. In July 1544 Holland paid a yearly sum of interest on hereditary and life annuities of only 47,000 guilders, which decreased to less than 30,000 guilders in 1553, while between 1552 and 1561 110,000 guilders again was added to the sum of interest payments, according to Steyn. From then on any further debt creation was felt to be impossible and in 1562 the provincial interest burden was reported to have been reduced again to 60,000[20].

Holland's interest burden had risen from about 70,000 guilders at the start of the Revolt to about 245,000 guilders at most in 1586[21], probably mainly as the result of forced loans, and only partly of (short-term) voluntary loans, both on so called 'obligations'[22]. In 1588 the province took over 1.5 million in urban annuities as provincial debt, by which the interest burden must have grown to about 345,000 guilders in that year. In July 1594 the decision was taken that annuities would again be sold on the credit of the province, as had been the case in the 1540s and 1550s. However, while Amsterdam's credit had already been recovered by the beginning of the 1580s[23], the States had to conclude as late as September 1598 that it was still very difficult to raise by way of 8.3%-annuities the 200,000 guilders they needed.

The source for Amsterdam's debt in 1514 is the so-called '*Informacie*', an enquiry into the state of the cities and villages of Holland and Friesland, mainly by way of an enquiry into their public finance. This '*Informacie*' had been called for by the ruler in order to revise the partition of the contributions required from these provinces to enable warfaring. It showed that Amsterdam had sold '*renten*' before 1514 partly to redeem older debts, partly to enable it to pay its part in extraordinary '*beden*', i.e. requests for money for warfaring[24]. The 24,777 Dutch pounds to be paid in interest on annuities in 1514 at that time was more than 70% of ordinary public revenue. This shows the importance of loan financing in Amsterdam's public finance in the beginning of the 16th century. During the 18th century the interest burden was at most about 30% of total revenue. In the first decades of the 16th century the role of Amsterdam's debt was comparable to that of Holland at the end

---

19 ARA, FH 797, "Memorie van het Finantiewezen van Holland" (1755).

20 ARA, FH 797, Memorie 1755, f3v; for a complete overview see J. Tracy,"The taxation system of the county of Holland during the reigns of Charles V and Philips II, 1519-1566", in *Economisch en Sociaal Historisch Jaarboek*, 48 (1985). Tracy's figures for Holland's interest payments on *renten* are somewhat different from those offered by Steyn. The difference will be due to the fact that Steyn's figures stemmed from research in the resolutions of the States of Holland and were most probably the amounts Holland *had to* pay, while Tracy collected his figures from the accounts, which means that these were probably amounts really paid.

21 J.W. Koopmans, *De Staten van Holland en de Opstand. De ontwikkeling van hun functies en organisatie in de periode 1544 tot 1588*, The Hague, 1990, Appendix, has an amount of 120,000 pounds; if one includes the interest on short term obligations issued in the same year, the burden was already about 245,000 guilders.

22 'Obligations' were originally the debt paper issued for short-term loans at sometimes very high rates of interest. In practice it could be prolonged, however, even at lower interest rates. The debt paper issued after the Revolt in case of 'forced loans' was also called an 'obligation'. Although Holland had the intention either to redeem the obligations or to consolidate them in the form of annuities (*losrenten*), holders often preferred obligations as they could be made out to bearer and could be transferred taxfree. For annuities (*renten*) ascription was compulsory and a transfer tax had to be paid when they were transferred to another holder. This was not applicable to obligations. In this way gradually the bulk of the Dutch debt came to consist in obligations and in the 18th century they were the normal form of long term debt.

23 M.'t Hart and M. van der Burg, "Renteniers and the recovery of Amsterdams credit (1578-1605)", see chapter 13.

24 R. Fruin (ed.), *Informacie up den staet, faculteyt ande gelegenthey van de steden ende dorpen van Hollant ende Vrieslant om daernae te reguleren de nyeuwe schiltaele gedaen in den jaere MDXIV*, Leiden, 1866, p. 172.

of the 18th century, when Holland's interest burden also amounted to more than 70% of provincial public revenue[25].

Much the same held probably still true for Amsterdam in the next decades of the 16th century. Tracy offers figures on interest payments by Amsterdam for the years 1531-1540, which fluctuated between 60% and 74% of income, with a magnitude fluctuating between 46,000 and 65,000 Dutch pounds[26]. 'T Hart and Van der Burg document Amsterdam's interest burden on long term debts in the 1570s at about 30,000 Dutch pounds (later = guilders) per year. Between 1590 and 1606 they found about 50,000 guilders funded on the revenue of the 'big excises' and about 37,000 on average per year on the revenue of the '50. penny'-tax, in total about 87,000 guilders[27].

Amsterdam's debt was therefore, relatively, much more important in the 16th than in the 18th century. The deficits before 1514 had moreover not been caused by local problems like the growing poverty at the end of the 18th century. '*Los*-' and '*lijfrenten*' (redeemable and life-annuities)[28] had then been sold by the city partly to redeem older debts, but partly also to enable it to pay its part in extraordinary '*beden*', i.e. requests for money by the king for his warfaring[29].

The conclusion to this section must be that in as far as the public debt had been important for stateformation before 1600 it had still been based on *urban* credit. After about 1600, however, *provincial* credit became obviously strong enough to sustain a rising public debt to finance warfaring[30].

1.3 The seventeenth century

Table I shows that Amsterdam's interest burden increased considerably especially during the second half of the 17th century past its level of about 90,000 guilders in 1600. The average amount of the interest burden for the years 1664-1678 was about 452,000 guilders, requiring then about 40% of average local revenue. The figure was mentioned in the results of an investigation into the finances of the city ordered for by the '*vroedschap*' (= city council) in 1678, and found in an overview for the years 1700 and 1701, which compared those years with the period 1664-1678[31].

Koenen mentions the amount of about 455,000 guilders for 1680. It is the amount before an interest reduction from 4% to 3.5% realised in that year[32]. Of this amount about 168,000 guilders was on life-annuities, 177,000 in redeemable annuities, 110,000 in interest on obligations. This means that the debt in obligations and renten must have been about seven million guilders as the interest rate on them was 4%. If the average rate on life-annuities during this period is set at about 8%, then the value of this part of the debt was about two million, which would amount to a total urban debt in 1680 of about nine million in a city of about 200.000 inhabitants. Part of this debt still outstanding in 1680 may have been caused by loans in the war years after the disastrous year 1672 when the Republic was attacked from four sides. Many of these loans were probably – short term – loans for Holland[33]. Urban expenditure in the decades before 1672 and after 1678 had been on average about 2 million per year. From 1672-1678 it rose to on average 4.4 million per year. Financial facilities available for the province from Amsterdam's city government do not seem therefore to have been unimportant for the

25 As Amsterdam may have had about 12,000 inhabitants in 1514, according to the '*Informacie*', interest payment per head was about 2 guilders. The year wage of an urban labourer was about 50 guilders, which means that the interest payment per head per year in 1514 was about 4% thereof, very comparable therefore with provincial interest payment in Holland around 1700.

26 Tracy, *A Financial Revolution,* p. 16.

27 't Hart and van der Burg, "Renteniers, see chapter 13.

28 See footnote 14.

29 Fruin (ed.), *Informacie up den staet*, p. 172.

30 This point will be elaborated in my "A 'financial revolution' reconsidered; public finance in Holland during the Dutch Revolt, 1568-1648", *Economic History Review* (forthcoming).

31 GAA, Thesaurieren ordinaris, inv.nr. 115, "Stadts Inkomen en Lasten volgens de Staetlijsten".

32 Koenen, *Voorlezingen,* p. 128.

33 Koenen, *Voorlezingen,* p. 123.

preservation of the state in these years. The report of 1795 (Table II item 5) showed that even at that time Holland had a debt to Amsterdam. However, compared to Holland's total debt (see Table I) the relief offered by Amsterdam was obviously really very small.

It is well known that great parts of the 17th were periods of huge building activity in Amsterdam: the enlargement of the city since 1613, the building of the Bourse in 1611, the repair of the New Church in 1644 and the building of the Women's Penitentiary in 1643 can be mentioned. For the years since 1648 until 1672 Koenen mentions as the most important expenditure-items:

- nearly 8 million guilders for the building of the new town hall since 1648,
- about 21 million guilders for the enlargement and fortification of the city in 1660[34].

The sum of these figures is noticeably higher than the figure of about nine million in outstanding long term debt in 1680. This implies that – like in the 18th century – much of Amsterdam's extraordinary expenditure in those years either had not to be financed by investment in a funded city debt or at least could be redeemed very soon.

Nevertheless the interest and debt burden were clearly felt by the city government as being too high. A policy of debt reduction was inaugurated after the financial report of 1678 and this resulted in a decrease of the interest burden from about 420,000 guilders in 1680 – which is the figure *after* the interest reduction mentioned above – to about 320,000 guilders by 1700.

Also in the 17th century, therefore, *urban* public debt was definitely no longer an important factor in state formation. How small Amsterdam's debt had become relatively, is again obvious from the comparison with Holland (Table I). Since the start of the 17th century Holland's interest burden rose continuously from about 0.4 million guilders in 1599 to 1.4 million in 1609, to 6.9 million in 1650 and to 8 million in 1700. Amsterdam's interest burden rose, as we saw, from about 90,000 in 1600 to a top of only about 455,000 guilders in 1680 and decreased to about 320,000 guilders in 1700.

2. Interest burden and taxation

As Amsterdam's long term debts turned out to have been much smaller in the 17th and 18th centuries than one would have perhaps expected, taxation to pay for the urban interest burden did neither have to be very extensive. The revenue of the so-called 'big excises' which had always been the fund for Amsterdam's debt raising exceeded the interest burden sometimes quite a lot in the first quarter of the 18th century (see Graph I).

Although this was temporarily not the case in the years after the big life-annuity-loan in 1723 mentioned above, the same situation came to prevail again between 1750 and 1790. Holland's interest burden, however, required ever increasing sums in taxation of a enormously higher magnitude. How was this taxation organised, what was collected by provincial receivers, what by urban receivers? What were the possibilities for the pursuit of particular local interests in Holland's financial system?

2.1 The earliest stage of the Revolt

In July 1572 the first 'free' assembly – i.e. not convened by the king of Spain – of the States of Holland had been held, which had recognised the Prince of Orange as its leader in the growing revolt against Spain. From that time on the province needed huge amounts of money to finance the Prince's army. At the same time it proved to be no longer possible to sell provincial annuities, a situation which would last for more than thirty years. To finance the war the States could at the start do no more than decide what amounts they were ready to make available for the Prince and partition these over the cities which had sided with the Revolt. Therefore, temporarily at least the provincial government was

34 Koenen, *Voorlezingen,* pp. 24; 27.

completely dependent on the financial autonomy of the cities. The Prince of Orange had even suggested leaving all the details of tax policy to the discretion of the cities. Under the Habsburg king the autonomy of the cities regarding excise taxation had been a bone of contention. Since Charles V the Habsburg princes had insisted increasingly on their prerogatives in this regard. The Prince of Orange hoped that the cities might be the more willing to do their utmost to find the money for the war 'by giving them a right, which they did not have before'[35].

In the States of Holland however the cities decided in 1574 that they preferred province-wide taxes on an equal footing. Perhaps they wanted to prevent a '*divide et impera*'-situation for the Prince, perhaps they had become convinced of the fiscal efficiency of '*common* means'. Three interesting differences compared to Holland's common excises in the decades before the Revolt, however, were, firstly, that they were now no longer restricted to the cities only. They now had to be paid in the countryside as well and on exactly the same footing, which means that only now these 'common means' became completely 'provincial'[36]. Secondly, their number and the tariffs at which they were raised were increased so much that their revenue became very soon tenfold the revenue realised in the decades before the Revolt yet rapidly increasing in the years thereafter. In 1578 – the year when Amsterdam joined the Revolt at last – the revenue of the 'common means' had already risen to more than 800,000 guilders, while in the 1560s this had been less than 60,000 guilders[37]. In 1608, shortly before the Twelve Years Truce in the war with Spain, it had already risen to even 4.4 million guilders[38]. Holland's population will have increased in the meantime only from about 400,000 to about 600,000.

The last difference between the 'common means' before and after the Revolt is that in these first decades since the start of the Revolt, they were no longer levied primarily as a fund for provincial loans, but now to finance the war directly. No doubt their huge receipts made it relatively easy for the receivers of the 'common means' to attract short term loans (obligations) for Holland's government, especially in the Amsterdam merchant community. This must have been one factor in the explanation why Holland's interest burden rose, despite the fact that in the last decades of the 16th century it was not able to sell annuities on the open market. The other explanation was the interest burden due to forced loans within the cities.

What should be stressed in the context of this article is, that, although in 1599 Holland's interest burden had increased in these ways to about 400,000 guilders, the revenue of the 'common means' had increased in the same time to no less than 2.7 million guilders per year. The addition to tax revenue by means of loans between 1574 and 1600 cannot have been much more, therefore, than, on average, only about 150,000 guilders per year[39]. The 'common means' had obviously become much more than only a fund for the interest burden. Evidently the early decades of Dutch state formation were not so much founded on – either urban or provincial – public *debt* as on provincial *taxation*[40].

2.2 De '*verponding*'

Taxation in Holland did not consist only in the 'common means'. As has been said already, at the start of the Revolt the States of Holland had voted amounts to be spent on the war which were partitioned over the cities. These were often levied by way of forced loans. Apart from these

35 Resolutions of the States of Holland 13.November 1574; quoted in ARA, FH, Memorie 1755, f16v.

36 They have to be called 'common means' instead of 'common excises' since then, because they no longer consisted only in excises, but also in direct taxes on for instance cattle and sown lands.

37 J. Tracy, "Keeping the wheels of war turning", in: G. Darby (ed.), *The origins and development of the Dutch Revolt*, London, 2001, p. 133-150, p. 139.

38 ARA, Oldenbarnevelt, inv.nr. 110.

39 If the interestburden rose from 1572 to 1599 from about 70,000 to about 400,000 at an interest rate of 8.3%; if the interest rate was on average higher the average amount in debtcreation per year was even lower.

40 This point will be elaborated in my "A 'financial revolution' reconsidered; public finance in Holland during the Dutch Revolt, 1568-1648" (in *Economic History Review*, febr. (2003).

'repartitions' in which each city had to pay its part or 'quote' and which were intended to be based on relative wealth, there were very soon also repartitions based on the value of real estate only (the '*verponding*')[41]. The receipts of these repartitions came into the coffers of the receiver-general of Holland who was charged with the payments to the army. In 1581 the decision was taken to form new registers and since 1584 a new 'land and house tax' (*verponding*), based on these new registers and on a new territorial repartition, was levied. It had to yield about 250,000 guilders per time, but in fact it was levied up to even six times per year.

Because the province was dependent on urban governments for the formation and maintenance of the registers, local officials became responsible for the collection of this '*verponding*. Amsterdam for instance appointed so called *thesaurieren extraordinaris* (extraordinary treasurers) for this tax, in addition to the existing 'ordinary treasurers' which handled *urban* public finance. These 'extraordinary treasurers' also sold incidentally life-annuities for the city, as can be seen in the paper of 't Hart and van der Burg. These were funded, however, not on the receipt of the provincial *verponding* but on a local addition levied on behalf of the same ledger of houses[42].

The revenue of the provincial *verponding* had to be handed over by the extraordinary treasurers directly to the receiver-general of Holland. Because the '*verponding*'-receivers were city-officials, urban governments, however, retained some control. They could be lenient, for instance, in the collection of arrears. Arrears on the *verponding* would in fact become notorious in the course of time. At the end of the 18th century it was normal for the *verponding* to be at least one year behind.

Two other inefficient, more or less paralysing characteristics of the *verponding* were, firstly that its revenue could be increased only by the very unpleasant decision to raise more than one '*verponding*' in the same year. This was directly felt by the taxpayers. The major part of the 'common means', on the contrary, were indirectly levied and thus became only noticeable through commodity-prices. Their revenue moreover increased automatically with population growth. A second point is that the key according to which the amount the '*verponding*' had to yield was divided across the cities, was changed only twice in the history of the old Republic. Once in 1632, when at the same time the amount one *verponding* had to yield was raised from 0.6 million to 2.4 million guilders and once in 1732, when this amount was at the same time raised to 2.7 million. Amsterdam with its growing number of inhabitants and houses always tried to prevent a change in the distributive key. A change was in the interest of cities with a declining number of inhabitants, a decline which had started to occur especially since the end of the 17th century[43].

The percentage in 'remissions' on the '*verponding*' was on average only about 10%[44]. During the 16th century rebates on what the cities had to pay to the Habsburg prince, the so-called '*gratiën*' on the '*bede*', had often amounted to more than 50%[45]. It is true that urban control over the collection of the '*verponding*' during the time of the Dutch Republic implied the possibility of local abuses. The difference in these percentages are an indication, however, that 'local particularism' *before* the Revolt was much more harmful for the financial possibilities of the state at that time, than in the 17th and 18th century. The *verponding* was a tax therefore which allowed 'local particularism' to play a certain role, but much less so than had been the case with the *bede* in the 16th century.

41 Tracy, "Keeping the wheels of war turning", pp. 133-150.

42 These sales of life-annuities occurred not only between 1588 and 1607, but also between 1653 and 1687.

43 J.A. Aalbers, "Holland's financial problems and the wars against Louis XIV", in A.C. Duke and C.A. Tamse (eds.), *Britain and the Netherlands* VI, The Hague, 1977, p. 88.

44 Database on Holland's public finance under construction.

45 Tracy, *A Financial revolution*, p. 53.

2.3 Differences between the 'common means' and the '*verponding*'

A difference between the '*verponding*' and the 'common means' which should be emphasised in the context of this paper was that the district-receivers of the common means (the *ontvangers-particulier*) were *provincial* officials appointed by the States of Holland, while the receivers of the *verponding* were appointed by *urban* governments. The first district receiver in the district Amsterdam was not even a burgher of Amsterdam, but Dordrecht's former receiver Reinier van Neck. The instruction of the district receivers of the 'common means' obliged them to make monthly reports to the central office of the 'Finance of Holland' in The Hague, not to urban governments.

In the course of time urban governments had at least some influence on the choice of these receivers, because the States asked them to report about new candidates[46]. It is also known that urban governments were very eager to have a district-receiver in their city and that attempts of the States to keep their number as low as possible for reasons of cost efficiency, failed[47]. Rotterdam, which was denied its own receiver, very soon succeeded in getting accepted by the States the one that they had appointed themselves[48]. In the course of time all eighteen cities which had the right to vote in the States of Holland would have their own district-receiver for the 'common means'[49]. An important reason for this was undoubtedly that these receivers were charged with the interest payments on Holland's debt. It was very inconvenient of course for debt-holders having to travel to another city to encash their interest.

From the start, however, there was one important provision, which prevented a possibly damaging consequence for the state of the Dutch Republic to arise from urban influence on these receivers. The farming out of the provincial taxes to be received by the district-receivers had to be organised under the responsibility of the district-receiver. Originally one, later two representatives from the States of Holland of other cities had always to be present at these occasions to prevent low yields, which would be advantageous to the burghers of the city in case[50]. This was an important difference with, for instance, the collection of the custom duties, the *convooien and licenten*. These were notorious for their low yields due to the fact that each city feared for its trade, if the weight of custom duties were too heavy.

As to the 'common means' a weak point remained that the jurisdiction was left to urban governments. High provincial officials suspected urban governments to be too lenient in their fiscal jurisdiction. A report on 'remissions' and arrears in payments on the 'common means' for the years 1736-1745 showed, however, that the amounts involved in this 'abuse' were, at least at that time, actually very low: less than 1% of total revenue in these years[51].

---

46 ARA, Staten van Holland, inv.nr.s 1789-1723 "Register der politieke commissiën van de Staten van Holland en Westvriesland".

47 Koopmans, *De Staten van Holland en de Opstand,* p. 223.

48 H. ten Boom, "De eerste ontvanger van de gemenelandsbelastingen in Rotterdam", in *Rotterdams Jaarboekje*, (1989), p. 295-304.

49 Until 1596 15 of the 18 cities represented in the States of Holland had district-receivers; in 1596 Gorinchem was added, in 1764 Schiedam and in 1788 Schoonhoven.

50 Already in 1574 it is stated that a controller from a different city should be appointed to control the receiver of provincial excises in each of the cities; resolutions of the States of Holland 10-12-1574, quoted in ARA, FH 797, Memorie 1755, f17r. From 1575 on the resolutions of the States of Holland list the members commissioned to be present at the tax farms (see for instance 22-6-1575 (p. 420), 19-10-1575 (p. 701), 12-3-1600 (p. 84-85). Later on there used to be detailed schedules which indicated which representatives of which two cities should be present at each of the tax farming occasions in other cities (see for instance resolutions States of Holland 14-3-1705).

51 ARA, FH 829 contains a "Staet van het jaerlijks beloop der remissiën, onkosten op het doen der verpagtingen en verdere onkosten gevallen op de verpagte gemeene middelen, welke niet van de specie-staeten zijn afgetrokken, en gevolgelijk een vermindering in het jaerlijks import van de zelve middelen over het Zuider Quartier komen te geeven. NB hier onder sijn ook begrepen de insolventien der pachters"; during 1736-1745 the total amount in 'remissions', insolvent farmers and some other expenses on average per year was less than 75,000 guilders on a total revenue of about 10 million guilders per year.

From the point of view of this paper a second important difference between the *verponding* and the 'common means' was of course the much bigger revenues of the 'common means'. They yielded for instance about 7 million in 1632 and about 10 million in 1732 quite a difference with the 2.4 and 2.7 million of the *verponding* in the same years. It was the most remunerative of the provincial taxes, one which played a vital role in the formation of the Dutch state, therefore, that was relatively free from the potentially pernicious influences of 'local particularism'.

The degree of 'centralised' *provincial* instead of *urban* control over the 'common means' is also illustrated by the perfect and neatly arranged way this tax came to be administrated in the course of time in the office of the 'Finance of Holland', the beating heart of Holland's public finance. Since 1650 this office was able to produce each year, on behalf of the members of the States and/or the city-governments, detailed printed surveys, broken down into all eighteen districts, of all the means involved, which could amount to more than thirty in one year.

The conclusion must be that, by having consented in the 'common means' and in the institutional arrangements through which they were levied, the cities had effectively let common interest prevail over particular interests in one of the most crucial aspects of 'state formation' in the Dutch Republic.

2.4 The '100. and 200. *penningen*' on wealth

The last tax to be discussed here is the complicated one of the '100. and 200. *penningen* (pennies)', which originally was an extraordinary tax on wealth of 0.5%-2%, levied incidentally in war years on assessment registers. The assessment registers, which had been made in the 1650s, were renewed in the 1670s, but never any more there after, although this so called 'extraordinary' tax had soon to be levied nearly each year. It was levied mostly at a rate of 1.5%, not only in the war years between 1672 and 1713, but also each year there after. This had been nesessitated by the tremendous increase in the interest burden that in the meantime had occurred.

Part of the revenue of this tax flowed also through the urban administration, just like the revenue of the ordinary '*verponding*'. In 1673 special commissioners for the receipt of the '100. and 200. *penningen*' had been appointed by Amsterdam's urban government which were responsible for the maintenance of the registers. The part of the '100. and 200. pennies'- tax handled by the urban commissioners consisted in the course of time mainly in the 1.5% on immoveable wealth. An important part of the amount one had to pay on moveable wealth according to the assessment-registers, however, was increasingly met by the 1.5% levied from debt-paper. As the interest on Holland's debt paper came to be paid by the district-receivers of the 'common means' the easiest way to 'levy' this part of the tax became, of course, to just pay only 2.5% instead of 4% on Holland's debt-paper. As the assessment registers were not renewed – and as Holland's debt continuously increased – taxpayers increasingly could 'liquidate' their assessment on moveable wealth with the amount already 'paid' on their debt-paper.

In this way this part of the assessment registers was made increasingly useless. In 1723 the practice was formalised, therefore, that the '100. and 200. *penningen*' consisted on the one hand in 1.5% of the value of land and houses, which part became designated in the 18th century as an 'extraordinary *verponding*' to be administrated by *urban* officials. On the other hand it consisted in the 1.5% of the nominal value of debt paper levied and amdinistrated by the *provincial* district-receiver. Figure I offers a simple diagram of the provincial and urban fiscal administration and the ways they were connected.

FIGURE I. **Diagram of Relations between Holland's and Amsterdam's Fiscal Administration**

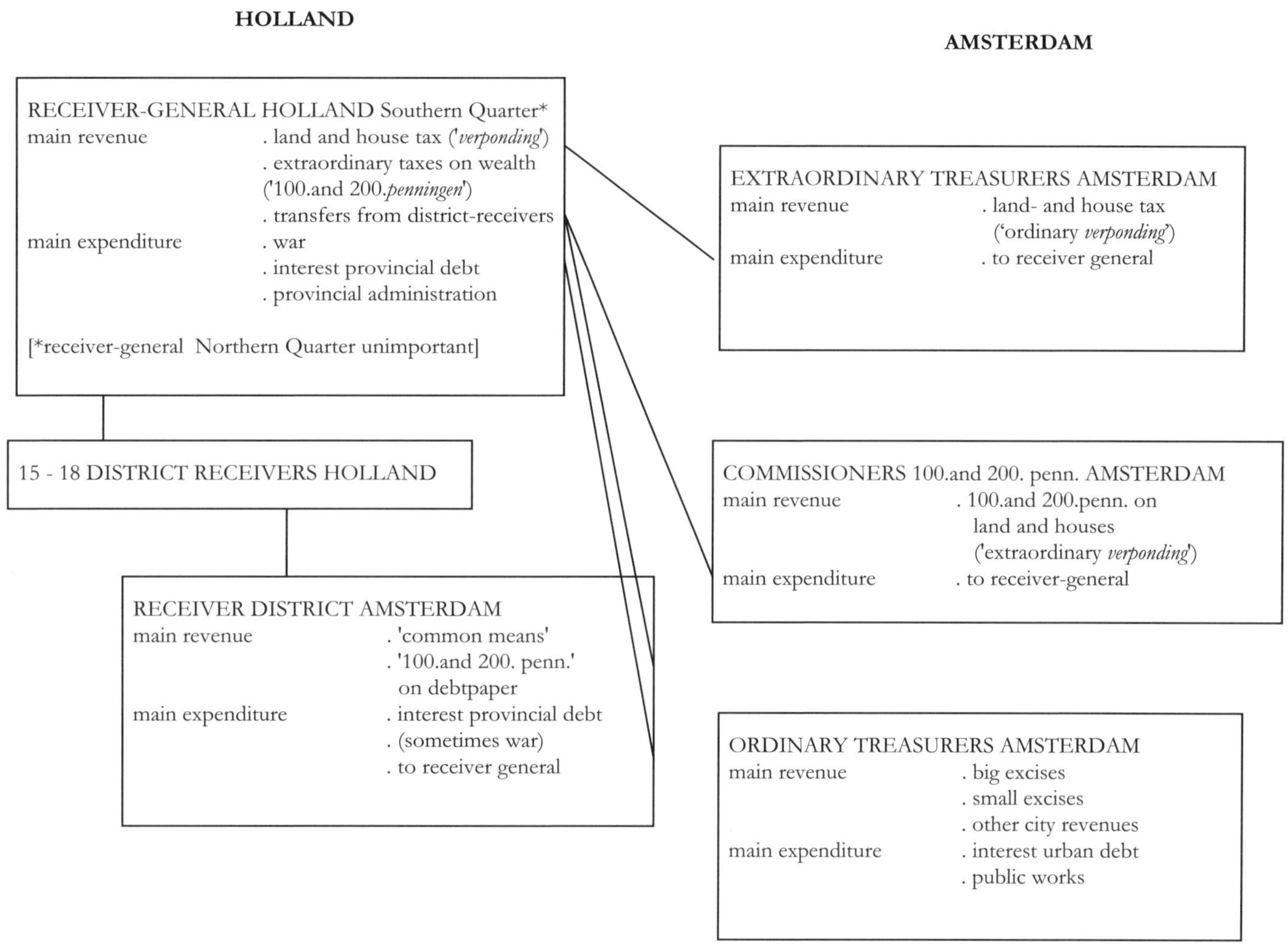

As was the case with the 'ordinary *verponding*', also in the case of the 'extraordinary *verponding*' cities with a declining population since the second half of the 17th century complained in vain that their share was too high and Amsterdam's share too low. Again Amsterdam bluntly refused to consent in a revaluation of the register of 1674 because it feared that this might drive wealthy merchants out of the city. The arrangements regarding this tax, which allowed the richest city to prevent necessary adaptations, obviously hampered its efficient exploitation, therefore.

Yet in another way Amsterdam could take advantage of urban control over the tax stream. In the city-accounts the receipt of the '100. and 200. *penningen*' on houses is to be found on the revenue side as well as on the expenditure side of the account, when its revenue was transferred to the Holland's receiver. As a side remark it should be noted that this means that the totals for Amsterdam's public expenditure and public revenue as they were published, and often been republished, by Koenen, are rather 'inflated' in fact. The degree to which this has been the case can be seen from Graph II.

GRAPH. II. **Role of Holland's Extraordinary Tax on Houses ('100. and 200. *penningen*') in Amsterdam's Public Finance, 1700-1792**
(guilders)

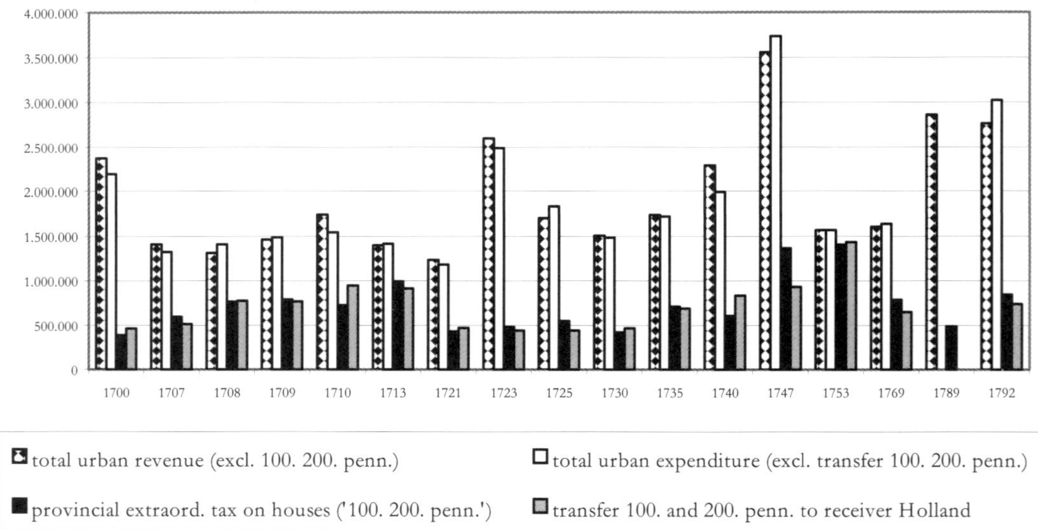

Source: GAA 5014, City Accounts

Most probably this administrative procedure was more an asset than a liability for the urban government, as it could function for instance as an easy source of short-term credit. A remarkable feature of Graph II is that the amounts on the revenue and expenditure side for this tax are not equal. Obviously the city decided at will when and in what measure the transfer to Holland's receiver was effectuated. This is confirmed by item 5) in the report of Amsterdam's debt in 1795 in Table II: Amsterdam had obviously decided not to pay the receipt of the '100. and 200. *penningen*' on houses due for the years 1793 and 1794 in order to balance a still outstanding debt of Holland to the city.

In the context of this paper it must be emphasised, however, that this was only true for that part of this tax, which had become the 'extraordinary *verponding*'. The other, and quantitatively more important part remained, as we have seen, under the control of the provincial receivers.

The 'common means' always remained the most important fund for Holland's debt because the main task of the district receivers of the 'common means' as to public expenditure was the payment of the interests. Only their *balance* had to be transferred to Holland's receiver-general for war expenditure. Now Graph III shows the development of Holland's interest burden and the revenue of Holland's 'common means'. Although less so than during the period of the Revolt against Spain (1572-1648), there needs to be no doubt that the last remained still well above the first even during the whole 17th century. In the 18th century, however, economic and demographic stagnation made considerable increases in the revenue of the 'common means' hardly feasible any longer. The graph shows that the growth of Holland's debt would evidently not have been possible any longer but for the interest reduction resulting from the tax on debt paper discussed in this paragraph. Graph III shows therefore how important this part of this tax became in fact for the preservation of the Dutch state especially in the 18th century.

GRAPH. III. **Interest Burden and Revenue 'Common Means' in Holland 1574-1794**
(guilders)

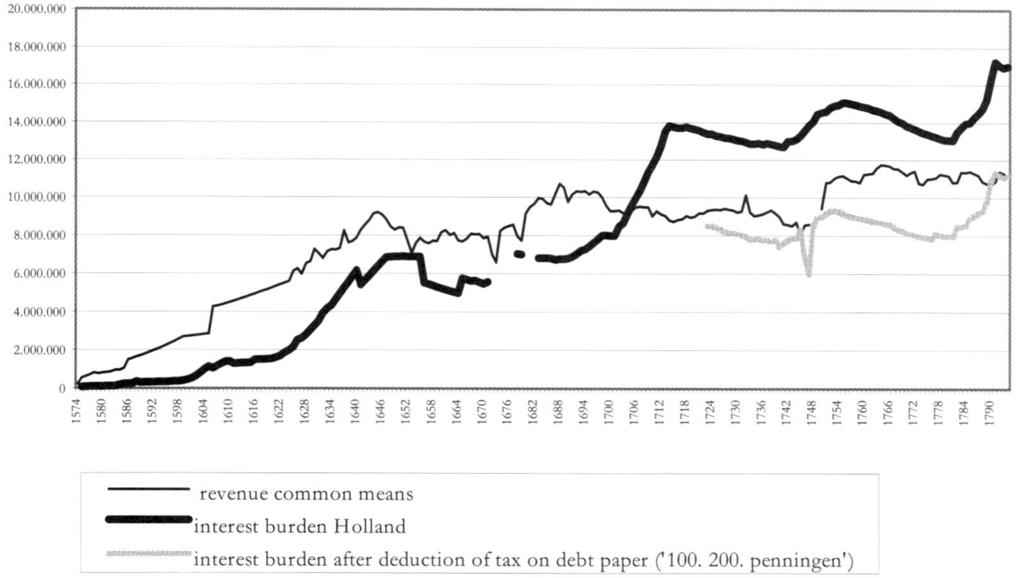

Source: Database under construction to be published in W. Fritschy and R. Liesker, *De gewestelijke financiën tijdens de Republiek der Verenigde Nederlanden. Deel V. Holland, 1572-1795* (forthcoming)

From this may be concluded that, although local jealousies and local particularism of course existed, it were the quantitatively most vital elements in the preservation of the Dutch state, Holland's debt and Holland's 'common means', which could be hardly damaged by them. Maybe the more interesting feature of the Dutch Republic, therefore, is not 'local particularism', but the institutional arrangements in public finance by which it was overcome.

Conclusion

In a historiographical overview of the theme of 'local jealousy in history' by P. Blaas in 1986 it was stressed that one of the results of the Dutch Revolt had been that the loose medieval state-system of the northern Netherlands was reinforced. Not only federalism, but also local autonomy was supposed to have become stronger after than before the Revolt. Holland after the Revolt, says Blaas, consisted in fact of 'a league of eighteen city-republics'[52]. Also J.L. Price saw 'the politics of particularism' as the most characteristic element of Holland and the Dutch Republic in the 17th century. The remarkable central argument of his book is 'that the political system of the old Dutch Republic worked so well *because* of its extreme decentralisation'[53]. 'T Hart has, on the contrary, stressed that 'the efficacy of the republic was seriously *limited* [my italics] because conflicting local and particularistic interests played such a large role in decision making.' Overall, however, her evaluation was already that nevertheless 'the meso-level of government (the provinces) came to dominate the cities in the republic'[54].

A comparison of urban debt and provincial debt and an analysis of the control over tax flows on the urban and the provincial level confirm this evaluation. The most important revenue sources for the preservation of the Dutch state can hardly have been harmed by 'local particularism'. The cities, Amsterdam included, had consented in 'common means' and their farming out under the supervision of commissioners of the States. This had enabled the subsequent growth of the provincial debt and the waning importance of local debts. In this way the cities had given up a crucial part of local autonomy in order to be able to serve the common best.

If public finance is the nerve of any state-system it is quite adequate, therefore, to describe the Dutch Republic as a league of seven '*province*-republics', much less so, however, to describe Holland after the Revolt as 'league of eighteen *city*-republics'. State-formation in the Dutch Republic was not successful because (or despite) of its extreme *de*centralisation, but, on the contrary, thanks to the remarkable extent of the *centralisation* of its public finance on the *provincial* level. This had minimised the pernicious influence of 'local particularism' on its two most important preconditions: its 'common means' and its public debt.

52 Blaas, "Stedelijke naijver", pp. 14-15.

53 J.L. Price, *Holland and the Dutch Republic in the seventeenth century. The politics of particularism*, Oxford, 1994, pp. 2-3.

54 M. 't Hart, "Intercity rivalries and the making of the Dutch state", in Ch. Tilly and W. Blockmans (eds.), *Cities and the rise of states in Europe A.D. 1000 to 1800*, Boulder, 1994, p. 208.

PUBLIC DEBT, STATE REVENUE AND TOWN CONSUMPTION IN ROME (16th-18th CENTURIES)

Fausto Piola Caselli
University of Cassino

Thanks to the rich archives still extant in Italy, there are many published studies on the history of the papal debt in the early modern period[1]. Since the amount of the global debt recorded in the Chamber balance sheets increased quickly from 1550 to 1680, scholars have usually considered the debt as a clear sign of misgovernment, owing to the disorder and decline of the papal public finances. As a matter of fact, figures assume a more realistic dimension in the long run, if they are indexed with the data of the State population. Furthermore, from the mid 16th century onward, the system of the papal debt was developed with great accuracy at the highest level of accounting techniques, in order to attract the investors' trust. Eventually, the policy of the debt was managed with far-sightedness by the Apostolic Chamber[2] and was entirely founded on the Roman fiscal return, which made political control over the capital town indispensable.

This paper will deal with some major topics concerning papal debt in the early modern age: the real weigh of the debt on the yearly balance sheets, the managing techniques worked out by the Chamber and the different rôles played by the periphery and by the capital town to sustain the debt.

Scope and growth of the debt.

The debt was started in 1526, the eve of the sack of Rome, with a loan of 200,000 gold ducats at the yearly rate of 10%. It was the *Monte Fede*, created to bear the military expenses of the Holy League[3]. According to Florentine terminology, *Monte* meant every issue of a loan approved with a relevant papal bull, while the *luogo di Monte* indicated the minimal amount that each saver could buy – generally 100 *scudi* – and which was concretely represented by a patent letter on parchment. As happened in all the *ancien régime* States, the papal debt was set up and increased to finance war expenditures, either in a direct and more often in an indirect way, with financial contributions granted to

---

ASR = Archivio di Stato di Roma
ASV = Archivio Segreto Vaticano
BAV = Biblioteca Apostolica Vaticana

1 A good survey of recent literature is F. Colzi, *Il debito pubblico del Campidoglio*, Rome, 1999, pp. 345-368. See also R. Masini, "Gli investimenti nei titoli del debito pubblico pontificio nella seconda metà del Seicento", in *Studi storici Luigi Simeoni*, 51 (2001), pp. 85-86.

2 Ministry of finances in the Papal State, with great political influence and power.

3 M. Monaco, "Il primo Debito pubblico pontificio: il Monte della Fede (1526)", in *Studi Romani*, 5 (1960), p. 562.

allied states. So it happened from the very beginning, and we often find in the issuing bull a quotation of the expenses 'for the war' or 'against the Turks'[4]. However, as the years passed, civic purposes became more evident in each issue of new *Monti*. Some *Monti* were also set up exclusively for financial reasons, so as to reimburse the title holders, as the new ones were issued at a lower rate of interest. During the reign of Sixtus V (1585-90) the *Monti* were multiplied for the general needs of the State due to the abolition of some tolls or for the system of the civic Chanceries, for the Archives, for public works and for minting new coins. Between 1606 and 1647, in order to complete the Basilica of Saint Peter, four *Monti Fabrica* (for building) were exclusively issued to bear the expenses for the works under the direction of Maderno and Bernini[5]. The *Monti dell'Annona*, set up for the acquisition of wheat during the frequent food shortages in the Papal State, were also great in number. In 1574 the first *Monte Province* was issued to help peripheral communities to pay off the loans lent by the Chamber for the purchase of wheat. For the same reason, in 1594 the first *Monte* dedicated only to the needs of Rome was issued. All in all the *Monti* set up for the acquisition of food remained active throughout the 18th century, because of the recurrence of famine. Though they were almost all extinguished by 1750, the *luoghi* still active after twenty years were just 12,500 and they moreover coincided with crises in agricultural and wheat production[6]. The public debt had been created to face the military expenses abroad, but gradually ended up being used for internal civil and town purposes.

The overall debt of the Apostolic Chamber progressively grew to reach the amount of ten million *scudi* in the first decade of the 17th century, 30 million *scudi* in the middle of the century, to then settle at between 40 and 50 million *scudi*. Nevertheless, growth was much less strong than it may appear at first sight, as between the end of the 16th and the mid 17th century prices had doubled or tripled almost everywhere. The greatest period of issuing loans took place between 1570 and 1650, when the central government was strengthening its power on the periphery. From 1526 to 1670 the Chamber issued 187 *Monti*: 23 for the Roman needs, 55 for the aristocracy and 71 for general purposes[7]. Afterwards, the issuing of state bonds became much more controlled and all the *luoghi di Monte* still in existence, which yielded a very different rate of interest varying according to the time of issue, were withdrawn and converted, between 1684 and 1685 into the *Monti di San Pietro* at a unified rate of 3%. From then onward and until the beginning of the Napoleonic period, the papal debt remained steady, with an expenditure for interest which shifted between 50% and 60% of the overall expenses of the papal budget.

Table I shows in global figures the progress of the public debt, in relationship to the yearly income and expense of the State. For the 16th and 17th centuries, all figures coming from the balance sheets still available have been quoted[8]. For the 18th century, only a few significant years have been carried in the table, because of the complete steadiness of the debt[9].

---

4 Printed papal bulls or decrees concerning the *Monti* are kept in ASV, *Misc. Armm. IV-VI* and *Bandi sciolti;* in ASR, *Bandi, Luoghi di Monte*. A precise inventory of the bulls from the early 16th century to 1676 has been published in seven volumes by the Municipality of Rome: *Regesti di bandi ed editti notificazioni e provvedimenti relativi alla città di Roma e dello Stato Pontificio,* vol. I-VII, Rome, 1920-1958.

5 F. Piola Caselli, "Public Finances and the Arts in Rome: the *Fabbrica* of St Peter's in the 17th Century", in M. North (ed.), *Economic History and the Arts*, Cologne/Weimar/Vienna, 1996, p. 63.

6 D. Strangio, *Crisi alimentari e politica annonaria a Roma nel Settecento*, Rome, 1999, pp. 173-75, 181.

7 ASR, *Camerale II*, *Archivio della Camera*, t. 10.

8 Papal balance sheets are mainly kept in ASR, *Camerale II. Conti di entrata e di uscita della Camera.* A few copies are also available in ASV, *Misc. Armm. IV-V*. From the beginning of the 18th century, the series of the balance is quite complete year by year, without gaps. Some of the yearly balance sheets (1592, 1619, 1657, 1689) have been published as quoted in the following note n. 10. In other cases, the literature reports only the global amounts of income, expenditures and interest.

9 1706: because of a big change in the Roman toll system; 1749: after Benedict XIV's administrative reform; 1789: end of political stability.

TABLE I. **Revenues, Expenditures and Interest**[10]
(Roman silver *scudi*)

Year	Revenue	Expend.(E)	Balance	Interest (I)	I/E %
1525	594,986	417,879	177,107	211,207	50.5
1576	945,315	901,660	43,655	404,227	44.8
1587	1,562,549	793,225!	769,324	?	
1589	1,546,279	1,056,946	489,333	639,779	60.5
1592	1,601,195	1,537,819	63,376	722,228	47
1599	1,440,842	1,464,547	-23,705	762,094	52
1605	1,558,308	1,599,979	-41,671	1,040,437	49
1619	1,790,520	1,673,162	-117,358	826,801	49.4
1632?	1,934,616				
1652	2,705,982	2,489,613	222,368	1,428,424	57.3
1654	2,509,558	2,223,476	286,101	1,473,676	66.2
1657	2,684,515	2,434,668	249,846	1,313,062	53.9
1660	2,673,530	2,472,965	200,564	1,353,494	54.7
1664	2,763,994	2,558,050	205,943	1,539,913	60.2
1667	2,772,628	2,604,647	167,980	1,530,276	58.7
1672	2,705,953	2,701,707	4,246	1,582,162	58.6
1673	2,419,981	2,609,006	-189,025	1,605,238	61.5
1677	2,408,500	2,578,106	-169,606	1,618,304	62.7
1678	2,541,039	2,493,491	47,547	1,643,573	65.9
1689	2,511,883	2,052,424	459,459	1,264,292	61.6
1691	2,321,139	2,220,984	100,155	1,270,342	57.2
1692	2,322,781	2,247,769	75,011	1,275,577	56.7
1706	2,469,005	2,896,225	-427,220	1,424,164	49.2
1749	2,178,268	2,144,036	34,231	1,353,792	63.1
1789	2,447,604	2,575,577	-127,973	1,379,516	56.4

In real figures, the increase of the papal debt for almost three centuries was much less strong than it may appear, mainly if one takes into account the demographic growth of the State. The total population of the Papal State, with the acquisition of Ferrara in 1598 and the annexation of Castro in 1649, went from 1,500,000 inhabitants at the beginning of the 16th century to 2,5000,000 at the end of

10 Sources for the years 1525 and 1526: P. Partner, "Papal Financial policy in the Renaissance and Counter-Reformation", in *Past and Present*, 88 (1980), pp. 49,51; for 1587 and 1691: L. Pezzolo, "Government Debts and Trust. French Kings and Roman Popes as Borrowers", 1520-1660, in *Rivista di Storia Economica*, 3 (1999), pp. 244-245; for 1589, 1657, 1672 and 1677: E. Stumpo, *Il capitale finanziario a Roma fra Cinque e Seicento. Contributo alla storia della fiscalità pontificia in età moderna (1570-1660)* , Milan, 1985, pp. 337,157; for 1592, 1599 and 1619: W. Reinhard, *Papstfinanz und Nepotismus unter Paul V. (1605-1621)*, Stuttgart, 1974, pp. 161-169, 342; for 1606: M. Monaco, *La situazione della Reverenda Camera Apostolica nell'anno 1525. Ricerche d'archivio (Un contributo alla storia delle finanza pontificie)*, Rome, 1960, pp. 68-69; for 1652, 1660, 1664 and 1667: G. Perugino, *Il bilancio pontificio del 1657*, Naples, 1999, p. 23; for 1654, 1673, 1678 and 1692: W. Reinhard, "Finanza pontificia e Stato della Chiesa nel XVI e XVII secolo", in A. De Maddalena and H. Kellenbenz (eds.), *Finanze e ragion di Stato in Italia e in Germania nella prima Età moderna*, Bologna, 1984, p. 361; for 1689: G. Lutz, "Zur Papstfinanz von Klemens IX. bis Alexander VIII. (1667-1691)", in *Römische Quartalschrift*, 74 (1979), p. 81; for 1706, 1749 and 1782: H. Gross, *Rome in the Age of Enlightenment: the post Tridentine syndrome and the ancient regime*, Cambridge, 1990, p. 197; for 1632, there is only a fragment in ASV, *Misc. Arm. IV*.

the 18th century[11]. Owing to the continuous decrease of the rates of interest, the *per capita* debt of the State in the three centuries quoted grew only four times. Annual expenditures followed more or less the same trend:

TABLE II. **Per Capita Yearly Expenditures and Interest**
(Roman *baiocchi*)

Year	Expenditures	Interest
1526	27.9	14.1
1576	48.7	21.8
1589	52.8	32
1619	83.7	41.3
1657	135.2	72.9
1689	108	66.5
1706	144.8	71.2
1749	99.7	62.9
1789	105.1	56.3

As one can clearly see in figure 1 the per capita curve of the interest paid reached a peak in the years of the reign of Urban VIII and of Innocent X (1623-1655). But already in the aftermath of the vast plague, which hit the entire State between 1656 and 1657, the behaviour of the interest paid had already shown a downward trend, which became more evident mainly during the whole 18th century. After all, the fiscal system had become more efficient especially regarding the consumption of goods[12]. The issue of public bonds for the everyday needs of the State was no longer necessary.

FIGURE I. **Per Capita Interest on Papal Debt**
(Roman *baiocchi*)

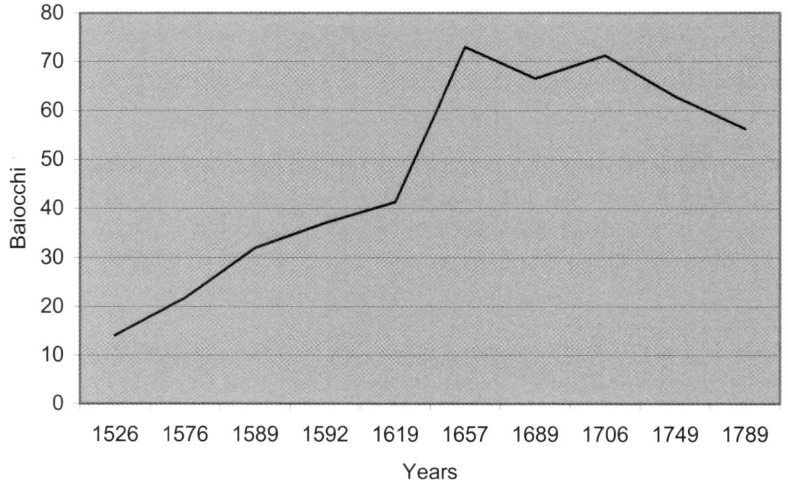

11 K.J. Beloch, *Storia della popolazione d'Italia*, Florence, 1994, pp. 628-629, 263.
12 E. Lo Sardo, *Le gabelle e le dogane dei Papi in età moderna*, Rome, 1994, pp. 26-27.

Eventually, the Papal debt – contrary to what has been recently stated[13] – was always kept under control and the State as such was never obliged to declare bankruptcy as had frequently happened in Spain and France. As a matter of fact, the Church state did not pass through a real financial revolution, which in the Netherlands, in England and even in the Kingdom of Naples deeply changed the central financial structure and the relationships between the citizens and the State[14]. Nevertheless, the public debt was in the Papal State an essential step towards the building of a centralised state and represented a sort of financial shift from the old medieval system to the new modern fiscal state.

Duration of the loans and redemption plans.

From a juridical point of view, the Chamber loans were assimilated to a contract of *censo consignativo*: the debtor borrowed a sum and had to reimburse it gradually – capital and interest – by the income of a specific source among the debtor's properties, whose yield was certain and guaranteed. But the Chamber itself, however, did not take on any obligation to pay off the borrowed capital. The *luoghi* were, accordingly, denominated *non vacabili* when, in fact, the debt was consolidated and the State would go on paying it back partially or totally as it pleased itself, according to cash availability. However, there also existed the *luoghi vacabili*, which represented a sort of life annuity with no capital repayment, which were awarded with a higher rate of interest. They were annulled at the moment of the death of the title holder, without any possibility of being bequeathed. In the case of sale, the owner of a *luogo vacabile* should demonstrate his good condition of health. For the holder, the higher rate of interest awarded to the *luoghi vacabili* compensated for the risk of losing the capital, in case of death. In the first period, the issue of *luoghi vacabili* and *luoghi non vacabili* were balanced: of the 55 different *Monti* issued between 1526 and 1590, for instance, 23 were *non vacabili* and 22 were *vacabili*[15]. However, the Chamber started to settle less rigid rules on the *luoghi vacabili*, allowing the *non vacanza* (making some of them not extinguishable) for a term of years without reference to the title holder's death; or permitting the titles to be transferred to the heirs *periculo mortis* (for danger of death). As time passed, the sale of *vacabili* between living persons became more and more usual with the grant of selling permissions, without special conditions. In fact, as far as their duration is concerned, it has been reckoned that the *Monti vacabili* of the Roman population had an average duration of 17 years and the *non vacabili* of the same category had an average length of 36 years[16]. The *vacabili* had a higher remuneration and a higher market price in comparison to the *non vacabili*, but the holders who had not been able to get special permission from the Chamber still could risk to lose the capital in case of death. About the mid 17th century the practise of the *Monti vacabili* disappeared because of their high cost and all the *luoghi*, beginning with the conversion into *Monte San Pietro*, were definitely issued as *non vacabili.*

The first reimbursement took place in 1597 and was carried out by the drawing of lots. From then on reimbursement by drawing lots, or the acquisition of *luoghi* on the free market, became more and more common. In the last two years of Urban VIII's reign, the Chamber ordered the general treasurer Antonfrancesco Farsetti to buy back two million *scudi* worth of the more lucrative *luoghi di Monte*, and between 1645 and 1650 two further million *scudi* were reimbursed by drawing lots. In 1661,

---

13 P. Partner, "The Papacy and the Papal States", in R. Bonney (ed.), *The Rise of the Fiscal States in Europe c. 1200-1815*, Oxford, 1999, pp. 363, 369.

14 Key studies on this topic are still J.D. Tracy, *A Financial Revolution in the Habsburg Netherlands*: Renten *and* Renteniers *in the County of Holland, 1515-1565*, Berkeley/Los Angeles/London, 1985; P.G. Dickson, *The Financial Revolution in England. A Study in the Development of Public Credit (1688-1756)*, London/Melbourne/Toronto, 1967; A. Calabria, *The Cost of Empire. The Finances of the Kingdom of Naples in the Time of Spanish Rule*, Cambridge, 1991.

15 F. Piola Caselli, "La diffusione dei Luoghi di Monte della Camera Apostolica alla fine del XVI secolo. Capitali investiti e rendimenti", in *Credito e sviluppo economico in Italia dal Medioevo all'Eta' Contemporanea*, Verona, 1988, pp. 198-200.

16 Colzi, *Il debito pubblico*, p. 59.

the Chamber decided to draw 6,350 *luoghi* of the *vacabili Monte Annona* in only one large lot with 735 different owner's names, with an average of 850 *scudi* paid back to each title holder. It is just the 17th century lots which can give a general idea of the amount of *luoghi* owned by the main representatives of the aristocracy and of the bankers operating in Rome. Orazio Falconieri, for example, a Roman banker of Florentine origin, the owner of a sumptuous villa at Frascati, had 1,127 *luoghi* drawn out of the 10,000 *luoghi vacabili* of the *Monte Sale*, he had invested four years before[17].

Between 1585 and 1672, the Chamber authorised also the issuing of 55 special *Monti*, to offer the opportunity to some great families of the Roman aristocracy to extinguish their debts. The dividends were guaranteed by the return of the real estate owned by the borrowing families, which were then blocked in favour of the creditors. The story of the noblemen's debts has to be mentioned for a strictly political reason on the one hand and a more technical one on the other. Some of the great Roman families resorted to loans not only for their unlimited penchant for luxury and grandeur, but also for their incessant fight, led for almost a century, against governmental centralisation. Between the end of the 16th century and the beginning of the 17th, the ancient traditional families of the Roman aristocracy were forced to give way to the new families who did not despise business, land and careers in the Curia. After taking power, the new emerging ruling class had no interest in exacerbating contrasts with the old aristocracy, by then almost extinguished. The instrument of their victory was not the imprisonment or physical destruction of the defeated families, but was more realistic and efficacious. It consisted of the issue of a new *Monte baroni* (issued for the noblemen), founded on the temporary seizure of the assets of the indebted family, to repay both the interest and capital of the debts. The public debt thus became the victorious weapon of the new *élites*, which were consolidating power without bloodshed. To guarantee a final payment of the debt, the Chamber required the drafting of a reimbursement plan, which was attached to the bull issuing each *Monte baroni*. This was a very new procedure, which was not requested for the usual Chamber loans, as the Chamber wanted to maintain greater freedom in repaying the capital. As a matter of fact, with the first *Monte Cesarini* (1585) the reimbursement plan foresaw a 14-year-long duration, a yearly instalment for 11 years beginning from the fourth year and repaying quotas for both interest and capital to be borne with the income from renting the Cesarini family's lands. A more precise reimbursement plan was set up in 1621 with the *Monte Giglioli*, reckoned for a length of 50 years. The Chamber requested the debtor to cash in only 70,000 *scudi* out of the 80,000 due to him as the total issued amount of the *Monte*. The remaining 10,000 *scudi* were put in a bank and compulsorily invested in a *moltiplico*, with the precise indication of the dividends to cash and to accumulate year after year, to pay the final debt[18]. This extraordinary precision bears witness to the high level of accounting techniques attained and readily adopted by the Apostolic Chamber which obviously drew on the experience and advice of its merchant bankers.

Interest paid and market prices. The role of bankers

Over three hundred years, the interest rates went from a peak of 12% down to a minimum level of 3% of the *Monti S. Pietro*. In around 1550, 8% was a usual figure, but in the second half of the 16th century the *Monti* yielded between 5% and 7% and progressively decreased to 3% at the end of the following century. The *Monti vacabili* instead, were awarded with a spread which could even reach 5 points: this happened with the *Monte Pace non vacabile* at 5.25% and the *Sisto vacabile* at 10% issued two

17 F. Piola Caselli, "Banchi privati e debito pubblico pontificio a Roma tra Cinquecento e Seicento", in *Banchi pubblici, banchi privati e monti di pietà nell'Europa preindustriale. Amministrazione, tecniche operative e ruoli economici*, Genoa, 1991, pp. 484-485.

18 F. Piola Caselli, "Una montagna di debiti. I Monti Baronali dell'aristocrazia romana nel Seicento", in *Roma moderna e contemporanea*, 2 (1993), pp. 43-45. With the *moltiplico* the banker was ordered to reinvest the interest in new bonds with which the title holder had no chance to interfere.

years later. In 1585, a *Lista dei Monti vacabili e non vacabili* registered the names of 4,430 different Roman title holders totalling a capital of 2,806,000 *scudi* owned, for an average of 633 *scudi* to each person[19]. The *Monti non vacabili* yielded an average of 6.5%, while the *vacabili* had a return of 10%. One hundred years later, in 1678, a report on some Offices and *Monti vacabili* explained that the rates of interest were much too high and that the Chamber had no return in keeping that level.

All in all, the nominal rates offered by the Chamber were even lower than those paid by other countries for similar issues. The French royal loans would offer 8.33% in 1594, 14.7% in 1660 and 11.9% ten years later. The level of the French rates of interest varied according the needs of war, as everywhere, but the trend toward a decline was clear and at the end of the century a good 5% was quite usual[20]. In Italy, public loans were issued at a reasonable price, since the late Middle Age, exception being made for war periods. In Florence, the *Seven percent fund* set up to provide dowries for girls, had a 7% return which was twice the official rate of interest paid on the public debt[21]. Later on, interest rates went near and below 5%. In Venice the *depositi in Zecca* were cut down to 3% in 1593, after a peak of 14% during the war[22]. Many public loans from Milan were issued at 5% in the mid 17th century, a level which was considered too high by the government[23]. In Naples forced reductions of interest were well known by savers during the 17th century, and in the 18th century the average was about 4%[24]. Actually, though, the real rates paid in Rome were lower than the nominal rate, as the *luoghi di Monte* would be negotiated from the very beginning at a market price which was higher than their face value. The *Monti vacabili* especially, despite the risk of loss of the capital, were particularly appreciated as a form of investment. After 1575 when the Genoese financiers had already been heavily damaged by Philip II's decree, Genoese capital investment, attracted by the prospect of good returns, flooded Rome with the result of increasing the market prices of the *luoghi*, as an anonymous commentator recorded:

...i Monti di Roma...sono comprati da tutte le nazioni, e specialmente da Genovesi, che per comprare all'ingrosso gli hanno fatto alzare di prezzo...[25]

(the Roman bonds... are bought by all the populations and mainly by the Genoese, who bought wholesale and increased prices).

The jurist Teodoro Amayden, who was at the time very popular in Rome, complained in 1641 that the Genoese exported dividends out of Rome, instead of reinvesting them on the spot[26]. Genoese demand for Roman bonds remained high for the whole 18th century, supporting faithfully each issue[27]. This was one reason for the high market prices, but not the only one.

Table III shows some market prices of *Monti vacabili* during 50 years between 16th and 17th centuries: prices tend to increase as long as the economic crisis of the beginning of the 17th century became more and more heavy:

19 ASV, *Dataria*, vol. 289. See also Table IV.

20 Pezzolo, *Governments debts*, p. 252.

21 J. Kirshner and J. Klerman, "The Seven Percent Fund of Renaissance Florence" in *Banchi pubblici*, p. 372.

22 L. Pezzolo, "*L'oro dello Stato. Società, finanza e fisco nella Repubblica veneta del secondo '500*", Venice, 1990, p. 178.

23 A. Cova, "Banchi e monti pubblici a Milano nei secoli XVI e XVII", in *Banchi pubblici*, p. 331.

24 I. Zilli, "*Imposta diretta e debito pubblico nel Regno di Napoli*", Naples, 1990, p. 94.

25 BAV, *Cod. Ott. Lat.*, t. 2484, n. 1.

26 BAV, *Cod. Vat. Lat.*, t. 7851, *Relatione della città di Roma*, ff. 378 r.–380 r.

27 G. Felloni, "*Gli investimenti finanziari genovesi in Europa tra il Seicento e la Restaurazione*", Milan, 1971, p. 169.

TABLE III. **Market Prices of The Most Popular Luoghi di Monte Vacabili, 1576-1621**[28]
(Roman silver *scudi*)

Monte	1576	1580	1593	1604	1608	1621
Pio	105	113	113	123	?	139
Lega	108	114	112	122	124	139
Giulio	107	117	118	124	125	139
Avign. I	111	115	116	123	124	139
Avign. II	109	114	114	123	126	139

The Apostolic Chamber would correctly take into account the market price. As a matter of fact, when in 1686 the old *Monti* were converted into the new *Monte san Pietro*, the owners had the opportunity to opt for the new issue with a rate of exchange 130:100, which was granted considering the real market price of the old bonds[29]. After one century, a sale of almost 4,000 *luoghi di Monte* at 3%, which took place in 1782 at the price of 127 *scudi* each, shows how the market price remained above the nominal price for a long time, even despite the low rate of interest[30].

The favour bestowed by investors on the *luoghi di Monte* was mainly due to the lack of alternative investments. Rome was a city almost completely devoid of handicraft activities that were not dedicated to the internal market. At the end of the 16th century the capital city of the Papal State restricted her export to a few luxury items: sumptuous carriages, musical instruments, statues and other *objets d'art*, draperies and some wool artefacts. According to J. Dulumeau, Rome imported everything, and exported art and the True Faith only[31]. In the 17th century the situation became even more stagnant if possible. If on the one hand it was not possible to invest in handicraft or commercial activities, investing in lands returned little and demanded great efforts in the management of the farms. Rents were low because of the only really productive activity in Rome: the building industry. Investing in agriculture was very dangerous because of the recurring famines and because it would often result in a net loss of the invested capital[32]. Therefore, everybody would invest their capital in *luoghi di Monte* despite the hardly flattering opinion on the public debt expressed by contemporary economic observers. At the beginning of the 18th century, Nuzzi thought that the investment in *luoghi di Monte* was the "...unhappiest and weakest of all investments and what is worse, fosters laziness and idleness in the souls making them contrary to fatigue and industry..."[33].

Eventually, savers investing in the papal debt were certain of its return. The interest paid every two months did not depend upon the whimsical will of a sovereign, but came from precise and guaranteed sources of income. Each bull setting up the *Monte* determined with absolute precision the sources for the payment of the debt, which were again mentioned also in the records of the Papal State balances, especially since Sixtus V's time. Interest for the papal debt mainly came from tolls whose income, put out to contract, was almost wholly directed towards the treasuries of the *Monti* in fixed time

28 Sources: Piola Caselli, *La diffusione*, p. 210; Reinhard, *Papstfinanz*, pp. 17, 47; Stumpo, *Il capitale finanziario*, pp. 250, 254-255; V. Reinhardt, *Kardinal Scipione Borghese (1605-1633). Vermögen, Finanzen und sozialer Aufstieg eines Papstnepoten*, Tübingen , 1984, pp. 248-250.

29 ASV, *Arm. V*, t. 258.

30 D. Strangio, "Debito pubblico e riorganizzazione del mercato finanziario nello Stato ecclesiastico del '700", in *Roma moderna e contemporanea*, 2 (1994), p. 188.

31 J. Delumeau, *Vie économique et sociale de Rome dans la seconde moitié du XVIe siècle*, Paris, 1957-59, p. 694.

32 D. Strangio, "L'amministrazione del debito pubblico pontificio nel Settecento", in *Archivio della Società romana di storia patria*, 122 (1999), p. 296.

33 F. Nuzzi, *Discorso...intorno alla coltivazione e popolazione della Campagna Romana. Alla Santità di Nostro Signore Papa Clemente Undecimo*, Rome, 1702, p. 34.

instalments. Moreover, the titles could freely circulate among private citizens, a characteristic enhancing the investors' favour. A transfer needed only a few administrative formalities and the payment of a rather modest fee[34]. Private people could sell the titles simply recording the transfer on the registry of the holders. They could also sell titles by proxy. It was also possible to make transfers to a person to be designated at a later moment, that is the possibility to choose successively a third person, as well as to buy the bonds back. There was no particular place or seat in Rome for negotiating the titles – Rome had no Stock Exchange – and it usually took place in private, at the home of the *Monte*'s secretary or at the seats of the major Roman banks.

As a matter of fact, the merchant-bankers played a role of absolute importance in the sophisticated system of the papal public debt. As the Curia did not have an adequate bureaucratic structure, the Papal State could not manage without the services of the great merchants and banking houses. The bankers did not lend money to the State, but carried out the services of treasury, cash and financial brokerage. They were acting as Treasurers in the Apostolic Chamber, or as bidders for tolls and for general services. This was according to a tradition which we can trace back to the times of Boniface VIII when the Chiarenti family from Pistoia, the Mozzi and Spini from Florence were steadily established in the Chamber Treasury. The tradition was later reinstated with the return of the Curia to Rome, after the Schism: in 1417, as a matter of fact, the General Treasurer was the Florentine Carlo Geri. This function of the bankers to act a treasurers of the Apostolic Chamber came to an end in 1745 when Benedict XIV entrusted the *Monte di Pietà* in Rome to act as the General Treasury[35]. The bankers also took the role of wholesale purchasers of the public debt, selling the bonds by retail with private investors and great Roman families. As they had acquired all the loans, they also had the right to hold the treasury of each *Monte* with its relevant cash flow and all connected economic consequences. It was the Florentines who began it all between the 15th and the 16th century, soon to be followed by the powerful Genoese. The Chamber would sell its own *luoghi* to the bankers at a higher value than the face one, well conscious that the market prices could permit it. The maximum was reached in 1600 with the *Monte Novennale* sold by the Chamber to the Guicciardini at 114.5 silver *scudi* per each *luogo*, and moreover for a long period the sale of the public debt to the bankers was always settled at two or three points over parity. In other countries instead, the sale was usually negotiated under parity as happened in France, before Colbert's times[36]. Later on, though, things began to change. In 1643 Orazio Falconieri bought the whole enormous loan of 10,000 *luoghi* of the *Monte del Sale*, sold by the Chamber at 98 *scudi* for each *luogo*[37]; as a matter of fact, from 1645 the Banco di Santo Spirito – established in 1605 – appeared in the papal bulls as both cashier and treasury in charge. It substituted little by little for the bankers' services, together with the Roman *Monte di Pietà*.

Rules, taxes and buyers.

The solidity of the papal debt is then to be explained by the lack of alternative investments, by the certainty of the interest matured and by a whole lot of norms, which had been drawn up to protect the buyers of the State. They were already well outlined from the beginning, at the moment when the first *Monte Fede* was issued[38]. Everyone could be a title holder, also minors and even the disabled. Even those under the death penalty could buy them, and in this case, if their capital had been confiscated, they could still cash in the interest which they could make use of until the day of their execution.

34 Colzi, *Il debito pubblico*, pp. 181-182.
35 Piola Caselli, *Banchi privati*, pp. 469-472.
36 Tracy, *A financial revolution*, p. 22.
37 ASR, *Camerale II, Luoghi di Monte*, t. 28.
38 Monaco, *Il primo Debito pubblico*, p. 562.

Little by little the habits and the administrative rules regarding the public debt were perfected and were diffused. It became necessary then, to sum them up in one written code: a peculiar forerunner of a code on paper published in 1615, which was used as a reference text by the investors and by the administrative staff (treasurers, secretaries, accountants) running each *Monte*[39]. Also stated were the taxation rules for the *Monti*, whose earnings were tax free, except for the fees to be paid for issuing certificates and statements. Taxes on bond transfers were very cheap: in 1615 one would pay 0.8% for the *non vacabili* and the 0.4% of the *capitolini* bonds which, however, generally yielded a lesser interest. It was established that the brokers could exact for their mediation rights, on buying and selling, three silver *giulii* for each *luogo* (0.3% on the face value) from the seller and 0.1% from the buyer. The broker, then would gain 0.4% of the face value which was in fact only a true 0.3%, if one takes into account the market value of the *luoghi*. Later on, an inheritance fee of three *giulii* for each *luogo* was introduced for relatives while still later, in 1689, the fees gradually increased from three *giulii* up to two *scudi* per *luogo* depending on the degree of relationship[40]. Tipping was also fixed for bankers, secretaries and so on: the residents in Rome would tip no more than one *baiocco* per *luogo* and those living outside Rome should tip two *baiocchi*[41]. In actual terms each single *luogo di Monte* could never be burdened by taxes by more than 2% of its face value during its whole period of validity, and this increased the favour enjoyed by the *luoghi* among savers.

Who were the savers who used to buy the *luoghi di Monte* in Rome? There has so far not been an overall attempt to answer this question, because of the great difficulty in tracing the documents of the *Monti* secretariats. We do have, however, some reports which yield some information. The *Lista* of 1585 informs us of the composition of the patrimony in *luoghi* of 4,430 owners, that is equivalent to 5% of the Roman population:

TABLE IV. **Luoghi owned by 4,430 Montisti**
(Rome, 1585)

Number of *luoghi*	Owners (% total)
0-5	72.7
6-10	15.2
11-50	11
over 50	1.1

Public bodies such as hospitals, churches, religious orders owned an average amount of 1,044 *scudi*, while private individuals had 900 *scudi*. Contrarily to what one might believe, the investors who had invested in the *luoghi di Monte* toward the end of the 16th century did not make up a small and rich elitarian group but a number of persons who would invest in one or two *luoghi*; these are the figures that recur more frequently in the *Lista*. Men constituted 66.5%, women 24.7%, and 6.2% belonged to various institutions. The remaining 2.6% were registered jointly to two or more people. As the institutions, or public bodies, appear on the list to a rather small extent, one cannot even state that the Church apparatus had been invited forcedly to acquire the Chamber debt. Eventually, one fourth of the title holders were women – registered mainly as the original proprietor and not as heirs by succession. This was a very high level, not far away from the proportion of women subscribing to the urban *renten*,

39 *Tasse e provisioni diverse sopra in governo dei Monti*, in ASV, *Arm. V*, t. 252.
40 ASV, *Armandio V*, t. 258.
41 ASV, *Armandio V*, t. 203.

investigated for the same period in a town of the County of Holland[42]. But this was a scenario which would be bound to change in the following decades.

From recent literature relevant to other cases it is possible to draft a comprehensive picture of the typology of the owners of the *luoghi di Monte* with reference to three different periods over almost two centuries:

TABLE V. **Owners of Luoghi di Monte in Rome**[43]
(in %)

	1593-1616	1684-1689	1793-1797
Public bodies or institutions	14	19	33
Laymen, not nobles	54	20	38
Noblemen and high clerks	32	61	29

The evident growth of the nobles as owners of the bonds – and the following drop – can be explained as the outcome of the practice of nepotism which around the middle of the 17th century had reached its maximum splendour. The Chigi family, to which pope Alexander VII (1655-1667) belonged, around 1660 had accumulated a patrimony of 500,000 *scudi* in *luoghi di Monte*[44]. Later on, at the end of the 18th century, only 16% of the holders were women, to a large extent then lower than two centuries earlier. Eventually, considering the number of *luoghi* owned, we realize that 62% of the title holders owned up to 5 *luoghi* each, 17% up to 10 and 19% up to 50 *luoghi* each.

The most evident fact consists in the slow but steady increased participation of public institutions such as brotherhoods, churches, convents, hospitals, charitable and pious institutions. There is also an increase of the 'big' owners of bonds. Private investors, noblemen and high ranking priests, though with various vicissitudes, seem gradually to lose their position, in favour of the public institutions. Anyway, the class of small proprietors of the *luoghi di Monte* still remained rather large, if not really popular. Roman labourers, craftsmen and artisans could only with difficulty save enough money to be able to invest even in one single *luogo di Monte*, unless they got together in associations or groups – which was permitted by the Chamber – registering a single bond to more than one person. Work in farms around Rome was paid between 15 and 22 *baiocchi* a day plus some food[45]. In the town, a generic labourer could make between 15 and 27 *baiocchi* a day, a master mason from 40 to 60 *baiocchi* and an expert craftsman such as a master tinsmith could even reach 80 *baiocchi* a day[46]. In a year, then, considering an average of 260 working days, they could have made about 70 or 150 or even 200 *scudi*, according to the type of craft. There was no possibility, then, of investing in bonds worth 100 *scudi* each. All in all, there was the opportunity for a Roman master mason to build his house slowly, but not that of investing his savings in the public debt. But at a higher level of income, however, this was possible. A professor at the Rome University 'La Sapienza' would earn only 300 *scudi* per annum and the chancellor 390, but the accountant of the Banco di Santo Spirito earned 650 *scudi* toward the mid 17th century and a cashier got 720 *scudi*[47]. There did quite possibly exist, for the public debt, a class of investors between the manual workers and the noble and mercantile aristocracy. It consisted of high-level priests, country

42 See chapter 12, tables and annotations of M. van der Heijden, "Renteniers and the public debt of Dordrecht (1555-1572)".
43 Sources: Colzi, *Il debito pubblico*, p. 204; Masini, *Gli investimenti*, p.95; D. Strangio, "Debito pubblico e deficit di bilancio dello Stato della Chiesa. Il Monte Nuovo della Difesa.", in *Studi romani*, 48 (2000), pp. 96-101.
44 M. Teodori, *I parenti del Papa. Nepotismo pontificio e formazione del patrimonio Chigi nella Roma barocca*, Padua, 2001, p. 157.
45 M. Petrocchi, *Roma nel Seicento*, Bologna, 1970, p. 176.
46 P. Scavizzi, "Considerazioni sull'attività edilizia a Roma nella prima metà del Seicento", in *Studi storici*, 9 (1968), pp. 184-186; M. Vaquero Piñeiro, "Ricerche sui salari nell'edilizia romana (1500-1650)", in *Rivista Storica del Lazio*, 5 (1996), pp. 131-158.
47 Colzi, *Il debito pubblico*, p. 147.

merchants, administrators, tradesmen and particularly qualified artisans: Gianlorenzo Bernini and his father owned numerous *luoghi di Monte vacabili*[48].

Role of the periphery and of the capital town.

The interest paid by the Chamber to the *luoghi di Monte* came mainly from tolls, plus some spiritual and patrimonial revenues. The fiscal sources got little by little a clear pre-eminence, but at the beginning of the period the contribution of the state periphery was much lower than what the Rome customs could yield. Figure II shows the source for interest coming from the periphery and from the capital town. Among all provinces, the North East area (Emilia, Romagna, Marche, Umbria) gave the largest amounts of money, with an increase which in the figure is more and more evident:

FIGURE II. **Sources of Interest for the Papal Debt**[49]
(Roman *scudi*)

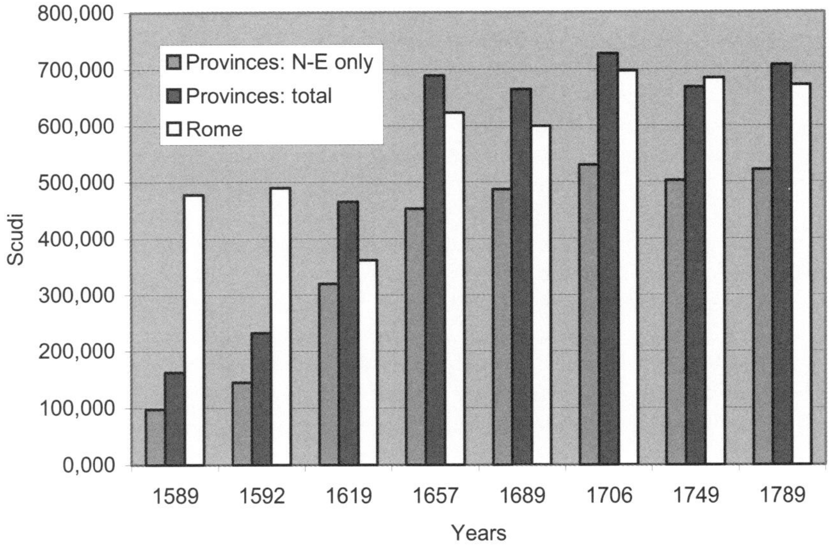

At the end of the 16th century, when the autonomy of the small towns was still strong, the Roman area paid 75% of the global interest for the debt. Later on, from the mid 17th to the end of the 18th century, a balance between the periphery and the Roman area seems eventually to have been reached.

But if we take into account the demographic data, the burden on the Roman area was – as a matter of fact – much higher than that put on the provinces. Figure III shows in full how the *per capita* contribution of each citizen from the periphery – which is to say from each tax payer, or each consumer

48 L. Nussdorfer, *Civic politics in the Rome of Urban VIII*, Princeton, 1992, p. 92.
49 Sources: ASR, *Conti di entrata e di uscita della Camera*, t. 1, 2, 3, 10, 15. For the Roman population, see Beloch, *Storia della popolazione*, pp. 196-197.

– was fifteen or twenty times lower than what a citizen from Rome would be asked to pay for the debt, through taxation or other sources:

FIGURE III. **Per Capita Burden for the Papal Debt: Periphery and Capital Town**
(Roman *baiocchi*)

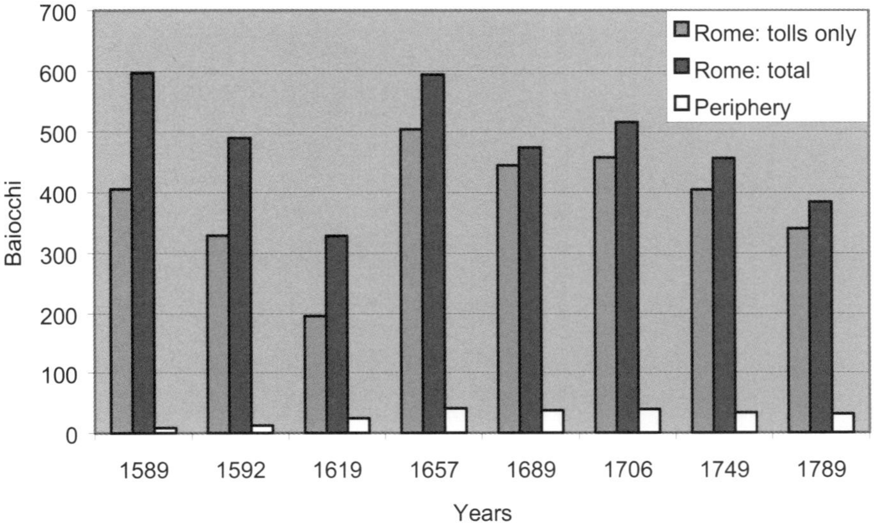

The figure shows a sharp decrease of the Roman *per capita* contribution for the debt during the first period, up to the first two decades of the 17th century. The trend is due to the demographic growth of the Papal State in the 16th century and to the annexation of the thickly populated territory of Ferrara in 1598. At the time of the big plague, the mid 17th century, the Roman contribution achieves again the old high levels, owing to the new strong taxation system on town consumption set up by the Chamber. From then onward, the *per capita* contribution of Rome initiates a slow decrease, still remaining within a ratio 15:1 in comparison to the *per capita* contribution of the periphery.

During the 18th century, spiritual incomes decreased quickly in the Chamber treasury and the debt was then entirely paid by tolls. A remark, signed by the book keeper in a record inside the 1706 balance sheet, reminds the reader that the whole interest of the *Monti St. Pietro* was at that time entirely paid from the Roman tolls. The State debt had become a mere urban debt, paid by only one town. As the literature has already stressed, consumption of food, building materials and a luxury standard of living in Rome reached a peak in the 16th century, still remaining on a high level even during the stagnation of the 17th and 18th centuries[50]. The good reputation of the papal debt was placed in the virtuous circle: high consumption, rich fiscal yield and regular interest paid. As an obvious consequence, the state needed iron control of the capital town, for economic reasons even before political and administrative strategies

50 J. Revel, "Les privilèges d'une capitale: l'approvisionnement de Rome à l'époque moderne", in *Annales E.S.C.*, 30 (1975), p. 567.

URBAN GOVERNMENTS, PUBLIC DEBTS AND ANNUITY MARKETS

THE SALE OF ANNUITIES AND FINANCIAL POLITICS IN A TOWN IN THE EASTERN NETHERLANDS ZUTPHEN, 1400-1600

Remi van Schaïk*
Rijksuniversiteit Groningen

For several reasons, the Guelders town of Zutphen occupies a special place among the towns in the eastern Netherlands which were engaged in international trade and therefore belonged to the Hanseatic League. Like Kampen, Deventer and Doesburg, it was situated on the river IJssel, the connection between the Rhine and the Zuyder Zee, which gave direct access to the North Sea and therefore constituted one of the major trade routes between the German Rhineland and the coastal regions of the northern Netherlands, northern Germany, and the Scandinavian and Baltic countries. Zutphen was also the capital of one of the four quarters of the Duchy of Guelders, in fact a federal 'state' (see Figure I). As an indication of the population, according to calculations for the last decade of the 15th century, Zutphen is estimated to have had about 4,000 inhabitants. It must be noted that this point in time was part of a period of severe economic and, according to some sources, demographic crisis. In any case, the population of Deventer was considerably larger[1].

For present-day researchers, the special place occupied by Zutphen can also be explained by the fact that, like Deventer, the town boasts an almost unbroken succession of municipal accounts dating back to relatively early times, which enable us to get a clear picture of the town's financial ins and outs and obtain a profound insight into its financial and economic development. The municipal or chamberlain's accounts of Deventer have been preserved from 1337 onwards[2]. Those of Zutphen, in addition to some earlier fragments, are partly preserved from 1381 and are virtually complete from 1445 onwards, with the exception of a few odd years[3]. However, a considerable part of Zutphen's

---

StA Zutphen = Stadsarchief Zutphen (Municipal Archives Zutphen)
OAZ = Oud-Archief Zutphen

* I wish to thank Mrs. Ingrid Sennema (Groningen) for translating this article and Dr. Vincent Tassenaar (Groningen) for his help in the graphic representation of the data.

1 On the population figures of Zutphen at the end of the 15th century (1492-1498), see R. van Schaïk, *Belasting, bevolking en bezit in Gelre en Zutphen (1350-1550)*, Hilversum, 1987, p. 149. Deventer c. 1470: J.F. Benders, "De demografische ontwikkeling van Overijssel 1369-ca. 1600", in *Overijsselse Historische Bijdragen*, 110 (1995), p. 39.

2 Municipal Archives Deventer, *Middeleeuws Archief*, n° 150. Edition of the accounts up to 1440, by J.I. van Doorninck, J. de Hullu, J. Acquoy (eds.), *De cameraars-rekeningen van Deventer, 1337-1393*, 7 vols. Deventer, 1885-1914, and by G.M. de Meyer (ed.), *De stadsrekeningen van Deventer* [1394-1440], 6 vols. Utrecht, 1968-1984.

3 StA Zutphen, *OAZ*, n° 865-974 and 1033-1160 (up to 1600). The accounts up to 1445 were edited by R. Wartena (ed.), *De stadsrekeningen van Zutphen 1364-1445/46*, Zutphen, 1977. W.J. Alberts also edited accounts of 1457/58 and 1472/73: "De overrentmeestersrekening van Zutphen over het jaar 1457-1458", in *Bijdragen en Mededelingen van het Historisch Genootschap*, 77 (1963), pp. 51-189, and "De overrentmeestersrekening van Zutphen over het jaar 1472-1473", in *Bijdragen en Mededelingen van het Historisch Genootschap*, 71 (1956), pp. 1-159.

annual accounts not preserved in the original is still known to us from 17th-century extracts[4]. Kampen, on the other hand, does not have any medieval annual accounts, while Doesburg only has municipal accounts for the years 1389 and 1400–1423 (although with many gaps) and then again from 1475 onwards[5].

Moreover, particularly with a view to the present study into urban annuity policies, another enormous advantage is the high degree of completeness, and thus representativeness and homogeneity, of the Zutphen books. Precisely for this reason Zutphen will be presented as a case study. The present report concerns the preliminary results of a study into long-term developments covering, for reasons of a labour-saving nature, a period of about two centuries after the oldest data, that is to say untill 1600. Undoubtedly, with the help of qualitative material from the Zutphen archives, more detailed analyses of the quantitative material will have to be made in order to be able to interpret the developments more accurately.

This study concentrates on the development of the organisation and scale of the sale of annuities *(renten)* as part of a town's finances and in relation to the economic and political climate. To this end a number of questions will be posed: how do these monies relate to the other monies in the town's finances, how systematically were annuity revenues recorded, which expenses were financed by this instrument, and which receipts were used to cover the payment of annuities? Was it a matter of ad hoc decision-making or was it a structural policy instrument? How large was the debt caused by this instrument of public financing through the years, and was the town government of Zutphen financially and politically able to control its consequences?

Urban annuity sales

First of all, it must be noted that there is no reason at all to suppose that the sale of annuities in Zutphen, or in other towns in the Duchy of Guelders, was subject to a princely concession or the granting of a special permit, as seems usual in many other region[6]. The town was undoubtedly free to sell annuities at will[7]. Attempts (but nothing more than that) to contain urban autonomy were made only by the Burgundian authorities, after the conquest and temporary occupation of Guelders during the years 1473-1477 and 1481-1492[8].

In general, the sale of annuities manifested itself as an instrument of public finance used by town governments in order to fund expenditures that could not be covered by a town's "normal" income. In this way capital investments could be made, the financing of which could be spread out over a period of ten to twenty years. Although what is referred to here are not loans in the proper sense – canon law was opposed to those – they were somewhat similar. Moreover, this instrument

---

4 StA Zutphen, *Handschriftencollectie Gerhard Kreijnck*, n° 15-16, 18. Kreijnck (1612-1692) was burgomaster of Zutphen from 1642 onwards.

5 Editions by A.J. van de Ven and L.S. Meihuizen (eds.), "De oudste stadsrekening van Doesburg (1373/74)", in *Bijdragen en Mededelingen Gelre*, 46 (1943), pp. 103-135, and R.A.D. Renting (ed.), *De stadsrekeningen van Doesburg betreffende de jaren 1400/1401 en 1402/1403*, Groningen, 1964 (Fontes Minores Medii Aevi XV). The dating of 1373/74 by Van de Ven was incorrect and should be 1389/90, as W. Zondervan quite rightly put forward in his "De datering van de oudste stadsrekening van Doesburg", in *Bijdragen en Mededelingen Gelre*, 60 (1961), pp. 117-126.

6 As was already been noted, correctly, by W.J. Alberts, "Beitrag zur Wirtschaftsgeschichte des Rheins in Zusammenhang mit der spätmittelalterlichen Wirtschaftsentwicklung der Niederlande", in *Rheinische Vierteljahrsblätter*, 26 (1961), p. 309.

7 J.H. Kernkamp (ed.), *Vijftiende-eeuwse rentebrieven van Noordnederlandse steden*, Groningen, 1961, p. 7 (Fontes Minores Medii Aevi XIII), who contended that the towns needed a special permit for selling annuities. However, this is not always crystal clear with regard to towns in Holland. In Leyden this probably was the case, but not so in Dordrecht before 1486 and the same was true of Hoorn; see J.W. Marsilje, *Het financiële beleid van Leiden in de laat-Beierse en Bourgondische periode. 1390-1477*, Hilversum, 1985, p. 285.

8 See R. van Schaïk, "Taxation, public finances and the state-making process in the late Middle Ages: the case of the Duchy of Guelders", in *Journal of Medieval History*, 19 (1993), pp. 262-266.

FIG. I. **The Duchy of Guelders, its Quarters and Capitals around 1450**
(Design: Willem Kuppers, Aurich)

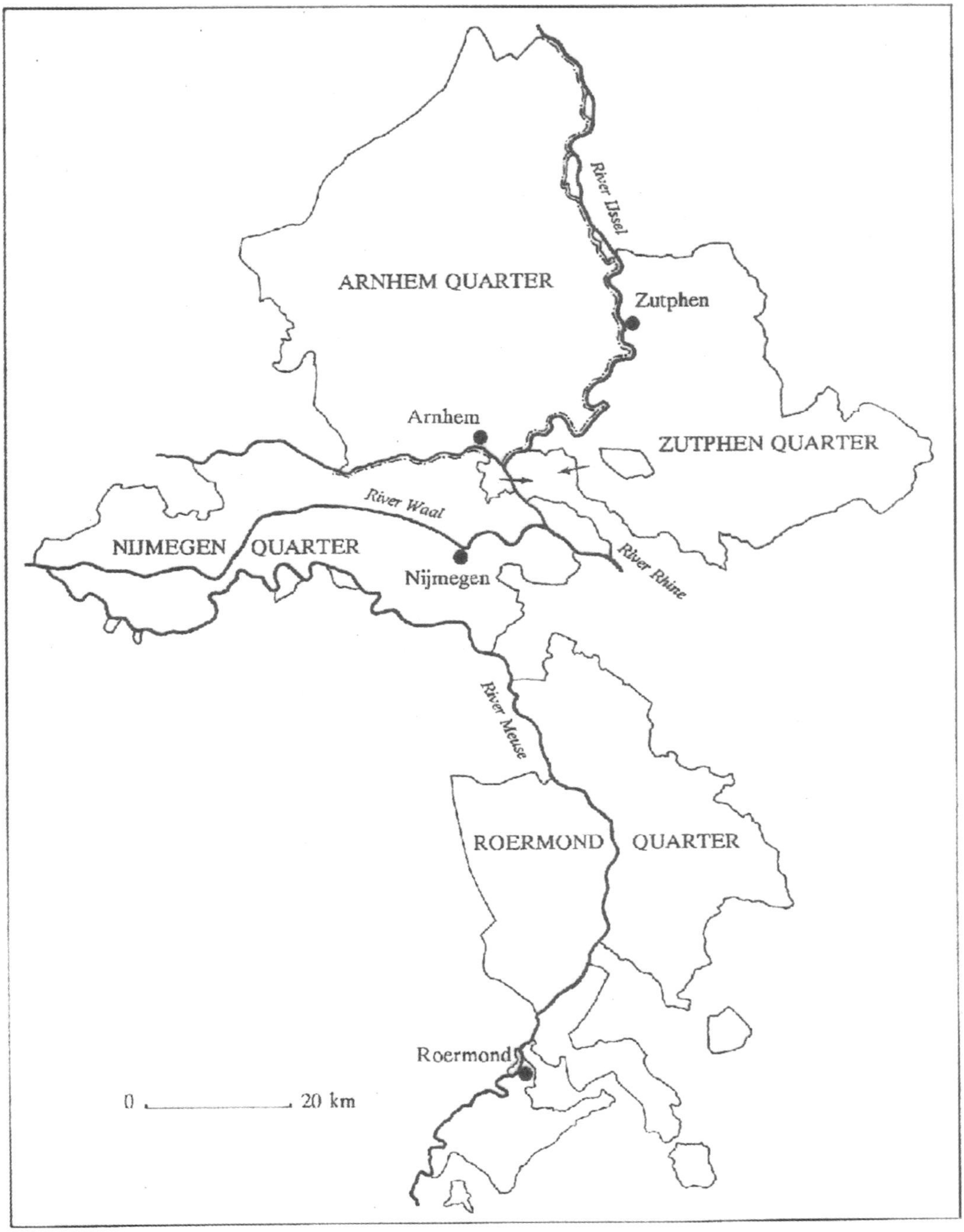

enabled the authorities to avail themselves of capital without having to turn to Jews or Lombards, who lent money at very high interest rates. Indeed, as I have pointed out elsewhere, by the beginning of the 15th century, in the Eastern Netherlands the role of Jews and Lombards as moneylenders had completely ceased, although until the last decades of the 15th century several Jewish families, living mainly in the borderland of Guelders and Cleves, apparently remained active by issuing loans on pledged security to customers from the lower social classes as well[9]. Finally, by using this instrument, direct taxation of the wealth of citizens or an increase in indirect taxes, such as excise tax – which could easily spark off social unrest – could be avoided. Therefore, the large-scale sale of annuities was used, particularly in towns where direct taxation and forced loans rarely occurred[10].

The acquisition of extra income and the resultant debt was not always motivated by an acute lack of liquid assets. Part of it could also be intended for the redemption of earlier loans by means of issuing new annuities at a lower interest rate. Whereas initially the payment of such annuities was charged to certain urban revenues, for example in Zutphen the sale of *gruit* (a herb mixture used in the preparation of beer), we can observe that, in time, for whatever reason, this particular basis was replaced by the town's total wealth. Two forms of annuities (*pensiones*, or *pensien* in Middle Dutch) can be distinguished: life annuities and perpetual annuities. Perpetual or heritable annuities (*erfrenten* or *erfgeld*, also called *pensie* in the municipal accounts) were only advantageous as a financing instrument if they were redeemable, otherwise a town would be landed with a debt for all time. The interest rate for perpetual annuities was always lower than that for life annuities. In Zutphen, the interest rate for perpetual annuities was generally 6.25%, although they were also sold at 5%, and that for life annuities 10%[11]. Life annuities (*lijfrenten* or *lijfgeld)*, issued for the duration of the life of the buyer or of his assignee, were finite. This also applied if two lives were covered under the terms of the contract, although the latter situation did not occur very often. Examples of this, all dating from 1459, include a sale to a married couple made on condition that if one of them passed away the amount would be halved, a sale to a woman on condition that if she died her niece would be the rightful assignee, and finally a sale to a mother and daughter covering both lives[12].

This is why life annuities were only sold to people over a certain age in some South-German towns in order to prevent the credits thus acquired from causing debts for too long a period thus putting the seller of the annuity at a disadvantage. In Augsburg in 1457, for example, it was decided that life annuities could only be sold to people aged 40 and over. In Nuremberg the town government took steps to ensure that life annuities were not sold to persons under 60. Such conditions, however, are not known in the case of Zutphen. The higher payment of interest – in other words, the higher interest rate – of life annuities compared to that of perpetual annuities, assuming they were sold at the same price, can be considered as an invisible amortisation rate of the standing debt. Therefore, life

9 R. van Schaïk, "On the social position of Jews and Lombards in the towns of the Low Countries and neighbouring German territories during the late Middle Ages", in M. Carlier a.o. (eds.), *Core and periphery in late medieval urban society. Proceedings of the colloquium at Ghent (22nd-23rd August 1996)*, Louvain/Apeldoorn, 1997, pp. 165-191 (Studies in urban social, economic and political history of the medieval and modern Low Countries 7). See also: Chr. Cluse, *Studien zur Geschichte der Juden in den mittelalterlichen Niederlanden*, Hannover, 2000, pp. 116-171 (Forschungen zur Geschichte der Juden, Abt. A 10). A comparable loss of function in money-lending in Swiss towns during the first decades of the 15th century was observed by H.-J. Gilomen, "Aufnahme und Vertreibung von Juden in Schweizer Städten im Spätmittelalter", in H.-J. Gilomen, A.L. Head-König, A. Radeff (eds.), *Migration in die Städte. Ausschulss – Assimilierung – Integration. Multikulturalität*, Zürich, 2000, pp. 93-118 (Schweizerischen Gesellschaft für Wirtschafts- und Sozialgeschichte 16).

10 An example of the opposite is the case of Geldern: W. Kuppers, *Die Stadtrechnungen von Geldern 1386-1423. Einführung, Textausgabe, Register*, Geldern, 1993, pp. 97, 101-105 (Geldrisches Archiv II), although there, too, annuities were sold since the late 14th century, albeit on a relatively small scale.

11 In 1451 one life annuity was, by way of exception, sold at 12.5%, because the buyer was an old woman.

12 StA Zutphen, *OAZ*, n° 1345.

annuities were sold from time to time in order to redeem perpetual annuities[13]. This was also the case in Zutphen.

Life annuities appear to have been especially popular with private persons, both clerics and laymen, mostly from Zutphen and its surroundings, but from more distant regions as well. The large number of women buyers is remarkable, as is illustrated by Table I.

TABLE I. **Life annuities in Zutphen**

year	number of *renteniers*	clerics	laymen total	women	%	men	%
1421	208	28	180	112	62	68	38
1436	349	50	299	178	60	121	40

Among the buyers of perpetual annuities or *renteniers* (recipients of rents), however, there was a considerable number of institutions, such as monasteries, parish churches, chapters, hospitals, and religious fraternities.

TABLE II. **Perpetual annuities in Zutphen**

year	number of *renteniers*	institutions	%	laymen	%
1421	76	27	36	49	64
1436	64	37	58	27	42

Random examples taken from later years during the 15th and 16th centuries indicate a large though not constant percentage of institutions of the total number of perpetual annuities buyers. Several institutions, notably monasteries, were situated far away from Zutphen: in the region of the Lower Rhine (Duchy of Cleves, Cologne), Westphalia and the so-called *Oversticht* (the present-day province of Overijssel).

The perpetual annuities under discussion here are clearly different from ground rents (also called *erfrenten* or *tijnsen*) in the sense of usage fees, fees levied on fructiferous goods and real property. This type of ground or house rent, private rent versus public or communal rent, provides insight into comparative values and changes in the market for real estate. Several studies of the market for these rents were conducted in the 1970s and 1980s (e.g. studies on Hamburg and Lübeck or Ghent)[14].

13 E. Isenmann, *Die deutsche Stadt im Spätmittelalter 1250-1500. Stadtgestalt, Recht, Stadtregiment, Kirche, Gesellschaft, Wirtschaft*, Stuttgart, 1988, pp. 174-176.

14 R. Sprandel, "Der städtische Rentenmarkt in Nordwestdeutschland im Spätmittelalter", in H. Kellenbenz (ed.), *Öffentliche Finanzen und privates Kapital im späten Mittelalter und in der ersten Hälfte des 19. Jahrhunderts*, Stuttgart, 1971, pp. 14-23. K. Richter, *Untersuchungen zur Hamburger Wirtschafts- und Sozialgeschichte um 1300, unter besonderer Berücksichtigung der städtischen Rentengeschäfte 1291-1330*, Hamburg, 1971; H.J. Werner, *Handelskonjunkturen und Rentenmarkt am Beispiel der Stadt Hamburg um die Mitte des 14. Jahrhunderts*, Hamburg, 1972; H. Haberland, *Der Lübecker Renten- und Immobiliënmarkt in der Zeit von 1283-1315*, Lübeck, 1974. About Ghent: M. Boone, M. Dumon, B. Reusens, *Immobiliënmarkt, fiscaliteit en sociale ongelijkheid te Gent, 1483-1503*, Kortrijk-Heule, 1981 (Standen en Landen LXXVIII).

The municipal accounts of Zutphen

In Zutphen, separate accounts were kept for the payment of annuities for which, at least from 1381 onwards, one of the two town receivers bore special responsibility, the so-called *pensieambt.* Until 1381, one alderman (*schepen*) was in charge of and accountable for the treasury. As far as we can gather, he collected all regular urban revenues except those from the excise tax on wine and from the sale of *gruit*[15]. The excise tax on hops was also collected by *gruit* masters. The accounts of wine masters have not been preserved, but it is likely that they were in the charge of a separate treasury as well. From 1397 onwards the holder of the *pensieambt* was accountable for the collection of the excise on wine.

For this reason, in 1381 a new, more comprehensive treasury was created with its own administrator. After that there was a *pensieambt* in addition to the office of receiver, while the urban finances comprised two separate treasuries, each with its own well-defined receipts and expenditures. The annual account of 1381 is the earliest municipal account for Zutphen that has been preserved in the original. The first original account of the other fund dates only from 1445[16]. In addition, there are 17th century extracts, already mentioned above, made by burgomaster Gerhard Kreijnck. There is a small fragment of an account dating from around 1364, while a sheet containing financial settlements of 1356 and 1359 between the city and the receiver with regard to the latter's administration during previous years, indicates that the urban accounts must have been in existence from an earlier date[17].

From 1460 onwards, the holder of the *pensieambt* was called the second receiver (*onderrentmeester*) and the administrator of the other fund the first receiver (*overrentmeester).* Although these titles suggest the subordination of one administrator to the other, in actual practice this was never the case. As long as two members of the twelve-strong college of aldermen were in charge of the financial administration (for changes with regard to the administration in 1526, see below), there were two treasuries, each administered and accounted for separately.

It can be demonstrated that, as of 1330, the town regularly sold annual annuities funded by the revenue from *gruit*[18]. The right to sell *gruit* was initially a princely monopoly. Many towns had managed to get hold of this right early on by means of leasing or pawnbroking, as had Zutphen. From 1330 onwards, there must have been a separate treasury administered by the *gruit* masters. In Zutphen the cash balance of this treasury was probably included in the overall municipal account administered by the town's only receiver who bore financial responsibility at the time. We cannot prove this assumption since none of the receiver's accounts have been preserved in the original before 1381. Thanks to a 17th -century extract, something is known about this *gruit* master's account, though only from 1395. Apparently, a similar situation existed in Münster. According to the chamberlain's account of 1447/48 – as in Deventer, Münster receivers were called chamberlain (*cameraar)* – one of the two chamberlains recorded revenues from the *gruit* masters (*'Boringhe van den gruetheren'*), while according to another source annuities used to be charged to *gruit* revenues[19].

As a result of the fact that during the second half of the 14th century and the beginning of the 15th century the use and, consequently, the sale of *gruit* fell rapidly in favour of hops – in 1403 *gruit* revenues amounted to 290 lb., in 1421 to 50 lb., and in 1435 to as little as 9 lb.! – the town government

15 Wartena (ed.), *De stadsrekeningen*, p. x-xi.

16 In Zutphen the financial year ran from 22 February to 21 February of the next year, which was connected with the annual election of aldermen. From 1586 onwards the financial year for the first receiver started on 1 or 3 April, but for the second receiver the starting date remained 22 February.

17 StA Zutphen, *OAZ*, n° 1290.

18 StA Zutphen, *OAZ*, n° 1313 (reg. n° 93). This is relatively early, because a large town such as Cologne turned to the sale of annuities on a large scale as late as the end of the 14th century; payments were made from a special treasury, the so-called *Samtagsrentenkammer*. F. Irsigler, "Kölner Wirtschaft im Spätmittelalter", in H. Kellenbenz (ed.), *Zwei Jahrtausende Kölner Wirtschaft*, Cologne, 1975, II, p. 300.

19 W.J. Alberts (ed.), *Die Kämmereirechnungen der Stadt Münster über die Jahre 1447, 1448 und 1458*, Groningen, 1960, pp. 83-84, note 9 (Fontes Minores Medii Aevi XI).

had to look for an alternative source of income in order to honour its financial obligations as the latter by far exceeded the revenues[20]. In 1403, an amount of 424 lb. still had to be paid in perpetual annuities as well as 226 lb. in life annuities.

As long as *gruit* masters still existed – although this office had not yet completely disappeared, by 1400 it seemed to have become more or less superfluous – they still charged annuity payments to *gruit* revenues, but those annuities were entered separately in the accounts of the *pensieambt*. In 1421 no beneficiaries of life annuities charged to the sale of *gruit* were left alive and no separate entries were necessary any more. A final integration of the old and new annuities took place in 1426 in the accounts of the second receiver[21]. Of course there were still beneficiaries of perpetual annuities, although their number also declined steadily: in 1445 only 18 lb. had to be charged to *gruit* revenues. This was approximately 4% of the total burden of perpetual annuities for that year; in 1421 this percentage had been well over 23%. For from 1416 onwards as many perpetual annuities as possible were redeemed by the sale of new life annuities, because perpetual annuities imposed a too heavy burden on the town's finances[22].

The currency and steadiness of annuities

R. Wartena has explained and argued how the Zutphen town government hedged against the continuous devaluation of the currency at the time, which particularly affected long-term financial agreements in an unstable currency, such as annuities, but also long-term rents and leases[23]. Between 1371 and 1391 the value of Zutphen's unit of account, the Zutphen pound, had declined to one third of its former value against the gold coin. In 1391, the town government recognised this fact and from the beginning of that year the pound (lb.) was tied to a fixed exchange rate with the gold coin, the écu (the so-called *oude gouden schild*). Holders of annuity certificates (*rentebrieven*) were henceforth paid the equivalent of a fixed number of grammes of gold. Apparently the town government of Roermond had already taken measures of the same kind. Probably following the example of those two towns, Duke Reinald IV of Guelders (1402-1423), implemented a similar policy for his duchy in 1405. On this occasion an exception was made for Zutphen and Roermond. The fact that Zutphen had decided in favour of this valuation so much earlier must have contributed to the appeal of its annuity certificates in a wide area, far beyond the boundaries of the town and of the duchy, for between 1391 and 1405 the pound, as it was used elsewhere, had devalued again by 25%. Holders of annuity certificates from Zutphen were not affected by this development.

The town government of Zutphen held on to this steady pound until into the 1520s, when a switch was made to the – equally steady – florin. At the time of the transition from pound to florin, 1 florin was equivalent to 2.5 lb. It will therefore be sufficient to multiply the receipts and expenditures in the books by 2.5 in order to be able to correctly compare the periods before and after the transition.

20 About the transition from *gruit* beer to hopped and *kuite* beer in the Netherlands, see E. Aerts and R. Unger, "Brewing in the Low Countries", in E. Aerts, L.M. Cullen, R.G. Wilson (eds.), *Production, marketing and consumption of alcoholic beverages since the Late Middle Ages*, Louvain, 1990, pp. 92-101.

21 R. Wartena (ed.), *De stadsrekeningen*, pp. x-xi.

22 The year 1416, contrary to R. Wartena, "Het Zutphens pond en de val van de groot", in *Ondernemende geschiedenis. 22 Opstellen geschreven bij het afscheid van mr. H. van Riel*, The Hague, 1977, p. 47, and Wartena (ed.), *De stadsrekeningen*, p. xi, who mentioned the year 1418.

23 Wartena, "Het Zutphens pond", pp. 45-48.

Analysis of the annuity revenues and expenditures until the 1490s

Judging by its financial obligations in 1381, the town must have received already 30,900 lb. from the previous sale of annuity certificates. It is assumed here that the annual payment of life annuities was 10% of the principal and that of perpetual annuities 6.25%. Otherwise, the earliest mentions of regular sales of annuities in Zutphen date back to 1330 already. Taking into account the annual interest burden in the course of the 15th century, we must draw the conclusion that for a town like Zutphen the sale of annuities was of major importance for funding extraordinary expenditures (see Figures II and III).

FIG. II. **Revenues from the Total Sales of Life and Perpetual Annuities in Zutphen, in Zutphen LB., 1380-1521**

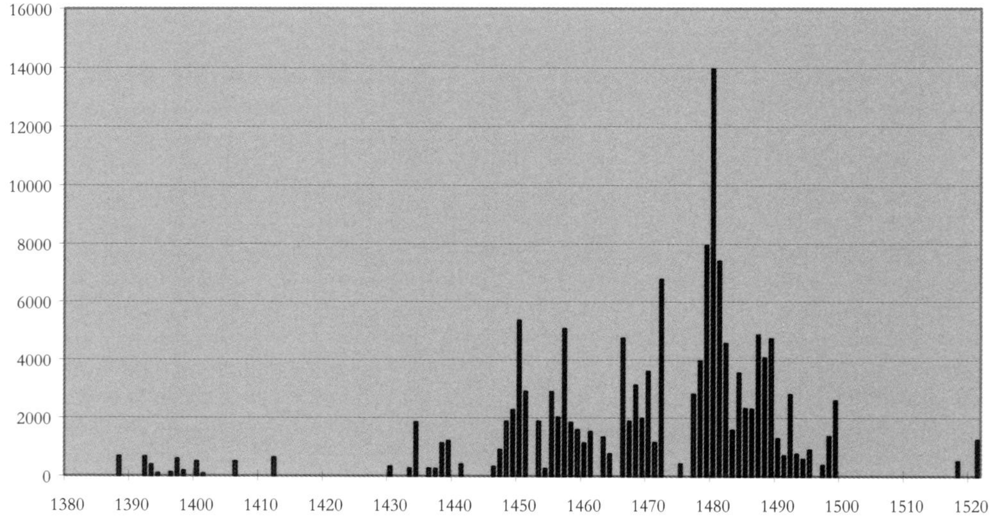

It can be demonstrated that from 1416 onwards, as I told, a start was made to redeem as many perpetual annuities as possible, because they imposed the heaviest burden on the town's finances as a result of their eternal character. The necessary funds came from the sale of new life annuities: '*van vercoften lijfgelde daer erfgelt weder mede gelost is*'[24]. The sale of life annuities entailed notably fewer risks as long as, on average, the beneficiaries did not live longer than could be expected on the basis of past experience. Apparently a temporarily heavier interest burden, which would decrease steadily with the decease of each beneficiary, was preferred to a lower but perpetual burden. Eventually, perpetual annuities were only paid to religious institutions, hospitals, etc. and similar foundations which were obviously ineligible for life annuities.

In around 1417 the town was still in a very strong position financially, which was reflected in the value of the Zutphen pound, which during that year reached its highest value in gold. In subsequent years, until 1422, the total interest burden showed a sharp decline. While the annuity

24 Wartena (ed.), *De stadsrekeningen*, pp. 242-243. This argument is also known from the case of Cologne during the years 1432-1473; see R. Knipping, "Das Schuldenwesen der Stadt Köln im 14. und 15. Jahrhundert", in *Westdeutsche Zeitschrift für Geschichte und Kunst*, 13 (1894), p. 361.

burden amounted to 5014 lb. by 1403, in 1422 it had decreased to 3780 lb. The rapid increase from 1423 onwards, on the other hand, may be related to the protracted political and military entanglements

FIG. III. **Revenues from the Sale of Life and Perpetual Annuities in Zutphen as a Percentage of the Total Urban Revenues, 1390-1521**

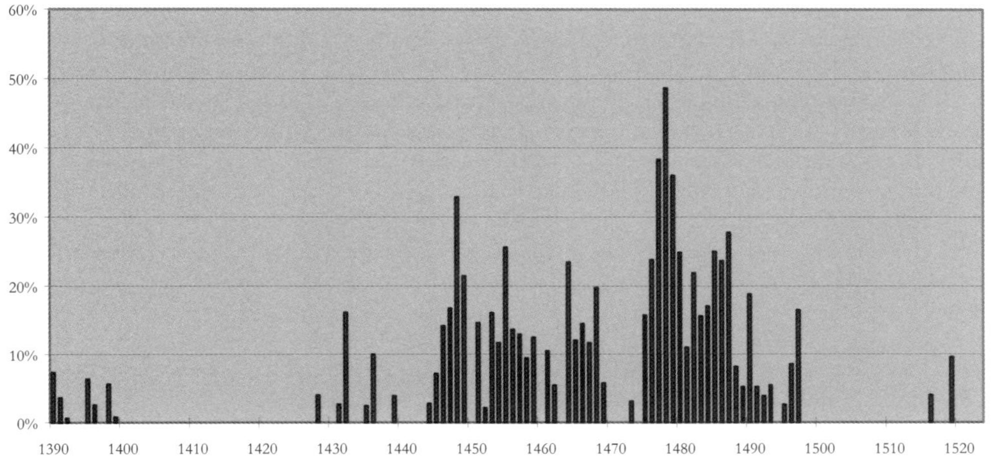

in the duchy since the accession of Duke Arnold of the House of Egmond. Thus, in 1445 the annuity burden had reached again the level of 1403 (Figure IV). In general, circumstances of this kind most often prompted town governments to look for additional sources of income.

FIG. IV. **Total Payments of Life and Perpetual annuities in Zutphen, in Zutphen LB., 1380-1600**

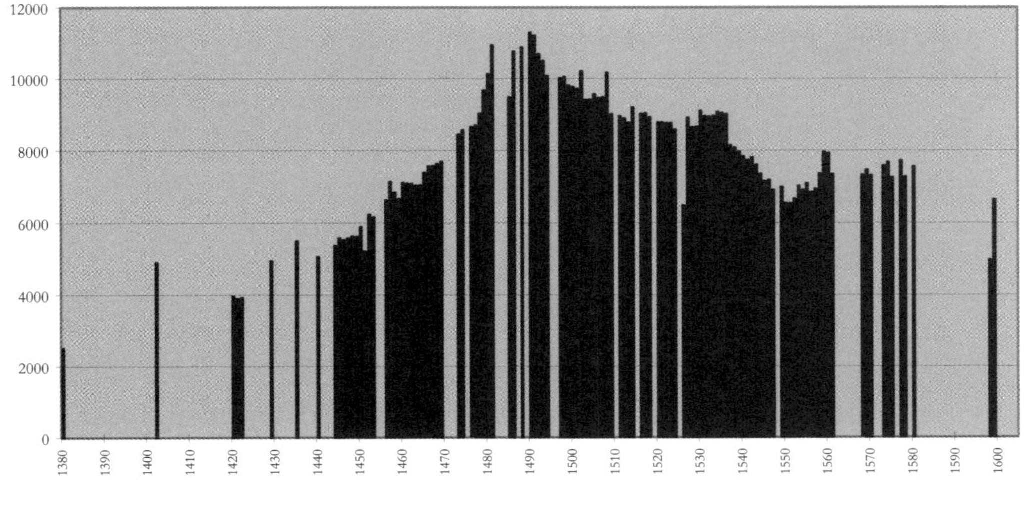

Nevertheless, other events or calamities could also occasionally lead to the decision to issue annuities. The following example is a case in point. According to an annuity certificate in the archives of the Spittaal, a convent in Zutphen that since the middle of the 15th century followed the third rule of St. Francis, on 30 April 1446 the convent community purchased a redeemable perpetual annuity of 5 Rhenish florins (*Rijnse guldens)* secured by urban receipts (*'uth onsser alingen stadtrenten, guederen ende opkommingen'*) which would be paid in biannual instalments, on St. Martin's Day (11 November) and May Day (in the accounts the entry was dated Whitsuntide). Judging from the contract this annuity could be redeemed at 5%. Mention was also made of the intention to use the capital thus received for the restoration of the Church of St. Walburg[25]. According to several narrative sources mostly written shortly after the event, for example an anonymous chronicle from Tiel (dated shortly before 1455) and the chronicle of the famous Thomas à Kempis from the monastery Agnietenberg near Zwolle (dated 1464-1471), on 10 April (Palm Sunday) the church tower had fallen down after being struck by lightning during stormy weather with hail, rain and sudden gusts of wind. More than ten lives were said to have been lost[26].

While during the first half of the 15th century there had been a strong preference for the issue of life annuities rather than perpetual annuities, during the second half of that century the tide turned (Figure V). Especially after 1447 a marked increase in the sale of annuities can be discerned (Figure II).

FIG. V. **Revenues from the Sale of Annuities, Life and Perpetual Annuities Separately in Zutphen, in Zutphen LB., 1440-1521**

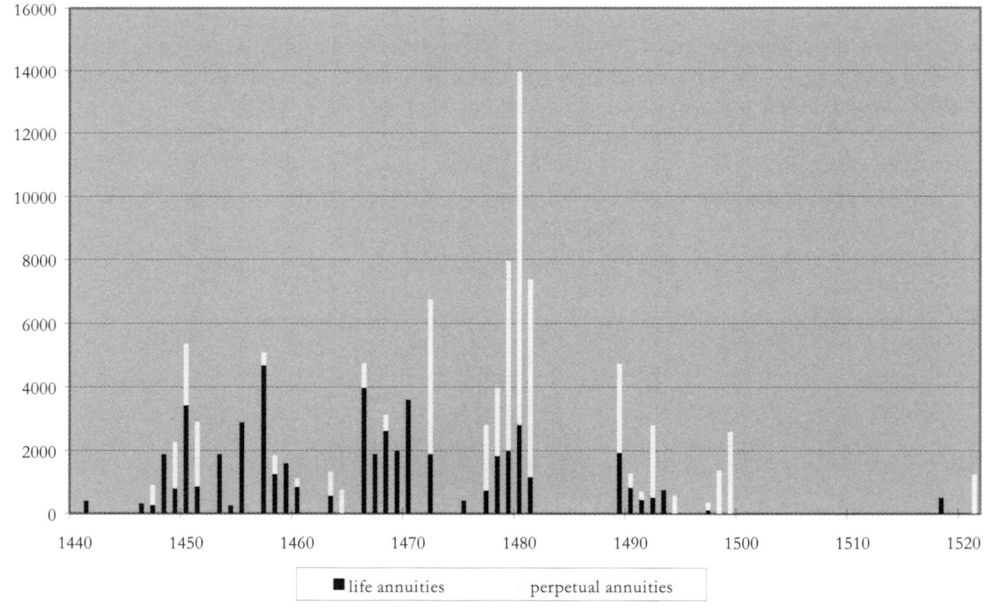

25 StA Zutphen, *Spittaal,* n° 112 (reg. n° 700): orig. (copy dating from c. 1500 in *Spittaal*, n° 1, and from the 2nd half of the 16th century in an urban copy book of annuity certificates, *OAZ*, n° 1331, fol. 47).

26 *Auctoris incerti Chronicon Tielense*, J.D. van Leeuwen (ed.), Utrecht, 1789, pp. 545-546, translation into Dutch with an introduction by J. Kuys a.o., *De Tielse kroniek. Een geschiedenis van de Lage Landen van de Volksverhuizingen tot het midden van de vijftiende eeuw, met een vervolg over de jaren 1552-1566*, Amsterdam, 1983, p. 170 (§ 868). "Chronicon Montis Sanctis Agnetis", in *Thomae Hemerken a Kempis Opera Omnia*, M.I. Pohl (ed.), Freiburg i.Br., 1922, VII, pp. 416-417. The Cologne chronicle of Johann Koelhof (1499), mentions 13 victims: edition in *Chroniken der niederheinischen Städte. Cöln*, Leipzig, 1877, III, p. 786.

The issue of perpetual annuities in particular entailed an increase in the town's indebtedness with long-term consequences, unless it was thought that perpetual annuities could somehow be redeemed soon. In any case, for one reason or another, Zutphen was not able to sustain its policy of avoiding the further sale of perpetual annuities. Whereas in 1445 only 530 lb. had to be paid in perpetual annuities, compared to 4,820 lb. in life annuities, by 1470 the interest burden for perpetual annuities already amounted to 1,373 lb., compared to 6,312 lb. for life annuities, and by 1500 to 5,467 lb. compared to 4,340 lb. for life annuities.

We must assume that in periods when the town's financial situation deteriorated, the purchase of life annuities stagnated or declined, whereas the issue of perpetual annuities – in spite of lower interest rates but thanks to the prospect of long-term payments – still attracted new financial backers.

In the period until about 1470, when the independence of the Duchy of Guelders – already under great pressure as a result of the continuous strife between Duke Arnold of Egmond and his son Adolf, who was eager to assume power – was increasingly threatened by the expansionist designs of Charles the Bold, Duke of Burgundy and his ally the Duke of Cleves, there was an enormous peak in the sale of annuities for the year 1460. This peak can be explained by the extra income the town had to obtain in order to comply with the Treaty of Batenburg of 13 October 1459, a treaty intended to maintain the unity of the duchy. In the Zutphen archives a record can be found of the annuities owed by the town as a result of the 3,000 Rhenish florins it had to raise in defense of the regional interest[27]. Within less than eight weeks, the town was to provide Adolf and his father Arnold with one third of the total sum of 3,000 florins which had been promised to father and son together (that is, 1,000 to Adolf and 2,000 to Arnold)[28]. The duchy's other three capitals had also committed themselves to paying 3,000 Rhenish florins each[29]. In other words, the town was in need of funds at very short notice. These funds were obtained by the sale of perpetual annuities, but, judging from the subscriptions, life annuities as well. As a matter of fact, this sum was later deducted from the next ducal direct tax, a so-called *pondschatting*, and was therefore considered an advance payment[30]. Receipts show that by 11 February 1460 Zutphen had in any case supplied Arnold with the full amount of 2,000 Rhenish florins[31]. According to entries in this register, which runs from 1478 to 1503, perpetual annuities were either sold at 6.25% or 5%.

The fact that after that time the sale of annuities (life annuities and perpetual annuities) continued unabated and debts accumulated can hardly come as a surprise, bearing in mind the political and military situation as well as the related economic circumstances during the last quarter of the 15th century (Figure VI). The interest burden for 1477, for example, amounted to as much as 50% and for 1479 to 85% (!) of the total expenditure (Figure VII). For that matter, the economic situation in a large part of the Netherlands during this period has been described as a time of crisis due to at least two or three periods of extremely high corn prices resulting from poor harvests, trade blockades and a number of severe epidemics[32]. The Duchy of Guelders – including Zutphen – had to endure two occupations by the Burgundians: from 1473 to 1477 and from 1481 to 1492. Zutphen was insolvent during the last decades of the 15th century. Many interests could not be paid in time and were postponed: complaints flooded in[33].

---

27 StA Zutphen, *OAZ*, n° 1345 (starting at the end of 1459 and continuing until 1503).
28 StA Zutphen, *OAZ*, n° 737.
29 See W.J. Alberts, *De Staten van Gelre en Zutphen*, Groningen-Djakarta, 1956, II, pp. 4-6 (Bijdragen van het Instituut voor Middeleeuwse Geschiedenis der Rijksuniversiteit te Utrecht XXIX).
30 I.A. Nijhoff, *Gedenkwaardigheden uit de geschiedenis van Gelderland*, The Hague, 1830-1875, IV, n° 345.
31 StA Zutphen, oaz, n° 737, 892 (reg. n° 834-836, 839).
32 W. Kuppers and R. van Schaïk, "Levensstandaard en stedelijke economie te Zutphen in de 15de en 16de eeuw", in *Bijdragen en Mededelingen Gelre*, 72 (1981), pp. 16-18, 20-24.
33 StA Zutphen, *OAZ*, *Brieven*, reg. n° 386a, 538, 825.

FIG. VI. **Payments of Annuities Life and Perpetual Annuities Separately in Zutphen, in Zutphen LB., 1420-1581**

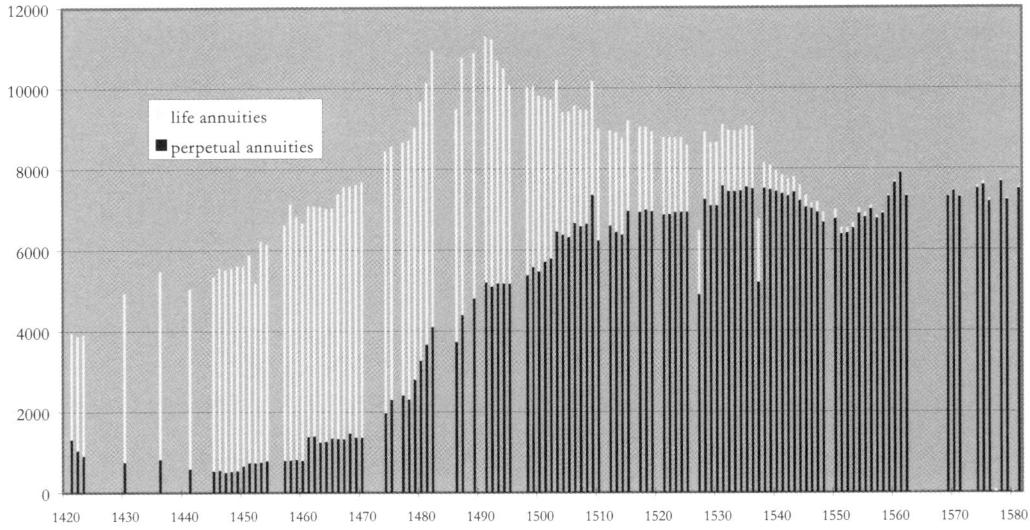

In summary, it has been found that from about 1460 onwards financial problems in Zutphen first came to a head as a result of the strife between the duke and his son, which led to the outbreak of war in Guelders. The crisis deepened due to the Burgundian threat, the Burgundian occupations and the ensuing struggle to throw off the Burgundian yoke.

FIG. VII. **Payments of Life and Perpetual Annuities in Zutphen as a Percentage of the Overall Urban Expenditure, 1400-1600**

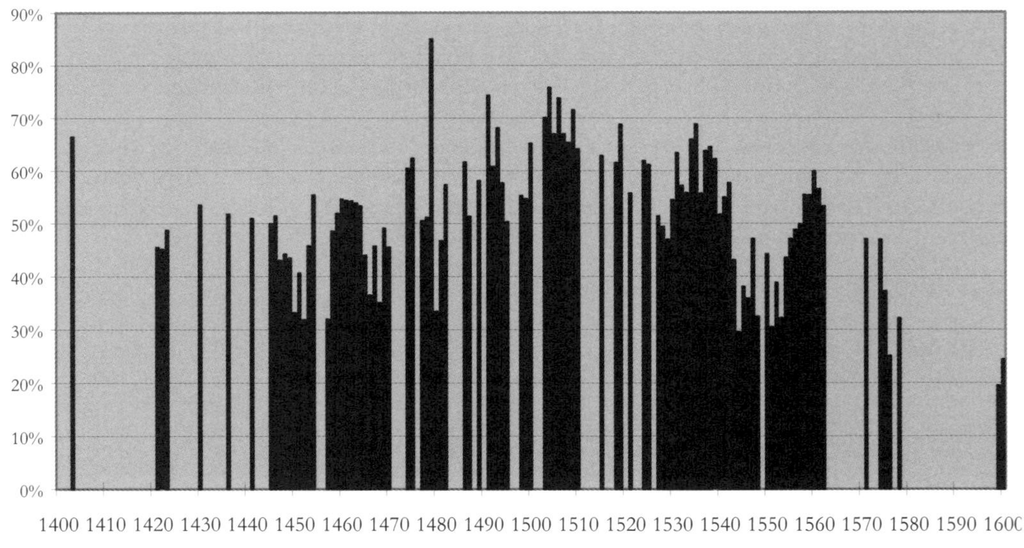

Annuity revenues and expenditures from the 1490s to 1543

Immediately after the duchy had regained its independence, as early as 1493, a sudden, radical change occurred in the town's financial policy. In 1493, no perpetual annuities were sold, although life annuities were sold to the amount of 758 lb. In 1494 perpetual annuities to the amount of 584 lb. were sold yet again, but no life annuities. The accounts for 1495 have not been kept. In the ledgers for 1496 both sections remained blank, therefore there were no transactions. In 1497, 258 lb. worth of perpetual annuities and 111 lb. of life annuities were sold. From 1498 to 1517 no more life annuities were sold; in 1518 sales amounted to 506 lb., and from 1519 into the end of the 16th century the sale of life annuities came to a standstill. Perpetual annuities were still sold in 1498 (1372 lb.) and 1499 (2583 lb.), but from then until 1600 (apart from an occasional issue in 1521 to the amount of 1253 lb.), no more annuities were sold (Figure V).

In 1492 annuity payments amounted to as much as 60.7% of the town's total expenditure for that year! The financial burden for the 1490s included, for example, the maintenance of the cavalry who were fighting in the war against the towns of the *Oversticht* and the payment of an unprecedentedly large series of direct taxes, levied on all the ducal lands, to ransom Bernard of Meurs who was held hostage by the French. Bernard had taken the place of Charles of Egmond so that the latter could be inaugurated as the new Duke of Guelders in 1492. Charles, however, had great difficulty in building on this regained independence[34]. His attempts entailed an enormously increased tax burden for the whole country, among other things through raising the number of direct taxes (*pondschattingen*), as well as through frequent military campaigns for which the towns of the duchy were expected to supply the material and financial means, if not the men to fight in the army, which was increasingly made up of mercenaries. The bottom of his own ducal coffers had long been reached.

As a consequence, in the short term the burden of Zutphen's public debt did not diminish at all. In long term, however, the debt diminished significantly, although slowly (Figure IV).

Zutphen's internal problems during the years 1493-1543

The sudden change of policy in the 1490s in the long tradition of continual annuity sales, resulting in the termination of new annuity issues until 1545, has to be related to the political troubles in Zutphen during 1493 and 1494. To a large extent those troubles originated in the complete failure of the town's financial policy which, in turn, was related to the long-lasting state of war. Generally speaking, political and social troubles often led to a hostile attitude to any form of credit. Many examples are known of towns that became bankrupt[35].

From the end of the 15th century onwards, the political influence of citizens' deputies or commons (*gemeenslieden*) was growing. Since 1446, the political activities of the college of commons, which had been in existence for quite a long time (its role in the town's financial audit was recorded for the first time in 1412), and of all craft guilds had been radically suppressed[36]. It was obvious that something was afoot around 1490, although it is not clear what was at the root of this development. It is certainly conceivable that general political changes at the time played a part. In fact there were first signs of a renewed political involvement with the town's government on the part of commons and

34 van Schaïk, "Taxation", pp. 264-271.

35 H.-J. Gilomen, "Anleihen und Steuern in der Finanzwirtschaft spätmittelalterlicher Städte, Option bei drohendem Dissens", in S. Guex, M. Körner, J. Tanner (eds.), *Staatsfinanzierung und Sozialkonflikte (14.-20. Jh.)*, Zürich, 1994, pp. 137-158 (Schweizerischen Gesellschaft für Wirtschafts- und Sozialgeschichte 12).

36 R. van Schaïk, "Zutphens geschiedenis: van de elfde tot het einde van de zestiende eeuw", in W.Th.M. Frijhoff a.o. (eds.), *Geschiedenis van Zutphen*, Zutphen, 1989, p. 74.

craft guilds. As is mentioned above, it had previously not been possible for pressure groups to influence the political and financial administration. This was the result of the essentially closed character of the town government[37]. In any case, it seems to be a fact that the rapidly increasing financial and military burden on the town's wealth, which already carried an enormous debt, led to protest on the part of the citizens. This can be gathered from documents dating back to 1493. There were probably disturbances. On this occasion the citizens demanded, among other things, the election of the first receiver for a four-year term of office instead of the usual annual changeover, a stricter control of urban finances, a limitation of expenses of office, a more effective enforcement of urban bylaws, and a more stringent maintenance of brewing privileges. This list of demands has been preserved[38]. Andries of Haaften, town secretary since 1486, was dismissed. In February 1494 he made a request to the magistrate that he should be allowed to stay on as an official of the chancellery[39]. It is conceivable that general disaffection with the dire economic situation of the time sought a political outlet and that the incumbent town government was made a scapegoat. Henceforth express mention was made of the citizenry when important administrative decisions were taken. On 11 March 1494 four citizens sealed a temporary, six-year increase of urban taxes on the use of mills and on the sale of wine and beer, agreed with the consent of the citizenry. It was also decided to sell off urban domains in order to obtain ready cash.

Apparently, the citizens' demand to elect the first receiver for a period of four years was not met – the newly appointed receiver Andries of Holthuizen only performed his duties in 1493/94 and then not again until 1496/97. Nevertheless, all this appears to have led to the establishment of the "college of the eighteen" made up of two church wardens together with four commons, who probably also represented the craft guilds, from each of the *vierdelen*. The *vierdelen* refer to the four quarters of the Old Town (Oudstad): Mommenhave, Waterstraat, Barleheze and Grote en Kleine Wand. Remarkably, the suburban quarters of Nieuwstad (dating from the late 13th century) and Spittaalstad (grown in the course of the 14th century) were not represented[40].

Meanwhile, the sixteen commons and two church wardens acquired such a measure of influence that they were also involved in external political and diplomatic matters. Internal and external political interests were closely interwoven. The crucial question, however, remained the supervision and control of the town's finances[41]. In particular, the town government had to fight hard for the implementation of new taxes to reduce the deficit. For that reason, in 1500 the commons were consulted about the introduction of a levy of surcharges on the existing beer excise (the so-called tax on firedogs). In 1502 representatives not only from the council but also from the craft guilds were invited to Arnhem in order to discuss military matters together with the towns of Arnhem and Nijmegen. There is a list dating from 1505 containing twenty commons, five for each quarter, appointed by the citizenry to discuss all important issues with the council. The fact that the deputation was made up of twenty people appears to have been coincidental. During the audit of the annual accounts for 1507, which did not take place until 1526 (!), "according to the old custom" (this probably refers to the practice since 1494), the college of eighteen were present. All this justifies the conclusion that the citizens had meanwhile managed to consolidate their influence and, formally speaking, had a say in political, military and financial matters. With regard to financial issues, no doubt the citizens and

37 See the comparative study on Ghent, Dordrecht, Rotterdam and Zutphen by W.P. Blockmans, "Mobiliteit in stadsbesturen 1400-1550", in D.E.H. de Boer and J.W. Marsilje (eds.), *De Nederlanden in de late middeleeuwen*, Utrecht, 1987, pp. 236-260, especially 251-254.

38 van Schaïk, "Zutphens geschiedenis", pp. 75-76.

39 J.F. Benders, "Andries van Haeften", in *Biografisch woordenboek van Gelderland*, Hilversum, 1998, I, pp. 46-48.

40 This could be an indication of a difference in (legal) status – as yet never studied in detail – between the citizens of the original city and those of the new quarters, built in the late 13th and 14th centuries; be that as it may, Oudstad and Nieuwstad had been legally united in 1312.

41 About the involvement of the commons in financial and political matters until 1543, see van Schaïk, "Zutphens geschiedenis", pp. 77-79.

craft guilds brought pressure to bear on the town government to put an end to the existing annuity policy with its disastrous outcome. This was however only a first step.

The fact that the accounts for 1507 were not finalised until 1526 may on the one hand be considered an omen. Apparently it required a lot of effort for outsiders to gain insight into the financial administration of earlier years. On the other hand, the year 1526 is significant because from exactly that year onwards the influence of the citizens increased further. Clearly the supervisory powers of the college of eighteen, which had to be consulted by the magistracy about all matters, were no longer considered sufficient. In fact, 1526 was the beginning of a new phase. In the course of that year the political problems only became worse and violent riots broke out when the population heard the news that one of the officials of Duke Charles had, on the latter's orders, begun to collect a *pondschatting* in Warken, a village near Zutphen, without previous consultation. According to the usual procedure, *pondschattingen* could only be levied after prior consent by each of the quarters of the duchy. Pent up aversion to the extravagant ducal policies was released in a serious incident. The official in question was captured and imprisoned in the town hall. Subsequently the duke declared Zutphen disloyal and perjurious. The town government was at a loss as to what to do and was caught in an awkward position between the two sides. On 7 December 1526 it asked the duke's forgiveness for the riots and begged him to have mercy on the imprisoned burgomaster Arnt Slindewater, who had, in all probability, been captured by the duke at Arnhem by way of reprisal. In order to face up to the opposition, the town government had to make concessions to the other side as well. On 18 December it was decreed by the burgomaster, aldermen, councillors, the "eighteen" and the entire citizenry that guild statutes had to be observed rigorously, and that judges had to return a verdict on all cases which subsequently had to be proclaimed to the commons. Although the guilds were mentioned explicitly, they did not yet acquire any formal political influence. That would not happen until 1538.

Remarkably enough, in 1526 the considerable political influence of the guilds in Utrecht was brought to an end after a period of heavy social unrest which had started at the end of 1521. Here, too, financial matters, notably the redeeming of the public debt and the control of the issue of annuities, were the bone of contention. The guilds had claimed full control of the municipal accounts for the years 1511 until 1525, but in August 1525 their influence was curtailed again[42]. In 1528, the guilds government was abolished as a whole by Emperor Charles V when he put an end to the secular power of the Bishop of Utrecht[43].

It is evident that the rebelliousness on the part of the Zutphen population was not only directed against the duke but also against its own town government. Henceforth four commons were to collect the rent of urban domains and administer the town's finances. In addition, two commons were also appointed first receiver and second receiver. In other words, the responsibility for the town's finances was taken away from the college of aldermen, while two commons took over as receivers without joining the college of aldermen themselves. This was really an important step. In Deventer the commons had not managed to attain a similar position, although here, too, the 24 commons had a considerable say in the town's financial affairs. From 1513 onwards, they were represented in the so-called *Achtenkamer*, a mixed committee of eight made up of aldermen, councillors and commons, appointed to make payments of annuities on behalf of the town government. In 1518 it was decided that four aldermen and councillors and eight commons would be members of this Achtenkamer, which

---

42 About the guilds revolt in Utrecht, see the two papers of C.A. van Kalveen: "De gildenbeweging van april 1525 en haar voorgeschiedenis", in *Jaarboek Oud-Utrecht*, 1972, pp. 93-114, and "Bijdrage tot de geschiedenis van de gildenbewegingen te Utrecht, mei-augustus 1525", in *Jaarboek Oud-Utrecht*, 1979, pp. 54-86.

43 P. Lourens and J. Lucassen, "De oprichting en ontwikkeling van ambachtsgilden in Nederland (13de-19de eeuw)", in C. Lis and H. Soly (eds.), *Werelden van verschil. Ambachtsgilden in de Lage Landen*, Brussels, 1997, p. 48.

would become a standing committee controlled by the 24 commons. Overall, however, the influence of the commons in financial affairs remained restricted[44].

From about 1532 onwards a new period of turmoil began in Zutphen. It is not necessary here to dwell on the ins and outs of this period of time. Suffice it to say that the foreign policy of Duke Charles with all its financial consequences provoked more and more resistance in his own duchy. More importantly, the financial doings of Zutphen's town government, which was no longer in charge of the financial administration, gradually threatened to lead the town towards bankruptcy. This was obvious to everyone, not only to the insiders. The magistrates were probably the last to sense that something was up. Whether or not pressurized by commons in their supervisory capacity, in 1535 the magistracy proceeded to draw up a centenary survey of the town's receipts and expenditure. A selection from the annual accounts for the years from 1402 to 1502 was used[45]. Apparently it was thought that the cause of the extremely high expenses could be traced back to this period. This is also implied by the fact that for a large number of years, particularly from 1480 to 1502, the amounts paid in annuities were written down. The survey is not very accurate in this respect – according to accompanying notes the majority of the amounts are qualified as "approximately". Even if the magistracy had been able to put their finger on the problem – contracting loans during the last quarter of the 15th century which would later lead to an unacceptably heavy interest burden could certainly qualify as a problem – it was simply not possible to eliminate this cause in order to nullify its pernicious effects. Obviously, conclusions of this kind were not limited to the "inner circle". Social unrest increased day by day. The direct influence of the guilds first manifested itself in 1538 when, after a violent occupation by ducal troops, the town government had been driven into a tight corner and skirmishes broke out between urban mercenaries and ducal troops. Agitation among the population in other towns in Guelders, such as Nijmegen, as well, finally forced Duke Charles to pack his bags and make way for his successor William, the son of the Duke of Cleves and Jülich. However, William was not able counter the widespread discord in his territory. This was the start of the third and last phase in the process of interference in politics.

On the face of it, external factors seem to have been decisive in provoking the revolt in Zutphen, but probably nothing was further from the truth. External factors may be regarded as a mere red herring. Hardly had the old duke died and the new duke been inaugurated when, in 1538, serious internal strife broke out in Zutphen[46]. This time the internal problems could come to the fore, and the last episode in the process of the growing political influence of citizens could unfold. It is possible that the revolutionary agitation in Deventer in the years 1526-1528 may have played a role, although there is no hard evidence of real influence from Deventer[47]. Maybe even the appearance of Anabaptists in numerous towns had to do something with these events. This cannot be proved in the case of Zutphen, although there are indications that Anabaptists were active in Zutphen around this time[48]. In any case, under the leadership of the guilds the magistracy was urged to put things right once and for all with regard to the town's finances, organisation of the craft guilds and the election of the magistracy[49]. By sweating it out, playing for time and making minor concessions, the incumbent magistracy staved off the inevitable for as long as possible. However, this only had the effect of making

44 C.A. van Kalveen, "De Deventer gemeente tijdens oorlog en burgeroproer 1482-1528", in *Overijsselse Historische Bijdragen*, 94 (1979), pp. 30-70. About the previous history of this college of commons: C.A. van Kalveen, "Uit de geschiedenis van de Deventer gemeente tot omstreeks 1481", in *Overijsselse Historische Bijdragen*, 92 (1977), pp. 25-59.

45 StA Zutphen, *OAZ*, n° 1332.

46 C.O.A. Schimmelpenninck van der Oije, "Het optreden der gemeenslieden te Zutphen, 1538-1543", in *Bijdragen en Mededelingen Gelre*, 65 (1971), pp. 39-83.

47 About the agitation of the commons in Deventer, see van Kalveen, "De Deventer gemeente", pp. 65-68.

48 H.D. Wessels, "Ketterij in de Graafschap. Uitingen van afwijkend kerkelijk-godsdienstig gedrag in de Graafschap Zutphen in de beginfase van de vroege Reformatie", in *Bijdragen en Mededelingen Gelre*, 71 (1980), pp. 63-65.

49 A comparable observation was made for Zwolle in the years 1523-1530; see F.C. Berkenvelder, "De gilden te Zwolle tot 1600", in *Overijsselse Historische Bijdragen*, 104 (1989), pp. 7-33, and F.C. Berkenvelder, "De gilden te Zutphen en Zwolle tot 1600", in *Zutphen*, 13 (1994), p. 31.

the radicals, led by Jan Pelser and Jan sGraven, more radical. By 22 February 1539 tensions were running so high that the magistracy found it had backed itself into a corner. First they met the demand for a sound system of financial accountability, followed by the demand for political recognition of ten craft guilds, in international context in fact a rather late phenomenon. However, the third demand, which concerned direct influence on the appointment of aldermen, affected the tradition which had existed since 1330 and therefore the very nature of the political system – the closed character of the town's government. On 22 February, 44 commons from the citizens, two from each of the ten guilds and six from each of the four urban quarters, confidently entered the council chamber in order to participate in the elections. The die was cast; as one man the town magistrates laid down their keys and retired to the nearby castle-town of Bronkhorst, which was assumed to be safe.

Duke William, who had announced that he would be present in Zutphen in order to "monitor" the election of aldermen, dared not show his face. A power vacuum had been created which was in fact to continue until 1543, when Emperor Charles V took control of the government of the duchy of Guelders and restored order. In this process the temporary political influence of the craft guilds was nullified while the influence of the college of commons was restricted. The old magistrate families could return to their soft seats in the council chamber. Meanwhile, the citizens' revolt had become bogged down in a fight over personal interests which increasingly stood in the way of the realisation of the original aims. Thus Zutphen's revolt suffered the same fate as so many revolutionary movements in the course of history. In other words, the position of the commons, which had previously been relatively strong, weakened after 1543[50].

Annuities since 1543

Under the new circumstances the traditional magistrate families appear to have learned from history. They did not revert to the same financial practices as those that had been abandoned decades earlier. The consequence of all this was that the total of Zutphen's indebtedness resulting from annuity payments, which had slowly declined since 1500, did not diminish further but stabilised until 1581 (see Figures IV and VI). No accounts of the second receiver are available for the years from 1582 to 1599. Most of these had probably already disappeared when Gerhard Kreijnck made his extracts in the second half of the 17th century. There are only extracts of the accounts for 1582 and for 1595 to 1598 to give us some compensation for this lack of data. The town's interest payments for life annuities accounted for in 1599 and 1600 amounted to zero, while those for perpetual annuities had diminished considerably – by one third – during the years 1581 to 1600. Some fluctuations in the annual payments can be ascribed to back debts.

It seems that Zutphen's traditional annuity policy gradually came to an end. It is unknown to what extent attempts were still being made to sell annuities in order to generate extra revenues, but if so, these attempts would have had little success. Zutphen's financial situation deteriorated during the 16th century and the town moved more and more towards insolvency. By the end of the 16th century Zutphen's economic condition was at its worst: the town was utterly impoverished and depopulated[51].

50 W.Th.M. Frijhoff, "Geschiedenis als strijdbijl. Burgerij, gemeenslieden en magistraat in Zutphen (vijftiende tot achttiende eeuw)", in B. Looper and J.C. Riemens (eds.), *Geschiedenis in Zutphen. Over geschiedschrijving, geschiedbeoefening en historisch besef. Opstellen aangeboden aan drs. M.M. Doornink-Hoogenraad*, Zutphen, 1988, pp. 44-46.

51 van Schaïk, "Zutphens geschiedenis", pp. 62-64, 66, 69, and W. Frijhoff, "Zutphens geschiedenis, 1591-1814", in Frijhoff a.o. (eds.), *Geschiedenis van Zutphen*, Zutphen, 1989, pp. 85-86.

Conclusions

In the course of the 14th century, which was comparatively early, the town of Zutphen started selling life annuities and perpetual annuities as a means to augment urban income. This happened at a time when, because of its commercial position, the town enjoyed a high degree of confidence not only with local citizens but also with citizens and institutions for miles around. From the accounts of selling prices and payments of annuities, which were kept meticulously, it appears that until the middle of the 15th century the level of indebtedness could be controlled reasonably well, although during the first half of the 15th century the burden of debt could already be considered substantial since it accounted for 40 to 50% of the town's total annual expenditure. As far as is known, these payments were disbursed from a separate treasury which had initially been fed by *gruit* revenues and excise tax on wine. Nonetheless, both treasuries, which together formed the overall urban finances, functioned as communicating vessels. In this early period the town government appeared to prefer life annuities, with their short-term effect, to perpetual annuities. In view of the frequency of the sales and the size of the interest burden it can be argued that already during this period the issue of annuities was used as a structural financing instrument. Although generally the extra revenues were earmarked for specific purposes, it is also evident that they were necessary to sustain the town's high levels of expenditure. Particularly the building and maintenance of public works and the town's contribution to the duchy's defence were important considerations, which, incidentally, did not mean that the town lost sight of its own interests as one of the duchy's capitals, which included building up an independent position vis-à-vis the Duke of Guelders.

During the second half of the 15th century the sale of perpetual annuities rapidly outstripped that of life annuities while, at the same time, annuity sales were being stepped up, thus causing a substantial long-term public debt. The intensification of annuity sales was closely related to increasing politico-military and economic problems in the region which would culminate in a full-scale crisis during the last quarter of the 15th century. The sale of annuities became ever more necessary in order to finance either the duchy's independence or the burden of enemy occupation, while the debt burden was increasingly felt as a millstone around the town's neck. In the 1490s the situation had in fact got out of control. From that time onwards the town government's financial management gave rise to opposition on the part of urban interest groups. In three phases between 1493 and 1543, the influence of those groups, represented by commons and, increasingly, the guilds, on financial and political matters gradually became more significant. In this entire process the restriction and subsequent cessation of annuity sales was an important issue. However, it would take the entire 16th century before the indebtedness resulting from the sale of life annuities was reduced to zero and that resulting from the sale of perpetual annuities to an acceptable level. At the same time, however, it can be established that by the end of the 16th century the economic power of Zutphen, once a flourishing Hanseatic town, had reached its nadir. Comparable conclusions are drawn in respect of the economic development of other IJssel-towns, as for instance Kampen and Deventer, but it is as yet the question whether their financial dependence on annuity sales was so large as in Zutphen[52]. Only parallel studies for other towns in the IJssel region can throw more light on this matter.

---

52 See C.A. Tamse, "Bijdrage tot de economische geschiedenis van Kampen in de middeleeuwen en de XVIe eeuw", in *Kamper Almanak*, 1963/64, pp. 204-279, B.M.J. Speet, *Historische Stedenatlas van Nederland*. 4: *Kampen*, Delft, 1986, pp. 23-25, and P. Holthuis, *Frontierstad bij het scheiden van de markt. Deventer: militair, demografisch, economisch; 1578-1648*, Deventer, 1993.

LA PRISE DE DÉCISION EN MATIÈRE D'EMPRUNTS DANS LES VILLES SUISSES AU 15e SIECLE.

Hans-Jörg Gilomen
Zürich University

En 1430, suite à une demande de Jean Nider, prieur des dominicains de Bâle, le fameux savant Job Vener de Strasbourg rédigea un avis sur la bulle '*Regimini universalis*' du pape Martin V, publiée cinq ans plus tôt[1]. Par cette bulle, le pape avait statué que les rentes constituées sur des biens immobiliers, au prix usuel et avec droit de réméré du vendeur, ne tombaient pas sous l'interdit canonique de l'usure. Cette bulle est considérée comme décisive dans la controverse concernant le caractère usuraire des rentes rachetables, qui agita les esprits dès la fin du 14e siècle[2]. Dans son commentaire, Vener répondait aux questions précises posées par Jean Nider, mais il formulait aussi des considérations plus générales[3]:

> '...puisque le Saint-Siège a décidé en ce sens, cela devrait suffire à ôter ses scrupules à tout chrétien. Mais à supposer que les rentes et les intérêts, et surtout ceux qui sont constitués dans de nouveaux contrats avec droit de réméré, ne soient pas suspects, mais plutôt licites, il me semble quand même – sous réserve des décisions et déclarations déjà promulguées ou futures du Saint-Siège – qu'il serait plus utile pour la société (*rei publicae*) de restreindre la constitution de telles rentes, quoique pas entièrement (c'est-à-dire sans discernement), mais quand même d'une certaine façon, et au moins de les interdire généralement aux simples laïcs plébéiens et rustiques (*simplicibus laycis plebanis et rusticanis*), s'il n'y a pas de raison particulière à l'encontre, car à cause du nombre immense de ces contrats, le commerce s'arrête, l'agriculture est désertée et c'est l'occasion de négligences, d'oisiveté et d'inertie, et même, si rien n'est entrepris à l'encontre, il pourrait s'ensuivre beaucoup d'inconvénients, comme nous l'avons déjà vu à Mayence et en quelques autres lieux. Et il est à craindre qu'il s'en suive bientôt meurtres et commotions des peuples parce que les terres ne peuvent plus supporter tant de charges de cens et d'intérêts[4].'

Il est à remarquer que parmi les problèmes résultant de l'endettement par des rentes constituées, ce texte désigne en premier lieu les conséquences funestes pour les paysans et pour

---

StAB = Staatsarchiv Basel-Stadt
StAW = Stadtarchiv Winterthur

1 H. Heimpel, *Die Vener von Gmünd und Strassburg 1162-1447*, 3 vols, Veröffentlichungen des Max-Planck-Instituts für Geschichte 52, Göttingen, 1982, p. 1367s. n° 34/I. Le texte de cette bulle se trouve aussi in le *Corpus Iuris Canonici*, *Extravagantes communes*, lib. 3, tit. 5 *De emptione et venditione*, c. 1. Ibid. c. 2: renouvellement de la bulle par Calixte III.
2 Sur cette controverse, voir H.-J. Gilomen, "Kirchliche Theorie und Wirtschaftspraxis. Der Streit um die Basler Wucherpredigt des Johannes Mulberg", in *Itinera*, 4 (1986), pp. 34-62.
3 Heimpel, *Die Vener*, pp. 1368-1371, n° 34/II.
4 Heimpel, *Die Vener* (cit. note 1), p. 1370: '*Et timendum est, quod in brevi ex hoc strages et commociones in populis orientur, quia territoria non sufficiunt ammodo tot gravamina censuum et reddituum supportare*'.

l'agriculture[5]. Par ailleurs, l'allusion à la ville de Mayence montre que notre savant était bien informé de l'actualité politique et tout aussi conscient des problèmes causés par les emprunts des villes. Surchargée par une dette publique constituée en rentes, Mayence avait connu en 1428/29 un renversement politique à la suite de son insolvabilité[6]. Le chanoine zurichois Félix Hemmerlin (1388/89 - 1458/1461), probablement l'homme le plus savant de la Confédération helvétique dans la première moitié du 15e siècle, indiquait comme l'une des causes primordiales de la destruction du royaume de Bohême par les troubles hussites la surcharge des terres par des redevances et des pensions, payables sous forme de rentes au clergé[7]. A tort ou à raison, il envisageait lui aussi l'endettement rural comme un facteur décisif du mécontentement profond menaçant l'ordre social au 15e siècle[8]. En jugeant le crédit sous forme de rentes aussi défavorablement, nos deux auteurs suivaient et dépassaient même peut-être le discours traditionnel des canonistes et des théologiens contre l'usure. Leurs mises en garde contre les conséquences sociales néfastes trouveraient un écho dans les tirades du réformateur Luther contre toute forme de crédit[9].

Mais le plus important, à mon avis, dans les deux témoignages cités, c'est le changement de ton. Après le rejet par le pape des arguments théologiques et canoniques contre l'aspect usuraire des rentes[10], les réserves exprimées contre cette forme de crédit se fondent dorénavant sur des considérations d'ordre purement économique et sociales. A cette époque, on note un glissement similaire du discours moral vers un discours économique concernant d'autres problèmes encore. Mais les scrupules moraux n'étaient pas complètement éliminés pour autant. En 1428, trois ans après la décision papale, Rudolf Graf, prieur provincial des ermites de saint Augustin, acheta pour 50 florins une rente de la ville de Bâle, avec la stipulation surprenante qu'il recevrait chaque année 5 florins jusqu'à ce que la somme totale lui ait été remboursée au bout de dix ans[11]. Il n'était donc pas question

---

5 En Alsace, région dont Vener avait une connaissance approfondie, l'endettement paysan augmenta de façon alarmante dans la seconde moitié du 15e siècle, après avoir connu une brusque flambée dans les années soixante-dix du 14e siècle. Voir C. Geissert, "Les rentes constituées de l'oeuvre Saint-Georges Haguenau (XIVe-XVIIe siècles)", in *Archives de l'Eglise d'Alsace,* 41 (1982), p. 32s.; F. Rapp, "Die soziale und wirtschaftliche Vorgeschichte des Bauernkrieges im Unterelsass", in *Schriften des Vereins für Reformationsgeschichte,* 189, année 82 (1975), p. 41, a relevé dans les cartulaires des centaines de contrats de rentes datant du 15e siècle et concernant des paysans.

6 J. Fischer, *Frankfurt und die Bürgerunruhen in Mainz (1332-1462),* Beiträge zur Geschichte der Stadt Mainz 15, Mainz, 1958, pp. 18-30.

7 "De novorum officiorum divinorum institutione", in *Clarissimi viri Juriumque doctoris Felicis Hemmerlin cantoris quondam Thuricensis varie oblectationis opuscula et tractatus*, Ex Basilea Jdibus Augusti M ccccxcvij [1497], fol. 61v-73v, surtout fol. 73r: '*Et hec indubitanter fuit primordialiter regni Bohemorum destructionis causa, quia multum impatienter videbatur laicis, immo terrarum particulas nimium gravatas per pensiones clero censuales. Nam vix fuit pedis passus per omnes regni districtus ubi clerus non habuerit tributorum vel aliarum pensionum fructus*'. Hemmerlin lui-même a écrit après 1454 un traité sur les rentes rachetables: F. Hemmerlin, "De emptione et venditione vnius pro viginti", in: *Clarissimi viri*, fol. 153v-156r. Il confirmait l'absence de toute tache d'usure et – un peu en contradiction avec l'opinion précitée – leur utilité pour la société. Voir H.-J. Gilomen, "Der Traktat *De emptione et venditione unius pro viginti* des Magisters Felix Hemmerlin", in J. Helmrath et H. Müller (éds.), *Studien zum 15. Jahrhundert. Festschrift Erich Meuthen*, München, 1994, pp. 583-605.

8 Les nombreuses mesures prises par les seigneurs et les autorités municipales contre l'endettement des paysans illustrent l'importance croissante accordée à ce problème: H.-J. Gilomen, "L'endettement paysan et la question du crédit dans les pays d'Empire au Moyen Age", in *Endettement paysan et crédit rural dans l'Europe médiévale et moderne*, Actes des XVIIe Journées Internationales d'Histoire de l'Abbaye de Flaran, Septembre 1995, Toulouse, 1998, p. 130ss.

9 G. Schmoller, "Zur Geschichte der national-ökonomischen Ansichten in Deutschland während der Reformations-Periode", in *Zeitschrift für die gesammte Staatswissenschaft*, 16 (1860), pp. 461-716, surtout pp. 554-571. H.-J. Prien, *Luthers Wirtschaftsethik*, Göttingen, 1992.

10 La question théologique ne fut d'ailleurs pas tout à fait close. Elle refaisait surface ça et là et fut encore traîtée au concile de Bâle, par exemple, voir *Concilium Basiliense. Studien und Quellen zur Geschichte des Concils von Basel*, VIII, Basel, 1936, pp. 58, 80-83, ici 101.

11 B. Harms (éd.), *Der Stadthaushalt Basels im ausgehenden Mittelalter. Quellen und Studien zur Basler Finanzgeschichte*, 3 vols., Tübingen 1909-1913, I, p. 121 ligne 97: '... *sol man im alle jar fünf guldin widergeben, uncz das er der bezalt wird*'. Déjà en 1425/26, il avait acheté une rente pour 100 fl., '*darumbe man im jaerlichs 10 guldin geben sol untz daz er der hundert guldin bezalt wirt*', Harms (éd.), *Der Stadthaushalt Basels*, p. 111 ligne 66. Une notice du scribe montre que ceci n'était pas considéré comme une vraie rente, mais

d'intérêt dans ce cas, mais de la mise en application de la vieille idée que le paiement des rentes devait servir à amortir le capital versé[12].

Le clergé n'était pas le seul à se défier du crédit. Parmi les marchands hanséates eux-mêmes, certaines opérations de crédit étaient considérées d'un mauvais oeil à cause des abus qu'elles pouvaient engendrer[13]. En 1399, les villes lituaniennes de Riga et de Réval défendirent aux marchands l'achat à crédit dans leur commerce avec les Russes[14]. En 1401, la diète de la Hanse à Lubeck interdit l'achat à crédit en Flandre[15]. Une prohibition de tout crédit commercial en Flandre fut décidée par la Hanse en 1417, et cette décision fut confirmée en 1422, 1434 et 1447[16]. En 1462, le comptoir de Londres demanda à la diète de la Hanse d'interdire toute opération de crédit dans le commerce avec l'Angleterre[17]. Pour des motifs différents[18], les rois d'Angleterre s'opposaient dans le cadre de leur *bullionist policy* à l'application du crédit dans le commerce de la laine[19].

Ces quelques remarques, que l'on pourrait aisément multiplier, n'ont d'autre but que de rappeler un fait quelque peu oublié, ou même démenti dans les travaux récents des historiens de l'économie du bas Moyen Age[20]: bien que dès le 13e siècle, le crédit se soit rapidement diffusé dans toutes les couches de la population sous de multiples formes[21], la mentalité dominante resta longtemps encore réservée, voir méfiante ou même hostile. Cette hostilité n'était pas toujours évidente dans la vie quotidienne, mais elle se manifestait fortement dans les moments de tensions sociales, dans les commotions urbaines[22] comme dans les soulèvements ruraux[23].

Mais qu'en pensaient les membres des conseils municipaux? Quelles expériences ont-ils vécu personnellement et de quelles expériences de leurs collègues d'autres villes ont-ils eu connaissance? Le cas de la véritable banqueroute de la ville de Mayence n'est pas isolé. J'ai donné ailleurs une longue liste de villes criblées de dettes jusqu'à l'insolvabilité[24]. L'expérience directe ou indirecte des conseillers a

---

comme un dépôt par les administrateurs de la ville. En versant la somme de 10 fl. en 1432/33, on notait que c'était à cause des 100 fl., que '*bruder Conrat Gräff den räten ze behalten geben hatt*'. in Harms (éd.), *Der Stadthaushalt Basels*, II, p. 188 ligne 98.

12 Concernant cette idée, voir H.-J. Gilomen, "Das Motiv der bäuerlichen Verschuldung in den Bauernunruhen an der Wende zur Neuzeit", in S. Burgharts, H.-J. Gilomen, G.P. Marchal, R.C. Schwinges et K.S. Muscheid (éds.), *Spannungen und Widersprüche. Gedenkschrift für Frantisek Graus*, Sigmaringen, 1992, p. 187 note 66. En 1475 encore, Antonius Perotti confirmait qu'il ne déduirait pas les intérêts payés de la somme prêtée: '... *quod non possit computtare fictum in predictis denaris...*' *Materiali e Documenti Ticinesi*, serie I, fascicolo 52, Leventina (1474-1477), Bellinzona, 2001, p. 2478 n° 1101, 8 janvier 1475.

13 Ph. Dollinger, *La Hanse (XIIe-XVIIe siècle)*, Paris, 1964, pp. 252-256: 'L'hostilité au crédit'; en allemand: *Die Hanse*, 3e éd., Stuttgart, 1981 (Kröner Tauschenausgabe 371), pp. 267-271: "*Der Kampf gegen das Kreditwesen*".

14 Le règlement du comptoir de Novgorod datant des années 1295 défendait déjà aux marchands allemands d'accepter des marchandises à crédit des Russes; Dollinger, *La Hanse*, p. 255 et document 31a, p. 506 f.; en allemand: Dokument 31a, p. 540.

15 *Hanserezesse. I. Abt.: Die Rezesse und andere Akten der Hansetage von 1256-1430*, adapté par W. Junghans und K. Koppmann, 8 vols., Leipzig 1870-1897, V, p. 16 Nr. 23, § 1. Dollinger, *La Hanse*, document 31b, p. 506s.; en allemand: p. 540.

16 Dollinger, *La Hanse*, p. 256; en allemand p. 271.

17 *Hanserezesse. II. Abt.: Die Rezesse und andere Akten der Hansetage von 1431-1476*, adapté par G. v.d. Ropp, 7 vols., Leipzig, 1876-1892, V, p. 190 n° 263, § 49 ; Dollinger, *La Hanse*, document 31d, p. 507s.

18 Voir plus bas.

19 M. Postan, "Credit in Medieval Trade", in *The Economic History Review,* 1 (1927/28), pp. 234-261: en 1430, une loi interdit aux marchands anglais de vendre leurs marchandises, surtout les draps, autrement qu'au comptant. L'"*Ordinance of Partition of Wool*" de 1430 ordonna pour le marché de Calais le paiement immédiat et au comptant de la laine. Ceci fut confirmé en 1437.

20 Voir par exemple S. Jenks, "War die Hanse kreditfeindlich?", in *Vierteljahrschrift für Wirtschaftsgeschichte,* 69 (1982), pp. 305-337; M. North (éd.), *Kredit im spätmittelalterlichen und frühneuzeitlichen Europa* (Quellen und Darstellungen zur hansischen Geschichte NF 37), Köln/Wien, 1991.

21 B. Kuske, "Die Entstehung der Kreditwirtschaft und des Kapitalverkehrs", in *Köln, der Rhein und das Reich*, Kölner Vorträge 1, Leipzig, 1927, réimpression Köln/Graz, 1956.

22 H.-J. Gilomen, "Anleihen und Steuern in der Finanzwirtschaft spätmittelalterlicher Städte, Option bei drohendem Dissens", in S. Guex, M. Körner et J. Tanner (éds.), *Staatsfinanzierung und Sozialkonflikte (14.-20. Jh.) - Financement de l'Etat et conflits sociaux (14e-20e siècles)* (Schweizerischen Gesellschaft für Wirtschafts- und Sozialgeschichte - Société suisse d'histoire économique et sociale 12), Zürich, 1994, pp.137-158.

23 Gilomen, "Das Motiv", pp. 173-189; Gilomen, *L'endettement paysan.*

24 Gilomen, *Anleihen*, pp. 137-140. En France, Beaumanoir avait déjà esquissé un programme pour régler les dettes des villes insolvables: Ph. de Beaumanoir, *Coutumes de Beauvaisis*, 2 vol., Paris, 1899-1900, réimpression Paris, 1970, II, p. 271s., n° 1527.

certainement influencé leur manière de voir les choses, leur perception du crédit et de l'emprunt, et cette perception a conditionné leur mode de décision et d'action. Que les hommes se comportent d'une manière tout à fait rationnelle en matière économique est un présupposé de la science économique qui est en train de s'effriter[25]. Car ce ne sont pas les faits eux-mêmes qui dirigent l'action humaine, mais bien la perception de ces faits. Outre l'expérience personnelle et la connaissance de faits non vécus, ce qui se dit conditionne également la manière de percevoir[26]. Notre propos est d'essayer de mieux comprendre comment les décisions ont été prises, de saisir le *decision making process* des autorités lors de l'émission d'emprunts au bas Moyen Age. Les sources sont presque muettes à ce sujet; il faut les scruter attentivement pour y trouver des allusions et des indications. Nous analyserons les sources urbaines du territoire de la Suisse actuelle et surtout, à cause de leur abondance en ce qui concerne les problèmes financiers, celles de la ville de Bâle, quoique pour de nombreux points abordés ici il faudra se tourner également vers d'autres villes[27].

Le choix entre l'impôt et le crédit

En cas de besoin de fortes liquidités – le plus souvent à cause de dépenses militaires – les autorités avaient le choix entre l'institution de nouveaux impôts ou l'aggravation de ceux qui existaient déjà d'une part et le recours à l'émission d'un emprunt de l'autre[28]. Pour prendre une telle décision, l'on ne disposait pas encore, à l'époque, de règles économiques stipulant que le financement par l'emprunt doit être réservé à des investissement rentables. Nous avons vu que le crédit était suspect et il le resterait encore longtemps, surtout dans le cadre des finances publiques[29]. Le financement par le crédit était considéré comme un palliatif, ou, pour le dire en des termes modernes, comme l'anticipation du

---

25 Voir la série d'articles sous le titre "Psychologische Grundlagen der Oekonomie" in la *Neue Zürcher Zeitung*, 2001; G. Schwarz et R. Nef (éds.), *Neidökonomie*, Zürich, 2000; E. Fehr et G. Schwarz (éds.), *Psychologische Grundlagen der Oekonomie*, Zürich, 2001. Voir déjà *Gablers Wirtschaftslexikon*, 11e éd., Wiesbaden, 1984, art. "Entscheidungstheorie", col. 1297: '*Die sozialwissenschaftliche Entscheidungstheorie verwirft die Annahme einer absoluten Rationalität menschlicher Entscheidungen, die als Konstruktion für wissenschaftliche Analysen oft verwendet wird. Im Einklang mit psychologischen und soziologischen Erkenntnissen bezieht sie die vielfachen individuellen und sozialen Begrenzungsfaktoren der menschlichen Rationalität in die Analyse ein*'.

26 G. Spiegel, *The Past as Text. The Theory and Practice of Medieval Historiography*, Baltimore, 1997.

27 Les comptes annuels de la ville de Bâle ont été publiés par Harms (éd.), *Der Stadthaushalt*. Sur base de cette édition, J. Rosen, un érudit de formation économique, a publié entre 1971 et 1987 plusieurs articles, qui furent réédités après sa mort en 1988 sous le titre: *Finanzgeschichte Basels im späten Mittelalter*, Stuttgart, 1989. Quelques travaux anciens ne sont toujours pas remplacés: G. Schönberg, *Finanzverhältnisse der Stadt Basel im Mittelalter im 14. und 15. Jahrhundert*, Tübingen, 1879; B. Harms, "Die Steuern und Anleihen im öffentlichen Haushalt der Stadt Basel 1361-1500", in *Zeitschrift für die gesamte Staatswissenschaft*, 63 (1907), pp. 627-681; E. Wackernagel, *Geschichte der öffentlichen Anleihen der Stadt Basel und ihrer rechtlichen Formen 1200-1830*, Basel, s.d. [1927] (typoscript); O. Feger, "Vergleichende Betrachtungen zur Finanzgeschichte von Konstanz und Basel", in *Finances et comptabilité urbaines du XIIIe au XVIe siècle. Colloque International Blankenberge 1962* (Pro Civitate 7), Bruxelles, 1964. Voir aussi U. Dirlmeier, "Stadt und Bürgertum. Zur Steuerpolitik und zum Stadt-Land-Verhältnis", in H. Buszello, P. Blickle, et R. Endres (éds.), *Der deutsche Bauernkrieg*, Paderborn/München/Zürich, 1984, pp. 254-280; G. Fouquet et U. Dirlmeier, "Probleme und Methoden der quantitativen Finanz- und Wirtschaftsgeschichte des Spätmittelalters: Oeffentliche Finanzen und städtische Militärpolitik in Basel und Hamburg während der Jahre 1460 bis 1481", in K.H. Kaufhold et J. Schneider (éds.), *Geschichtswissenschaft und elektronische Datenverarbeitung* (Beiträge zur Wirtschafts- und Sozialgeschichte 36), 1988, pp. 175-228; G. Fouquet, "Die Finanzierung von Krieg und Verteidigung in oberdeutschen Städten des späten Mittelalters (1400-1500)", in B. Kirchgässner et G. Scholz, *Stadt und Krieg*, Sigmaringen, 1989, pp. 41-82.

28 Puisque j'ai traité de ces problèmes ailleurs de manière détaillée, je peux être bref sur ce premier point. Voir Gilomen, *Anleihen*, pp. 137-158.

29 D'après J. Landmann, "Geschichte des öffentlichen Kredits", in *Handbuch der Finanzwissenschaften*, 2e éd., Tübingen, 1968, III, p. 3: Jusqu'à la fin du 18e siècle, les emprunts étaient considérés comme un '*im Rahmen einer gesunden Finanzwirtschaft im Grunde ungehöriges Deckungsmittel*'. C'était un '*Not- und Velegenheitsausweg, dessen sich die Finanzverwaltung ohne irgendwelche Beziehung zur Art des Bedarfes bedient ...*'

produit d'impôts futurs[30]. Le recours à l'emprunt était un expédient efficace pour se procurer rapidement des liquidités importantes; c'était plus efficace que la perception d'impôts, qui entraînait toujours des complications. Ça et là, il ressort des sources que l'on opérait un choix explicite entre l'émission d'emprunts et la perception d'impôts, en étant conscient du lien étroit entre ces deux moyens de financement. La perception d'impôts extraordinaires fut souvent justifiée soit par l'urgence d'acquitter des dettes, soit par la volonté d'éviter le gonflement de la dette par un nouvel emprunt[31]. Parfois, les autorités s'engageaient à supprimer le nouvel impôt aussitôt que la dette serait acquittée[32].

Au vu des réserves existant à l'encontre du crédit et plus particulièrement de l'émission d'emprunts, pourquoi les autorités avaient-elles recours à ce moyen de financement, alors même que l'endettement de la ville était déjà fort lourd? Il est vrai que l'aggravation des impôts existants ou l'institution de nouvelles contributions pouvait entraîner quelques risques. L'évasion fiscale pratiquée par les riches – et parfois même par les gens modestes[33] – entraînant l'épuisement du substrat imposable n'était qu'un moindre mal. Les réactions violentes des bourgeois constituaient le danger majeur. Les émeutes urbaines ont été très fréquentes aux 14e et 15e siècles. La cause, ou à tout le moins l'occasion récurrente, était d'ordre fiscal. Dans bien des cas, l'aggravation des impôts en vue de réduire la dette agissait comme un détonnateur[34]. Le lien étroit entre impôts et emprunts se vérifie là aussi: il arrivait, en effet, que les émeutiers ne visent pas seulement la destruction des registres d'impôt, mais aussi celle des titres des créanciers de la ville[35].

---

30 G. Espinas, *Les finances de la commune de Douai des origines au XVe siècle*, Paris, 1902, p. 303: '... les causes d'émission des emprunts se confondent avec les motifs de perception des assises qui, on ne l'ignore pas, sont levées, en principe, pour payer la dette'.

31 Le 1er décembre 1338, le conseil de la ville de Berne confirmait que le prieur des Clunisiens de Rüeggisberg lui avait permis d'imposer ses sujets '*in subsidium nostrorum debitorum*'. *Fontes rerum Bernensium*, Bern, 1891, VI, p. 453. En 1401, le conseil de la ville de Bâle justifiait la perception d'une assise nouvelle par la réduction projetée de la dette publique: '*Wondt wir von gemeiner stette wegen gross gelt vffgenommen hand, daz wir swarlich zinsent, ..., so habent wir ... ein gemein vngelt vffgeleit ..., mit dem die schulden, so vffgenomen sint, ..., so verr wir mugent, ab zetragende*'. StAB, *Steuerakten* A1. En 1425, la perception d'un impôt extraordinaire fut motivée par le conseil de la ville de Zurich de la manière suivante: '*Anno domini MCCCCoXXVto ... haben wir ... von der schulden wegen, so wir alle von unser gemeinen statt wegen schuldig sind, uns erkennet und geeinbert, umb dass wir nit schaden an schaden nemmen muessen, das wir dis jares stueren soellen*'. H. Nabholz, F. Hegi, E. Hauser et W. Schnyder (éds.), *Die Steuerbücher von Stadt und Landschaft Zürich des XIV. und XV. Jahrhunderts*, 8 vols., Zürich, 1918-1958, II, Zürich, 1939, p. 9. La ville de Berne réservait en 1449 le produit de la nouvelle capitation (Wochenangster) à l'amortissement de la dette publique et au paiement des intérêts: '... *enpfangen und wider uss geben allein an hobtgut und jerlich zinss als die stat uff dis zit schuldig ist* ...' Archives d'Etat de Berne, B VII 2477. Les administrateurs de cet impôt jurèrent: '... *nützit [du produit] ze geben, denn an die schulden und zinse*...'

32 La ville de Berne, par exemple, s'engageait en 1449 en ce sens envers la ville de Zofingen: '*Das Stadtrecht von Zofingen*', *Sammlung Schweizerischer Rechtsquellen*, 16. Abt., I, V, Aarau, 1914, p. 131s.

33 Il est aisé de trouver des documents concernant les riches; la fuite de pauvres est moins évidente. Dans la liste des contribuables de Zurich de 1442 on note concernant un certain Burkart von Konstanz, compagnon: '*ist die stür geflochen*'. Schnyder (éds.), *Die Steuerbücher*, II, p. 503, maison no. 9.

34 R. Barth, *Argumentation und Selbstverständnis der Bürgeropposition in städtischen Auseinandersetzungen: Lübeck 1403-1408, Braunschweig 1374-1376, Mainz 1444-1446, Köln 1396-1400*, Köln/Wien 1974, p. 2s.; R. Endres, "Zünfte und Unterschichten als Elemente der Instabilität in den Städten", in *Revolte und Revolution in Europa* (Historische Zeitschrift, Beiheft 4), München, 1975, p. 163s.; R. Rotz, *Urban Uprisings in 14th Century Germany: a Comparative Study of Brunswick (1374-80) and Hamburg (1376)*, Princeton, 1970, p. 22; F. Graus, *Pest - Geissler - Judenmorde. Das 14. Jahrhundert als Krisenzeit* (Veröffentlichungen des Max-Planck-Instituts für Geschichte 86), Göttingen, 1987, pp. 499 et 514ss.; pour la France, voir A. Léguai, "Les troubles urbains dans le nord de la France à la fin du XIIIe et au début du XIVe siècle", in *Revue d'histoire économique et sociale*, 54 (1976), p. 303; B. Chevalier, "Corporations, conflits politique et paix sociale en France aux XIVe et XVe siècles", in *Revue historique*, 543 (1982), p. 32s.; Ph. Wolff, "Les luttes sociales dans les villes du Midi français du XIIIe au XVe siècles", in *Annales ESC*, 2 (1947), pp. 443-454 (aussi dans Wolff, *Regards sur le Midi médiéval*, Toulouse, 1978, p. 81); pour l'Angleterre et l'Italie, voir A.H. Hibbart, "The Economic Policies of Towns", in *The Cambridge Economic History*, III, Cambridge, 1965, pp. 196f. et 206. Ceci est vrai aussi pour les émeutes des paysans, voir J. Heers, *Le clan familial au Moyen Age*, Paris, 1974, p. 9: '...un peu partout, en Europe occidentale, les émeutes rurales suivent de près l'institution ou l'aggravation de l'impôt royal...'

35 Pour l'émeute fiscale de Bâle en 1402, voir StAB, *Ratsbücher* A3, *Leistungsbuch* 2, f. 40v. Un meneur de l'émeute disait: '...*dass man gan sölle von huse zu huse, nemlich in der hüser, die gulte und zinse an den reten hettend, und solle man denen ir brieff und ingesigel zer brechen, so bezalte man.*', et un autre: '...*hette yederman sinen sin, sy giengent fur das richthuse und nemment allen denen ir brieff, die guot und zinse an den reten hettent.*' Pour Braunschweig 1374, voir *Die Chroniken der deutschen Städte* 6, Leipzig, 1868, Reprint Göttingen, 1962, p. 347.

A mon sens, c'est avant tout la crainte de troubles sociaux qui poussait les autorités à emprunter au lieu d'imposer, même quand la situation financière d'une ville était déjà obérée au point de risquer l'insolvabilité. Je ne pense pas – comme on l'a affirmé – que les autorités avaient l'intention d'offrir par des emprunts une possibilité d'investissements rentables aux capitaux bourgeois[36] ou d'assumer le rôle d'une caisse d'épargne[37]. Les sources n'en donnent aucune preuve. Un taux d'intérêt de 5%, ou moins encore, pour des rentes rachetables n'était d'ailleurs pas tellement alléchant pour les investisseurs. L'hypothèse que les investissements peu rentables en rentes viagères n'avaient d'autre but que de mettre l'argent à l'abri du risque en cas d'incendie ou de vol, n'est guère convaincante[38]. Les sources montrent sans équivoque que pour beaucoup des créanciers les rentes faisaient fonction de pension de vieillesse[39], mais cela n'implique pas que les autorités aient consciemment émis des emprunts à cette fin et les aient administré comme une caisse d'épargne. On a même suggéré – à tort, me semble-t-il – qu'il fallait voir l'endettement des ville sous l'aspect de cette fonction sociale[40]. Pour de petites gens, la somme à verser pour une rente était trop élevée. Dans la plupart des villes, on ne vendait pas de rentes rachetables pour des sommes inférieures à 100 florins[41]. Quelques chiffres pour Bâle peuvent illustrer ceci:

TABLEAU I. **Les emprunts de la ville de Bâle sous forme de rentes rachetables, de 1420/21 à 1429/30**

Année	somme, fl.	rentes, fl.	taux, %	tranches, fl.	moyenne, fl.
1420/21	1.750	71	4,06	3 de 100 – 850	583,3
1421/22	3.390	167,5	4,94	8 de 340 – 850	423,8
1422/23	850	42,5	5	2 de 300 – 550	425,0
1423/24	1.650	82,5	5	5 de 200 – 480	330,0
1424/25	11.530	576,5	5,01	7 de 150 – 1.700	678,2
1425/26	18.660	905,5	4,85	26 de 100 – 3.000	717,7
1426/27	3.662	176	4,81	6 de 50 – 2.300	610,3
1427/28	5.000	240	4,80	4 de 800 – 2.200	1.250,0
1428/29	6.850	342,5	5	9 de 200 – 2.500	761,1
1429/30	7.853	342,5	4,36	14 de 70 – 1.600	560,9
1420-29	61.195	2.946,5	4,81	94 de 50 – 3.000	651,0

Voir aussi p. 333. Pour Barcelone en 1285, voir M. Mollat et Ph. Wolff, *Ongles Bleus, Jacques et Ciompi. Les révolutions populaires en Europe aux XIVe et XVe siècles*, Paris, 1970, pp. 48-50.

36 Voir J. Landmann, "Zur Entwicklungsgeschichte der Formen und der Organisation des öffentlichen Kredits", in *Finanz-Archiv*, 29 (1912), p. 13.

37 R. Sohm, "Städtische Wirtschaft im fünfzehnten Jahrhundert", in *Jahrbücher für Nationalökonomie und Statistik*, 34 (1879), p. 265.

38 B. Kuske, *Das Schuldenwesen der deutschen Städte im Mittelalter* (Zeitschrift für die gesamte Staatswissenschaft, Ergänzungsheft 12), Tübingen, 1909, p. 22. Les termes utilisés dans les sources pour les rentes rachetables sont '*kouffzins, ze widerkouff, gült*', les rentes viagères sont désignées par le terme '*lipgeding*', les rentes perpétuelles par '*ewigzins, ewiggült*'.

39 Je ne citerai qu'un seul exemple bâlois de cette forme d'épargne-vieillesse. Un certain Hans Schmid et sa femme Anna achetèrent le 23 août 1469 pour 100 fl. une rente viagère de 10 fl. Le 13 décembre 1472, par un versement supplémentaire de 20 fl., Anna augmenta la rente à 12 fl. Devenue veuve, elle versa le 24 juin 1479 encore 80 fl. et porta ainsi la rente à 20 fl. StAB, *Finanz* AA 4.20, 105v, voir aussi Finanz AA 4.17, 81v, AA 4.21, 33v, ainsi que Harms (éd.), *Der Stadthaushalt Basels*, I, p. 233 ligne15, p. 242 ligne 93, p. 264 ligne 82. En 1451, son mari avait déclaré une fortune de 300 fl.: Schönberg, *Finanzverhältnisse*, p. 589; P. Koelner, *Die Safranzunft zu Basel*, Basel, 1935, p. 404. La rente échut en 1484/85, au décès de Anna Schmid.

40 Voir G. Wunder, "Die Stadt als Darlehenskasse am Beispiel der Reichsstadt Hall im 16. und 17. Jahrhundert", in B. Kirchgässner et E. Naujoks (éds.), *Stadt und wirtschaftliche Selbstverwaltung* (Stadt in der Geschichte. Veröffentlichungen des Südwestdeutschen Arbeitskreises für Stadtgeschichtsforschung 12), Sigmaringen, 1987, p. 120.

41 Ceci ne vaut pas seulement pour les villes de la Suisse alémanique. A Hambourg, par exemple, la somme moyenne des rentes rachetables était, au 14e siècle, de 240 marcs et dans la deuxième moitié du 15e siècle de 350 marcs, voir H. Reincke, "Die alte Hamburger Stadtschuld der Hansezeit (1300-1563)", in *Städtewesen und Bürgertum als geschichtliche Kräfte. Gedächtnisschrift für Fritz Rörig*, Lübeck, 1953, p. 504. A Nuremberg, les rentes viagères contractées en 1388 s'élevaient à 556 fl. en moyenne, la médiane étant de 450 fl. Les rentes vendues par des particuliers, par contre, étaient parfois très faibles.

Peu de villes ont vendu des rentes d'un faible montant, et ce furent surtout des rentes viagères[42]. Cependant, le cas de Bâle montre que les montants plus modérés de ces rentes étaient encore trop élevés pour des gens peu fortunés:

TABLEAU II. **Les emprunts de la ville de Bâle sous forme de rentes viagères, 1420/21-1429/30**

Année	somme, fl.	rentes, fl.	taux,%	tranches, fl.			moyenne, fl.
1470/71	4.855	236	4,86	12	de	25 – 1.000	404,6
1471/72	8.250	330	4	14	de	50 – 2.050	589,3
1472/73	4.923	198	4,02	15	de	48 – 1.300	328,2
1473/74	27.303	1.328	4,86	68	de	67 – 1.200	401,5
1474/75	10.584	497	4,70	23	de	50 – 2.000	460,2
1475/76	18.386	916	4,98	31	de	20 – 2.000	593,1
1476/77	15.253	726,5	4,76	39	de	20 – 2.000	391,1
1477/78	5.913	276,5	4,68	11	de	63 – 2.000	537,5
1478/79	2.222	89	4,01	11	de	50 – 672	202,0
1479/80	1.900	76	4,00	3	de	100 – 1.400	633,3
1470-79	99.589	4.673	4,69	227	de	20 – 2.050	438,7
1420-29	61.195	2.946,5	4,81	94	de	50 – 3.000	651,0

La comparaison de cet échantillon de la première moitié du 15e siècle avec un second, un demi-siècle plus tard, est fort instructive:

TABLEAU III. **Les emprunts de la ville de Bâle sous forme de rentes rachetables,1470/71-479/80**

Année	somme, fl.	rentes, fl.	taux,%	tranches, fl.			moyenne, fl.
1470/71	4.855	236	4,86	12	de	25 – 1.000	404,6
1471/72	8.250	330	4	14	de	50 – 2.050	589,3
1472/73	4.923	198	4,02	15	de	48 – 1.300	328,2
1473/74	27.303	1.328	4,86	68	de	67 – 1.200	401,5
1474/75	10.584	497	4,70	23	de	50 – 2.000	460,2
1475/76	18.386	916	4,98	31	de	20 – 2.000	593,1
1476/77	15.253	726,5	4,76	39	de	20 – 2.000	391,1
1477/78	5.913	276,5	4,68	11	de	63 – 2.000	537,5
1478/79	2.222	89	4,01	11	de	50 – 672	202,0
1479/80	1.900	76	4,00	3	de	100 – 1.400	633,3
1470-79	99.589	4.673	4,69	227	de	20 – 2.050	438,7
1420-29	61.195	2.946,5	4,81	94	de	50 – 3.000	651,0

42 Pour les rentes viagères, voir W. Ogris, *Der mittelalterliche Leibrentenvertrag* (Wiener rechtsgeschichtliche Arbeiten 6), Wien/München, 1961. Au tournant du 14e au 15e siècle, les villes de Brunswick, Göttingen, Hannovre et Lüneburg vendaient des rentes viagères d'un montant de 2 à 4 marcs, voir A. von Kostanecki, *Der öffentliche Kredit im Mittelalter nach Urkunden der Herzogtümer Braunschweig und Lüneburg* (Staats- und Socialwissenschaftliche Forschungen 9), Leipzig, 1889, I, p. 40. D'après Espinas, les petites rentes ont disparu à Douai au cours du 14e siècle, voir Espinas, *Les finances,* p. 331s. A Cologne, de très petites rentes étaient disponibles à côté de montants très élevés, voir R. Knipping, "Das Schuldenwesen der Stadt Köln im 14. und 15. Jahrhundert", in *Westdeutsche Zeitschrift für Geschichte und Kunst,* 13 (1894), pp. 340-397. Knipping évoquait déjà le rôle de ces emprunts comme caisse d'épargne. A Regensburg, on fixa la somme minimum pour des rentes viagères à 7 livres, voir K.Th. von Inama-Sternegg, *Deutsche Wirtschaftsgeschichte*, 3 Bde., Leipzig, 1879-1901, p. 492.

1° La somme totale des rentes rachetables vendues par la ville a augmenté de plus d'un tiers (de 61.000 à 99.500 fl.).

2° Comme partout en Europe, le taux d'intérêt a diminué. De 1470 à 1479, la moyenne ne s'élève qu'à 4,69% au lieu de 4,81% de 1420 à 1429. Alors que la somme totale des ventes a augmenté de 38,6%, celle des rentes ne s'est accrue que de 36,9%.

3° La différence la plus prononcée concerne la moyenne des sommes versées pour une rente. Les rentes modestes sont très rares, la moyenne assez élevée le montre. Parmi celles-ci, quelques unes ne représentent qu'une augmentation de rentes plus importantes, constituées quelques années plus tôt. Mais il reste que la moyenne a diminué d'un tiers (32,6%). La possibilité d'investir dans des rentes urbaines rachetables s'est donc élargie à des personnes moins nanties. Mais ceci demande une vérification ultérieure par une analyse prosopographique des créanciers.

4° La ville bénéficie d'une réduction du prix du crédit par la diminution du taux d'intérêt, mais elle subit aussi une augmentation des frais d'administration par l'augmentation des rentes et des rentiers.

TABLEAU IV. **Les emprunts de la ville de Bâle sous forme de rentes viagères, 1470/21 - 1479/80**

Année	somme, fl.	rentes, fl.	taux,%	tranches, fl.			moyenne, fl.
1470/71	2.207	192,5	9,59	6	de	87 – 1.000	367,8
1471/72	3.327	301,5	9,06	8	de	85 – 1.450	415,9
1472/73	757	74	9,78	5	de	20 – 200	151,4
1473/74	778	70	9	3	de	140 – 440	259,3
1474/75	200	20	10	1	de	200 – 200	200,0
1475/76	280	28	10	3	de	80 – 100	93,3
1476/77	430	43	10	3	de	80 – 200	143,3
1477/78	-	-	-			-	-
1478/79	630	58	9,21	2	de	80 – 550	315,0
1479/80	-	-	-			-	-
1470/79	8.609	787	9,36	31	de	20 – 1.450	277,7
1420/29	55.829,5	5.209	9,33	179	de	40 – 1.600	311,9

Pour les rentes viagères, la comparaison des deux échantillons donne des résultats dissemblables:

1° La somme encaissée par la ville pour la vente de rentes viagères a fortement diminué (47.220 fl., soit 85% de moins). Il y a même des années d'absence totale de cette forme de crédit.

2° Le taux des rentes viagères est resté stable (il a même légèrement augmenté).

3° Quoique la somme moyenne versée pour une rente viagère ait diminué elle aussi, cette diminution n'est pas aussi accentuée que dans le cas des rentes rachetables (une diminution de 11% seulement). Mais ces moyennes ne signifient pas grand chose: que dire d'une moyenne de 315 fl. pour deux rentes, l'une de 80 et l'autre de 550 fl.?

Rentes rachetables ou rentes viagères?

La décision d'émettre un emprunt étant prise, il fallait en définir les modalités. Et d'abord: quelles rentes choisir, des rentes rachetables ou des rentes viagères? Les tableaux I - IV donnent des indications importantes concernant ce choix. Le taux d'intérêt plaidait en faveur des rentes rachetables. En général, il était moitié plus bas que celui des rentes viagères (par exemple, 5% au lieu de 10%). Comme la somme avancée par l'acheteur d'une rente viagère ne devait pas être remboursée, le taux d'intérêt plus élevé comprenait en fait une quote-part d'amortissement. La rentabilité des contrats de rentes viagères était aléatoire: pour une rente de ce type acquise pour la somme de 100 florins à un taux de 10%, la ville devait débourser au bout de vingt ans 200 fl. en vingt annualités de 10 fl., somme qu'elle devait verser aussi dans le même laps de temps pour une rente rachetable en vingt annualités de 5 fl., y compris le prix du rachat de 100 fl. Par une rente viagère, la ville obtenait 100 fl. et devait – en 20 ans – en dépenser le double. Le solde s'élevait donc à 100 fl. Le taux réel payé pour le loyer d'une somme de 100 fl. pendant 20 ans était donc de 5%, tout comme pour une rente rachetable. Dans cet exemple, toute rente viagère dont le titulaire expirait avant les 20 ans consécutifs à la passation du contrat était donc plus avantageuse pour la ville qu'une rente rachetable. En revanche, chaque année de survie de rentiers au-delà de ce laps de temps entraînait pour la ville une perte considérable.

Comme les autorités ignoraient le mode de calcul de l'espérance de vie et comment repartir les risques entre un grand nombre de contractants, l'issue financière de ce genre d'emprunts restait très aléatoire. Bien entendu, entre les souscripteurs potentiels on accordait la priorité à ceux dont l'âge avancé laissait prévoir une échéance rapprochée[43]. Mais on vendait aussi des rentes viagères sur plusieurs corps, et ceci déjà très tôt[44]. Nous ne savons pas grand chose de l'échéance des rentes viagères[45]. Il est rare que les sources nous en donnent des indications. Entre 1470/71 et 1479/80, la ville de Bâle a vendu 31 rentes viagères pour un montant total de 8.609 fl. Pour 17 de ces rentes, atteignant un montant de 5.870 fl. (68,2% de la somme totale), j'ai réussi à reconstruire les dates d'échéance. Pour plus de la moitié de cet échantillon de rentes viagères, il est donc possible de calculer le taux d'intérêt réel (voir le Tableau A en annexe).

De ces calculs, il résulte que la ville a encaissé la somme totale de 5.870 fl. pour la vente de ces rentes. Par ailleurs, elle a dépensé 9.571 fl. pour les paiements annuels. Le solde est donc négatif: on a payé 3.701 fl. de plus que ce qui a été reçu. Ces 3.701 fl. représentent l'intérêt réel payé par la ville. Pour trois rentes seulement, le taux réel a dépassé 4,69%, soit le pourcentage qu'on aurait dû payer pour des rentes rachetables (il s'agit du taux moyen des rentes rachetables contractées pendant ces années; voir le Tableau A en annexe). Neuf rentiers n'ont reçu aucun intérêt; pour certains d'entre eux, l'investissement a même été déficitaire. Si la ville avait emprunté la même somme sous forme de rentes rachetables à 4,69%, elle aurait dû dépenser 11.325 fl. pour les intérêts et le rachat au lieu de 9.571 fl., soit 1.754 fl. (18,33%) de plus.

Si cet échantillon est représentatif (ce qu'il faudrait évidemment vérifier par des analyses ultérieures), il s'ensuit que la dette sous forme de rentes viagères était plus avantageuse pour la ville que sous forme de rentes rachetables. On aurait donc mieux fait de pousser la vente des rentes viagères au

---

43 En 1457, la ville d'Augsbourg vendit des rentes viagères pour une somme totale de 4.000 fl. Les créanciers devaient être âgés de 40 ans au moins. E. Leiber, *Das kanonische Zinsverbot in den Städten des Mittelalters*, Ueberlingen, 1926, p. 108.

44 Ainsi, dès 1286 on trouve des rentes sur plusieurs corps à Lübeck, voir Kuske, *Das Schuldenwesen*, p. 26; 1323 à Regensburg, voir *Regensburger Urkundenbuch*, I, Monumenta Boica 53, NF 7, München, 1912, n° 454.

45 J'ai donné un tableau des rentes viagères vendues par la ville de Munich en 1374 et en 1390 d'après F. Blendinger, "Münchner Bürger, Klöster und Stiftungen als Gläubiger der Reichsstadt Augsburg im 14. und 15. Jahrhundert", in *Archive und Geschichtsforschung. Studien zur fränkischen und bayerischen Geschichte, Fridolin Solleder zum 80. Geburtstag dargebracht*, Neustadt a.d. Aisch, 1966, pp. 80-109, voir H.-J. Gilomen, "Die städtische Schuld Berns und der Basler Rentenmarkt im 15. Jahrhundert", in *Basler Zeitschrift für Geschichte und Altertumskunde,* 82 (1982), p. 22s.

lieu de celle des rentes rachetables. En réalité, dès le milieu du siècle, au plus tard, on a fait le contraire. Les administrateurs n'ont pas pu prendre leur décision en connaissance de cause. Nous en savons plus qu'eux. C'est un problème sérieux pour les historiens de l'économie, qui ont pour tâche d'expliquer les actions et les décisions dans le passé à la lumière de faits que les contemporains ignoraient.

Pour les administrateurs des finances de Bâle, le coût du crédit était pourtant décisif. N'ayant pas à leur disposition de bases statistiques pour calculer les risques, ils s'efforçaient d'en tenir compte en pratiquant des taux différents selon l'âge des créanciers. Pour examiner cela, nous allons élargir notre échantillon à l'ensemble des rentes vendues au cours de ces dix années, c'est-à-dire aux 31 rentes viagères (v. le Tableau B en annexe). Le taux maximum de 10% a été accordé dans 18 cas. C'était le taux normal. Ces rentes étaient fondées sur un seul corps (10 cas), sur les deux corps d'un couple de mariés (7 cas) ou sur ceux d'un frère et d'une soeur (1 cas). Il y a lieu de croire que ces créanciers étaient assez âgés. Ainsi, deux femmes étaient déjà veuves. Gerhard Mekynch, le scribe de la ville, était certainement d'un grand âge, puisqu'il est déjà mentionné comme notaire au concile de Bâle en 1445[46]. Hans Ysenlin et sa femme avaient déjà acheté deux rentes viagères en 1455/56 et 1456/57, au taux réduit de 7, 69%[47]. Dix-huit ans plus tard, en 1473, on leur concéda 10%[48]. Heinrich Vogt était devenu membre de la corporation des merciers dès 1435[49]. Il acheta une première rente viagère en 1466[50]. Peter-Hans Rotenburg était entré dans la même corporation en 1451[51]. Hans Pirry est attesté de 1461 à 1477 comme procureur du monastère de Gnadental[52]; en 1469, il acheta une première rente viagère rapportant 9,09%[53]. Par ailleurs, il y avait des rentes sur un corps d'un taux plus faible (9,09 et 9.41%) et d'autres sur les corps d'un couple marié produisant également un intérêt plus réduit (8,33% dans deux cas et 8,66% dans un cas). On ne s'étonnera pas du taux peu élevé de 8% pour la rente de deux enfants (Ennelin et Afra). Trois rentes sur deux corps ont été vendues à un taux de 10%, mais avec la clause que ce taux diminuerait de la moitié ou d'un tiers après la mort d'un des rentiers. D'autres rentes du même genre ont été vendues pour des taux encore plus faibles. Une rente sur trois corps n'est émise qu'à un taux de 7,5%.

Comme les rentes viagères n'étaient pas résiliables, la ville ne pouvait rien entreprendre contre les gains excessifs dus à la longévité de certains rentiers[54]. Les autorités de la ville de Berne s'en aperçurent avec amertume en 1390. Dans une instruction pour mener des pourparlers avec Anna Billung de Bâle, ils rappelaient qu'elle avait déjà perçu la somme énorme de 5.400 fl. en rentes annuelles[55]. La même rentière est visée par le chroniqueur Conrad Justinger qui, racontant les efforts fournis pendant les années quatre-vingt du 14e siècle pour amortir la dette publique, constata qu'on avait réussi à racheter toutes les créances sauf celles de deux vieilles femmes de Bâle, auxquelles on

---

46 Voir A. Bernoulli (éd.), *Basler Chroniken*, IV, Leipzig, 1890, p. 137; P. Koelner, *Die Zunft zum Schlüssel in Basel*, Basel, 1953, p. 235.

47 Harms (éd.), *Der Stadthaushalt*, I, p. 200 ligne 1 et p. 202 ligne 89.

48 Harms (éd.), *Der Stadthaushalt*, I, p. 245 ligne 72 et Finanz AA 4.20, fol. 104v.

49 Koelner, *Die Zunft*, p. 250.

50 Harms (éd.), *Der Stadthaushalt*, I, p. 224 ligne 94.

51 Koelner, *Die Zunft*, p. 244.

52 B. Degler-Spengler, *Das Klarissenkloster Gnadental 1289-1529*, Quellen und Forschungen zur Basler Geschichte 3), Basel, 1969 p. 104.

53 Harms (éd.), *Der Stadthaushalt*, I, p. 230 ligne 72.

54 En principe, le rachat de rentes viagères était impossible sans le consentement des rentiers. Çà et là, on trouve cependant des rentes viagères rachetables et des rachats. La ville de Bâle, par exemple, racheta en 1466/67 pour 150 fl. une rente viagère vendue en 1425 pour 312 fl. Pendant 41 ans, une annuïté de 26 fl. avait été versée, ce qui donne un total de 1.066 fl. En ajoutant les 150 fl. du rachat et en déduisant les 312 fl. du versement de 1425, cette rente a coûté à la ville la somme coquette de 904 fl., sans les frais d'administration. Voir StAB, *Finanz* AA 4.17, fol. 124r. Mais il y a des exemples en sens contraire. En 1454/55, on racheta pour 20 fl. une rente viagère qui avait été vendue en 1449/50 pour 40 fl. La rente annuelle s'élevait à 4 fl., payés cinq fois, soit 20 fl. au total. Dans ce cas, la ville avait emprunté à titre gratuit. Harms (éd.), *Der Stadthaushalt*, I, p. 182 ligne 40, et II, p. 282 ligne 82.

55 *Fontes rerum Bernensium*, X, Bern, 1956, no. 1402.

devait près de 100 fl. de rente viagère par an[56]. Cette expérience négative a eu des conséquences importantes: tout au long du 15e siècle, les autorités de Berne n'ont plus jamais vendu de rentes viagères[57]. D'autres villes, au contraire, ont vendu en même temps des rentes rachetables et viagères[58]. Dans quelques villes, on a même donné – du moins pour un temps – la préférence aux rentes viagères[59]. Prenons encore une fois la ville de Bâle comme échantillon:

TABLEAU V. **Les formes de rente dans la ville de Bâle, 1420/21 - 1429/30**

année	rachetables, fl.	%	viagères, fl.	%	total,fl.	100%=11702 fl.
1420/21	1.750	38,8	2.760	61,2	4.510	38,5%
1421/22	3.390	32,1	7.174	70,4	10.564	67,9%
1422/23	850	9,2	8.374	90,8	9.224	78,8%
1423/24	1.650	36,0	2.933	64,0	4.583	39,2%
1424/25	11.530	79,7	2.930	20,3	14.460	123,6%
1425/26	18.660	56,2	14.533	43,8	33.193	283,7%
1426/27	3.662	51,7	3.417	48,3	7.079	60,5%
1427/28	5.000	41,9	6.938,5	58,1	11.938,5	102,0%
1428/29	6.850	62,2	4.170	37,8	11.020	94,2%
1429/30	7.853	75,1	2.600	24,9	10.453	89,3%
1420/29	61.195	52,3	55.829,5	47,7	117.024,5	

Plusieurs faits méritent d'être mis en évidence:

1° L'ampleur des déficits comblés par des emprunts diffère énormément d'une année à l'autre: de 4.510 fl. en 1420/21 à 33.193 fl. en 1425/26, c'est-à-dire du simple au décuple. Si la somme moyenne des dix années (11.702 fl.) est prise pour base (100%), l'écart se situe entre 30,8% et 283,7%.

2° Pendant la période envisagée, les administrateurs des finances Bâloises n'ont pas hésité à emprunter sous forme de rentes viagères, contrairement, par exemple, à ceux de Berne.

3° Sur l'ensemble de la période, le rapport entre rentes rachetables (52,3%) et rentes viagères (47,7%) est équilibré, mais il y a des différences énormes d'une année à l'autre: en 1424/25, les rentes viagères représentent moins du quart du montant total emprunté, tandis qu'en 1429/30 elles dépassent 90%.

56 G. Studer (éd.), *Die Berner-Chronik des Conrad Justinger*, , Bern, 1871, p. 159.

57 La conviction que la rente viagère est nuisible pour les finances urbaines se rencontre aussi dans quelques autres villes: en 1484, Cologne interdisait la vente de rentes viagères, voir Leiber, *Das kanonische Zinsverbot*, p. 116.

58 A Breslau, par exemple, entre 1357 et 1418, 76% des sommes investies l'étaient en rentes héréditaires (*Erbrenten*) et 24% en rentes viagères. Voir O. Beyer, *Schuldenwesen der Stadt Breslau im 14. und 15. Jahrhundert mit besonderer Berücksichtigung der Verschuldung durch Rentenverkauf*, Diss. Breslau, 1900, Breslau 1901, pp. 19 et 28. L'affirmation de Espinas, *Les finances*, p. 307, est contestable: 'partout la vente de rentes viagères était le mode d'emprunt le plus usité et les rentes formaient de beaucoup la partie la plus considérable de la dette'.

59 C'est, par exemple, le cas à Bâle pendant les deux premières décennies du 15e siècle. Pour Nuremberg dans les années soixante-dix et quatre-vingt du 14e siècle, voir *Die Chroniken der deutschen Städte*, I, p. 294. Les rentes vendues par la ville de Wetzlar entre 1351 et 1368 étaient presque sans exception des rentes viagères, voir A. Schoenwerk, "Der Bankrott der Reichsstadt Wetzlar 1369", in *Geschichtliche Landeskunde, Mitteilungen des Instituts für geschichtliche Landeskunde der Rheinlande an der Universität Bonn, Rheinische Heimatblätter*, 4 (1927), p. 520. D'après Espinas, *Les finances*, p. 305, la grande majorité des rentes payées par la ville de Douai aux 13e et 14e siècles étaient viagères. A Cologne, à partir de la deuxième moitié du 14e siècle, on a préféré presque exclusivement les rentes viagères, voir Knipping, *Das Schuldenwesen*, p. 357s.

4° A en juger par cet échantillon, c'est surtout lorsque le montant total de l'emprunt est faible que les rentes viagères atteignent une proportion élevée.

Le fait que le service de l'intérêt s'éteignait quasi automatiquement à la mort du ou des titulaires formait incontestablement un argument de poids en faveur des rentes viagères. Cet argument était tellement évident qu'on ne le trouve que rarement formulé explicitement dans les sources[60]. Les tentatives pour remplacer les rentes rachetables par des rentes viagères visaient au même but[61]. On pourrait même se poser la question de savoir si la mortalité élevée au milieu du 14e siècle et le retour périodique de la peste ont encouragé les autorités de certaines villes à accorder la préférence aux rentes viagères.

Pour beaucoup d'acheteurs, les rentes viagères assuraient leurs frais de subsistance. On trouve beaucoup de femmes et surtout de veuves parmi ces rentiers. Lors de leur entrée en religion, moines et moniales étaient dotés de préférence au moyen d'une rente viagère. A Zurich, les deux tiers des rentes viagères étaient payées à des membres du clergé[62]. Dans le premiers tiers du 15e siècle surtout, les rentes viagères étaient également recherchées par des personnes nanties. Parmi les rentiers de la ville de Bâle, on trouve des membres des familles Burggraf, Nygebur et Prüss de Francfort[63], von Veenhove de Cologne[64], von Gelren de Spire[65], von Perrimon (Praroman) de Fribourg en Suisse[66], zum Gelthus, zer Eich, Gossenhofer zu Schenkenberg, zem Jungen, Windeck de Mayence[67], Mensler et Müge de Strasbourg[68], Bubenberg, Diesbach, Scharnachtal, Senn von Bremgarten de Berne[69], Russ et von

60 A Krakau, par exemple, on préférait en 1460 vendre une rente viagère en se basant sur cette considération: voir B. Lesinski, "Les rentes comme instrument de crédit dans la Pologne médiévale", in *Studia Historiae Oeconomicae*, 3 (1968), p. 57: La vente était motivée par le fait qu'on '...*der stat evigen getwang nicht machen mögen und gleichwol aus czeitlicher bürde czeitlichen leichtlicher komen möchte*'.

61 Dans les années 1432-73, les autorités de Cologne s'efforçaient de convertir la dette, et le conseil municipal ordonnait à l'administration financière '*lijfrente zo verkouffen ind erfflich gelt, dae die stat mit besweirt is, affzolegen*.' Knipping, *Das Schuldenwesen*, p. 361.

62 W. Frey, *Beiträge zur Finanzgeschichte Zürichs im Mittelalter*, Zürich, 1910, p. 157.

63 Sifrid Burggraf, StAB, *Finanz* AA 4.16, fol. 116r, 153r; Harms (éd.), *Der Stadthaushalt*, I, p. 176 ligne 52; sa femme Yrmel, StAB, *Finanz* AA 4.16, fol. 99v.; Henne Nygebur, StAB, *Finanz* AA 4.16, fol. 116r, 138r; Johann Prüss et sa femme Gred pour leurs enfants Gred et Johann, StAB, fol. 116v, *Finanz* AA 4.17, fol. 125r, voir aussi *Urkundenbuch der Stadt Basel*, VI, Basel, 1902, p. 525 no. 188.

64 Gerhart von dem Veenhoue et sa femme Gerdrut, StAB, *Finanz* AA 4.16, fol. 117r, 138r; Harms (éd.), *Der Stadthaushalt*, I, p. 112 ligne 5.

65 Claus von Gelren et sa femme Anne, StAB, *Finanz* AA 4.16, fol. 118v, 138r.

66 Anna, femme de Jacob von Perrimon, Harms (éd.), *Der Stadthaushalt*, I, p. 81 ligne 28.

67 Heinrich Gelthus, Harms (éd.), *Der Stadthaushalt*, I, p. 111 ligne 12 et 15; StAB, *Finanz* AA 4. 14, fol. 68v; AA 4.16, fol. 11 Or, 138r; *Urkundenbuch der Stadt Basel*, VIII, n° 6 ligne 36. Götz et Jecklin zer Eich, Harms (éd.), *Der Stadthaushalt*, I, p. 111 ligne 95; StAB, *Finanz* AA 4.16, fol. 119v, 153r; *Urkundenbuch der Stadt Basel*, VI, n° 237. Ort zer Eich pour ses enfants Salomon et Else, StAB, *Finanz* AA 4.16, fol. 112v, 113r, AA 4.17, fol. 123v. Clas Gossenhofer pour ses enfants Adam et Gred, StAB, *Finanz* AA 4.16, fol. 114r, AA 4.17, fol. 123v, AA 4.20, fol. 151r, AA 4.21, fol. 51r, AA 4.22, fol. 157r. Clas Gossenhofer pour ses filles Else et Katharina, StAB, *Finanz* AA 4.16, fol. 114 r, AA 4.17, fol. 124r. Katharina, femme d'Arnold zem Jungen, Harms (éd.), *Der Stadthaushalt*, I, p. 111 ligne 19; StAB, *Finanz* AA 4.16, fol. 119r. Peter zem Jungen et sa fille Katharina, StAB, *Finanz* AA 4.16, fol. 110r, AA 4.17, fol. 123 r. Jaeklin zem Jungen pour sa fille Else et la moniale Katharine Summerowin, StAB, *Finanz* AA 4.16, fol. 108v, 152v, 153r. Jecklin zem Jungen pour sa femme Lise et sa fille Else, StAB, *Finanz* AA 4.16, fol. 108r. Les frères Henni et Herman Windeck, StAB, *Finanz* AA 4.16, fol. 111v, AA 4.17, fol. 123r, AA 4.20, fol. 151r; *Urkundenbuch der Stadt Basel*, VIII, n° 6/37.

68 Hans Mensler, Harms (éd.), *Der Stadthaushalt*, I, p. 180 ligne 22, p. 184 ligne 72; StAB, *Finanz* AA 4.16, fol. 138v, 192v; *Urkundenbuch der Stadt Basel*, VIII, n° 6/5. Peter Müge, Harms (éd.), *Der Stadthaushalt*, I, p. 75 ligne 42.

69 Johann von Bubenberg, Harms (éd.), *Der Stadthaushalt*, I, p. 72 ligne 16, p. 83 ligne 72, p. 102 ligne 13; StAB, *Finanz* AA 4.14, fol. 57r, AA 4.16, fol. 89rv, 153r. Niclaus von Diesbach und seine Frau Margaretha, Harms (éd.), *Der Stadthaushalt*, I, p. 75 ligne 82; StAB, *Finanz* AA 4.16, fol. 80r, 152v. Heinrich und Franz von Scharnachtal, Harms (éd.), *Der Stadthaushalt*, I, p. 75 ligne 21; StAB, *Finanz* AA 4.16, fol. 79v, 152v, AA 4.17, fol. 94r; *Urkundenbuch der Stadt Basel*, VIII, n° 6/19. Jacob Senn von Bremgarten, Harms (éd.), *Der Stadthaushalt*, I, p. 139 ligne 1; StAB, *Finanz* AA 4.16, fol. 75r, 152v.

Langnau de Lucerne[70]. De véritables fortunes étaient investies en rentes viagères. La Bâloise Gred zem Wolf, veuve d'Ulman Vitztum, touchait chaque année une rente de 600 fl., qu'elle avait achetée en plusieurs tranches pour un montant total de 6.260 fl[71].

TABLEAU VI. **Les emprunts de la ville de Bâle sous forme de rentes, 1470/71 - 1479/80**

année	rachetables, fl.	%	viagères, fl.	%	total,fl.	100%=10.800 fl.
1470/71	4.855	70,8	2.007	29,2	6.862	63,5%
1471/72	8.250	71,3	3.325	28,7	11.575	107,2%
1472/73	4.923	86,7	757	13,3	5.680	52,6%
1473/74	27.303	97,2	778	2,8	28.081	260,0%
1474/75	10.584	98,1	200	1,9	10.784	99,9%
1475/76	18.386	98,5	280	1,5	18.666	172,8%
1476/77	15.253	97,3	430	2,7	15.683	145,2%
1477/78	5.913	100	-	0,0	5.913	54,8%
1478/79	2.222	77,9	630	22,1	2.852	26,4%
1479/80	1.900	100	-	0	1.900	17,6%
1470/79	99.589	92,2	8.407	7,8	107.996	
1420/29	61.195	52,3	55.829,5	47,7	117.024,5	

1° De 1470/71 à 1479/80, l'écart entre la somme la plus basse et la plus haute s'est encore creusé: il se situe entre 17,6% et 260% de la moyenne décennale (au lieu d'un écart compris entre 30,8% et 283,7% en 1420/29).

2° Les rentes viagères n'ont plus la cote auprès des administrateurs des finances urbaines Bâloises.

3° La somme encaissée par la vente de rentes rachetables ne tombe jamais au-dessous de 70%. Pour l'ensemble de la période considérée, elle se situe au-dessus de 90%.

4° Dans la deuxième moitié du 15e siècle, les autorités Bâloises ont affiché une préférence marquée pour les rentes rachetables. A mon sens, cette option n'était pas motivée, comme dans le cas de Berne, par l'idée qu'en fin de compte les rentes viagères seraient beaucoup plus coûteuses pour la ville que les rentes rachetables. Les autorités étaient surtout sensibles au fait que sous cette forme, la dette publique offrait plus de liberté dans la conduite de la politique financière. A Bâle, on avait acquis très tôt une grande souplesse dans l'administration de la dette publique.

D'autres villes n'ont pas été aussi heureuses. Le choix du conseil municipal pouvait même se limiter soit à des rentes rachetables, soit à des rentes perpétuelles. Ces dernières, qui en théorie du moins se perpétuaient jusqu'à la fin des temps, ne se prêtaient absolument pas au financement des

70 Anton Russ und seine Frau Anna von Küssenberg, Harms (éd.), *Der Stadthaushalt,* I, p. 102 ligne 1; StAB, *Finanz* AA 4.16, fol. 80v, 97r, 138rv; *Urkundenbuch der Stadt Basel,* VIII, n° 6/2. Benedicta von Langnau, Harms (éd.), *Der Stadthaushalt,* I, p. 86 ligne 40.

71 StAB, *Finanz* AA 4.16, fol. 63v. Grede murut le 22 juillet 1439, voir StAB, *Finanz* AA 4.16, fol. 152v. Pour cette rente Gred a payé durant plusieurs années des tranches de 110 à 410 fl. Le 15 juillet 1430, la ville lui donna un acte pour la somme de 3.400 fl. et une rente de 336 fl. D'autres versements suivirent de 1432 à 1437/38. Le 7 juillet 1438, un nouveau diplôme fut établi pour la somme de 6.260 fl. et une rente annuelle de 600 fl. Harms (éd.), *Der Stadthaushalt,* I, p. 71 ligne 83, p. 76 ligne 1, p. 83 ligne 86, p. 93 ligne 5, p. 95 ligne 49, p. 98 ligne 74, p. 108 ligne 31, p. 115 ligne 24, p. 119 ligne 37, p. 124 ligne 52, p. 125 ligne 52, p. 131 ligne 62, p. 142 ligne 99, p. 147 ligne 93, p. 150 ligne 73, p. 150 ligne 77, vol. 2, p. 212 ligne 83; StAB, *Finanz* AA 4.16, fol. 63v, 64r, 152v.

besoins d'une ville. Pourtant en 1425, Conrad zem Haupt, l'agent représentant les intérêts financiers de la ville de Winterthur à Bâle et à Strasbourg, conseilla de vendre des rentes perpétuelles afin de rassembler la somme nécessaire au rachat d'une dette contractée plus d'un siècle auparavant auprès de plusieurs financiers Strasbourgeois[72] et dont on voulait se débarasser[73]. La ville suivit ce conseil: en 1427, on vendit deux rentes perpétuelles pour la somme totale de 5.150 fl. L'intérêt annuel s'élevait à 150 fl., soit à peine 2,9%. On n'abandonnait cependant pas l'espoir de racheter un jour cette dette perpétuelle: une stipulation dans le contrat visait au droit de préemption si jamais les rentiers ou leurs héritiers avaient l'intention de vendre ces titres[74]. Avec la somme acquise, on racheta des rentes pour lesquelles on avait payé 5 à 6% d'intérêt[75].

L'emprunt sous forme d'un simple prêt à intérêt auprès de financiers juifs, lombards ou autres, encore assez courant au 14e siècle, ne se rencontre plus qu'exceptionnellement au 15e siècle. En 1424 par exemple, la ville de Zurich accueillit deux Juifs pour une durée de douze ans, à condition qu'ils lui prêtent 250 fl.[76]. Ce rôle modeste est peut-être une conséquence des amortissements de dettes effectués par le roi Wenzel, qui ont appauvri les financiers juifs[77]. Devenus pour la plupart de petits prêteurs sur gages, ceux-ci furent chassés des villes suisses au cours du 15e siècle[78]. La ville de Berne, par exemple, qui en 1384 encore avait emprunté une somme de 2.060 fl. auprès des Lombards de Soleure[79], chassa en 1427 Lombards et Juifs du territoire sous sa juridiction. Cette expulsion était motivée par une idée mercantiliste avant la lettre, que nous rencontrons aussi concernant les rentes[80]: Par leur usure, Lombards et Juifs étaient considérés comme très nuisibles pour la ville et la campagne, parce qu'ils auraient exporté à l'étranger d'immense sommes d'argent comptant[81].

Quels créanciers?

Restait à décider où il fallait chercher des créanciers. En cas de besoins financiers, les conseils municipaux se tournaient de préférence vers les bourgeois et habitants de leur propre ville. En règle générale, on évitait autant que possible le recours à des créanciers étrangers (c'est-à-dire des personnes

72 Sur cette dette voir K. Hauser, "Winterthurs Strassburger Schuld (1314-1479). Mit Beilagen (1405-1477)", in *Jahrbuch für Schweizerische Geschichte*, 28 (1903), pp. 1-59.

73 StAW, *Urkunde* Nr. 639, 19: '*Man fint an fil enden 40 gulden um 1 gulden ewig, da gienge üch der halb zins ab*'.

74 StAW, *Urkunde* Nr. 642, 19 mai 1427: '*Waere dz der obgenant Ruodolff von Ringeltingen, sin erben ald naechkomen den obgenanten jaerlichen zins deheinest verkoeffen woeltint samenthaft oder ein teil, von was sachen wegen sich dz fuogti oder gefuogen moechti, das soent sy vns den obgenanten von Wintterthur als vnseren naechkomen ze wissent vnd kunt tun*'. Voir aussi *Urkunde* Nr. 1121: proposition pour le rachat d'une rente perpétuelle. Evidemment, le plus souvent les villes ont évité de vendre des rentes perpétuelles. Mais le cas de Winterthur n'est pas tout à fait isolé. En 1480/81, par exemple, la ville de Zofingen a vendu une rente perpétuelle de 34 fl. pour la somme de 1.020 fl, l'intérêt s'élevant donc à 3,3%. Stadtarchiv Zofingen, 1, *Stadtbuch*, fol. 45v: '... *ewigs zins sind nitt widerkoüffig...*' Avec cette somme, on racheta le 24 février 1481 une autre rente; Stadtarchiv Zofingen, 1, *Stadtbuch*, fol. 45r.

75 StAW, B 2, 1, *Ratsprotokoll 1405-1460*, fol. 74v.

76 H. Zeller-Werdmüller (éd.), *Die Zürcher Stadtbücher des XIV. und XV. Jahrhunderts*, II, Leipzig, 1901, p. 166s. n° 196, 16 août 1423; p. 186 n° 225, 15 mai 1424; p. 192s. n° 229, 24 juin 1424; Staatsarchiv Zürich, *Urk. Stadt und Land*, Nr. 290, 2 mars 1425.

77 A. Süssmann, *Die Judenschuldentilgungen unter König Wenzel* (Schriften der Gesellschaft zur Förderung der Wissenschaft des Judentums), Berlin, 1907.

78 H.-J. Gilomen, "Aufnahme und Vertreibung von Juden in Schweizer Städten im Spätmittelalte", in: H.-J. Gilomen, A.-L. Head-König et A. Radeff (éds.), *Migration in die Städte. Ausschluss - Assimilierung - Integration - Multikulturalität / Migration vers les villes. Exclusion - assimilation - intégration - multiculturalité* (Schweizerische Gesellschaft für Wirtschafts- und Sozialgeschichte - Société Suisse d'histoire économique et sociale 16), Zürich, 2000, p. 93-118.

79 J.J. Amiet, "Die französischen und lombardischen Geldwucherer des Mittelalters namentlich in der Schweiz", in *Jahrbuch für Schweizerische Geschichte*, 1 (1876), pp. 177-255; 2 (1877), pp. 141-328, ici p. 241. Sur le prêt d'un juif de Renzheim, voir *Deutsche Reichstagsakten*, II, p. 45.

80 Voir plus bas.

81 G. Tobler, "Zur Geschichte der Juden im alten Bern bis 1427", in *Archiv des Historischen Vereins des Kantons Bern,* 12 (1889), p. 361: Juifs et Lombards '*von der statt und land unmessig barschaft hant gefüret, darumb ouch si wol ze vermidene sint*'.

habitant hors de la ville et de sa juridiction) et l'on se débarrassait le plus tôt possible de tels engagements[82]. En 1478, par exemple, après une délibération sur le budget, le conseil de Bâle décida le rachat des rentes à 5% et surtout de celles payables à des étrangers[83].

On peut discerner plusieurs raisons pour cette préférence. Prenons l'exemple assez instructif de la ville de Berne. Commentant les difficultés à trouver en 1384 des créanciers en ville, le chroniqueur Conrad Justinger remarque qu'on aurait bien pu trouver l'argent chez les Bernois eux-mêmes, mais que personne ne voulait le prêter à la ville parce que celle-ci n'honorait pas ses engagements[84]. Il faut sous-entendre qu'en cas de retard ou de refus de paiement, les créanciers locaux n'avaient pas à leur disposition les moyens de contrainte dont pouvaient se servir les étrangers. Durant les années quatre-vingt du 14e siècle, les autorités Bernoises se soucièrent de l'endettement important envers des créanciers étrangers, surtout Bâlois. Nous avons les chiffres de l'engagement de la ville envers les Bâlois: en 1397, on payait 334 florins en rentes viagères et 1.226 florins en rentes rachetables[85]. Le conseil de Berne aurait préféré que l'or et l'argent payés sous forme de rentes restent en ville et ne soient pas dépensés ailleurs[86]. Cette idée mercantiliste, très répandue à l'époque, est attestée maintes fois dans les sources: l'écoulement de métaux précieux à l'extérieur était considéré comme une perte pour l'économie de la ville. Des restrictions à l'exportation furent promulguées dans beaucoup de villes. La 'faim de métaux précieux' (*bullion famine*) – causée avant tout par la nécessité d'alimenter le monnayage municipal – resta forte jusqu'aux années soixante du 15e siècle[87]. Par conséquent, l'interdiction faite aux particuliers de vendre des rentes à des étrangers fut décrétée dans certaines villes[88].

Un édit du 12 mars 1384 laisse transparaître d'autres facteurs exprimant la préférence des Bernois pour les créanciers locaux. Les autorités s'engageaient à continuer en toutes circonstances le paiement des rentes, même si un rentier local avait commis un méfait quelconque[89]. D'après un autre édit, daté du 1er août 1389, les conseillers promettaient de continuer le paiement en faveur de ceux qui auraient fui la ville à cause d'une poursuite pénale[90]. Par ailleurs, on s'efforçait également de mettre les nouveaux créanciers à l'abri de critiques anti-usuraires en défendant d'attenter à leur honneur et de les

---

82 Pour l'époque considérée, il est inexact d'affirmer que l'on aurait préféré des créancier étrangers '*um der eigenen Bürgerschaft keinen Grund zu noch stärkerer Einmischung in die Verwaltung der Stadt zu liefern*'. Voir Landmann, "Geschichte des öffentlichen Kredits", p. 41.

83 StAB, *Finanz* R 1, fol. 7r: '*Zum besten vnd zum furderlichesten abzelosen vnd sunderlich was vsserthalb der stat ist, wa das sin mag, mit nammen was da stat von 20 einen, vnd daneben vffzenemmen als vor stat*'.

84 *Die Berner Chronik des Conrad Justinger*, par G. Studer (éd.), Bern, 1871, p. 158.

85 Gilomen, *Die städtische Schuld Berns*, p. 7.

86 *Fontes rerum Bernensium*, X, Bern, 1956, n° 502, 12 mars 1384: '... *want ouch das selb guot an silber und golt und andern dingen dester bas und fuorer in unser stat mag beliben ...*'

87 P. Spufford, *Money and its use in medieval Europe*, Cambridge, 1988, pp. 339-362: *The Bullion-Famines of the Later Middle Ages*. Voir aussi les thèses critiques de N. Sussman, "The Late Medieval Bullion Famine Reconsidered", in *The Journal of Economic History*, 58 (1998), pp. 126-154.

88 Par exemple, dans le pays de Zoug en 1412: *Sammlung Schweizerischer Rechtsquellen*, Zug 1, Aarau, 1971, p. 230, 12. mars 1412. Dans le pays de Schwyz, l'engagement de terres à des étrangers en vue d'acquérir des rentes fut interdit en 1454; J.J. Blumer, *Staats- und Rechtsgeschichte der schweizerischen Demokratien oder der Kantone Uri, Schwyz, Unterwalden, Glarus, Zug und Appenzell*, I: *Das Mittelalter*, St. Gallen, 1850, p. 457s. En 1488, le conseil de Berne ordonnait à ses sujets dans la vallée de la Simme de racheter les rentes payables aux bourgeois de Lucerne et autres, dont ils avaient grevé les terres. Lettre adressée au bailli dans la vallée de la Simme, Staatsarchiv Bern, *Missiven* E, fol. 324r: '*Lieber getruwer, wiewol wir dir vormolen ernstlich beuolchen vnnd gantzen gewalt habenn geben, mitt den vnnsern bi dir, so merclich summen gelts zü Lutzern vnd anderswo vff järlige verzinsung genommen haben, zu verschaffenn, die selben zü ledigen, so verstan wir doch, wie seligs nitt beschechen vnd das sich etlich dem widerwertig erzöugen, das vnns vast missvallet. Vnd also vss grund des, so beuelchend wir dir ernstlichen, nochmalen mitt allen denen, so vsserthab vnnsern landenn vnd gebiete gelt vff gebrochen vnd dadurch ihre güter beladen haben, zueuerschaffen vnd si an die heiligen tün schweren, solig zinß vnd houbtgüt zü den zilen vnd tagen, wie die an dem bescheiden sind, abzülösenn, ir güter zü ledigen und darinn dehein verzug noch widerred zübruchen*'.

89 *Fontes rerum Bernensium*, X, Bern, 1956, n° 502, 12 mars 1384: '...*ob ioch der selben personen, so uns das guot lüwen deheine missetete und ützit vershulte, noch denne süllent wir inen oder ir erben oder an die stette, da si das selb ir guot hin ordnoten oder beschigken, geben, berichten und bezalen...*'

90 *Fontes rerum Bernensium*, X, n° 1180.

qualifier d'usuriers ou de voleurs[91]. Ces efforts montrent l'importance que les autorités attribuaient au choix de créanciers locaux. Mais tous ces mesures restèrent sans effet: à quelques exceptions près, les Bernois se sont abstenus d'acheter des rentes de leur propre ville pendant tout le bas Moyen Age. La ville était contrainte de s'adresser surtout aux Bâlois et aux Strasbourgeois, parfois à d'autres étrangers encore[92].

Cette préférence accordée aux bourgeois du cru s'explique aussi par le fait que les frais d'administration et de contrôle (*handling costs*), ainsi que les risques étaient moindres pour des créanciers locaux. D'ordinaire les rentes étaient payables au domicile du créancier. Les frais de paiement à des créanciers étrangers pouvaient être assez élevés et l'on courait des risques supplémentaires à cause du transport de l'argent[93]. A chaque échéance, il fallait envoyer un courrier avec l'argent vers des destinations parfois assez lointaines[94]. Dans la première moitié du 15e siècle, la ville de Bâle, par exemple, avait des créanciers à Masevaux, Mulhouse, Brisach, Fribourg et Neuenburg en Brisgau, Zurich, Strasbourg, Mayence, Spire, Worms, Francfort et ailleurs encore[95].

TABLEAU VII. **Les emprunts en rentes rachetables de la ville de Bâle à Francfort au 15e siècle.**

Année	somme, fl.	rentes, fl.	taux,%	tranches		moyenne, fl.
1410/11	4.600	200	4,35	1 de	4.600 fl.	4.600
1425/26	2.300	115	5	3 de	400-1.000 fl.	767
1438	4.700	235	5	7 de	400-1.000 fl.	671
1446/47	4.540	227	5	3 de	340-3.000 fl.	1.513
1474	7.440	372	5	17 de	200-1.200 fl.	438
1476	500	25	5	1 de	500 fl.	500

En 1410/11, une somme de 4.600 fl. fut versée en une seule tranche par Guete Knoblouchin et son fils Brand. Le taux d'intérêt (une rente de 200 fl.) était fort modeste, puisqu'il atteignait à peine 4,35%[96]. La somme de 2.300 fl. fut versée en 1425/26 en trois tranches; la rente annuelle de 115 fl. correspond à un taux d'intérêt de 5%. L'emprunt important contracté le 24 novembre 1438 à Francfort s'élevait à 4.700 florins d'or, versé en sept tranches individuelles valant de 400 à 1.000 florins[97]. Les rentes – 235 florins au total, soit 5% de la somme versée – étaient payables pour moitié le dimanche de Letare (aux mois de mars/avril) et pour moitié à la décollation de Saint Jean-Baptiste (le 29 août). Ces termes tombaient donc à la mi-temps des deux messes (du dimanche Oculi au dimanche des rameaux

91 *Fontes rerum Bernensium*, X, n° 502.

92 Gilomen, *Die städtische Schuld Berns*, pp. 57-60.

93 Dans le formulaire des contrats de rentes viagères conclus avec des rentiers de Strasbourg, la ville de Bâle s'engageait, '*jnn die [30 fl. de rente] gen Strassburg in die statd on jren [des créanciers] costen vnd schaden ze werende vnd ze antwürtende*'; StAB, *Finanz* AA 4.16, fol. 141r-141v. D'après le formulaire des rentes de Mayence, ces paiements étaient effectués '*vff vnsern [der Stadt] costen schaden vnd verlust jn der stat Mentz jn yren sichern gewalt...*'; StAB, *Finanz* AA 4.16, fol. 145r-146r. La ville de Bâle consentit au paiement extraordinaire d'une rente à Mayence au lieu de Bâle, à condition que les rentiers supportent seuls le risque d'une perte en cours de route: '*Vnd were sach, dz solich gelt vnderwegen genommen würde, sol inen genommen sin vnd der stat nit, als der brief wiset*'. StAB, *Finanz* AA 4. 16, fol. 153v; voir aussi fol. 72r, rente du 22 février 1427.

94 Pour mieux étaler les besoins de liquidité au cours de l'année, les administrateurs Bâlois préféraient stipuler le paiement des rentes en quatre versements. Mais pour les créanciers étrangers cela était trop coûteux. On paierait donc la rente de Heinrich Keller à Wil en Thurgauvie en un seul versement à la Pentecôte, mais on prévoyait un paiement en quatre versements si jamais il venait habiter Bâle: '*Zuge er aber har, so sollte man jm die 50 guldin glich geteilt zue den vier fronuasten geben*'. StAB, *Finanz* AA 4.16, fol. 96v.

95 Gilomen, *Die städtische Schuld Berns*, p. 58.

96 StAB, *Finanz* D 1, fol. 115r.

97 StAB, *Finanz* AA 4, 16, fol. 35v-37r.; M. Rothmann, *Die Frankfurter Messen im Mittelalter* (Frankfurter Historische Abhandlungen 40), Stuttgart, 1998, n'a pas exploité ces sources. Voir aussi Harms (éd.), *Der Stadthaushalt*, II, p. 211 ligne 45.

au printemps et du 15 août au 8 septembre en été)[98]. D'autres termes – la nativité de la Vierge (le 8 septembre) et le dimanche des rameaux étaient prévus dans des contrats du 15 octobre 1446[99], du 1er avril[100] et du 7 septembre 1447[101]. Ces emprunts s'élevaient à une somme de 4.540 florins et les rentes annuelles à 227 florins (5%). Les 372 florins de rentes de l'important emprunt contracté le 23 mars 1474 (7.440 florins en 17 tranches de 200 à 1.200 florins) étaient eux aussi payables pour moitié le dimanche de Letare et pour moitié à la décollation de Saint Jean-Baptiste[102].

Les exemples d'emprunts placés à Francfort montrent qu'on ne s'adressait à des créanciers étrangers que pour des sommes assez élevées. L'urgence de se procurer vite de grosses sommes liquides influait donc sur la décision d'approcher des marchés financiers importants: pour Bâle, c'était en premier lieu celui de Strasbourg; pour les autres villes de la Suisse alémanique c'était celui de Bâle même[103]. En de rares occasions seulement, les Bâlois se dirigeaient vers Francfort, Mayence ou Spire[104]. Pour conclure ces emprunts à l'étranger, il fallait avoir recours aux services coûteux d'un agent financier sur place. En 1448/49, par exemple, on avait eu l'idée d'approcher le marché financier de Spire, mais l'agent des Bâlois établi à Spire dut s'avouer vaincu: bien que d'autres villes aient racheté leurs rentes, les capitaux remboursés furent aussitôt réinvestis sans que l'agent puisse s'en procurer une partie pour la ville de Bâle. D'autres rachats étant imminents, il proposa de renouveler ses efforts. Mais il ajouta qu'il ne pourrait pas s'agir d'une somme correspondant aux besoins des Bâlois parce que leur ville était trop éloignée pour les créanciers[105].

Les autorités municipales préféraient des créanciers d'envergure qui pouvaient verser des sommes considérables. Il ne semble pas que le taux d'intérêt ait influé sur la décision d'approcher les marchés étrangers[106]. Les conditions à Francfort n'étaient pas plus favorables qu'à Bâle. Dès le deuxième quart du 15e siècle, le taux de 5% offert par la ville de Bâle à ses propres bourgeois pour des rentes rachetables était le plus élevé du marché; et le niveau du taux moyen s'abaissa encore pendant la deuxième moitié du siècle[107]. Dans les années 1448/49, à un moment où l'argent était rare dans la Confédération et dans les environs[108], le conseil de Bâle continuait à conclure avec ses bourgeois des rentes rachetables à 5[109] voir 4%[110], alors qu'il payait jusqu'à 6%[111] et même 6 2/3%[112] à Strasbourg, parce que des sommes importantes pouvaient y être empruntées. Cependant, ces taux excessifs furent réduits

98 Rothmann, *Die Frankfurter Messen*, p. 102.

99 StAB, *Finanz* AA 4, 16, fol. 25r.

100 StAB, *Finanz* AA 4, 16, fol. 119r.

101 StAB, *Finanz* AA 4, 16, fol. 118v. Voir Harms (éd.), *Der Stadthaushalt*, II, p. 242 ligne 40.

102 StAB, *Finanz* AA 4, 17, fol. 125v-126v. Voir Harms (éd.), *Der Stadthaushalt*, I, p. 246 ligne 70, p. 247 ligne 6.

103 Le rôle du marché financier de Bâle s'accrut encore au 16e siècle, voir M. H. Körner, *Solidarités financières suisses au XVIe siècle. Contribution à l'histoire monétaire, bancaire et financière des cantons suisses et des Etats voisins* (Bibliothèque historique vaudoise), Lausanne, 1980.

104 Pour le marché financier à Spire voir "Nach Speyrer Recht und Gewohnheit. Von Struktur und Funktion des Speyrer Kapitalmarktes im Spätmittelalter", in H. Ammerich et O. Roller (éds.), *Festschrift zum 100jährigen Bestehen der Pfälzischen Hypothekenbank, 1886-1986,* Teil II: *Beiträge zur Pfälzischen Geld- und Finanzgeschichte*, 1986, pp. 47-69, et aussi dans B. Kirchgässner, "Wirtschaft - Finanzen - Gesellschaft, Ausgewählte Aufsätze" (Festgabe zu seinem 65. Geburtstag), Sigmaringen, 1988, pp. 40-56.

105 StAB, *Finanz* AA 8 (sans date, ca. 1448/49).

106 Ceci contredit l'affirmation pour le 13e siècle de G. Sivéry, "Mouvements de capitaux et taux d'intérêt en occident au XIIIe siècle", in: *Annales ESC.*, 38 (1983), p. 138: 'Chaque fois qu'il y a déplacement des circuits financiers, le taux d'intérêt joue un rôle: investisseurs et prêteurs quittent en masse cités ou foires où le taux s'affaiblit pour des places où le loyer de l'argent est plus favorable'.

107 Voir la courbe du taux d'intérêt des rentes contractées par la ville de Bâle, dans: Gilomen, *Die städtische Schuld Berns*, p. 14.

108 "Die Chroniken Heinrichs von Beinheim. 1365-1452 sammt Fortsetzung 1465-1473", in *Basler Chroniken*, V, Leipzig, 1895 p. 400: '*Umb die selb zyt [il s'agit de la fin de l'année 1447] was das gold und gelt fast genaem und thür zu Basel, und under Basel hinab; woren die edlen fast arm worden, des Delphin und kriegs halb*'.

109 5%: par exemple Harms (éd.), *Der Stadthaushalt,* I, p. 179 ligne 59ss.

110 4%: par exemple *Urkundenbuch der Stadt Basel*, VII, p. 401 no. 245, 17 octobre 1449.

111 6% à Strasbourg voir B. Harms (éd.), *Der Stadthaushalt,* (cit. note 11), I, p. 182 ligne 35 ss.

112 6 2/3% à Strasbourg voir B. Harms (éd.), *Der Stadthaushalt,* (cit. note 11), I, p. 178 ligne 96 ss.

dans les années suivantes, d'abord à 5%, puis – par des versements supplémentaires – à 4,35%[113]. L'échéance de ces rentes était fort différente. La plupart furent rachetées après deux à cinq années[114], d'autres en 1471 après 22 années[115], en 1476 après 28 années[116] et même en 1506 après 57 années[117]!

Qu'un besoin urgent et extraordinaire de liquidités ait déterminé la décision de faire appel aux financiers de Francfort s'explique aisément par les difficultés politiques. En 1410, les autorités Bâloises s'attendaient à la fin de l'armistice conclue entre leur ville et Catherine de Bourgogne. En 1424/26, années d'emprunts très importants (voir le tableau III), la ville était en guerre avec le margrave Bernard de Bade et avec Thiébaut de Neuchâtel sur le Rhin. La décision de l'emprunt de 1438 fut prise en pleine crise financière: le ravitaillement de la ville, surpeuplée par l'afflux de participants au Concile, posait de graves problèmes. A cause du blocus du Sundgau par les Autrichiens et des régions plus basses de l'Alsace par Strasbourg, une commission du conseil municipal fut chargée d'acheter de grandes quantités de grain à Nuremberg, Ulm, Spire et Worms. Les troupes des Armagnacs menaçaient l'Alsace. Les décisions prises dans les années quarante et à nouveau dans les années soixante-dix le furent dans une situation de guerre pénible: la Guerre dite de Saint Jacques ou de Zurich contre l'Autriche en 1443-1450[118] et la Guerre de Bourgogne en 1474-1477[119].

On s'est d'ailleurs débarrassé au plus vite de ces engagements: l'emprunt de 1410/11 fut remboursé en 1412/13[120]. Pour ce faire, le financier Bâlois Henman Offenburg, doyen des métiers, avança à la ville 1.168 fl., somme qui lui fut rendue en 1413/14[121]. Les contrats de novembre 1438 furent rachetés au printemps de l'année suivante[122], ceux de 1446/1448 pendant les années 1450-1454[123] et ceux de 1474 au bout d'un an déjà[124]. Que l'on se soit servi de rentes rachetables pour des emprunts ayant une échéance aussi courte à de quoi surprendre. Il est très vraisemblable que pour parer à toutes éventualités on avait amassé beaucoup trop d'argent liquide et, la menace de guerre passée, on a donc pu rembourser rapidement.

Outre les données usuelles comme la date du contrat, la somme versée, le montant de la rente, les termes de paiement, les registres de rentes de Bâle mentionnent également d'une manière succincte les sûretés juridiques prévues dans les contrats de 1446/47 à Francfort. Il s'agit plus précisément des moyens coercitifs accordés aux créanciers en cas de retard de paiement[125]. Ceci démontre l'importance accordée à ce problème. Les sûretés concédées aux étrangers différaient de celles que l'on accordait aux rentiers locaux. Le droit d'arrêter des marchands Bâlois et leurs marchandises, par exemple, n'était concédé qu'aux étrangers[126]. Le paiement des rentes aux propres

---

113 Pour ces versements supplémentaires, voir par exemple B. Harms (éd.), *Der Stadthaushalt,* (cit. note 11), I, p. 193 ligne 59ss. On appelait ces versements supplémentaires 'steigerung' parce que le rapport entre le capital et la rente était augmenté (il était, par exemple, augmenté de 15 fl. pour 1 fl. de rente annuelle, soit 6,66%, ou de 20 fl. pour 1 fl., soit 5%, ou de 25 fl. pour 1 fl., soit 4% (4,35% équivaut à un rapport de 23 à 1). Voir pour un versement supplémentaire du même genre B. Harms (éd.), *Der Stadthaushalt,* (cit. note 11), I, p. 185 ligne 30-33: '... *5 gulden zu irem vorderen houptguot, daz von 20 eyner stat*'.

114 Par exemple B. Harms (éd.), *Der Stadthaushalt,* (cit. note 11), II, p. 262 ligne 1.

115 B. Harms (éd.), *Der Stadthaushalt,* (cit. note 11), II, p. 351 ligne 42.

116 B. Harms (éd.), *Der Stadthaushalt,* (cit. note 11), II, p. 396 ligne 51.

117 StAB, *Finanz* AA 4.22, fol 152r.

118 A. Niederstätter, *Der Alte Zürichkrieg. Studien zum österreichisch-eidgenössischen Konflikt sowie zur Politik König Friedrichs III. in den Jahren 1440 bis 1446* (Forschungen zur Kaiser- und Papstgeschichte des Mittelalters 14), Wien, 1995.

119 C. Sieber, *Spätmittelalterlicher Nationalismus. Die Burgunderkriege am Oberrhein und in der Eidgenossenschaft* (Veröffentlichungen des Max-Planck-Instituts für Geschichte 116), Göttingen, 1995.

120 B. Harms (éd.), *Der Stadthaushalt,* (cit. note 11), II, p. 120 ligne 9.

121 B. Harms (éd.), *Der Stadthaushalt,* (cit. note 11), II, p. 122 ligne 74.

122 B. Harms (éd.), *Der Stadthaushalt,* (cit. note 11), II, p. 210 ligne 69, 78; p. 212 ligne 18, 25.

123 B. Harms (éd.), *Der Stadthaushalt,* (cit. note 11), II, p. 262 ligne 7, p. 277 ligne 39, p. 282 ligne 42.

124 B. Harms (éd.), *Der Stadthaushalt,* (cit. note 11), II, p. 382 ligne 72 - p. 383 ligne 17.

125 Par exemple StAB, *Finanz* AA 4, 16, fol. 25r: '*mit anegriffen an juden oder kawerschen ze nemmend mit lüte vnd guete zu verbietende*'.

126 La formule est la suivante: '... *so mogent die obgenanten kouffer, ir erben vnd die person, als vorstat, vnd wer jnen des helffen will, vns, die vorgenanten von Basel, die verkouffer, vnd alle vnser burger vnd die vnsern vnd vnser vnd derselben luten guete, ligende vnd varende, wa oder an welhen enden si die ankomment, es were jn stetten, jn dorffern, vf wasser oder vf lande, darumb wol angriffen, phenden, verhefften, verbieten vnd bekumbern,*

bourgeois n'était pas non plus garanti par la détention d'otages, qui devaient en cas de retard de paiement se présenter dans une auberge à Bâle ou dans la ville du rentier[127]. Dans ce même registre étaient transcrits les formulaires de rentes rachetables et de rentes viagères et ces contrats diffèrent selon le lieu de résidence des créanciers: '*Forma der kouffzinsbriefen, so die stat den vßern git*'[128], '*Forma kouffbrieff, als man sij hie in der statt git*'[129], '*Forma eyns koufbriefes mit eynem angriff vnd one bürgen*'[130], '*Forma lipgeding brieue gen Strasburg*'[131], '*Forma lipgeding in der stat*'. Sans entrer dans les détails[132], il suffira de souligner ici l'importance attachée aux différences entre ces stipulations dans les contrats.

Les rentes viagères vendues à des étrangers ou à des titulaires qui changeaient de domicile posaient des problèmes de contrôle spécifiques. Prenons l'exemple de Diemut von Heidegg née de Gradeneck, veuve de Werner von Heidegg. Le 18 mars 1470, elle se plaignit de ce que le conseil de Winterthur n'avait pas payé sa rente viagère depuis deux ans déjà, et ceci bien qu'elle eût fait envoyer par le conseil de la ville de Pettau (Ptuj près de Maribor en Slovénie) une déclaration selon laquelle elle était toujours en vie. Les autorités de Winterthur lui avaient répondu ne pas connaître le sceau de Pettau. Elle insista une nouvelle fois en faisant remarquer avec sarcasme qu'elle était bien vivante, Dieu merci, et qu'elle n'avait pas l'intention de quitter ce monde avant d'être appelée par le Seigneur, n'en déplaise aux conseillers de Winterthur[133]. Cette ignorance concernant la vie ou la mort des rentiers pouvait jouer en faveur du débiteur. En 1422, Elisabeth von Baldegg, moniale du monastère de Königsfelden, avait acheté à la ville de Bâle pour 100 fl. une rente viagère de 9 fl. La rente était payable à Bâle. Il semble bien que personne ne l'ait revendiquée pendant de longues années, car en 1448 un scribe notait: 'Je pense qu'elle est morte depuis longtemps'[134].

Les thèses formulées ici sur base de petits échantillons devraient être vérifiées par une analyse approfondie des sources sérielles, surtout celles de la ville de Bâle que j'ai déjà rassemblées et que je me propose d'exploiter dans les années à venir.

---

mit gerichte, geistlichen oder weltlichen, oder one gerichte, vnd die phande triben vnd fueren in welhe gericht si wellent, si versetzen, verkouffen, an sich ziehen vnd damitte gefarn, wie sich daz daselbes rechtlich vnd von billicheit wirt geheuschen, one allen vnsern zorn, jntrag vnd wider rede, so lange vnd so vil vntz daz jnen der geuallen vnd vßstanden zins, darummb si gephendet vnd anegriffen haben, mit dem costen der anegriffung gar vnd gentzlich bezalt ist worden'. StAB, *Finanz* AA 4.16, fol. 147r.

127 La formule est la suivante: '... *wenn denn nach jegklichem solichem zyl die egenanten vnser bürgen von dem obgenanten koüffer, sinen erben oder der personen, als vorstat, gemant werden zuo huse, zuo hofe oder vnder ougen, von munde oder mit briefen, so sollent sy alle vnd jr jegklicher jnsunders, der also gemant wirt oder gemant werdent, jn den nechsten acht tagen nach solicher manunge by iren geswornen eyden, so sy harumb gesworn vnd getan hand liplich zuo gott vnd den heiligen, haruff ein recht offen gewonlich giselschaft zuo Nuremberg halten vnd leisten jr jegklicher mit sin selbs libe oder mit einem erbern knechte vnd müssigen pherde an siner statt, ze veilem kouff vnd ze rechten molen tägelichs vnuerdinget jn eins offenen wirtes huß, das jnen in der manunge benempt wirt*'. StAB, *Finanz* AA 4.16, fol. 142r-143v. Sur le droit de caution et d'otage en Suisse, voir A. Lechner, *Das Obstagium oder die Giselschaft nach schweizerischen Quellen*, Bern, 1906 et P.R. Walliser, *Das Bürgschaftsrecht in historischer Sicht dargestellt im Zusammenhang mit der Entwicklung des Schuldrechts in den schweizerischen Kantonen Waadt, Bern und Solothurn bis zum 19. Jahrhundert*, Basel/Stuttgart, 1974.

128 StAB, *Finanz* AA 4.16, fol. 142r-143v.

129 StAB, *Finanz* AA 4.16, fol. 147v-148r.

130 StAB, *Finanz* AA 4.16, fol. 146v-147r.

131 StAB, *Finanz* AA 4.16, fol. 141r-141v; voir StAB, *Städt. Urk* 1029, 17.7.1425.

132 StAB, *Finanz* AA 4.16, fol. 144rv. Je prépare la publication d'un article analysant ces formulaires de contrats.

133 '*Fueg ich ew aber zewissen, das ich von gots gnaden noch im leben pin und durch ewern willen nicht ee, denn wann got vber mich verhenget, von dieser welt schaiden will*'. StAW, *Urkunde* n° 969, 18 mars 1470.

134 StAB, *Finanz* AA 4.14, fol. 63r: '*Ich gloube sy sie langes tod*'.

Annexes

TABLEAU A. **Echéances des rentes viagères de Bâle, 1470/71 - 1479/80**

année date du contrat nom du/des rentier/s somme	rente	taux	date d'échéance	années	rentes payées	solde	taux,réel	rente 4,69%
<u>1470/71</u>								
5-2-1471								
Jacob Waltenhein								
1.000	100	10	1478/79	8	800	200	-2,5	1.375,2
1-6-1471								
Clara Steynenbrunnen, veuve								
200	20	10	26-6-73	2	40	160	-40,	218,68
<u>1471/72</u>								
28-9-1471								
Heinrich Harwart et son fils								
1.450	140	9,66	1479/80	8	1.120			
	100	6,9	6-11-16	37	3.700	-3.370	6,28	4.510,23
25-1-1472								
Mathis Karlistein et sa femme								
240	20	8,33	14-9-1475	3,5	70	170	-20,24	279,4
1-2-1472								
Ennelin Vischer, fille naturelle du chapelain Johann Vischer, et sa demi-soeur								
250	20	8	1490/9	119	380	- 130	2,74	472,78
4-5-1472								
Gerhart Meckingk, scribe de la ville								
452	45,2	10	26-11-74	2,5	113	339	-30,	505,0
<u>1472/73</u>								
11-7-1472								
Hans Gründelin et sa femme								
200	18	9	1485/86	13	234	- 34	1,31	321,94
13-12-1472								
Hans Schmid et sa femme								
20	2	10	1484/85	12	24	-4	1,67	31,26
<u>1473/74</u>								
15-9-1473								
Heinrich Vogt et sa femme								
200	20	10	1489/87	13	260	-60	2,31	321,94

année date du contrat nom du/des rentier/s somme	rente	taux	date d'échéance	années	rentes payées	solde	taux,réel	rente 4,69%
19-10-1473 Hans Yselin et sa femme 138	13,8	10	1483/84	10	138	0	0,0	202,17
10-11-1473 Dietherich Krebs et sa femme 440	36	8,18	1482/83	9	324	116	-2,93	625,72
1474/75 23-8-1474 Peterhans Rotenburg 200	20	10	1486/87	12	240	-40	1,67	312,56
1475/76 9-8-1475 Hans Pirry et sa femme 100	10	10	1501	26	260	-160	6,15	221,94
1476/77 7-9-1476 Hans Lurtzsch 200	20	10	1486/87	10	200	0	0,0	293,80
4-11-1476 Conrat von Miltenberg 150	15	10	1484/85	8	120	30	- 2,5	206,28
1478/79 24-4-1479 Hans Hiltprand 550	50	9,09	20-5-1509	30	1.500	-950	5,76	1323,85
24-6-1479 Ennelin Schmid, veuve 80	8	10	1484/85	6	48	32	- 6,67	102,51
Total: 5.870					9.571	-3.701		11.325,26

TABLEAU B. **Des rentes viagères, 1470/21 - 1479/80.**

Noms des rentiers	somme	rente	taux
Cristen Burckart et après sa mort sa soeur	87	8,7	10
Joß Hug von Nürnberg et sa femme	600	52	8,66
Heinrich Junghein	200	20	10
Caspar Tuenower et sa femme	120	12	10
Jacob Waltenhein, conseiller	1.000	100	10
Clara Steynenbrunnin, veuve	200	20	10
Claus Vischer, sa femme et Heinrich Ysenhuet de Fribourg	600	45	7,5
Heinrich Harwart et son fils	1.450	140	9,66
après la mort d'un d'eux		100	6,9
Conrat von Tellsperg et sa femme	150	15	10
après la mort d'un d'eux		10	6,67
Mathis Karlistein et sa femme	240	20	8,33
Ennelin Vischer, fille naturelle du chapelain Johann Vischer, et sa demi-soeur	250	20	8
Gerhart Meckingk, scribe de la ville	452	45,2	10
Margreth Schmidin von Säckingen	85	8	9,41
Heinrich Bamnach et sa femme	100	8,33	8,33
Hans Gründelin et sa femme Gredlin	200	18	9
si Gred meurt avant Hans		12	6
Burckhart Christen et Claus Büwman	200	20	10
après la mort de Burckart		10	5
Hans Schmid et sa femme	20	2	10
Claus Vischer et Heinrich Ysenhut de Fribourg en Suisse	200	20	10
après la mort d'un d'eux		10	5
Heinrich Vogt et sa femme	200	20	10
Hans Graf et sa femme	136,75	13,68	10
Dietherich Krebs et sa femme Ennelin	440	38	8,18
si Dietherich meurt avant Ennelin		30	6,81
Hans Yselin et sa femme	137,93	13,79	10
Peterhans Rotenburg	200	20	10
Hans Smid von Werr et sa femme	80	8	10
Hans Pirry et sa femme	100	10	10
Margreth Smidin	100	10	10
Heinrich Gruber	80	8	10
Hans Sturler	200	20	10
Conrat von Miltenberg	150	15	10
Ennelin Schmid, veuve	80	8	10
Hans Hiltprand	550	50	9,09

LA DETTE DE LA VILLE DE HUY AU 17e SIECLE

Denis Morsa
Dexia Banque

A l'instar des Etats, communautés urbaines et rurales ont été confrontées de manière récurrente au financement de leurs dépenses par voie d'emprunt[1]. En particulier, la ville de Huy au 17e siècle constitue un champ d'observation privilégié des structures et de l'évolution d'une dette municipale ancienne[2]. Toutefois, il convient de dépasser l'évocation des événements et des circonstances locales. Ceux-ci doivent servir de révélateurs d'une série de réalités plus cruciales et de traits caractéristiques du crédit public sous l'Ancien Régime; c'est pourquoi nous insisterons aussi bien sur la nature des instruments financiers auxquels avaient recours les protagonistes que sur le processus de formation des taux d'intérêt. Au préalable, esquissons le cadre dans lequel s'insère notre propos. Située au cœur du pays mosan, Huy appartenait à la constellation des vingt-trois bonnes villes de la principauté épiscopale de Liège[3]. Elle était au 17e siècle dirigée par un gouvernement ou conseil; renouvelé chaque année, cet organe était composé de vingt-deux membres issus des corporations de métiers[4]. Le nombre de conseillers fut réduit à douze par l'ordonnance du prince Maximilien-Henri de Bavière promulguée le 15 juin 1686[5]. Bien que les grandes options en matière financière fussent de la compétence du conseil urbain, la gestion quotidienne était déléguée à un receveur nommé à l'occasion de l'élection du magistrat et qui portait le titre de 'rentier'[6]. La stagnation, sinon le déclin des principales

---

Sans l'amicale insistance de M. Paul Janssens, cet article n'aurait jamais été rédigé; qu'il veuille bien trouver ici l'expression de nos plus vifs remerciements.

Les équivalences métrologiques et monétaires sont les suivantes: un florin de Brabant-Liège = 20 patards ou sous = 0,667 florin de Brabant; un muid mesure de Huy = 8 setiers = 266,169 litres (12 muids mesure de Huy = 13 muids mesure de Liège); une tonne = 104,28 litres. (B. Demoulin, *Les finances d'un pays d'Etats aux marches de l'Empire, la principauté de Liège (1688-1728)*, Bruxelles, 1986, pp. 32-33; F. Discry, "Notes de métrologie hutoise", in *Anciens pays et assemblées d'Etats*, LXII, 1973, pp. 151-199). Pour la facilité des calculs, nous avons décimalisé les sous-multiples des mesures anciennes. Toutes les sommes relatives aux finances hutoises sont exprimées en florins de Brabant-Liège.

AEH = Archives de l'Etat à Huy

1 M. Körner, "Le crédit public", in *Systèmes économiques et finances publiques*, Paris, 1996, pp. 515-548.

2 Les quelques pages consacrées à la dette hutoise à la fin du 17e et au début du 18e siècle par J.-P. Rorive, *Les misères de la guerre sous le Roi-Soleil. Les populations de Huy, de Hesbaye et du Condroz dans la tourmente du siècle de malheur*, Liège, 2000, pp. 232-236, n'épuisent pas le sujet.

3 G. Hansotte, *Les institutions politiques et judiciaires de la principauté de Liège aux Temps modernes*, Bruxelles, 1987, pp. 243-272. Les bonnes villes disposaient du privilège d'être représentées aux assemblées d'Etats; leurs délégués formaient l'Etat tiers. Sur la principauté épiscopale de Liège, renvoyons à la synthèse de B. Demoulin et J.-L. Kupper, *Histoire de la principauté de Liège. De l'an mille à la Révolution*, Toulouse, 2002.

4 L'organisation politico-administrative de la ville de Huy sous l'Ancien Régime est l'objet du livre de F. Discry, *Archives et institutions hutoises de l'Ancien Régime*, Heule, 1965.

5 *Recueil des ordonnances de la principauté de Liège*, 3e partie, I, pp. 66-71.

6 A Huy et dans la principauté de Liège sous l'Ancien Régime, le 'rentier' n'est pas un individu qui tire des revenus d'un capital; c'est le receveur municipal et partant le chef de l'administration financière, même s'il est arrivé, comme nous le verrons, que plusieurs titulaires de la fonction aient possédé des créances sur la ville qui furent converties en rentes. A Huy, contrairement à ce

activités économiques, tangibles dès la fin du 16e siècle[7], s'étaient répercutés sur le volume de la population, dont les effectifs, compris entre 6.000 et 7.000 âmes[8], ne cessaient de se contracter[9]. A cet égard, Huy suivait une trajectoire singulière, puisque la conjoncture urbaine générale dans l'espace belge entre 1600 et 1700 était scandée par les rythmes qu'imprimait un régime de croissance lente.

Pourquoi l'emprunt?

Les praticiens des comptabilités urbaines anciennes connaissent les difficultés inhérentes à la mise en œuvre rigoureuse de ces documents[10]. D'entrée de jeu surgit l'incontournable exigence d'un effort de clarification, de manière à identifier l'objet même de l'enquête, en l'occurrence, les notions de dette et d'emprunt. Par exemple, à côté des emprunts proprement dits, dont le produit était consigné dans les comptes municipaux, on observe que la ville a quelquefois institué des rentes à l'intention des receveurs qui avaient couvert des déficits à l'aide de leurs fonds propres. Voilà assurément des formes de crédit et des catégories de prêteurs qui appellent un traitement distinct.

Au 17e siècle, la ville de Huy a contracté des emprunts pour corriger des déséquilibres imputables à l'inélasticité de son système fiscal[11]. A ce propos, nous retiendrons quelques indices explicites. On a conservé les comptes de 74 exercices[12] inscrits dans l'intervalle chronologique 1606-1690[13]. Ce n'est qu'en dix occurrences que les recettes fiscales ont été supérieures aux dépenses[14]. La

---

qui se passait à Liège, la charge n'était pas un office octroyé au plus offrant (D. Henry, "Les finances de la Cité de Liège au XVIIIe siècle", in *Finances publiques d'Ancien Régime. Finances publiques contemporaines en Belgique de 1740 à 1860. Processus de mutation. Continuités et ruptures*, Bruxelles, 1975, pp. 194-196).

7 A. Joris, *Huy, ville médiévale*, Bruxelles, 1965, pp. 176-179.

8 Eléments d'information chez D. Morsa, "La population de Huy au XVIIIe siècle", *Annales du Cercle hutois des sciences et beaux-arts*, 46 (1992), pp. 77-138 et D. Morsa, "L'urbanisation de la Belgique (1500-1800). Taille, hiérarchie et dynamique des villes", in *Revue du Nord*, 320-321 (1997), pp. 303-330. Les structures sociales de l'entité, qu'on ne peut ignorer lorsqu'on envisage la question de la dette urbaine, restent pour l'essentiel à découvrir. Notre essai "Niveaux de vie, professions et espace urbain. La ville de Huy aux débuts des Temps modernes", in *Les niveaux de vie au Moyen Age. Mesures, perceptions, représentations*, Louvain-la-Neuve, 1999, pp. 175-203, n'avait d'autre ambition que d'ouvrir le chantier .

9 Rorive, *Les misères de la guerre*, pp. 65-71 et "Les occupations militaires à Huy durant les guerres de Louis XIV", in *Annales du Cercle hutois des sciences et beaux-arts*, 54 (2000), pp. 29-30, a contesté nos évaluations de la population hutoise. Or, contrairement à ses assertions, nos chiffres ne reposent pas sur des documents fiscaux! Ils ont été obtenus par la mise en œuvre d'un procédé élémentaire de rétroprojection. Notre contradicteur est un virtuose du paradoxe, puisque après s'être récrié, il n'hésite pas à utiliser nos données. Si celles-ci sont à ce point inconsistantes, que diable attend-il pour en proposer de plus robustes? Critiquer sans apporter des contre-propositions dûment étayées est un exercice stérile.

10 R. De Roover, "Les comptes communaux et la comptabilité communale à Bruges au XIVe siècle", in *Finances et comptabilité urbaines du XIIIe au XVIe siècle*, Bruxelles, 1964, pp. 86-102; W. Prevenier, "Quelques aspects des comptes communaux en Flandre au Moyen Age", in *Finances et comptabilité*, pp. 111-145; M. Körner, "Les dépenses", in *Systèmes économiques*, pp. 401-402.

11 D. Morsa, "Etude sur les finances de la ville de Huy au XVIIe siècle", in *Finances publiques d'Ancien Régime*, pp. 137-171. Notre article "Les fruits amers de la nécessité. Les impôts de consommation à Huy au XVIIIe siècle", in *'Proeve 't al, 't is prysselyck', Consumption in European Towns (13th-18th Century). Liber amicorum Raymond Van Uytven*, Anvers, 1998, pp. 245-273, analyse les facteurs de blocage au sein du système fiscal hutois d'Ancien Régime; bien que l'examen porte sur le 18e siècle, les conclusions peuvent s'appliquer au siècle précédent.

12 Les comptes sont conservés pour les exercices 1606-1607 (n.s.) à 1612-1613 (n.s.), 1617-1618 (n.s.) à 1620-1621 (n.s.), 1622-1623 à 1625-1626, 1627-1628 à 1639-1640, 1641-1642 à 1659-1660, 1661-1662 à 1664-1665, 1667-1668 à 1689-1690 (AEH, *Comptes des rentiers*, n°170-182).

13 Nos données se fondent exclusivement sur les 74 comptes conservés pour l'intervalle considéré. Grâce aux *Actes du Conseil* (AEH, n°12-28), nous avons mention de quelques autres rentes vendues entre 1606 et 1690, mais nous ne pouvons vérifier que les capitaux ont été réellement encaissés ni qu'ils n'ont pas servi à financer des opérations 'débudgétisées', c'est-à-dire qui n'étaient pas consignées dans les comptes. Précisons que nos données sont corrigées de l'inégalité des exercices financiers. En effet, de 1606 à 1621, l'année financière prend cours à Noël; de 1622 à 1676, elle débute le 18 novembre; de 1676 à 1686, elle commence le 20 mai; enfin, à la suite du règlement de Maximilien-Henri de Bavière de 1686 déjà évoqué, l'année financière s'ouvre le 1er juillet. Autrement dit, le compte de 1675-1676 ne couvre qu'un exercice de 6 mois, tandis que celui de 1686-1687 s'étend sur 13,5 mois. Il s'indiquait par conséquent de redresser les données pour tenir compte de l'inégalité des exercices.

comparaison recettes-dépenses est éloquente. Pour la période considérée, les premières se montent à 1.332.400,87 florins, tandis que les secondes s'élèvent à 1.856.321,67 florins. Autrement dit, sur base annuelle, la ville encaissait 18.005,42 florins par des moyens fiscaux, or les dépenses se fixaient à 25.085,43 florins. En moyenne, chaque exercice requérait 7.080,01 florins en sus des impôts pour parvenir à l'équilibre. Certes, il existait des recettes non fiscales, mais leur apport était insuffisant[15].

Chronologie et modalités de l'emprunt

Poursuivons en examinant rythmes, formes et circonstances des emprunts émis par la ville de Huy au 17e siècle. Des 74 exercices envisagés, 12 signalent le recours à l'emprunt, pour un montant global de 302.298,95 florins. En moyenne, l'appel au marché des capitaux se répétait tous les 6,17 ans et rapportait 25.191,58 florins (tableau I).

TABLEAU I. **Emprunts de la ville de Huy au 17e siècle**

Exercices	Montant (florins)	Exercices	Montant (florins)
1607-1608	3.000	1675-1676	68.212
1611-1612	600	1676-1677	40.569
1628-1629	15.148	1678-1679	56.196,05
1638-1639	3.000	1679-1680	1.916,70
1649-1650	18.000	1688-1689	10.566
1674-1675	83.428,55	1689-1690	1.662,65

Source: AEH, Ville de Huy, *Comptes des rentiers*, n° 170-181bis.

Ces 302.298,95 florins ont été réunis par des procédés divers notamment par la constitution de 23 rentes 'héritables' et 'rédimibles', compromis entre les rentes perpétuelles et les rentes viagères[16]. Elles ont drainé 124.552 florins, soit 41,20% de l'ensemble. Les capitaux récoltés par la vente des rentes s'étagent entre un minimum de 800 florins et un maximum de 20.000 florins. La moyenne qui s'établit à 5.415,30 florins est affectée d'un fort coefficient de variation (83%). La dispersion est due autant à la variabilité des besoins de la trésorerie communale qu'à l'inégale capacité financière des prêteurs. Notons également que la série manifeste une dissymétrie positive (1,63) qui atteste de la fréquence des valeurs situées sous la moyenne arithmétique. Les achats de rentes d'un montant modeste étaient la règle; à 14 reprises les capitaux prêtés sont en deçà de la moyenne générale.

Le solde, soit 177.746,95 florins, a été obtenu via des emprunts à très court terme[17], des avances consenties par le receveur, des prêts sans intérêt et surtout, la mise en gage des recettes des

14 Le déficit financier structurel n'était pas une spécificité hutoise; c'était un attribut largement partagé (F. Braudel, *Civilisation matérielle, économie et capitalisme, XVe-XVIIIe siècle*, II, *Les jeux de l'échange*, Paris, 1979, pp. 462-465).

15 Ces recettes non fiscales consistaient pour l'essentiel en produits issus du domaine de la ville ou de ventes diverses.

16 '... vendons, engageons et transportons audit France Miess pour luy, ses hoirs et ayans cause, ladite rente de cents siex florins et traises pattars huict soulz Braibant annuels ... à rachapt au quinsième deniers, lesquels cents siex florins traises pattars huicts soulz de Braibant héritables susdits, nous et nos successeurs ou par noz rentiers et recepveurs ou l'ung d'eulx, payerons et ferons payer chascun an audit France Miess, ses successeurs et ayants causes et à deux terminnes ... et ainsy continuellement d'an en an et sy longuement qu'avons icelle rente rachapté et rédimé, ce que faire pourrons à toujours quant bon nous semblerat ... faisant vendre et rembourser une seule fois laditte somme ...' (AEH, *Actes du Conseil*, f°5 r°, à la date du 20 septembre 1601). Ainsi que le stipule ce texte (confirmé par d'autres), la périodicité des intérêts était bisannuelle. En garantie du paiement régulier des intérêts, la ville hypothéquait l'ensemble de ses biens et de ses ressources.

17 'Item, d'avoir receu des sieurs Godefroid Bernard et Dieudonné Dawans, au nom et partie faisant pour le mestier des merciers le 11e d'avril 1676, la somme de quattres cents florins que la Ville debverat restituer sans intérests lorsque ledit mestier en aura besoing' (AEH, *Comptes des rentiers*, n°178, *1675-1676*, p. 7). De même, en 1676-1677, la ville emprunte 40.569 florins dont une

institutions de charité, à raison de 200 muids d'épeautre en 1674-1675 et de 238 muids 5 setiers d'épeautre en 1678-1679. Ces deux opérations, qui rapportèrent successivement 52.628,55 florins et 51.177,05 florins[18], ne s'assimilent pas *stricto sensu* à des constitutions de rentes; elles méritent dès lors qu'on s'y arrête[19]. Confronté aux exigences des Impériaux puis des Français, le magistrat avait imaginé dans un premier temps recourir aux moyens traditionnels. La démarche fut vaine, car les investisseurs se dérobèrent[20]. Leurs réticences s'expliquent par le contexte général: la guerre battait son plein et le prix des vivres s'envolait[21]. Dans ces conditions, des rentes qui rapportaient 5 ou 6,67% ont dû apparaître bien peu attrayantes. Enfin, depuis le début des hostilités en 1672, les appels au crédit s'étaient multipliés dans la principauté; le marché s'était tari[22]. Puisque ses propositions de vente de rentes demeuraient sans écho, le magistrat n'eut d'autre solution que d'engager les recettes en grains des institutions de charité[23]. Il y parvint non sans d'âpres discussions avec les administrateurs de la bienfaisance publique[24] et après avoir obtenu le consentement du prince. En contrepartie, la ville s'obligeait à payer chaque année aux organismes de charité l'intérêt des muids engagés évalués d'après l'effraction. La somme nécessaire à cet usage devait provenir d'un nouvel impôt de 10 patards sur chaque tonne de bière brassée dans le périmètre urbain; le surplus éventuel de la recette devait être assigné au rachat[25]. En cas de rachat, une prime correspondant à un an d'intérêt au denier 20 (5%) était attribuée aux prêteurs[26]. Grâce à la mise en gage de recettes en grains, la ville obtint rapidement les capitaux qui jusque-là lui avaient été refusés; en 1674-1675, la demande fut même supérieure à l'offre[27]. Reste à expliquer pourquoi les investisseurs qui avaient dédaigné les propositions d'achat de rentes réservèrent bon accueil aux recettes en muids d'épeautre. Suggérons à ce sujet quelques éléments de réponse. En premier lieu, les preneurs de muids n'appartenaient pas à la même sphère que les preneurs de rentes constituées. Nous y reviendrons. Selon toute vraisemblance, ils furent sensibles au fait que les recettes en grains étaient indexées sur le coût de la vie. L'actif conservait le pouvoir d'achat du capital qui s'y était investi. Ce comportement était rationnel en phase d'incertitude et d'inflation aiguë. L'hypothèse d'une capacité de hiérarchisation des possibilités d'action des agents économiques se

---

partie (14.522 florins) sera remboursée au cours de l'exercice même (AEH, *Comptes des rentiers*, pp. 12, 77-78). Voir aussi AEH, *Comptes des rentiers*, n°179, *1679-1680*, pp. 21-22.

18 AEH, *Actes du Conseil*, n°22, f°21r°-21v°, 122r°-122v°; n°24, pp. 84-85, 128-130; AEH, *Comptes des rentiers*, n°177, *1674-1675*, p. 11; n°179, *1678-1679*, pp. 27-35.

19 Une autre ville principautaire, Sint-Truiden a procédé à des mises en gage analogues (E. Heynen, "Het beheer van de stedelijke financiëen te Sint-Truiden (1711-1731)", in *Historische Bijdragen opgedragen aan Monseigneur Dr. H. Kesters*, Saint-Trond, 1971, p. 121.

20 'Le 18 janvier 1677, au Conseil de Huy, nous ayant esté faict rapport qu'on ne peut treuver argent en laditte cité de Liège, ny ailleurs pour subvenir aux rations nous demandées par les puissances estrangères ...' (AEH, *Actes du Conseil*, n°22, f°122r°); '... ne se treuve personne qui veuille en cette considération avancer la moindre somme ...' (AEH, *Actes du Conseil*, n°24, pp. 129-130, à la date du 13 mars 1679).

21 A Liège, le prix du setier seigle (30,712 litres) passe de 2,67 florins en 1673 à 4 florins en 1674 et à 7,20 florins en 1675 (J. Pieyns et W. Tijms, "De graanprijzen van Luik (1400-1940). De effracties van de schepenen (1400) 1409-1792, de clericale effracties (1528-1793) en de effracties van het département de l'Ourthe en de provincie Luik sedert 1794", in *Studies over de sociaal-economische geschiedenis van Limburg*, 38 (1993), p. 139). A Huy, le setier de seigle (33,271 litres) est estimé à 5,18 florins en 1677-1678 contre 4 florins l'année précédente (D. Morsa, recherches inédites).

22 Demoulin, *Les finances d'un pays d'Etats*, pp. 198-201, dresse la liste des créanciers de l'Etat liégeois pour la période 1671-1674: durant ce laps de temps, 55 prêteurs ont avancé aux Etats une somme de 1.025.615 florins.

23 Sur l'organisation de la bienfaisance publique à Huy sous l'Ancien Régime, on se reportera à R. Van der Made, *Le Grand Hôpital de Huy. Organisation et fonctionnement (1263-1795)*, Louvain-Paris, 1960; N. Haesenne-Peremans, *La pauvreté dans la région liégeoise à l'aube de la révolution industrielle. Un siècle de tension sociale (1730-1830)*, Liège, 1981; N. Terwagne, *L'hôpital des Grands Malades à Huy aux Temps modernes (1750-1795)*, mémoire de licence inédit, Université catholique de Louvain, 2000.

24 AEH, *Actes du Conseil*, n°22, f°18r°.

25 AEH, *Actes du Conseil*, n°24, p. 89. Le montant du rachat, sans la prime, devait correspondre au prix acquitté par le preneur.

26 AEH, *Actes du Conseil*, n°24, p. 137.

27 Une recette de 1.800 florins est enregistrée dans le compte de l'exercice 1674-1675 provenant de dépôts de candidats acquéreurs de muids, dont la demande n'avait pu être honorée mais qui n'avaient pas réclamé leur avance (AEH, *Comptes des rentiers*, n°177, *1674-1675*, p. 11).

trouve renforcée dès lors que l'on constate que les acquéreurs des muids étaient pour la plupart ceux-là mêmes qui étaient débiteurs à l'égard des institutions de charité[28]. La mise en gage des recettes en nature leur ménageait l'occasion de réduire une partie des dettes qu'ils avaient contractées antérieurement[29].

Les circonstances qui ont incité la ville à emprunter ressortissent en ordre principal à des facteurs externes, où les événements militaires tiennent le haut du pavé[30]. Des 302.298,95 florins amenés par l'emprunt dans les caisses municipales, 295.698,95 florins (soit 97,82%) ont financé, directement ou non, dégâts, réquisitions ou départ des troupes qui occupaient la cité ou la principauté. A dater de la guerre de Hollande, on assiste à une recrudescence des emprunts. De 1674 à 1679, ils rapportent 250.322,30 florins, soit 82,81% des sommes empruntées au 17e siècle. Il tombe sous le sens que l'emprunt n'a pas comme contrepartie le financement d'investissements productifs. La ville s'y résout dans l'urgence, pressée par des circonstances contre lesquelles elle est impuissante. Elle emprunte parce qu'elle n'a pas d'autre issue; il ne s'agit nullement d'une gestion planifiée de sa trésorerie.

Dès lors que le besoin de ressources supplémentaires s'est fait sentir, pourquoi l'emprunt a-t-il pris le pas sur l'impôt? Nous l'avons évoqué, le système fiscal en vigueur à Huy sous l'Ancien Régime était doté d'une faible élasticité[31]. Articulé autour d'impôts de consommation assis sur des biens de première nécessité (accises), il se révélait incapable de générer rapidement les flux additionnels que la situation commandait. Par surcroît, la technique d'affermage des recettes, dont la perception était souvent concédée pour plusieurs années, allongeait les circuits financiers. Or, rançons et réquisitions qui motivaient le recours à l'emprunt devaient être versées et exécutées sans délai[32]. Concédons qu'à diverses reprises le magistrat a tenté d'instaurer des taxes nouvelles, principalement des impôts directs[33]. Mais la structure des fortunes et des revenus dans une ville gangrenée par le fléau de l'indigence vouait ces tentatives à l'échec. Il n'est pas exclu non plus que les édiles aient été sensibles à l'impopularité de l'impôt dont l'accroissement portait en germe la rupture de la cohésion sociale à laquelle l'idéologie corporative dominante attachait grand prix, voire aux menaces de troubles[34]. Après tout, les émeutes

---

28 Nous connaissons l'identité des apporteurs de capitaux pour l'opération réalisée en 1678-1679: AEH, *Comptes des rentiers*, n°179, *1678-1679*, pp. 27-35; AEH, *Actes du Conseil*, n°24, pp. 109-103. Du total de l'opération, 9.591,38 florins (soit 22,38 muids) ne furent pas affectés à des 'rachats' de redevances dues par les preneurs des recettes en grains.

29 Etant donné la nature de l'opération, la mise à prix était élevée: 200 florins le muid; aux mêmes dates (1678-1679), le muid d'épeautre se négociait à 8 florins sur le marché de Liège (B. Demoulin, *La principauté de Liège et l'Europe. Analyse du mouvement général des prix agricoles (1678-1728)*, p. 24; Pieyns et Tijms, "De graanprijzen van Luik", p. 139). A Huy, le muid d'épeautre est également coté à 8 florins à la même période (Morsa, recherches inédites). Rappelons que les mesures de capacité liégeoises et hutoises n'étaient pas identiques.

30 A ce sujet, voir J.-P. Rorive, *La guerre de siège sous Louis XIV en Europe et à Huy*, Bruxelles, 1998.

31 Voir Morsa, "Les fruits amers de la nécessité". Le rendement du système fiscal hutois était directement corrélatif aux revenus des habitants et à leur capacité à consommer. Or, la pauvreté structurelle emportait le sort de près d'un quart de la population; cette proportion augmentait bien entendu en cas de crise. Il est inexact d'écrire comme Rorive, *Les misères de la guerre*, p. 232, que la fiscalité était plus lourde à Huy qu'à Liège. S'il est vrai qu'il existe une correspondance entre le niveau de la population urbaine et la puissance financière d'une municipalité (G. Saupin, *Les villes en France à l'époque moderne (XVIe-XVIIIe siècles)*, Paris, 2002, p. 223), la pression fiscale était plus élevée à Liège qu'à Huy. La première comptait quelque 50.000 habitants et encaissait en moyenne 330.000 florins (Henry, "Les finances de la Cité de Liège", p. 202); la seconde abritait au maximum 7.000 habitants pour un produit fiscal de 18.000 florins.

32 '... Monsieur Dumonceau, intendant pour Sa Majesté très Chrestienne dans les villes de Mastreck (Maastricht), Huy, citadelle de Liège et provinces de Limbourg, auroit par son ordre du 27 novembre dernier demandez aux bourguemaistres et principaux bourgeois de cette ville (de Huy), aussytôt ledit ordre receu, l'ustensille de deux batallions composez de dix-septs compaignies chascun ...' (AEH, *Actes du Conseil*, n°22, f°61v°-62r° à la date du 20 décembre 1675).

33 Les impôts directs extraordinaires revêtaient la forme de tocages (impôts sur les cheminées et pièces à feu), taxes personnelles ou taxes sur les immeubles. Leur apport fut toujours médiocre. Nous en avons donné la liste et le produit dans "Etude sur les finances", pp. 170-171.

34 La ville fut le théâtre de désordres au début de 1681 en raison de l'augmentation des impôts sur les grains (AEH, Ville de Huy, *Correspondances*, n°67). Ajoutons à ces risques celui de délocalisation d'activités économiques que certains entrepreneurs estimaient surtaxées; ainsi, en 1631, le Conseil constate qu'à la suite de la prorogation d'un impôt exceptionnel sur les bières voté

fiscales ne sont pas une légende. Emprunter offrait l'avantage de ménager le présent en étalant le paiement des charges sur plusieurs générations.

Attachons-nous à présent aux rentes constituées par la ville au bénéfice des receveurs communaux sortis de charge. Le receveur était tenu d'avancer la différence entre recettes et dépenses[35]. Quand le découvert n'était pas trop considérable, le receveur était défrayé au cours d'un exercice ultérieur. Néanmoins, quand l'avance avait été trop importante au regard des disponibilités immédiates de la ville, le receveur était remboursé par une rente dont le capital correspondait à sa mise de fonds personnelle[36]. Nous avons repéré neuf rentes de cette nature: leur capital cumulé s'élevait à 38.243 florins soit en moyenne 4.249,26 florins. Pareilles valeurs confirment que ce mode de remboursement n'intervenait que si les sommes avancées par le receveur excédaient des seuils élevés (>1.000 florins). La solution agréait les deux parties: le receveur avait la garantie de recouvrer son dû et la ville diluait son déficit courant en le reportant dans les dépenses d'exercices futurs. Ce faisant, elle accroissait néanmoins la charge de la dette.

Les prêteurs

Qui étaient les bailleurs de fonds de la ville de Huy au 17e siècle? La question, d'apparence anodine, ne peut trouver de réponse entièrement satisfaisante, en raison de l'inconsistance documentaire. Trop de prêteurs ne sont connus que par leur seul patronyme, à l'exclusion de tout autre mention. Dans ces conditions, il est chimérique de s'attacher à dresser un profil ou une typologie. Au mieux, sommes-nous en mesure d'esquisser quelques traits à propos de 23 rentes vendues au 17e siècle à 22 prêteurs différents[37]. Quoiqu'il ne soit guère étoffé, l'échantillon révèle des tendances: 8 rentes ont été achetées par des bourgeois de Liège, 5 par des autochtones, 1 par un noble de Namur et 9 par des personnages dont l'origine est inconnue. Une rente a été achetée conjointement par deux prêteurs qui ont amené chacun la moitié du capital, tandis qu'à deux reprises, deux rentes ont été constituées au profit d'un même prêteur[38]. L'apport moyen par prêteur était de 5.661,45 florins. Ces opérations de crédit consacrent la supériorité de la gent masculine: on ne dénombre que trois femmes au sein de l'échantillon, dont deux ont le statut de veuves. Fait à souligner, les créanciers sont sans exception des personnes privées; les institutions laïques ou ecclésiastiques n'ont pas souscrit aux rentes émises par la

---

pour trois ans en 1622, un certain nombre de brasseurs ont quitté la ville: '... ce nonobstant, noz prédecesseurs, depuis le terme expiré (dudit impôt) en auroient continué la collecte, avec grands grieffs et plainctes des compagnons dudit mestier (des brasseurs) de sort qu'aucuns auroient quitté non seullement le mestier mais aussi la ville' (AEH, *Actes du Conseil*, n°19, f°142v°).

35 Au 18e siècle, le montant des avances que le rentier devait consentir à la caisse communale en cas de besoin sera limité à un maximum de 1.000 florins sans pouvoir exiger aucun intérêt (M. Bastin, "Les finances de la ville de Huy au XVIIIe siècle", in *Annales du Cercle hutois des sciences et beaux-arts*, 23 (1950), p. 225). Rien de tel au siècle antérieur; tout dépendait de la capacité individuelle du titulaire de la fonction. L'entrée en charge du rentier était subordonnée au versement d'une caution, en nature ou en argent (AEH, *Actes du Conseil*, n°26, f°13v°-14r°; Discry, *Archives et institutions hutoises*, pp. 177-178). Le dépôt de pareille caution fut régulièrement éludé.

36 AEH, *Actes du Conseil*, n°19, f°54 r°; '... ordonnons et accordons ... à nostre renthier, tant moderne que futtur, de paier audit Coppée (rentier sorti de charge), les courans et interetz desdits milles septz centz florins au denier quinse, prendant course audit seizième de novembre dernier (1629), jusques à refurnissement du capital ...' (AEH, *Actes du Conseil*, n°19, f°123 v°). Le rentier Denis Coppée avait en effet au cours de son mandat avancé 1.500 puis 200 florins pour acquitter des débours qui incombaient à la ville.

37 Sont exclues de cet échantillon les rentes constituées en faveur des receveurs afin de les rembourser de leurs avances à la caisse communale.

38 Le 13 août 1650, une rente de 600 florins est constituée au profit de Robert de Tru, échevin de Huy et de Vincent delle Neuville, bourgeois de Huy, qui ont apporté le capital à raison de 4.500 florins chacun (AEH, *Actes du Conseil*, n°20, pp. 233-238). En décembre 1674, la veuve d'Eustache Donnay, capitaine d'une compagnie bourgeoise de Huy, apporte par deux fois 8.000 florins en contrepartie de deux rentes de 400 florins (AEH, *Comptes des rentiers*, n°177, *1674-1675*, p. 9). Le 23 décembre 1675, l'échevin de Grady, de Liège prête à la ville 12.002 florins contre une rente de 706 florins; il récidive le 13 février de l'année suivante par un prêt de 10.000 florins assorti d'une rente de 625 florins (AEH, *Actes du Conseil*, n°22, f°63r°-64r°, 68v°-69v°).

ville[39]. Du point de vue socio-professionnel, les crédirentiers se recrutent en majeure partie dans le cercle des marchands et dans une moindre mesure dans le giron de la petite noblesse[40]. A vrai dire, le marché du crédit apparaît segmenté; en effet, la ville ne pouvait rivaliser avec des organismes dotés d'une assise financière beaucoup plus imposante, tels les Etats ou la cité de Liège. Ceux-ci avaient accès à des espaces de marché où se mouvaient la bourgeoisie de robe, les grands officiers de l'Etat, voire au marché des Provinces-Unies[41]. La ville de Huy, qui présentait un risque débiteur plus élevé et dont les besoins étaient plus modestes, devait quant à elle chercher des pourvoyeurs de fonds au sein de strates sociales moins prestigieuses, aux encaisses monétaires plus chiches[42]. La recherche de prêteurs *intra-muros* ne soulevait pas de problème spécifique; en revanche, l'approche de prêteurs extérieurs générait des coûts de négociation et des frais de voyage. La plupart du temps, cette délicate besogne était dévolue à des membres du magistrat[43], qui parfois avaient été précédés par des envoyés en mission exploratoire pour sonder les intentions[44]. Le mot d'ordre était immuable: vendre des rentes au meilleur prix pour la ville, c'est-à-dire au taux d'intérêt le plus bas[45]. Il est probable qu'avant d'entamer leurs démarches, les délégués avaient pris soin de dresser la liste des personnes qu'ils comptaient solliciter. On soupçonne l'existence d'un réseau de relations tissées à l'occasion d'activités professionnelles ou d'événements politiques (participation aux journées d'Etats).

Comme nous l'avons indiqué, les acquéreurs des recettes en grains de la bienfaisance publique composent un groupe qui épouse une configuration spécifique. Leur éventail social les distingue des acheteurs de rentes constituées. Nous avons affaire à des individus clairement insérés dans le réseau de la rente foncière. Au nombre de 25 en 1678-1679, ils ont apporté en moyenne 2.047,10 florins correspondant à 9,54 muids d'épeautre. L'implication d'ecclésiastiques est un autre trait saillant; on en recense 7 qui se partagent entre un souscripteur individuel et six communautés religieuses[46].

39 Rorive, *Les misères de la guerre*, p. 226, fait état de 100 florins prêtés à la ville par l'abbaye du Val Saint-Lambert en 1678; cette transaction n'apparaît pas dans les comptes.

40 Exception faite de la rente de 200 florins au denier 15 (capital de 3.000 florins) vendue le 11 août 1629 à Jean de Groesbeeck, gouverneur de Huy (AEH, *Actes du Conseil*, n°19, f°105v°-107r°). Jean de Groesbeeck était un de conseillers du prince-évêque Ernest de Bavière (1581-1612), voir Demoulin et Kupper, *Histoire de la principauté de Liège*, p. 152. Le gouverneur commandait au nom du prince la garnison qui occupait le château; il ne jouait aucun rôle dans l'administration de la cité.

41 Voir la pénétrante analyse de Demoulin, *Les finances d'un pays d'Etats*, pp. 178-206. A la fin du 17e siècle, les Provinces-Unies qui avaient un excédent de capitaux par rapport à leurs investissements intérieurs et des taux d'intérêt peu élevés devinrent les banquiers de l'Europe et exportèrent une grande quantité de capitaux sous la forme de prêts à des Etats étrangers (F. Crouzet, *Histoire de l'économie européenne, 1000 -2000*, Paris, 2000, pp. 124-125).

42 A dater de la guerre de Hollande, les appels au crédit émanant des organismes publics se multiplient; outre les Etats, nombre de localités victimes de la tourmente financière sont à la recherche de prêteurs, ainsi, Verviers, autre ville de la principauté de Liège, emprunta 90.000 florins en 1678 (D. Berlamont, "Occupations militaires et finances urbaines aux XVIIe et XVIIIe siècles: l'exemple verviétois", *Annuaire d'histoire liégeoise*, 37 (1978), pp. 59-106; J. Lejaer, "Histoire de la ville de Verviers depuis son érection en ville jusqu'à la fin de l'Ancien Régime, 1651-1794", *Bulletin de la Société verviétoise d'archéologie et d'histoire*, 38 (1951), pp. 7-381). Par ailleurs, le fait que la dette municipale hutoise était moins 'aristocratique' que celle des Etats de la principauté pouvait jouer en faveur de la ville: il était moins risqué de surseoir au paiement des intérêts quand les créanciers étaient d'humbles marchands plutôt que de puissants personnages installés au sommet de l'Etat ou qui y avaient des relais.

43 AEH, *Actes du Conseil*, n°22, f°90r°, à la date du 3 mai 1676.

44 AEH, *Comptes des rentiers*, n°178, *1675-1676*, f°23; *Actes du Conseil*, n°22, f°90r°.

45 '... ordonnons par cette au sieur Jean del Creyr, rentier, de prendre à frais la somme de deux mille florins Brabant, voir à moindre frais que faire se pourat, permettant le descharger ou luy tenir en comptes lesdis deniers capitaux et intérests' (AEH, *Actes du Conseil*, n°17, f°110r°, à la date du 23 avril 1622).

46 Les six communautés étaient les carmes, les croisiers et les jésuites de Huy, les dames d'Andenne, l'abbaye de Saint-Hubert et les archidiacres de Stockem.

La formation des taux d'intérêt

Avant de s'enquérir des motivations des crédirentiers, il importe de saisir les mécanismes de formation des taux d'intérêt, puisque ceux-ci sont des facteurs fondamentaux du marché du crédit[47]. A ce stade, nous devons acter l'organisation rudimentaire des marchés d'emprunts publics dans la principauté de Liège sous l'Ancien Régime. La détermination des taux directeurs n'était pas l'apanage de praticiens de la finance[48]. Les autorités politiques de la principauté fixaient le taux maximum[49]. Ce mode de détermination ne résultait que de manière lâche d'un mécanisme de marché placé sous la double contrainte de la défense de la parité de la devise nationale et d'un niveau acceptable de l'activité économique[50]. Fondamentalement, imprégné des préceptes d'une 'économie morale', le pouvoir avait pour objectif avoué de réprimer l'usure. En outre, aucune distinction n'était formellement opérée entre taux à court terme et taux à long terme[51]. Cette ambiguïté ne manquait pas de se répercuter sur les taux appliqués aux rentes, car la rente à prix d'argent était toujours rachetable au gré de l'emprunteur. Or, parce qu'elle était héritable, la rente était considérée par les investisseurs comme un placement à longue échéance. Cette indétermination a dû renforcer chez les prêteurs l'exigence d'une prime de risque afin de se prémunir contre l'irruption d'événements imprévus. Prime de risque augmentée également pour se protéger contre les défaillances éventuelles de l'emprunteur. Bien que la constitution de rentes donnât lieu à l'établissement d'un contrat en bonne et due forme assorti de garanties, il n'était pas rare que la ville suspende ses paiements[52] ou sollicite un moratoire[53].

---

47 Des ouvrages d'initiation guident le néophyte dans cette matière complexe et ardue: F. Aftalion et P. Poncet, *Les taux d'intérêt*, 3e éd., Paris, 1994; A. Bénassy-Quéré, L. Boone et V. Coudert, *Les taux d'intérêt*, Paris, 1998. Pour nos régions sous l'Ancien Régime, voir P. Servais, *La rente constituée dans le ban de Herve sous l'Ancien Régime*, Bruxelles,1982, pp. 125-135.

48 Les taux nominaux à court terme sur lesquels agissent aujourd'hui les autorités monétaires répercutent leurs modifications sur les taux réels à long terme qui président aux décisions d'épargne et d'investissement.

49 La fixation du taux par les autorités est un phénomène général dans l'Europe des 16e et 17e siècles, à l'exception des Provinces-Unies (A.-M. Piuz, "De la marchandise à la banque", in *L'économie genevoise, de la Réforme à la fin de l'Ancien Régime, XVIe-XVIIIe siècles*, Genève, 1990, p. 577).

50 B. Belletante, *Dictionnaire de la bourse et des marchés*, Paris , 1996, pp. 300-301.

51 La distinction n'était pas opérée car il n'existait pas d'actifs financiers de maturité différente à partir desquels on aurait pu inférer une courbe structurée des taux (voir *Bulletin hebdomadaire de la Kredietbank*, 17 (1996), pp. 1-2). Les agents économiques étaient privés de références adéquates. Le taux de base était en réalité déterminé par les pouvoirs publics supérieurs: ainsi, les Etats de la principauté de Liège avaient en 1592 fixé le taux des rentes au denier 15 (6,67%), mais la mesure ne fut régularisée qu'en 1659 (Demoulin, *Les finances d'un pays d'Etats*, p. 193). Insistons sur le fait qu'il s'agit d'un taux maximum (Servais, *La rente constituée*, pp. 125-127). Ajoutons que nous n'envisageons que le cas du crédit public dans la principauté de Liège. Les taux à court terme n'étaient pas inconnus en matière de crédit privé (Y. Leclercq, *Histoire économique et financière de la France d'Ancien Régime*, Paris , 1998, p. 152). D'autre part, nous savons que Charles Quint a introduit une nouvelle forme de la dette publique, matérialisée par des emprunts à court terme placés sur le marché international d'Anvers au taux compris entre 10 et 24% (W. Blockmans, "Finances publiques et inégalité sociale dans les Pays-Bas aux XIVe-XVIe siècles", in *Genèse de l'Etat moderne. Prélèvement et redistribution,* Paris, 1987, p. 87). Mais Anvers était une place beaucoup plus évoluée que la principauté de Liège en matière de crédit (H. Van der Wee, "Antwerp and the new financial methods of the 16th and 17th centuries", in *The Low Countries in the Early Modern World*, Cambridge, 1993, pp. 145-166).

52 Le 14 septembre 1688, un créancier se plaint que la ville lui est redevable de douze années d'arriérés (AEH, *Comptes des rentiers*, n°181, *pièces justificatives*). Fréquemment, certains créanciers qui n'avaient pas reçu leur dû faisaient arrêter des bourgeois de Huy (AEH, *Actes du Conseil*, n°25, f°81r°) ou obtenaient la saisie du produit des recettes fiscales de la ville (AEH, *Actes du Conseil*, n°22, f°133r°).

53 Le moratoire, sollicité auprès du prince, donnait une assise légale à la suspension du service de la dette. Tantôt, la suspension est totale pendant un an, d'avril 1677 à mars 1678 (AEH, *Actes du Conseil*, n°22, f°133v°-134r°), tantôt partielle comme en 1684-1685, quand la ville s'engage à honorer une échéance sur deux et à payer une échéance d'arriérés (AEH, *Actes du Conseil*, n°25, f°32v°-33r°; n°26, f°27v°-28r°). Bien que accordé par le prince, le moratoire n'empêchait pas les créanciers les plus déterminés de continuer à menacer des bourgeois de Huy ou de saisir le produit des impôts: '... Son Altesse Sérénissime ... at bien voulu par son apostille du dixiesme avril dernier leurs accorder un respis et terme d'un an pour les debtes communes d'icelle (ville de Huy) ... et nonobstant laquelle il y at divers créanciers lesquels ne se laissent que d'user des menaces de faire arrester les bourgeois de laditte ville de Huy et de les faire arrester en cette citté de Liège, d'autres ont faict ou menassent de faire des arrests sur des deniers publicques, qui causeroit une enthière désolation de laditte ville ...' (AEH, *Actes du Conseil*, n°22, f°134r°-134v°).

Un autre élément n'est pas demeuré sans conséquences. La ville de Huy a emprunté lors de phases conjoncturelles très défavorables, quand les prix étaient emportés par de vives hausses annuelles. Ainsi que l'indique le tableau suivant, parmi les 12 exercices où la ville a eu recours au crédit, 6 s'insèrent dans des séquences de progression du prix du seigle de l'ordre de 16 à 80% d'une année à l'autre[54].

TABLEAU II. **Ecarts en % des cours du seigle entre deux années de récolte**

1606/07-1607/08	+ 25,56	1674/75-1675/76	+ 80,00
1610/11-1611/12	+ 27,97	1675/76-1676/77	- 44,44
1627/28-1628/29	+ 15,59	1677/78-1678/79	0,00
1637/38-1638/39	- 4,58	1678/79-1679/80	- 15,73
1648/49-1649/50	+ 55,84	1687/88-1688/89	0,00
1673/74-1674/75	+ 49,81	1688/89-1689/90	- 6,99

Source: J. Pieyns et W. Tijms.

Il n'est dans ces conditions pas interdit de poser l'hypothèse que les prêteurs ont intégré au taux qu'ils exigeaient non la hausse séculaire des prix, mais une fraction de l'inflation du moment, de manière à immuniser leur placement[55]. Un comportement de ce type serait logique chez des individus qui étaient familiarisés avec le commerce de l'argent.

Bref, contrainte d'emprunter à des dates qui n'étaient ni désirées ni prévues, la ville de Huy a contracté une dette onéreuse bien que les taux pratiqués n'eussent rien d'usuraire: de 1600 à 1667, les rentes se vendent d'ordinaire au denier 15 (6,67%)[56], ensuite, la période des guerres de Louis XIV inaugure une ère de plus grande variabilité: alors que fin 1674 et début 1675, le taux était tombé au denier 20 (5%)[57], les besoins de financement consécutifs au conflit renchérissent le loyer de l'argent; en décembre 1675, on enregistre des ventes de rentes au denier 16 (6,25%); dans les semaines qui suivent, le denier 15 redevient la référence. Comme tels cependant, les taux n'ont qu'une signification limitée. Indicateurs du loyer de l'argent, ils doivent être interprétés à l'aune d'une série de variables économiques parmi lesquelles se détache le taux d'inflation[58]. En l'état actuel des recherches, il n'est pas possible de restituer le taux d'inflation général dans la principauté de Liège au 17e siècle. A défaut, on usera d'un *proxy*, le cours du seigle enregistré sur le marché de Liège[59]. Si l'on veut bien se souvenir de la place que tenaient les achats d'aliments à base de grains dans les budgets des ménages sous l'Ancien Régime[60] et que le marché de Liège commandait les marchés régionaux des céréales[61], l'approche à travers le prisme de ce substitut n'est pas illicite. Le taux d'inflation est mesuré par une régression

La mention de versements d'intérêts dans le compte de l'exercice 1677-1678 n'est pas contradictoire avec le moratoire puisque le comput financier et le calendrier de la suspension du service de la dette ne coïncidaient pas. Le magistrat a réactivé les paiements quand il est entré en possession du produit de l'affermage de plusieurs recettes.

54 Les prix utilisés sont ceux de l'effraction du clergé de Liège publiés par Pieyns et Tijms, "De graanprijzen van Luik", pp. 67-154, en particulier pp. 137-139.

55 Autrement dit, les prêteurs ont toujours exigé le taux maximum légal et se sont montrés intraitables. Cette attitude explique aussi pourquoi les taux d'intérêt ont pu remonter après les mesures de réduction des taux appliquées par le pouvoir urbain.

56 Fait exception la rente constituée en 1649 au profit d'un certain Théodore Braibant: capital de 1.000 florins, intérêts annuels de 73 florins soit un taux de 7,30% (AEH, *Comptes des rentiers*, n°173, *1649-1650*, p. 7).

57 Le 20 septembre 1667, le magistrat avait décidé une diminution du taux des rentes existantes du denier 15 au denier 20, quitte à rembourser les créanciers qui auraient refusé cette modification (AEH, *Actes du Conseil*, n°21, p. 213).

58 *A fortiori* quand la détermination du taux légal s'opérait sans guère de rapports avec les fondamentaux de l'économie.

59 Pieyns et Tijms, "De graanprijzen van Luik", pp. 137-139.

60 Les cours céréaliers influençaient directement le prix du pain et celui de la bière qui étaient l'aliment et la boisson populaires.

61 Demoulin, *La principauté de Liège et l'Europe*, p. 19; J. Ruwet, "Prix, production et bénéfices agricoles. Le pays de Liège au XVIIIe siècle", in *Cahiers d'histoire des prix*, II, 1957, pp. 69-108, republié in *Pays-Bas et principauté de Liège aux Temps modernes. Recueil d'études*, Louvain-la-Neuve, 1981, pp. 43-77.

linéaire après transformation de la série des prix en logarithmes népériens[62]. Pour la période 1600-1689 on vérifie l'équation:

ln Prix seigle = - 11,62 + 0,01 T, avec T = temps
prob (0,00) (0,00)
R^2 = 0,31; R^2 ajusté = 0,283.

Soit pour la période d'observation un taux annuel d'inflation de 1% en moyenne, qui à l'examen de la courbe lissée des données est négatif dans la seconde moitié du siècle[63]. Le témoignage des prix confirme que la ville avait contracté une dette onéreuse; elle rétribuait les prêteurs à un taux supérieur de 4 à 5% à l'inflation[64]. Est-ce à dire que du point de vue du prêteur, la rente était un placement sûr? On se gardera d'être catégorique. La rente était un instrument financier peu élaboré qui ne rapportait que des intérêts simples, non des intérêts composés[65]. Par ailleurs, les prêteurs étaient à la merci aussi bien des défaillances de l'emprunteur qui n'honorait pas régulièrement toutes les échéances (les arriérés étaient légion), que des rachats. En cas de rédemption, le prêteur, qui n'avait pas automatiquement l'assurance de replacer son capital à un taux équivalent ou supérieur, s'exposait à une perte financière[66]. Un autre danger menaçait les prêteurs, principalement les bailleurs étrangers à la principauté, à savoir la détérioration du taux de change. En effet, les constitutions de rentes étaient libellées en monnaie de compte (florins de Brabant-Liège)[67]. Le fléchissement de la parité du florin liégeois vis-à-vis des monnaies réelles se traduisait aussi bien par une perte de pouvoir d'achat des intérêts que par une diminution de la valeur du capital au moment de sa restitution[68].

Comment expliquer que la ville ait toujours trouvé les capitaux dont elle avait un pressant besoin? Ne perdons pas de vue que dans les sociétés d'Ancien Régime, la rente était la clef de tout[69]; entrée dans les mœurs, largement répandue, elle était un des modes d'irrigation normal du système économique. En dépit des innombrables controverses quant à sa licéité (*pecunia pecuniam non parit*), le

62 P.E. Gaynor et R.C. Kirkpatrick, *Introduction to time-series modeling and forecasting in business and economics*, New York, 1994, p. 127. Les logarithmes des prix sont régressés sur le temps par la méthode des moindres carrés ordinaires. Le coefficient associé à la variable 'temps' donne immédiatement la pente de la tendance. Les valeurs de *prob* indiquent que les coefficients de régression sont statistiquement significatifs; le coefficient de détermination (R^2) corrigé définit la proportion de la variabilité totale du prix expliquée par la régression en tenant compte des degrés de liberté du modèle.

63 Pour la période 1650-1689, l'équation devient: lnPrix seigle = 33,49 - 0,02T, soit un taux annuel négatif moyen de 2%. Pour une traduction graphique de l'évolution des prix liégeois au 17e siècle, voir M. P. Gutmann, *War and rural life in the early modern Low Countries*, Assen, p. 117.

64 L'inflation, c'est-à-dire la hausse des prix, provoque une chute des revenus des titulaires de revenus fixes tels que les rentes, voir M. Flament, *L'inflation*, 4e éd., Paris, 1977, p. 48; G. Quaden, *La crise des finances publiques*, Liège, 1984, p. 104. A l'inverse, l'inflation soulage les débiteurs de revenus non indexés sur le coût de la vie.

65 Un capital est placé à intérêts composés lorsque à la fin de chaque période, l'intérêt est incorporé au capital pour produire à son tour des intérêts (M. Boissonade et D. Fredon, *Mathématiques financières*, Paris, 2000, p. 27).

66 La décision du pouvoir liégeois de limiter le taux légal à 6,67% a rencontré des résistances. Ainsi , Servais, *La rente constituée*, p. 127, observe des taux qui peuvent atteindre 10% au début du 18e siècle. La possibilité donnée aux prêteurs de replacer à un taux supérieur au taux légal un capital qui leur aurait été restitué n'est donc pas une hypothèse à exclure.

67 '... laditte somme de siex mille florins at esté réellement comptée à Jean de Lamalle nostre renthier en belles et notables pièces d'or et d'argent; lorsqu'il serat question de refurnir icelle somme, l'on ne pourrat donner aucunne pièce de moindre valeur que d'un rix daller valant présentement cinquant huictz patars Brabant, laquelle restitution touttefois se ferat à telle évaluation que les ors et argent auront course au jour de laditte restitution ...' (AEH, *Actes du Conseil*, n°19, f°98r, à la date du 29 avril 1629). Demoulin, *Les finances d'un pays d'Etats*, p. 183, rapporte à ce propos le litige qui opposa en 1690 l'Etat liégeois à un prêteur citoyen des Provinces-Unies.

68 L'évolution du cours et de la valeur des monnaies liégeoises est donnée par Pieyns et Tijms, "De graanprijzen van Luik", pp. 75-91. Voir aussi Demoulin, *Les finances d'un pays d'Etats*, pp. 32-33. Retenons que le florin de Brabant-Liège est stable de 1649 à 1759 (Demoulin et Kupper, *Histoire de la principauté de Liège*, p. 88).

69 L'expression est de P. Goubert, *L'Ancien Régime*, I, *La société*, Paris, 1969, p. 103.

prêt à intérêt avait conquis droit de cité[70]. Surtout, il existait une catégorie d'individus relativement fortunés, qui cherchaient à se ménager un revenu garanti autant que possible, pour eux-mêmes ou dans une perspective dynastique, *a fortiori* lorsque les temps s'assombrissaient. En souscrivant à des rentes urbaines[71], les bailleurs de fonds s'employaient à sécuriser un capital monétaire contre les menaces de spoliation et à récupérer une somme d'un pouvoir d'achat identique à leur placement au terme d'une vingtaine d'années toutes choses restant égales[72]; au-delà de cette échéance, ils tablaient sur un gain net grâce aux intérêts qui continuaient de courir ou à un rachat.

La gestion de la dette

Les autorités municipales ont tâché à plusieurs reprises de diminuer le coût de la dette. En 1615, la ville céda aux 11 métiers le droit de percevoir à leur profit exclusif les impôts qui les frappaient (les gabelles). En contrepartie, les corporations s'engageaient à acquitter les rentes dues par la ville à concurrence de 4.997 florins[73]. Le soulagement ne fut qu'éphémère. Dès les années 1620, la charge des intérêts retrouve ses niveaux antérieurs; en 1667, le magistrat abaissait au denier 20 le taux d'intérêt de toutes les rentes[74]. Il récidivait en 1673, ajoutant que les arriérés impayés seraient dorénavant acquittés non au taux d'origine, mais au denier 20[75]. Il renouvela la mesure en 1681, soucieux d'atténuer les conséquences des emprunts contractés à prix fort durant la guerre de Hollande[76]. Peine perdue: la charge ne fléchissait pas[77] d'autant que les amortissements n'étaient pas systématiques[78] (voir graphique). Après 1641, les intérêts de la dette franchissent 17 fois le seuil de 10.000 florins; ils

70 P. Goubert, "Les rentes constituées et le crédit: nature et rôle économique des constitutions de rentes dans la France du Nord au XVIIe siècle", in *Le siècle de Louis XIV*, Paris, 1996, pp. 115-123.

71 *A priori*, les collectivités urbaines ne présentaient pas un profil de risque supérieur à celui des particuliers et leurs appels de fonds, plus considérables, induisaient une masse d'intérêts plus élevée. A titre de comparaison, le montant ordinaire des capitaux de rentes répertoriés dans le protocole d'un notaire liégeois du 17e siècle s'étageait entre 500 et 650 florins; à l'inverse du crédit public, le crédit privé ne délivrait qu'un revenu annuel médiocre (C. Desama, "Les rentes en argent fournissent-elles un diagnostic de l'activité économique? Enquête dans un protocole liégeois au XVIIe siècle", *Annuaire d'histoire liégeoise*, 34 (1967), p. 29).

72 C'est ici qu'intervient l'inflation qui déprécie la monnaie. Supposons un individu qui prête à la ville 10.000 florins au denier 20 (5%), qui thésaurise les intérêts annuels et un taux d'inflation moyen annuel de 1%. La valeur du capital après 20 ans est obtenue par la formule $10.000/(1 + 0{,}01)^{20}$, soit 8.196 florins. Cette somme correspond à l'addition des intérêts annuels thésaurisés exprimés en valeurs futures. Autrement dit, compte-tenu des taux d'intérêt pratiqués et d'une inflation annuelle moyenne de 1%, les prêteurs pouvaient récupérer en thésaurisant les intérêts annuels une somme au pouvoir d'achat identique à leur capital initial après 25 ans environs. Bien entendu, si le prêteur replaçait systématiquement les intérêts et obtenait un rendement supérieur au taux d'inflation, la récupération d'un montant égal au capital initial en termes de pouvoir d'achat constant était plus rapide.

73 AEH, Ville de Huy, *Gabelles*, n°273, f°37v°-41r°.

74 AEH, *Actes du Conseil*, n°21, f°213.

75 AEH, *Actes du Conseil*, n°21, f°311v°-312r°.

76 AEH, *Actes du Conseil*, n°25, f°64r°.

77 En 1639, aux dires du magistrat, les intérêts annuels de la dette s'élevaient à 9.500 florins et les arriérés à plus de 30.000 florins (AEH, *Comptes des rentiers*, n°172, pièces *justificatives*). En 1678, les montants avaient grimpé respectivement à 14.000 et 100.000 florins (AEH, Ville de Huy, *Actes du Conseil*, n°23, f°49v°-50v°). En fonction de ces données et de l'évolution des taux d'intérêt, on peut proposer une estimation grossière de l'encours de la dette, à l'exclusion des arriérés: 142.500 florins en 1639 et 280.000 florins en 1678, soit une augmentation de 137.500 florins ou 96,49% en 39 ans, ou un taux moyen d'accroissement annuel de 1,73%. Ces ordres de grandeur sont confirmés par une contre-épreuve: de 1639 à 1678, la ville a emprunté 162.600 florins (à l'exclusion des deux opérations d'engagement des recettes en grains de la bienfaisance qui sont de nature spécifique) et a amorti à concurrence de 19.761 florins, soit une croissance nette de 142.839 florins. Evidemment, la solidité des évaluations est fonction du degré d'exactitude dont a fait preuve le magistrat; ne perdons pas de vue non plus que la série des comptes urbains est lacunaire, de sorte que quelques emprunts peuvent avoir échappé (voir note 13). Mais la relative concordance des évaluations de la croissance de la dette est *a priori* rassurante.

78 Durant la période observée, on comptabilise 12 opérations d'amortissement pour un montant total de 52.206,05 florins. Ces chiffres constituent des minima absolus puisque la série des comptes communaux est lacunaire et que les rachats de rentes n'étaient pas systématiquement consignés dans d'autres sources que les comptes, par exemple dans les recès du magistrat.

concentraient près du tiers des dépenses: 31,06% en moyenne pour les exercices étudiés. Le poids de la dette empêchait aussi la ville de financer des investissements productifs[79]; circonstance aggravante, l'importance de la dette extérieure entraînait un transfert de ressources au profit d'étrangers qui ne réinvestissaient pas ou ne dépensaient pas sur place. Les paiements d'intérêts à 'l'étranger' constituaient une perte nette de pouvoir d'achat pour l'économie hutoise puisqu'ils ne contribuaient pas au soutien de la demande solvable locale et par surcroît, ne généraient aucune recette fiscale[80]. Signalons que le projet d'un emprunt forcé de 15.000 florins à répartir sur les habitants, proposé par le magistrat le 22 décembre 1674, n'aboutit pas[81].

GRAPHIQUE: **Intérêts annuels (florins)**

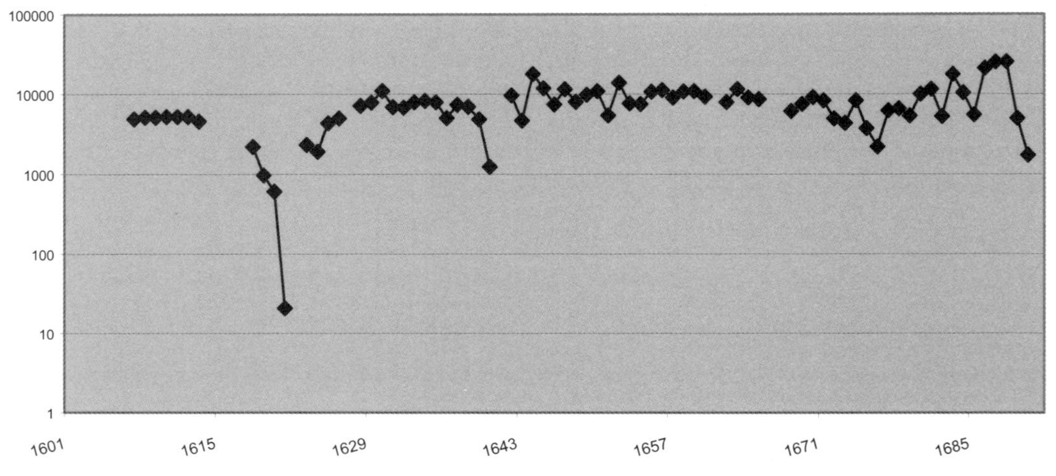

Exercices (1601=1600/1601)

Conclusion

L'endettement de la ville de Huy ne date pas du 17e siècle; ses racines sont beaucoup plus anciennes[82]. Mais l'intervalle 1600-1700 ponctue une séquence majeure dans le développement de la dette publique de la ville mosane. Entre 1600 et 1700, la dilatation du volume de la dette urbaine se conjugue avec l'incapacité du magistrat d'assainir ses finances. Eprouvée par le choc exogène des guerres, la ville a été l'otage d'un appareil fiscal insuffisant. L'augmentation de la dette procède en première instance de l'impasse où était condamnée une municipalité démunie des moyens de prélever

79 Par exemple, la ville dut confier à un organisme d'économie mixte, la Société du pont, le rétablissement du pont franchissant la Meuse qui avait été endommagé par les Français en 1676 (N. Rouche, "La ville de Huy sans pont pendant dix ans: 1676-1686", *Annuaire d'histoire liégeoise*, 37 (1972), pp. 1-57; N. Rouche, "Le pont de Huy entre 1686 et 1716", *Annuaire d'histoire liégeoise*, 39 (1973), pp. 55-101). Sur l'activité économique et financière de cette société, voir D. Morsa, "Initiative publique et services collectifs à Huy sous l'Ancien Régime. Contribution à l'histoire de la politique économique", in *L'initiative publique des communes en Belgique. Fondements historiques (Ancien Régime)*, Bruxelles, 1984, pp. 152-172.

80 Eu égard aux nécessités, la ville aurait pu imaginer de taxer les intérêts versés aux prêteurs étrangers.

81 AEH, *Comptes des rentiers*, n°177, *pièces justificatives*.

82 La situation financière de la ville paraît critique dès la fin du 14e siècle (A. Joris, *La ville de Huy au Moyen Age. Des origines à la fin du XIVe siècle*, Paris, 1959, p. 445).

une part du produit brut à la hauteur des nécessités. Bien entendu, le cordon de privilèges qui étouffait la société rendait illusoire la perspective d'une réforme fiscale d'envergure, en particulier l'élargissement de l'assiette. La vraie richesse, matérialisée par la propriété foncière, se dérobait à l'emprise du fisc[83]. Sanglé dans l'uniforme d'une stricte idéologie corporative, le système fiscal cherchait moins à maximiser le produit des impôts qu'à minimiser la charge qui pesait sur ceux que l'état ou la naissance astreignaient à supporter le fardeau contributif[84]. La préservation du consensus social était à ce prix. Dans un tel environnement, il ne fallait pas s'attendre non plus à une restriction drastique des dépenses ni à leur réallocation en vue d'une efficacité optimale. La gestion de la dette témoigne de l'absence de perspectives. Peu enclins à s'affranchir de leur inertie et de remèdes empiriques, les édiles n'eurent ni l'imagination ni l'audace de concevoir et d'appliquer un sévère programme de réduction de l'endettement[85]. L'équité commande de porter à leur actif quelques velléités qu'illustrent la cession de certaines recettes publiques aux métiers en contrepartie de la prise en charge d'une fraction du service de la dette ou la réduction *motu proprio* des taux d'intérêt. Toutefois, ces timides thérapeutiques ne permirent pas de corriger le déséquilibre structurel de la comptabilité urbaine. En revanche, nous devons acter l'inexistence de mesures énergiques capables d'éradiquer définitivement le mal. La création d'une caisse d'amortissement ou une opération de conversion de la dette ne furent jamais inscrites à l'agenda des responsables[86]. Enfin la croissance poussive, sinon négative du produit de l'économie hutoise au 17e siècle a constitué un handicap supplémentaire[87]. L'industrie drapière qui avait assuré la fortune médiévale de la cité s'était depuis longtemps effondrée, tandis que la métallurgie qui lui avait succédé au titre d'activité majeure manifestait des signes non équivoques d'essoufflement qui préludaient à un irréversible déclin[88]. Au surplus, la persistance de taux d'intérêt réels sensiblement supérieurs au taux de croissance de l'économie locale achevait de dégrader les finances municipales. Bref, d'omniprésents facteurs de blocage contraignaient la ville à l'endettement au point de mettre en péril sa solvabilité[89]. A rebours, le déficit excessif des finances hutoises générait un flux permanent de revenus pour les bailleurs de fonds. La fonction redistributrice de l'impôt aboutissait à un transfert continu de ressources en faveur des mieux nantis et des privilégiés et renforçait le caractère régressif du régime fiscal[90]. Les strates de la société qui avaient la capacité d'épargner et d'investir captaient une

83 Une partie substantielle de la richesse foncière appartenait au clergé, qui ne contribuait que marginalement à l'impôt; or la ville de Huy abritait non moins de 14 paroisses, 18 communautés religieuses et un chapitre collégial (*Huy, trésors d'art religieux*, Bruxelles, 1984). Les exemptions et exonérations dont pouvaient se prévaloir les gens d'église coûtaient cher à la fiscalité communale.

84 L'augmentation spectaculaire de la dette publique hutoise est imputable à la sous-imposition et au rendement médiocre du système fiscal. Illustrons notre propos par un simple exemple. Au cours des 74 exercices observés, la ville a emprunté une somme totale de 293.532,95 florins et a procédé à des amortissements pour 52.206,05 florins, soit une croissance nette de la dette de 241.326,90 florins. En moyenne, la charge fiscale annuelle par habitant se montait à 3 florins, soit 3 journées de travail d'un artisan qualifié. Un doublement de la charge aurait suffi pour résorber l'accroissement de la dette dans un délai de quinze à vingt ans pour autant que les recettes supplémentaires eussent été exclusivement affectées à cette fin.

85 Les mesures d'assainissement ne seront mises en œuvre qu'au 18e siècle, voir Bastin, "Les finances de la ville de Huy au XVIIIe siècle", pp. 248-252.

86 A contrario, la politique mise en œuvre par les Etats de la principauté constitue un remarquable exemple de gestion efficace (Demoulin, *Les finances d'un pays d'Etats*, pp. 186-198).

87 Comme la panne de croissance allait de pair avec une diminution de la population, le produit *per capita* est vraisemblablement demeuré constant.

88 Le nombre de forges implantées dans la vallée du Hoyoux aux portes de la ville qui était de 23 en 1570, recule à 17 en 1630 et à 3 en 1700 (G. Hansotte, "L'implantation géographique de l'industrie métallurgique des Pays-Bas et du pays de Liège, et son évolution aux Temps modernes", in *Implantations industrielles, mutations des sociétés et du paysage*, Bruxelles, 1986, p. 41; R. Leboutte, "La métallurgie dans la région liégeoise du XVe siècle à l'aube du XIXe siècle", in *Mutations de la sidérurgie du XVIe siècle à 1960*, Namur, 1997, pp. 57-83).

89 Huy offre un saisissant contraste par rapport à Verviers, ville liégeoise de taille comparable au 17e siècle, où la dette est restée sous contrôle (F. Bovy-Lienaux, "Les dépenses de la ville de Verviers au XVIIIe siècle", in *Finances publiques d'Ancien Régime*, pp. 175-178). Il est vrai que Verviers a pu s'appuyer sur l'essor de son industrie lainière.

90 Nous souscrivons aux remarques de Blockmans, "Finances publiques", pp. 78-79.

partie de la masse fiscale constituée par des prélèvements aux dépens de la frange numériquement majoritaire de la population qui ne pouvait se soustraire à l'impôt. En outre, une proportion des montants ainsi transférés n'était pas recyclée dans les circuits de l'économie hutoise. Reconnaissons que la ville ne pouvait se soustraire aux frais consécutifs aux occupations militaires et n'excluons pas que les besoins de financement public aient provoqué un effet d'éviction[91]. L'augmentation des dépenses municipales se serait accompagnée d'une baisse des dépenses privées, soit de ceux qui prêtaient des fonds au magistrat, soit de ceux qui auraient autrement emprunté ces fonds. Voilà pour la théorie. Cependant, l'incidence de la crise financière sur l'économie de la cité mosane ne doit pas être surestimée. A supposer que l'effet d'éviction se soit manifesté, plusieurs raisons donnent à penser qu'il n'a pas été total[92]. En effet, nous n'avons pas d'information sur l'investissement *ex-ante,* c'est-à-dire l'investissement qui se serait concrétisé en l'absence d'emprunts publics. Or, on serait bien en peine d'énumérer avec précision les projets d'investissements commerciaux ou industriels auxquels le secteur privé a renoncé[93]. Par surcroît, la mobilisation de capitaux pour venir en aide aux finances publiques n'a eu qu'une influence marginale sur le niveau des taux d'intérêt qui dépendait moins des mécanismes de marché que de décisions discrétionnaires des pouvoirs politiques supérieurs. Un autre fait significatif incite à relativiser l'impact des guerres et de leur cascade d'emprunts: les prêteurs n'ont jamais manqué à l'appel. La ville a trouvé des interlocuteurs quand elle proposait des rentes ou lorsqu'elle s'est résolue à aliéner les recettes en grains de la bienfaisance publique. N'est-ce pas le signe que les capitaux ne faisaient pas défaut au 17e siècle, y compris au sein des couches sociales intermédiaires où se recrutaient au premier chef les détenteurs des titres de la dette urbaine? L'existence de surplus d'épargne n'est pas un phénomène anodin[94]. L'abondance de capitaux nous incite à nous interroger quant à la validité de certaines notions propagées par l'historiographie, principalement celles qui insistent sur la dimension tragique des années 1600 à 1700. Qu'on ne s'y méprenne pas: rompre avec les schémas pessimistes n'implique pas qu'on leur substitue une version idyllique. Le 17e siècle consacre indéniablement un durcissement des hiérarchies sociales et accentue le partage inégal des ressources[95]. Cependant, le réduire à un siècle de malheur[96] et l'enrôler sous la bannière d'une légende noire relève d'une lecture de l'histoire singulièrement myope.

---

91 Sur l'effet d'éviction, voir C. De Boissieu, *Principes de politique économique*, 2e éd., Paris, 1980, pp. 415-419; M. Baslé, *Le budget de l'Etat*, Paris, 1997, pp. 84-85.

92 A Paris, du milieu du 18e au milieu du 19e siècle, l'effet d'éviction est de l'ordre de 30 à 40% (P. Hoffman, G. Postel-Vinay et J.-L. Rosenthal, "Les marchés du crédit à Paris,1750-1840", *Annales. Histoire, sciences sociales*, 49 (1994), pp. 82-83).

93 Ce serait plutôt l'inverse qui se serait produit; en l'absence d'incitation à investir dans le secteur privé productif, les détenteurs de capitaux ont souscrit aux emprunts publics. L'hypothèse d'un effet d'éviction à l'encontre du crédit à titre privé n'est pas non plus réaliste, car ce type de crédit mettait en cause des capitaux modestes (P. Servais, "De la rente au crédit hypothécaire en période de transition industrielle. Stratégies familiales en région liégeoise au XVIIIe siècle", *Annales. Histoire, sciences sociales*, 49 (1994), pp. 1393-1409. Voir aussi Desama, "Les rentes en argent" et note 71).

94 C'est à dessein que nous utilisons le terme de surplus, car il est hautement probable que les agents économiques qui souscrivaient aux emprunts publics avaient conservé une épargne de précaution.

95 On lira à ce propos l'exposé bienvenu de D. Terrier, *Histoire économique de la France d'Ancien Régime*, Paris, 1998, pp. 152-188. Voir également P. Verley, *L'échelle du monde. Essai sur l'industrialisation de l'Occident*, Paris, 1997, p. 95.

96 Bien que vigoureusement suggestives, ces formules à l'emporte-pièce sont réductrices et inaptes à rendre compte d'une réalité qui se décline tout en nuances.

Cities and Annuity Buyers

THE PUBLIC ANNUITY MARKET IN BRUGES AT THE END OF THE 15TH CENTURY

Laurence Derycke
Ghent University

As the management of public finances has important implications for the broad political and economic reality, public debt and public debt management have been discussed by several political and social-economic historians in reference to a wide variety of places and periods. Until very recently, however, public debt has always been treated as a side aspect of a broader issue, and research on the people who invested in the public debt has remained limited. Nevertheless, I believe that research on the public debt can lead to new perceptions in different fields of the historical research, and therefore I want to contribute to filling this gap in scholarly research. In this article I will analyse the functioning of the *renten* market in Bruges in the last quarter of the 15th century by focussing on the people who invested in the public debt by buying annuities on the urban domain. By combining a qualitative and a more quantitative approach I intend to unravel the specific composition of the public annuity market and to offer a clear picture of the socio-economic, political and geographic background of the people who participated in the public debt. This methodological approach will enable me at the same time to indicate any changes in the public annuity market and place these evolutions against the background of the broader political, social and economic context.

In order to approach the public *renten* market in Bruges from different sides, I singled out two specific topics that will be further discussed. First, I will analyse the geographic origin of the annuity purchasers and sketch the popularity of the Bruges public *renten* market. Second, I want to assess the socio-economic and political background of the annuity purchasers. In order to carry out this project I worked with a restricted number of *renten* buyers whom I subjected to in-depth prosopographic research. By selecting a sample of annuity purchasers, I was also able to take into consideration aspects concerning representativeness and possibilities for comparison. In this context it was obvious that the three different kinds of annuities that were issued on the Bruges domain – life annuities on one life, life annuities on two lives and heritable annuities – would be represented. Besides, since I am particularly interested in the dynamics and changes in the public annuity market and the impact of the broad historical context, it was crucial to select issues that took place under different conditions. As the last decades of the 15th century are a particularly interesting period given the major changes that occurred on the political, social and economic level, I selected three issues for the years 1472-1492 that can be situated in a completely different historical context: the sale of life annuities on one life for an annual amount of 105 lb. gr. started on the 26th of October 1472, the issue of 200 lb. gr. heritable annuities in June 1489 and the sale of 100 lb. gr. life annuities on two lives in July 1492[1]. These three issues cover a

SAB = Stadsarchief Brugge

total of 190 purchase transactions contracted by 155 different persons who compose the sample of *renten* buyers that I worked with and on whom I carried out extensive prosopographical research[2].

Private investment and the public annuity market: the international attractiveness of the Bruges *renten* market

In the case of Bruges, it is very difficult to shed any light on the geographical origin of the annuity purchasers because of serious methodological problems set by the available source material. Unlike the administration in most other towns, the authorities in Bruges did not hand down sources in which the origin of the *renten* buyers is systematically mentioned. The urban accounts – as the most important source for studying Bruges's consolidated public debt – only sporadically state someone's residence, and unlike in other towns the names of the *renteniers* are not grouped by the place of payment. Although some *renten* sales are better documented since specific accounting documents are available providing us with more information about investors and beneficiaries, even in these cases geographical aspects remain sporadic and far from systematic. As a consequence, the following discussion on the origins of the *renten* buying public will not be based on absolute figures and must inevitably remain approximate. Although the restricted data of the Bruges *renten* administration could be supplemented by using information from onomastics and scattered prosopographic data on other towns and specific social groups[3], only a rough picture could be sketched given the fragmentary and arbitrary state of this kind of secondary source material. Notwithstanding these shortcomings, the reliability of my observations and conclusions is increased since the provisional information on the Bruges public *renten* market leads to a picture confirming the results of studies about annuity purchasers in other major cities in the Low Countries such as Ghent, Lille, Louvain, Brussels and Mechelen[4].

As in the other large Flemish and Brabantine towns, the public *renten* market was not restricted to the inhabitants of the issuing city, and therefore the origin of the *renten* buyers was sometimes very diverse. Whereas a large number of people investing in urban public debt were indeed

---

1 As regards the revenues from the sale of annuities, the issues that I have selected can be considered as average issues. In October 1472 945 lb. gr. were collected, in June 1489 3,000 lb. gr. and in July 1492 1,000 lb. gr. These sums are relatively low in comparison with the revenues from the most important issues of the 15th century, namely the issues dating from 1438 and 1493 amounting respectively to 16,000 lb. gr. and 8,950 lb. gr.

2 In 1472 thirty-seven life annuities were sold to nineteen different persons; in 1489 one hundred twenty-nine heritable annuities were sold to as many persons, and in 1492 thirteen individuals bought twenty-four life annuities.

3 Some examples of studies that were useful for my prosopographical research: F. Prims, *Geschiedenis van Antwerpen. V. Onder Vlaanderen (1356-1405) en VI. Onder de hertogen van Burgondie- hertogen van Brabant (1406-1477)*, Antwerp, 1934; D. Clauzel, "Le renouvellement de l'échevinage à la fin du Moyen Age: l'exemple de Lille (1380-1500)", in *Revue du Nord*, 77 (1995), pp. 365-385; J. Gailliard, *Bruges et le Franc ou leur Magistrature et leur Noblesse avec des données historiques et généalogiques sur chaque famille*, Bruges, 1857-1864, 6 vol.; "Recueil ofte Bijeenvergaerderinghe van alle de heeren hier voortydts geweest hebbende Schepenen van den lande van den Vrijen alsoo men de selve naer groodt onderzoeck heeft connen vinden uyt de archiven ende erfchartres van d'abdyen, capitels, kercken, en hospitaelen deser stede van Brughhe, als over de selve erfvenissen gestaen hebbende, ende dat 't sydert den jaere 1228 voorwaerts, wanneer nogh geen burghemeesters en waeren ende schepenen sonder nomber", R. Marcoen, *Prosopografie van het wereldlijk openbaar ambt te Aalst in de XVe eeuw*, Ghent, unpublished master's thesis, 1963-64; F. Priem (ed.), *Documents extraits du dépot des Archives de la Flandre Occidentale à Bruges. Deuxième série. Tome septième*, Bruges, 1850, pp. 1-288; I. Schoups, an unedited CD-rom with prosopographical data concerning Ghent in the 15th century.

4 Interesting data on the spread of public annuities issued by other cities in the Burgundian realm can be found in M. Boone, "'Plus dueil que joie'. Renteverkopen door de stad Gent in de Bourgondische periode: tussen private belangen en publieke financiën", in *Driemaandelijks tijdschrift van het Gemeentekrediet van België*, 176 (1991), pp. 14-18; D. Clauzel, *Finances et politique à Lille pendant la période bourguignonne*, Lille, 1982, p. 181; C. Dickstein-Bernard, "La gestion financière d'une capitale à ses débuts: Bruxelles, 1334-1467", in *Annales de la Société royale d'Archéologie de Bruxelles fondée à Bruxelles en 1887*, 54 (1977), pp. 193-194; J.W. Marsilje, *Het financiële beleid in Leiden in de laat-Beierse en Bourgondische periode, 1390-1477*, Hilversum, 1985, p. 121; R. Van Uytven, *Stadsfinanciën en stadsekonomie te Leuven van de XIIe tot het einde der XVIe eeuw*, Brussels, 1961, pp. 217-218.

citizens of the issuing city, they were never alone and sometimes even not in the majority. As will be demonstrated later, the level of participation of citizens in the public debt of their hometown was liable to sharp fluctuations connected to a complex set of political, economical and financial aspects such as the city's creditworthiness and the means of coercion the urban government could use.

Outside the city, a large group of investors could be found in the close vicinity to the issuing city. Judging by the number of *renteniers*, the Franc of Bruges – which is the large rural area surrounding the city – and the smaller towns in the quarter of Bruges such as Damme, Sluis, Veurne, Nieuwpoort and Sint-Winoksbergen appear as important markets for the annuities issued by the Bruges government. Yet the spread of the Bruges *renten* was much wider than the direct political and administrative hinterland of the town. By any issue of annuities on the urban domain, Bruges's officials were sent to the major cities in the county, namely Ghent and Ypres, and also smaller towns such as Kortrijk, Oudenaarde, Aalst and Dendermonde could expect an official delegation from Bruges. Looking at the structure of this fund-raising web, it is interesting to observe that the market for Bruges annuities reflects to a considerable extent the hierarchy in the Flemish urban network. The money markets appealed to correspond to the lively economic, demographic and regional administrative centres in 15th-century Flanders. Besides the three major Flemish cities that were an important pool for *renteniers*, a considerable number of creditors were recruited in the flourishing harbour towns Nieuwpoort and Sluis, in regional centres like Sint-Winoksbergen and Veurne and even the developping industrial town of Hondschoote is represented. In the Ghent quarter on the other hand the river towns Oudenaarde, Kortrijk and Dendermonde were attractive markets just as was Aalst, the centre of gravity in the region of the river Dender[5].

As it was the case in cities like Ghent, Louvain, Leiden and Lille, the sale of urban annuities was not restricted to the principality alone, but also savings and financial markets outside the county were appealed to[6]. A considerable number of annuities issued on the Bruges domain were sold in the major Brabantine cities Brussels, Antwerp and Louvain, and in Holland's commercial and industrial towns Dordrecht, Rotterdam, Gouda and Amsterdam a ready market was found too. Other important centres in Bruges's fund-raising network were Lille and Tournai where large numbers of *renten* were sold. The remarkable position of Lille as a flourishing market for Flemish *renten* – it is clearly demonstrated that in Lille not only Bruges annuities were popular as *renten* issued by the government of Ghent and of some smaller Flemish cities were equally bought[7] – can largely be explained by the city's important administrative position within the Burgundian complex. As the residence of the *chambre des comptes* there were regular contacts between Lille and the Flemish towns which had important effects on the climate of investment and the readiness to participate in the public debt fund-raising for the benefit of other cities. Moreover, the wealth and the means of investment of the officials present made Lille extraordinary attractive as a financial market[8]. The success of *renten* in Tournai, on the other hand, was more closely linked to religious aspects as Tournai was the seat of the bishop and a prominent

5 P. Stabel, *Dwarfs among Giants. The Flemish Urban Network in the Late Middle Ages*, Louvain/Apeldoorn, 1996, pp. 264-266 (Studies in Urban Social, Economic and Political History of the Medieval and Modern Low Countries, 8).

6 Leiden was used to place life annuities with investors in Antwerp, Bruges, Brussels, Louvain and Mechelen. J. Bangs, "Holland's civic lijfrente loans (XVth century): some recurrent problems", in *Publication du centre européen d'études Burgundo-Médianes. Rencontres de Mons 24 au 26 septembre 1982*, 23 (1983), p. 79. In the case of Ghent during the period 1453-1458 only 5% of the annuities issued on the urban domain were sold within the city. 33% of the annuities were sold in other places in the county whereas a majority of 63% was sold outside Flanders. Boone, "'Plus deuil", p. 14. The same is true for many German cities that sold a substantial part of their annuities – sometimes even the majority – in far-away cities. Köln for example found investors in Mainz, Aachen, Frankfurt, Dortmund, South Germany and Holland. B. Kuske, *Das Schuldenwesen der deutschen Städte im Mittelalter*, Tübingen, 1904, p. 58.

7 Boone, "Plus dueil", pp. 23-24.

8 In his study on the personnel of the central institutions in Lille, J. Dumolyn clearly demonstrates that the officers of the *chambre des comptes* and the *conseil de Flandres* invested large amounts in the purchase of public annuities. J. Dumolyn, *Het hogere personeel van de hertogen van Bourgondië in het graafschap Vlaanderen (1419-1477)*, Ghent, unpublished Ph.D., 2001, II, pp. 381-384.

religious centre. The frequent contacts with other urban centres in the diocese and the strong concentration of wealthy religious people, for whom the purchase of *renten* was one of the rare possibilities for financial investment, made of Tournai an important centre in the fund-raising network of many Flemish cities.

Although it is clear that the Bruges annuities were sold in a wide range of towns and principalities, the character of the available source material makes a reliable assessment of the significance of foreign capital for the funding of Bruges's consolidated public debt impossible. The information is too fragmentary to serve as a starting point for calculating the volume of foreign money attracted to the city by the selling of *renten* or for defining the relative importance of the different financial markets for the funding of Bruges's public debt.

The widespread popularity of the annuities issued by the Bruges government is largely connected with the radiation of the city as the most important economic, commercial and financial centre in north-western Europe during the 15th century. As long as Bruges could retain its leading position, the city had few problems with the funding of its long-term public debt. The city's economic success that lasted well into the 15th century strengthened the general confidence in Bruges's prosperity and solvency, and therefore people easily invested in its public debt. By the end of the century, however, the situation would radically change. From the accession of Charles the Bold in 1467 onwards, the fiscal pressure of the central government on the county rose sharply which shortly afterwards resulted in the drastic reduction of the financial freedom that the major Flemish cities had enjoyed for a long time. Like other towns, Bruges got gradually caught in the financial stranglehold of the central authority, and the management of its rising public debt became increasingly problematic. In the 1480s the difficult situation further deteriorated as the already long-lasting conflict with Maximilian of Austria degenerated into an armed confrontation. The outbreak of the civil war in Flanders had deregulating effects on the urban finances, and the Bruges government completely lost control over its public finances. The city could no longer pay off its creditors, payments of annuities were stopped, and the *renten* charges accumulated in a very short time to two and a half times the annual urban revenues. Confidence in Bruges and the annuities sold on the urban domain therefore declined remarkably, and during the last decades of the 15th century it became extremely difficult to find purchasers for the newly issued annuities. Not only foreign investors gave up, even inside the city, people were no longer willing to invest in the urban public debt. A large number of annuities remained unsold and – as will be discussed later – one may assume that most of the persons still active in the public *renten* market acted mainly out of political pragmatism or were pressured by the urban government. The complete disruption of the public finances and the financial distrust resulting from it had far-reaching effects on the economic stability in Bruges and undoubtedly played a part in the shift of the economic centre in north-western Europe from Bruges to Antwerp.

From the very end of the 15th century onwards and especially during the first decades of the 16th century – when the state of the urban finances was still worrisome but less acute because of an official settlement of Bruges's finances and public debt[9] – the number of foreign *renteniers* was reduced by an active policy initiated by the urban government itself[10]. The driving motives for this decision were first, concern about the economically undermining effects of the public debt policy pursued

9 As the city was virtually bankrupt, the Bruges government asked Maximilian of Austria for a moratorium that was granted to the city on the 11th of December 1494 for a period of seven years. The urban receipts and expenses were minutely regulated by officers of the central government and the Bruges administration had the prince's authorisation to stop the payment of renten arrears for the next seven years. Since the financial crisis just dragged on, this charter had to be renewed several times by the end of the 15th and in the first decade of the 16th century. SAB, reeks 99, Politieke charters, 1e reeks, nr.1251.

10 The urban authorities did not have the exclusive right on the forceful redemption of annuities possessed by foreigners. As the whole community was responsible for the payment of the public annuities, every single inhabitant had the right to take over an annuity that was in the hands of a foreigner simply by reimbursing the capital amount invested at the time of the purchase. Ph. Godding, *Le droit privé dans les Pays-Bas méridionaux du 12e au 18e siècle*, Brussels, 1987, pp. 247-248. (Académie Royale de Belgique. Mémoires de la Classe des Lettres. Collection in-4°-2° série T. XIV).

heretofore, and second, awareness that a public debt financed from inside the city was more easily manageable and could somewhat relieve the financially suffocating situation. As much as possible, therefore, *renteniers* from outside the city were reimbursed, and the redeemed annuities were resold within the city. By reducing the share of foreigners in the public debt, the imminent threat of confiscation and imprisonment – legal instruments often used by unpaid *renteniers* to exert pressure on the defaulting government in order to accelerate the payment of the outstanding debts – could be diminished[11]. Besides, in the case of a reissue the government often managed to obtain a more favourable interest rate than the original one[12], for the resale of the redeemed annuities was generally less urgent and took place in serener conditions than the original issue. Given the relative stability of the situation, the urban government was also in a stronger position and could exert considerably more pressure on its citizens to buy expensive *renten* than it could have done in an emergency situation or on foreigners. By this manoeuvre an additional profit accrued, and thus extra money was brought in.

The urban government clearly used a broad spectrum of strategies to reduce the overall public debt and the immense charges of annuities in particular. From the 1490s onwards, several payments to the urban government such as the purchase of minor public offices and lottery tickets, for example, could occur in annuities, obligations and other kinds of official arrears. By this means, the urban government succeeded in paying off an important number of *renteniers* and creditors. For the moment, given the in progress state of our research and the vagueness of the sources, it still remains unclear whether or not other and more important transactions such as payments for the rent of indirect taxes on wine, beer and grain could also be discharged via arrears and annuities. This is an interesting question for investigation since a clear interconnectedness can be demonstrated between a select group of major investors in Bruges's public debt and the city's political and socio-economic elite, as will be discussed in one of the following sections. It would be interesting, therefore, to know if and to what extent this specific financial method contributed to a further strengthening of the grip of a select group of major *renteniers* on the political and financial administration of the city.

The international merchants and their strategies of investment

An important group of *renteniers*, whom I would like to treat separately, is the foreign merchants active in the market for Bruges's annuities. Since the international merchants are expressly represented in the endless lists of *renten* buyers, it is interesting to have a close look at the background of these *renteniers*, their motives to operate in the local annuity market and their financial significance for the management of the public debt in Bruges.

As the leading commercial and financial centre in north-western Europe, Bruges had attracted a considerable number of international traders from the beginning of its economic success onwards. Whereas international merchants were originally very mobile, more and more merchants came to Bruges for longer periods as the nature of trade changed. They began to play an increasingly important role in public life, a role that was no longer restricted to their purely economic business activities. They

11 One of the characteristics of annuities sold by an urban government was the common responsibility of the whole urban society for the due payment of the annuities issued on its domain. Therefore unpaid *renteniers* could claim their payment on each individual burgher of the issuing city. W. Ogris, *Der mittelalterliche Leibrentenvertrag. Ein Beitrag zur Geschichte des deutschen Privatrechts*, Vienna/München, 1961, pp. 265-268. Since by the end of the 15th century, the financial situation of Bruges deteriorated very rapidly implying that many *renteniers* remained unpaid for a longer period, the devastating effects of this practice would become clear. The economy suffered great losses as Bruges's burghers and merchants travelling outside the city constantly ran the risk of being captured by unpaid *renteniers* and seeing their goods confiscated.

12 A rate of interest was not a self-evident fact the urban government could define autonomously. On the contrary, the formation of a rate of interest was subject to a complex number of factors among which were the solvency of the city, the availability of other means of credit, the degree of financial trouble, the means of pressure the issuing institution could exert on potential purchasers, the situation in the city's private annuity market and the renten market in other towns.

got more closely involved in local social networks and politics as the different organisations of foreign merchants had developed into well institutionalised nations active in the different levels of the urban society and contributed to the characteristic shape of Bruges as a commercial metropolis. At the same time merchant nations which were more and more generally seen as one of the fundamental constituents of Bruges's society beside the craft-guilds and the burghers were also appealed to for financial support, and as the urban public debt administration indicates individual merchants started to participate in the city's consolidated debt.

If we take a look at the names of the foreign merchants buying *renten* on the Bruges domain, it immediately becomes clear that they were essentially merchants coming from the Hanseatic world, Portugal and Italy[13]. They were all merchants who resided in Bruges for a longer period which is not surprising given the sort of investment concerned since the purchase of an annuity was always intended as a long-term investment. Nevertheless, it remains an intriguing question what the motives of these foreign merchants were to invest in the public debt of what was, in many cases, a temporary place of residence. In the first place it is generally known that the international merchants often had at their disposal substantial means that could be used for investment. As the possibilities for investment in medieval society apart from trade were limited, urban annuities were one of the few available and attractive alternatives[14]. Our investigations, however, reveal that the wealth of the international traders was in many cases not the only or most decisive motive to operate in the *renten* market, even if a heavy purse was a necessary condition given the expensiveness of the annuities. Their involvement in the public and social life in Bruges played an equally important part. As noted earlier, the international merchants considered here all resided in the city for a longer period. They were involved in local social networks and had achieved a certain degree of integration. It is therefore not surprising that the majority of these international merchants operated in the public *renten* market by buying life annuities for the benefit of a local business partner or to support a concubine or an illegitimate child a merchant had by a Bruges women[15]. As they were excluded from succession by customary law, life annuities were a very convenient and frequently used instrument to benefit illegitimate children not only for the indigenous population but also for foreigners[16].

Since these foreign *renteniers* were international merchants, they were especially concerned about a good economic climate, and therefore relative stability in the field of the public finances was of primordial importance for them too. As these merchants had a clear economic interest in the good administration of the Bruges finances and the public debt, buying annuities was not merely a financial investment. At the same time it was an investment that could favour the overall economic climate and therefore the merchant's own business and trade. The same reasoning is applicable for other forms of financial support that were regularly granted to the Bruges government by individual merchants and merchant nations as loans and gifts. The sometimes large amounts of money contributed in cases of serious financial trouble were not inspired by the preservation of good relations with the urban

---

13 An important example of a Hanseatic merchant buying annuities on the Bruges domain is Albrecht van Vickenhuuse, a merchant from Lubeck who was also active in the amber industry in Bruges. In 1472-73, 1478-79, 1481-82 and 1486-87 he even occupied the position of dean of the craft-guild of the *paternostermakers* (SAB, Reeks 114, Wetsvernieuwingen). Examples of Italian merchants investing in the Bruges' public debt are several members of the family Arnolphini and the important merchant-banker from Florence Tomasso Portinari. (M. Boone, Apologie d'un banquier médiéval: Tomasso Portinari et l'État bourguignon, in *Le Moyen Âge*, pp. 31-54.)

14 Apart from trade which was a more risky form of investment, the most important possibilities for investment in medieval society were essentially the purchase of immovable property especially rural estates and houses on the one hand and the purchase of heritable and life annuities issued by both private and public bodies on the other. Dumolyn, *Het hogere personeel*, pp. 358-359 and 381.

15 M. Carlier, *Kinderen van de minne? Bastaarden in het vijftiende-eeuwse Vlaanderen*, Brussels, 2001, pp. 78-87. (Verhandelingen van de Koninklijke Academie van België voor Wetenschappen en Kunsten. Nieuwe Reeks, nr.3).

16 Carlier, *Kinderen*, pp. 182-183.

government alone as they were equally very important for the international merchants and the foreign nations from an economic point of view.

In the end there are indications to suppose that on specific occasions foreign merchants were asked or at least encouraged by the Bruges government to buy annuities on the urban domain. In this context it was especially the Italian merchants who were appealed to, probably as a result of their traditional function as financiers of public institutions. One of these occasions was in March 1471 when the government issued heritable annuities to an annual amount of 500 lb. gr. Whereas all annuities were sold at an interest rate of 5%, Tomasso Portinari was the only purchaser for whom an interest rate of 6.25% applied. This higher and more favourable interest rate was clearly a concession on the part of the urban administrators in order to persuade Portinari to invest a large sum in the purchase of annuities. Although 1,320 lb. gr. was indeed a considerable amount, especially in comparison with the average wage level in Bruges[17], for Tomasso Portinari on the other hand this must have been a rather small investment. As a banker and as a private person he was dealing with sums of much larger proportions, and the profits he made from other business and financial transactions were substantially bigger[18]. One may assume, therefore, that Portinari's investment in the Bruges public debt was not inspired by the gain of profit alone. His involvement in the social networks and his familiarity with political decision-making in Bruges must have played an important part too.

Although a large number of the international merchants and especially of those residing in Bruges for a longer period actually invested in urban annuities, they were not the big and most important financiers of the city's consolidated public debt. Apart from some exceptions of Italian merchants apparently asked to support the urban government for larger amounts, their investments were essentially small and very often directed at the benefit of illegitimate children, concubines and other relatives. In order to find out who were the most important share-holders of the Bruges consolidated public debt, we will have a closer look at the *renten* buyers in my sample and especially at the Bruges residents and those investors who were closely connected to the city.

A sociographic analysis of the Bruges *renten* buyers

In the sample of *renteniers* that I have selected as the basis for my prosopographic research, a wide range of different socio-economic strata is represented. Apart from the international traders I have discussed above, three specific groups of annuity buyers can be distinguished on an abstract socio-economic level: first a large group of *renteniers* that were professionally active as craftsmen, second an important number of *poorters*[19] and third a group of annuity buyers who belonged to noble families that had important links to the city.

If we take a look at the craftsmen who were active in the Bruges public annuity market, it is clear that whereas a significant number of craft-guilds are actually represented, they essentially belonged to the more powerful and richer crafts in Bruges as those connected to the textile, building, leather and luxury industries and the craft-guilds producing for the local market such as butchers, fish sellers and bakers. It is interesting to observe that all the specific craft-guilds mentioned here were not only the most prestigious ones on the social scale, they were also politically important as they had

17 In Bruges, the daily wage of a skilled worker amounted to 12 d. gr. C. Verlinden (ed.), *Dokumenten voor de geschiedenis van prijzen en lonen in Vlaanderen en Brabant. II.: XIVe-XIXe eeuw. A. Vlaanderen*, Bruges, 1965, p. 92.

18 As the agent of the Medici bank in Bruges, Portinari granted Charles the Bold several loans to a total amount estimated between 9,500 lb. gr. and 16,150 lb. gr. In 1470 he farmed the toll at Gravelines for an annual sum of 2,700 lb. gr., and he was personally engaged in the alum trade. In 1469 he possessed a quantity of alum with a market value of at least 10,000 lb. gr. Boone, "Apologie", pp.39, 43-44 and 47.

19 The *poorters* or *burghers* in Bruges were members of the urban high society who formed a specific social category that was politically privileged.

permanent representation in the Bruges government and could actually take part in the urban administration[20].

The largest and financially most important socio-economic group among the *renten* buyers includes the drapers, brokers-hostellers and wholesalers who were active in the public annuity market. Whereas this select group of wealthy Bruges *poorters* who belonged to the urban social, economic and political high society is already the largest group among the *renten* buyers, the number of *poorters* who participated in the public debt was possibly even larger than the number I have been able to establish so far since I have been confronted with a major methodological problem in the collection of prosopographic data on the Bruges population. The specific political reality in medieval Bruges had important repercussions on the reliability of the written documentation and was responsible for the fact that a lot of sources that are of primordial importance for the collection of prosopographic data on the Bruges society – like the lists of the annually renewed urban magistracy – are not fully reliable with regard to the socio-economic indications that they contain. Practically speaking, this implies that it happens very regularly that *poorters* are not recorded in the source material as members of the *poorterij* but as representatives of a craft-guild. The strictly formal organisation of the political life in Bruges brought a large number of *poorters*, and particularly those active in trade and in the textile industry, to enter one or more craft-guilds that were closely connected to their business in order to occupy positions in the urban government that were legally reserved to real craftsmen[21]. As a result of this manoeuvre, many more positions in the urban government were held by *poorters* than officially established in urban customary law and than directly observable in the available source material. Since *poorters* who held a seat in the government as representatives of a craft were officially recorded as craftsmen and not as members of the *poorterij*, it is clear that methodological problems arising from this historical practice are inevitable and can only be circumvented by bringing together data from different sources and by extensive prosopographical research.

The third significant socio-economic group that can be distinguished among the *renten* buying public is a select group of noblemen who participated in the Bruges consolidated public debt. Whereas many noblemen operating in the public annuity market did not actually live in the city, yet the majority belonged to lineages that were closely connected to the urban society. Prosopographic research clearly indicates that most of the noble creditors in the sample belonged to powerful families that had an important political tradition in the different administrative levels of the county and whose members had participated in the Bruges urban government on several occasions[22].

These rudimentary observations on the socio-economic background of the people who operated in the urban public *renten* market are in accordance with the findings on the organisation of the consolidated public debt in other major cities in the Low Countries[23]. In all the cases that have been studied, the richer craft-guilds and the *poorterij* were time and again the socio-economic circles par excellence where enough money was available to buy public *renten*, as urban annuities were relatively

---

20 In Bruges as in the other Flemish cities, participation in the urban government was not restricted to the urban high society as in the aftermath of the events of 1302, the urban government was opened to members of the craft-guilds too. From 1304 onwards, the assignment of the offices in the magistracy was officially regulated and would happen according to a fixed distributive code between the members of the craft-guilds and the *poorterij*. Eighteen of the twenty-six seats in the urban government were legally reserved for representatives of the crafts whereas four seats were kept by members of the *poorterij*. M. Ryckaert and A. Vandewalle, *Brugge. De geschiedenis van een Europese stad*, Tielt, 1999, pp. 41-42; K. Vanhaverbeke, *Het stadsbestuur in Brugge in de periode 1375-1407: Sociaal-institutionele benadering aan de hand van een prosopografische methode*, Louvain, unpublished master's thesis, 1997, pp. 74-76; J.A. Van Houtte, *De geschiedenis van Brugge*, Tielt, 1982, pp. 298-300.

21 As the seats in the urban magistracy were allocated to craftsmen and *poorters* according to a fixed distributive code that was established in urban customary law, one of the best ways for a *poorter* to circumvent this formal regulation was by entering a craft-guild and by occupying political positions as a representative of that craft.

22 The most important examples are the families *de Baenst* and *de Voocht*. J. Gaillard, *Bruges et le Franc ou leur magistratures et leur noblesse*, Bruges, 1857-1860, I, pp. 22-40 and II, pp. 3-19.

23 Boone, "'Plus dueil", p. 18; R. Marquant, *La vie économique à Lille sous Philippe le Bon*, Paris, 1940, pp. 220-221; Mertens, "Financieel beheer", pp. 165-175.

expensive and not attainable for everyone. The cheapest annuity that was sold on the occasion of the three issues studied in this article cost 9 lb. gr., an amount that corresponded on the Bruges labour market to the wage of a skilled mason for nine full months of labour[24]. This implies that participation in the public *renten* market was a priori restricted to a limited section of the urban population, especially since we know that only an extremely small number of the Bruges annuities were bought communally by several persons, a practice that could have lowered the financial threshold and broadened the demand for the urban *renten*[25]. The lower layers of the population were even unable to buy a cheap annuity and therefore were fully excluded from participation in the consolidated public debt.

The Bruges annuity purchasers belonged to the same socio-economic strata as those from which the members of the urban government were recruited. While the public annuity market was open for both *poorters* and richer craftsmen, the same is true for the urban magistracy since access to the political game in late medieval Bruges was not restricted to the small group of families that made up the urban *poorterij*. For in 1304 Bruges's political institutions had been drastically reorganised which implied that from that moment on broader layers of the population too, could take part in the city's political life. The absolute power of the *poorterij* was legally broken, and the craft-guilds were officially represented in the urban government according to a fixed distributive code[26]. In spite of this official regulation that should have guaranteed a broad and varied representation of the craft-guilds in urban politics, the Bruges government quite quickly regained its more closed character as it became increasingly dominated by an alliance of the *poorterij* on the one hand and the rich and powerful craft-guilds on the other. This evolution further continued, and by the beginning of the 15th century the Bruges administration was almost exclusively in the hands of the city's commercial and industrial elite[27]. As will be more fully discussed in the following section, my research on the public debt administration in Bruges demonstrates that the members of this commercial and industrial elite not only dominated the urban political life. At the same time, they succeeded in getting an iron grip on the public finances as they were the city's most important creditors and public debt shareholders and had monopolised the key financial positions in the government.

As a starting point for a more profound analysis of the specific composition of the *renten* buying public in Bruges during the last quarter of the 15th century, I calculated the total amount of money that the 155 persons in the sample had ever spent on the purchase of annuities issued on the Bruges domain[28]. By doing this, I was able to follow a more quantitative course and to introduce a refined classification in my research population since this strategy offered me the opportunity to group

---

24 J.P. Sosson, *Les travaux publics de la ville de Bruges XIVe-XVe siècles. Les matériaux. Les hommes*, Brussels, 1977, p. 301. (Crédit Communal de Belgique. Collection Histoire Pro Civitate, série in-8°, n°48).

25 Only two of the hundred-ninety annuities in the sample were bought by more than one person: in the first case a couple of tutors acted in favour of a minor, and in the other case two brothers jointly bought a heritable annuity for the amount of 30 lb. gr.

26 See note 20.

27 After a period characterised by a more or less strict application of the fixed distributive code between members of the craft-guilds and the *poorterij* for the assignment of the seats in the urban government, this regulation was less observed during the 15th century. In addition, an increasing number of *poorters* active in trade and in the textile industry entered craft-guilds and by these means occupied positions in the urban government that were legally reserved to members of the crafts. In this way, the powerful commercial and industrial elite in Bruges succeeded in strengthening its grip on the urban political life and in establishing its domination over the urban government. J. Dumolyn, *De Brugse Opstand van 1436-1438*, Kortrijk/Heule, 1997, pp. 75-87 (Standen en Landen, 101); A. Greve, *Hansen, Hosteliers und Herbergen. Studien zum Aufenthalt hansischer Kaufleute in Brügge im 14. und 15. Jahrhundert*, Ghent, unpublished Ph.D., 1998, p. 86; D. Van Den Auweele, *Schepenbank en schepenen te Brugge (1127-1384). Bijdrage tot de studie van een gewone stedelijke rechts- en bestuursinstelling*, KUL, unpublished Ph.D., 1974, pp. 398-402; K. Vanhaverbeke, Het stadsbestuur in Brugge in de periode 1375-1407: Sociaal-institutionele benadering aan de hand van een prosopografische methode, Louvain, unpublished master's thesis, 1997, pp. 121-123 en J.A. Van Houtte, "Makelaars en waarden te Brugge van de 13e tot de 16e eeuw", in *Bijdragen voor de Geschiedenis der Nederlanden*, V (1950), pp. 19-20.

28 As is clear, all the annuities issued on the Bruges domain bought by *renteniers* in the sample are considered regardless of the moment on which they were issued. As a consequence, the perspective taken here is much larger than the restricted number of annuities sold on the occasion of the three issues chosen as the basis for the present sample of *renteniers*.

the 155 *renten* buyers studied here in different and clearly defined financial categories. In order to guarantee sufficient differentiation, I distinguished six categories of *renteniers*, namely those investing a capital amount of between 1 lb. gr. and 100 lb. gr., of between 101 lb. gr. and 200 lb. gr., of between 201 lb. gr. and 300 lb. gr., of between 301 lb. gr. and 400 lb. gr., of between 401 lb. gr. and 500 lb. gr. and a sum above 500 lb. gr. As it must be possible to connect these numerical data with more qualitative information on the annuity purchasers, I expected this approach to lead to a more refined picture of the background of the Bruges *renten* buyers and a better assessment of the impact of the consolidated public debt on the power structures in the city.

The minimum that was spent by someone in the sample was 15 lb. gr. whereas the maximum expenditure amounted to 2.510 lb. gr., sums that correspond to a fixed annual revenue of respectively 1 lb. gr. and 190 lb. 10 s. gr. The wide gap between both extreme values clearly demonstrates that the *renten* buying public did not constitute a financially homogeneous group but that there existed a remarkable difference in the degree of involvement in the public debt among the individual creditors. An interesting question arising from this observation, and one that will be treated later on, is what the main reasons for these differences in involvement were and whether they can be related to a difference in motivation to operate in the public *renten* market or not.

The average annual income that was accumulated from *renten* bought on the Bruges domain by the people in my research population was 8 lb. 3 s. gr. whereas the median amounted to 2 lb. gr. If we take a look at the capital sums that the 155 creditors in my sample invested in the purchase of Bruges *renten*, the median lies at 30 lb. gr., and the average reaches 107 lb. 13 s. 10 d. gr. It is clear that these values are relatively low and must be situated in the first category and on the borderline between the first and the second category of invested capital I distinguished[29]. This implies that the conclusions I made in the previous section on the occasion of the minimum and maximum amounts are confirmed as the average and the median, too, indicate that there existed a clear financial difference between the individual annuity purchasers. The *renten* buying public falls into two different bodies namely a large group of *renteniers* buying annuities for a relatively small amount and a limited group of major creditors investing considerable sums in the public debt.

These findings are also confirmed by figure I, an illuminating diagram that shows the relative financial importance of the individual annuity buyers. On the vertical axis of the diagram the contribution of the *renteniers* to the total amount that was invested in the consolidated public debt is indicated in accumulated percentages, and on the horizontal axis the number of *renteniers* is given also in an accumulated form. The diagonal visualises the imaginary situation of an equal investment in the public debt by all *renteniers* whereas the curve corresponds to the real historical situation. The curve that indicates which share of the *renteniers* was responsible for which percentage of the invested capital is quite explicit and points to a marked inequality in the level of investment. Eighty percent of the *renteniers* were responsible for only 25% of the money spent on the purchase of annuities whereas the five most important creditors invested 36% of the total capital. Once again, and from a different point of view, the financial discrepancy in the group of *renteniers* is demonstrated. All available figures point unanimously to the division of the *renten* buying public into two different groups: first a large group of small creditors who operated in the public annuity market for just a limited amount and second a select number of *renteniers* who invested in the city's consolidated public debt on a large scale. It is clear that the *poorters* and richer craftsmen who were active in the domestic public annuity market did not constitute a uniform entity but formed a largely polarised group that was characterised by a broad base of modest investors and a small top of rich creditors. A few magnates towered above all the other *renteniers* and actually dominated the public debt administration. The extreme social and financial

29 In comparison to the average level of wages and prices in Bruges, these values are obviously high as the average and the median correspond to the wage of a skilled mason for respectively 9 and 2.5 years of full-time labour. C. Verlinden (ed.), *Dokumenten voor de geschiedenis van prijzen en lonen in Vlaanderen en Brabant. II.: XIVe-XIXe eeuw. A. Vlaanderen*, Bruges, 1965, p. 92.

inequality that characterised not only the urban society as a whole but also the composition of the wealthy upper classes, as has previously been established by W. Blockmans, finds here another demonstration[30].

FIGURE I: **Investment in the public debt**

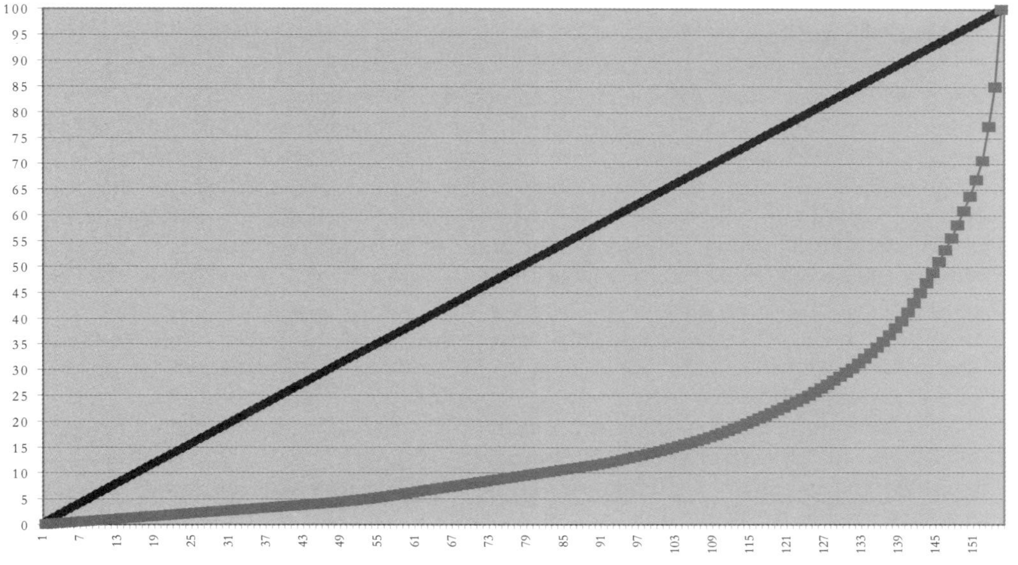

In close connection with the discrepancy in the level of investment, I found a striking difference in the number of annuities that was bought by the individual *renteniers*. Whereas 77% of the *renteniers* possessed just one or two *renten*, a select group of only 3% enjoyed the annual income of ten or more annuities[31]. Besides, the number of annuities was in proportion to the degree of investment which implies that the financially most important creditors also owned the largest number of annuities. As the major investors possessed a wide range of annuities that they had bought on different occasions, this select group of *renteniers* appears as a well-practised financial elite whose presence in the Bruges public *renten* market was not 'accidental'. To gain more insight into the motives of this select group, it would be interesting to have some information on the full strategies of investment applied by these persons. This kind of information, however, is very exceptional, and only for a few unique examples will it be possible to work this aspect out[32].

For a better assessment of the reasons that underlie the striking differences in the financial participation of the individual *renteniers*, I connected the preceding and mainly quantitative data with the information on the socio-economic background of the annuity buyers. For almost 80% of the *renteniers* in the sample some additional prosopographic information could be gathered which makes it possible

30 Studies of some tax accounting documents dating from the end of the 15th century demonstrated that Bruges's society was extremely polarised. There existed not only an important difference between the lower and the upper layers of the society, the wealthy middle classes too were extremely differentiated. W. Blockmans, "Nieuwe gegevens over de gegoede burgerij van Brugge in de 13e en vooral 15e eeuw", in W. Blockmans, I. De Meyer, J. Mertens e.a. (eds.), *Studiën betreffende de sociale structuren te Brugge, Kortrijk en Gent in de 14e en 15e eeuw*, Heule, 1971, p. 151. (Standen en Landen, LIV).

31 The *rentenier* in the sample who bought the largest number of annuities issued on the Bruges urban domain was Willem Oudmaert. He invested 1,279 lb. 10 s. gr. and enjoyed the annual profit from twenty-two renten.

32 This topic will be fully explored at a later stage of my research.

to characterise their socio-economic background to at least a certain extent. For the remaining 20% of the annuity buyers, on the other hand, no further data could be found. Since these *renteniers* belonged in essence to the financially most modest category of investment, namely the category of *renteniers* who bought annuities for an amount of between 1 lb. gr. and 100 lb. gr., it is an attractive idea to connect the silence of the source material with socially lower or middle class character of the *renteniers* concerned. However plausible this argumentum *ex silentio* might be, its validity can not be proved, and therefore the substantial group of *renteniers* who can not be identified will remain a factor of uncertainty in the following discussion.

By bringing together the financial data and the prosopographic information on the *renten* buyers in the different financial categories some new and illuminating conclusions could be drawn. A first trend that is clearly observable implies that the number of middle class people and members of the craft-guilds decreased as the amount of money that was invested in urban annuities increased[33]. Although craftsmen were still present in the higher financial categories, their relative importance, more specific in comparison to the industrial and commercial elite, decreased. An analogous evolution can be observed when the degree of participation in urban political life that could be attested for the different categories of investment is examined. Although urban treasurers and annuity purchasers with an important political career are present in all the distinguished categories, they are more markedly represented in the higher financial categories than in the lower[34]. The same is true for the noblemen and the persons with family ties to noble lineages who operated in the urban public *renten* market since they are all to be found in the highest investment categories.

These major trends are confirmed when the average and the median that can be calculated for the money that was spent on the purchase of annuities by specific socio-economic and political groups in Bruges are compared. For the representatives of the craft-guilds both the average and the median value fall under the overall figures[35]. As the number of craftsmen operating in the public annuity market indicates, the craft-guilds were an important market for the funding of the public debt. The figures on the size of the amounts that were invested, however, reveal that the numerical significance of the craft-guilds did not translate into an equally important financial involvement in the public debt. From a financial point of view, the participation of the craftsmen in the public annuity market was at a markedly lower level than their number would lead one to suspect since the individual craftsmen preferred to invest mainly small amounts. This is not true for the *poorters* in the sample whose situation is slightly different. Whereas the median for this specific group of *renten* buyers comes at 30 lb. gr. and corresponds with the general median, the average lies at 146,5 lb. gr. and is higher than the average that applies for the entire group of *renteniers*. These figures clearly indicate that *poorters* generally invested larger sums in the purchase of urban annuities than craftsmen were accustomed to do. Besides, in comparison to the median and overall average the markedly higher level of the average that applies for the group of *renten* buying *poorters* must be attributed to the financial activities of a small number of *poorters* who towered above the others and belonged to the select group of major investors who operated in the public annuity market for huge amounts.

If the level of investment in the public debt of some well-defined social, economic and political groups is taken as a starting point for a further analysis of the financial power structures in Bruges, three specific groups catch our attention: the leading politicians who exercised more than six

33 Whereas at least one in four renteniers in the lowest category of investment (between 1 lb. gr. and 100 lb. gr.) was a member of a craft-guild, none of the *renten* buyers investing more than 400 lb. gr. was.

34 In the category between 1 lb. gr. and 100 lb. gr. fourteen of the 123 *renteniers* belonged to the select group of politicians who exercised more than six offices in the urban government whereas five of the eight *renteniers* investing 400 lb. gr. and more were politicians of the highest level.

35 The average for the representatives of the craft-guilds comes at 61 lb. 8 d. gr. and the median amounts to 22,5 lb. gr. whereas the overall values are 107 lb. 13 s. 10 d. gr. and 30 lb. gr.

offices in the Bruges' magistracy[36], the urban treasurers and the group of noblemen and *renteniers* who were linked to noble families by marriage. These creditors occupied an exceptional position among the *renten* buying public as the figures that are available or could be calculated for these specific socio-political groups were at a remarkably higher level than those applying for the group of *renteniers* as a whole[37]. It is not surprising, however, that people who were largely involved in the urban administration and had important political and financial interests in the welfare of the urban establishment also played an important part in the field of the urban public debt seeing its importance for the political and financial stability in the city. By investing huge amounts in the public debt, some of the leading and wealthy figures in the city formed a select club of major investors whose participation in the city's public finances was essential especially from the 1460s onwards when the level of expenditure began to increase rapidly. By the end of the 15th century, Bruges went through a political and economic crisis that lead to the complete disruption of the public finances and at the same time strengthened the position of the leading urban creditors. As the burden of the *renten* charges grew, they played an increasingly crucial and indispensable role in the preservation of the political independence and the financial survival of the city, and therefore participation in the public debt could develop into an important weapon to strengthen the grip of a small group of creditors on the administration of the public means and further increase their political power. For the Bruges government had sold annuities on the urban domain with increasing frequency from the 1460s onwards, and payments for *renten* had become the largest entry of regular expenditure by the following decade[38]. In the last quarter of the century, the magnitude of the *renten* charges had assumed such proportions that the revenues from indirect taxes that were the most important constituents of the regular urban income had to be reserved almost completely for the annual payment of annuities[39]. This means that a select group of investors could claim the major flows of regular urban income and obtained a strong hold on the backbone of urban revenue. The close interconnection of the tax system and the administration of the public debt resulting from it had important financial, political and social consequences as it strengthened the position of a small group of investors to the extent that they could determine the course of the city's political life.

36 The administration in the major Flemish cities was characterised by a high rhythm of change in the assignment of the seats in the urban government. Broad layers of the population could take part in the urban government but only a small number of people dominated the political life and developed important and long-lasting political careers. In Bruges, an average politician exercised three functions in the urban government whereas the magistracy was dominated by the select political elite of politicians who exercised at least more than six public offices. W. Blockmans, "Het wisselingsproces van de Gentse schepenen tijdens de 15de eeuw", in *Handelingen van de Maatschappij voor Geschiedenis en Oudheidkunde van Gent*, XLI, 1987, pp. 78-79; W. Blockmans, "Mutaties van het politiek personeel in de steden Gent en Brugge tijdens een periode van regimewisselingen: Het laatste kwart van de 15de eeuw", in *Bronnen voor de geschiedenis van de instellingen in België*, Brussels, 1977, pp. 92-103.

37 The median and the average that could be calculated for the prominent politicans in the sample come at 45 lb. gr. and 341 lb. 15 s. 3 d. gr., for the treasurers at 130 lb. gr. and 370 lb. 2 s. 6 d. gr. and for the noblemen at 534 lb. gr. and 807 lb. 10 s. gr.

38 Up to the end of the 1480's, the Bruges *renten* charges always fluctuated between 35% and 50% of the total urban income. The civil war against Maximilian of Austria however fully deregulated the city's public finances and the burden of the consolidated public debt increased rapidly. Between 1490 and 1495 the *renten* charges increased to 130% of the urban revenues and attained a climax in the period 1494-1496 when they even equalled two and a half times the annual revenues. In the financial year 1496-97 the situation stabilised again and the *renten* charges fell back to a normal level of less than half the total revenues. This decline however was only apparent as it was a direct effect of the moratorium that the city had obtained in December 1494. As the city was virtually bankrupt, Maximilian of Austria had indeed authorised the Bruges government to stop the payment of *renten* arrears for a period of seven years.

39 In Bruges as in other Flemish cities, most of the regular annual income came from indirect taxation. During normal years revenue from indirect taxes amounted in Ghent to 70-80% of the global income, while in 15th century Bruges excises generally produced 60% of the total urban income. M. Boone, *Geld en macht. De Gentse stadsfinanciën en de Bourgondische staatsvorming (1384-1453)*, Ghent, 1990, pp. 134 (Verhandelingen van de Maatschappij voor Geschiedenis en Oudheidkunde te Gent, XV) en J. Merlevede, *Stad, vorst en schatkist. Het Brugse en Ieperse financiewezen tussen Middeleeuwen en Nieuwe Tijden (1405-1555)*, Brussels, unpublished Ph.D., 1985, pp. 265-266.

Dynamics and changes in the Bruges annuity market

In the final section of this article, I examine the three annuity issues that constitute the basis of my study against the background of the political circumstances prevailing at the dates of their issuance. The resituation of these three issues in their politico-historical context is an ideal point of departure for analysing the potential shifts in the composition of the *renten* buying public and the impact of the turbulent political events that characterised the last quarter of the 15th century on it. The first issue I selected dates from October 1472 and falls within a period of relative political stability. Notwithstanding the fact that Charles the Bold's autocratic behaviour and oppressive fiscal policy caused a growing displeasure among the citizens in the Low Countries, the central government remained unaffected and could maintain its authority during his reign. The power of the major cities had been restricted considerably, and as far as the situation in Bruges is concerned, the city's autonomy had been broken as its government was highly dominated by urban factions that were favourable to the cause of the central authority. The political climate of the second issue is completely different. This issue occurred in June 1489 and took place against the turbulent background of the armed conflict between the major Flemish cities and the central government for the authority in the county. This long-lasting conflict had started in 1477 and was rooted in the firm reactions that were caused by the centralising policies of Charles the Bold and his successor Maximilian of Austria. During this period of political instability, the composition of the Bruges government changed on several occasions as it was by turns dominated by radical and rebellious groups and more peace minded factions. The last issue took place in July 1492 and was set up to finance the reparations of the war damage and to pay the indemnities that Bruges was condemned to by the peace treaty of Damme. This peace treaty had brought an end to the armed conflict that had lasted for more than a decade between Maximilian of Austria and Bruges. The authority of the central government over the city was restored, and more than ever before, Bruges was in the grip of the central government as it became largely controlled by its officials.

If the average and the median cost price of the *renten* are compared for the three issues studied in this article, it immediately becomes clear that the highest values concern the issue of July 1492 followed by the values for the issue of 1472 and those for the issue of 1489[40]. The available figures clearly indicate that the annuities that were sold in 1492 were the most expensive and lay at a higher price-level than the *renten* issued in 1472 and certainly than those sold in 1489. A short analysis of the figures on the level of capital investment by individual *renten* buyers points in the same direction and demonstrates that the largest sums per individual *renten* buyer were paid in 1492[41]. The smallest level of investment per individual purchaser could be observed for the issue of 1489 whereas the figures on the issue of 1472 lay somewhere in between. Although it is true that the official conditions of sale were more favourable in 1492 than in 1472 and especially than in 1489 – as the urban government sold life annuities on one life at an interest rate of 9% in 1472, heritable annuities at an interest rate of 6,7% in 1489 and life annuities on two lives at an interest rate of 10% in 1492 – this can not fully explain the clear differences that were found especially when other figures are taken into consideration. As we know, the type of *renten* and the interest rate that were offered on the occasion of a new issue were not the only factors that affected the average value of the annuities that were sold and

40 The average and median that I calculated for the issue of October 1472 come at 25 lb. 10 s. 9 d. gr. and 18 lb. gr., for the issue of June 1489 at 23 lb. 5 s. gr. and 15 lb. gr. and for the issue of July 1492 at 41 lb. 10 s. gr. and 30 lb. gr.

41 The average and the median that could be calculated for the level of capital investment of the individual annuity purchasers come at 52 lb. 10 s. gr. and 4 lb. gr. for the issue of October 1472, at 23 lb. 5 s. gr. and 15 lb. gr. for the issue of June 1489 and at 83 lb. 6 s. 8 d. gr. and 80 lb. gr. for the issue of July 1492.

the extent to which people were willing to invest. Several indications suggest that the broader political, economic and financial context played a determining role too.

A first indication that justifies a more contextual interpretation can be found in the figures on the average number of *renten* that was bought by the individual *renten* purchasers who participated in the three issues studied in this article. Whereas the purchasers who operated in the public annuity market in 1472 and 1492 generally possessed several annuities on the Bruges domain, the vast majority of the people who invested in the public debt in 1489 did not buy any *renten* on other occasions. Unlike the *renten* buyers of 1472 and 1492, their participation in the public annuity market was a once-only action. The comparison of the average annual *renten* income and the corresponding median that apply for the *renten* buyers in the three different issues points in the same direction and reveals a marked difference between the *renteniers* who operated in the public *renten* market in 1472 and 1492, on the one hand, and the annuity purchasers who bought *renten* in 1489, on the other[42]. Whereas the figures concerning the annual income from annuities on the Bruges domain of the *renten* buyers who participated in the issues of 1472 and 1492 differ little and are relatively high, an important contrast can be observed in the case of the average annual *renten* income of the annuity purchasers in 1489 that lay at a significantly lower level. A possible explanation for these marked differences could be found in the specific political and financial context in which the issue of 1489 took place. As has been said before, the public finances in Bruges were exhausted by the end of the 1480's because of the long-lasting and extremely expensive war efforts of the preceding years. The financial situation had become hopeless, and the urban government was urged to raise money in every possible way to be able to prolong the civil war. Placed against this background of dire financial need, the available figures suggest an important shift in the funding of the public debt. Because the public government had repeatedly increased the fiscal burden and appealed to its major creditors in the previous years, it saw itself now forced to focus on broader sections of the population for the funding of the consolidated public debt and tried to sell its *renten* to as many citizens as possible. Given the urgency of the situation there is a good chance that the urban government exerted pressure on reluctant inhabitants. Besides, one may not exclude the possibility that some citizens who usually did not participate in the public debt were moved by specific political motives as they felt involved in the power struggle against the central authority and therefore bought *renten* to support the rebellious government.

In order to refine this provisional picture that is mainly based on numerical data, I analysed the composition of the *renten* buying public from a more socio-economic point of view for the three issues separately. This analysis once again confirms that the public annuity market was absolutely not static but on the contrary could be subject to significant and sometimes radical changes. A first important observation is that the group of purchasers showed the highest level of heterogeneity on the occasion of the *renten* sale in 1472. This heterogeneity refers to the socio-economic background of the annuity purchasers while at the same time a marked diversity in gender and geography could be observed too. The fact that broad layers of the urban population participated in the city's public debt is clear since not only the *poorterij* but also a significant number of craft-guilds were represented among the annuity purchasers. The most important feature of the composition of the *renten* buying public in 1472 however was that a lot of foreigners participated in the public debt, both international traders and inhabitants of neighbouring cities and also a remarkable number of women especially widows. This observation proves that the Bruges public *renten* market had preserved its attractiveness to investors from inside as well as from outside the city and that considerations about financial investment and gain of profit were important motives to participate in the consolidated public debt. International traders

42 The average annual income from *renten* issued on the Bruges domain and the corresponding median come to 265 lb. 12 s. gr. and 90 lb. gr. for the issue of October 1472, to 88 lb. 1 s. gr. and 30 lb. gr. for the issue of June 1489 and to 240 lb. 5 s. gr. and 85 lb. gr. for the issue of July 1492.

and widows were indeed very often wealthy individuals who were looking for investment possibilities as they possessed the means that were necessary for participation in the public *renten* market.

By June 1489, the composition of the *renten* buying public had altered. Whereas still diverse layers of the urban society were represented among the annuity purchasers as both *poorters* and richer craftsmen participated in the public debt, a major change had occurred concerning the geographic attractiveness of the Bruges *renten* and the aspect of gender. The number of foreign investors had decreased strikingly in comparison to 1472, and the area of recruitment had become much smaller. Notwithstanding the fact that still a small number of *renten* were sold in the close vicinity to the city, neither foreign merchants nor non-Flemish purchasers could be found among the *renten* buying public. Besides, the figures also indicate that the level of participation among the female part of the population had dropped. Whereas women were important *renten* buyers in 1472, they were no longer present in the public annuity market in 1489. It is clear that the character of the public annuity market had changed since some specific social groups that were mainly looking for opportunities for profitable investment had opted out not the least because most of the public *renten* remained unpaid. As the preceding figures suggest, considerations about investment had receded into the background as main motives to operate in the public annuity market and were replaced by more political arguments such as involvement in the power struggle against the central government and pressure exerted by the urban government.

By 1492, the situation had changed once again, and a completely different picture must be sketched. The annuities that were sold on the Bruges domain in July 1492 were all bought by citizens who occupied a leading position in the Bruges society and by powerful officials who worked for the central government. The *renten* buying public had an obviously more exclusive and closed character than in the previous issues as neither common craftsmen nor foreigners and women could be found among the annuity purchasers. Seeing the high level of capital investment per individual annuity purchaser and the exclusiveness of the *renten* buying public, I assume that the annuity purchasers who invested in the public debt at this crucial moment in the political history of Bruges were basically driven by considerations revolving around politics and personal power positions. In contrast with the situation of 1472 and 1489, the strengthening of one's position in the changed power structures had by 1492 become the most important motive to operate in the public annuity market.

Conclusions

In cases of acute financial shortage, an urban government could have recourse to different fiscal and parafiscal instruments to raise the urban income[43]. From the 1460's onwards, as the level of public spending increased very drastically, the Bruges government chose with a growing regularity for the funding of a consolidated public debt consisting of heritable *renten* and life annuities. This strategy of financing through the sale of *renten* had the advantage of attracting in a short term large amounts of foreign money towards the urban treasury as these annuities had great popularity and were sold in a wide area. Research on the origin of the annuity purchasers has indeed clearly indicated that the market for the Bruges' annuities was not restricted to the city itself nor to the county of Flanders but that *renten* buyers were also recruited in the neighbouring principalities.

In order to guarantee the participation of large groups of the urban population in the public annuity market a substantial number of small *renten* were sold[44]. By this fiscal strategy, investment in the

43 The major financial instruments an urban government could have recourse to, in order to cover unforeseen or growing expenses were the introduction of new and increased indirect taxes, the imposition of direct taxes and forced loans, the contraction of loans and the sale of annuities.

44 In his study on Mechelen in the 15th century, W. Mertens observed a certain tendency towards "democratisation" in the public annuity market. Whereas in the 14th century participation in the consolidated public debt was restricted to the small financial upper-classes, urban annuities became smaller and cheaper in the course of the 15th century by which the social middle classes

purchase of annuities became financially attainable for the broad middle classes that could now be appealed to for the funding of the public debt. Induced by the attractiveness of a fixed annual income for oneself, a relative or a friend, numerous craftsmen were indeed ready to buy *renten* on the urban domain, and therefore the broad middle classes could develop into one of the most important pillars for the funding of the public debt. By the end of the 15th century moreover their significance for the financial survival of the city became even more crucial as they remained active in the public *renten* market at the time when a lot of foreign investors drew back in reaction to the lasting political and economic instability. Since large groups of the urban population could operate in the public annuity market, the city government ensured itself of a broad basis to rely on in case of acute financial problems without being forced to increase immediately the already highly oppressive taxes. Selling annuities became an attractive and alternative way to involve people who were already heavily burdened in the administration of the public means as the urban government could appeal to people's inclination for financial profit.

At the same time a second group that was particularly important for the funding of the public debt in Bruges was the international traders who resided in the city for a long and continuous period as they operated very regularly in the public *renten* market. As their pattern of investment is largely similar to the one assessed for the majority of the autochthonous *renten* buyers, foreign traders invested preferably small sums in the purchase of public *renten*, and their appearance on the public annuity market was usually part of a broader strategy of investment. Like most of the other *renten* buyers, international traders were particularly interested in life annuities because these were ideal instruments to endow illegitimate children, concubines, relatives and friends with a fixed annual income. However, as the political tensions mounted very quickly after the death of Charles the Bold, the international traders disappeared from the public annuity market. Most of the foreign merchants had left the city during the period of the civil war, and since political and economic instability continued unabated, the public *renten* market lost its overall attractiveness to foreign investors. As a consequence, the public annuity market began to shrink, and it became increasingly dominated by autochthonous *renten* buyers who were probably coerced to invest in the city's public debt.

Finally, as we have seen a limited group of large creditors operated in the public annuity market for substantial amounts for whom pure financial investment was not the only nor the main reason to buy *renten* on the urban domain. This small group of major investors was a select company of urban high society members as most of them were prominent brokers-hostellers, drapers and wholesalers. They were all individuals with important offices in the urban government who were largely involved in the administration of the public finances. As this select company of leading figures dominated the public annuity market and monopolised it at politically crucial moments, one may assume that their participation in the public debt has to be understood within a broader context of consolidating political and financial power structures in the city. Since large investments in the public debt could lead to an increased grip on the urban government and the public finances, considerations about the strengthening of personal power positions were of decisive importance in the strategies of investment of these leading figures.

too could enter the annuity market. As they operated very regularly in the public *renten* market, the wealthy middle classes even became the most important creditors of the urban government. Mertens, *Financieel*, p. 174.

RENTENIERS AND THE PUBLIC DEBT OF DORDRECHT (1555-1572)

Manon van der Heijden
Vrije Universiteit Amsterdam

Introduction

Discussing *Coercion, Capital and States*, Charles Tilly claimed that in Early Modern Europe warmaking and statemaking reinforced each other, both leading to the extraction of resources from local population[1]. Indeed, the national debt of the Habsburg monarchs ruling the Netherlands (1477-1572) arose largely from the imposition of taxes and borrowing for and during wars. The enormous sums for the ongoing wars of Charles V and Philip II against France were largely raised (58% of the total) by the urban centres of Holland[2]. With the Dutch Revolt against the Spanish ruler in 1572, Holland's taxes were no longer imposed by the Habsburg monarchy, but from then on by the government of the new republic: the States General. Now Holland's urban governments were pressured to raise sums for the military costs of the revolt against Spain. Providing the city large amounts of money in a short time, selling *renten* (bonds) was the most effective and commonly used method of raising urban capital[3]. Holland's cities did so with either the city's collective estate or parts of the provincial estates as collateral. Playing the most significant role in Holland's network of trade, in the 15th century Dordrecht's credit had been strong enough to be exploited directly by the central government[4]. Although losing it's dominant position as a trade centre, Dordrecht still had the reputation as Holland's first city and still retained its strong creditbase during the sixteenth century. Thus, by selling *renten* on the urban market, purchasers of Dordrecht *renten* made substantial contributions first to the funding of the Habsburg wars, and after 1572 to the funding of the revolt[5]. However, who were those investors in urban public debt?

Scholars have not devoted much effort to determining what sorts of people invested in Early Modern urban debt. This may be surprising, especially when one realises that the selling of *renten* absorbed an essential part of both the total urban revenues and expenses. Who actually subscribed to the urban annuities? And did investors freely choose to entrust their money to urban securities or did

---

1 C. Tilly, *Coercion, Capital, and European States, AD 990-1990*, Cambridge/Oxford, 1990, p. 97.

2 J.D. Tracy, *A Financial Revolution in the Habsburg Netherlands. Renten and Renteniers in the County of Holland, 1515-1565*, London, 1985, pp. 12-27; "Emigré and Ecclesiastica Property as the Sheet-Anchor of Holland Finance, 1572-1584", in Ph. Benedict, G. Marnef, H. van Nierop and M. Venard, *Reformation, Revolt and Civil War in France and the Netherlands, 1555-1585*, Amsterdam, 1999, pp. 255-266, 257.

3 M. van der Heijden, "Stadsrekeningen, stedelijke financiën en historisch onderzoek", in *NEHA-Bulletin voor de economische geschiedenis*, 14 (1999), pp. 129-166. See also the findings of L. Derijcke in chapter 11.

4 Tracy, *A Financial Revolution*, pp. 16-17.

5 L.M. Verloren van Themaat, H.W. Dokkum, E.C. Dijkhof, J.T. Roggen and N. Sanderson, *Oude Dordtse Lijfrenten. Stedelijke financiering in de vijftiende eeuw*, Amsterdam, 1983, pp. 7-15; J.H. Kernkamp, *Vijftiende-eeuwse rentebrieven van Noordnederlandse steden*, Groningen, 1961, p. 6 (*Fontes minores medii aevi*, 13). Both authors refer to P.J. Blok, *Een Hollandsche stad,* The Hague, 1910, I, p. 250; J.W. Marsilje, *Het financiële beleid van Leiden in de laat-Beierse en Bourgondische periode, 1390-1477*, Hilversum, 1985, pp. 285-288.

the urban government pressure them in any way? For the Netherlands, James Tracy and Marjolein 't Hart raised some of these questions with regard to buyers of provincial *renten* and subscribers to Union loans (the Generality)[6]. More specifically, Bowsky and Molho debated the issue of forced loans in late medieval Italy[7]. Flemish scholars who point out the importance of the political interests of investors in urban *renten* have offered another interesting angle. Marc Boone proposed that *renten* buyers viewed their investment as a means to support the politics of the central government[8]. Finally, Jeremy Bangs suggested that Early Modern urban annuities might be seen as the exchange of a financial service for a military or social service[9].

Such larger questions can only be answered by determining the social-economic and political background of investors. In order to describe the characteristics of the urban elite, historians have used the method of collective biography. However, it is exactly this kind of information that is often difficult to retrieve. This article also deals with the problems that scholars meet when identifying investors in urban debt during the Early Modern period. The most important aim is to determine the political backgrounds of the buyers of Dordrecht *renten* in two specific years, before and during the revolt: 1555 and 1572. Did purchasers belong to the urban political elite, as often assumed by other historians? Could Dordrecht's public debt fully rely on the investments of wealthy citizens, or did the city largely depend on non-resident purchasers? We also raise the question of the sex ratio. Were women (widows especially) as much involved in urban debt as in other towns[10]? Finally, did the revolt of 1572 in any way affect the profile of buyers of Dordrecht *renten*? So, were there any significant differences between 1555 and 1572 in the proportion of officeholders and their kin, in the proportion of female buyers, and in the proportion of non-resident purchasers? Before answering these questions, we will briefly discuss the procedure of urban *renten* sales.

The procedure of urban *renten* sales

When selling annuities, the city usually issued both life- and redeemable annuities, which could be bought by citizens as well as buyers from outside the city. The latter paid the city an amount of money and received an annual income in return. The amount, the rate, the name of each buyer, and the beneficiaries were all written down on individual certificates. Where life-annuities were concerned, the contract ended the moment the buyer died. Redeemable or perpetual annuities, however, could be redeemed whenever the city wished to buy off the agreement. In these cases the buyers usually received the original amount. However, without being bought off the redeemable annuities were heritable, and could therefore last for several generations. Accordingly, redeemable *renten* were often referred to as heritable or perpetual annuities. The word 'perpetual' refers to the lasting nature of the agreement[11].

In the life annuity the city issued an amount, engaging to pay the buyer a specified annuity for the life of someone nominated by the buyer. The moment the nominee died the annuity ceased. As a

6 Tracy, *A Financial Revolution*; M. 't Hart, "Public loans and money lenders in the seventeenth century Netherlands", in *Economic and Social History of the Netherlands,* 1989, I, pp. 119-139.
7 A. Molho, *Florentine public finances in the early Renaissance, 1400-1433*, Cambridge, 1971, pp. 60-112; W. M. Bowsky, *The Finance of the Commune of Siena, 1287-1355*, Oxford, 1970, pp. 166-188.
8 M. Boone, "'Plus deuil que joie'. Renteverkopen door de stad Gent in de Bourgondische periode: tussen private belangen en publieke financiën", in *Gemeentekrediet van België: driemaandelijks tijdschrift*, 45 (1991/2), pp. 3-25, 13.
9 J.D. Bangs, "Holland's civic lijfrente loans (XVth century): some recurrent problems", in *Publication du Centre Européen d'études Burgondo-médianes*, 23 (1983), pp. 75-82.
10 Boone, "Plus deuil", p. 13. These questions were also raised in the article of M. van der Burg and M. 't Hart in chapter 13.
11 During the period examined in Dordrecht redeemable *renten* were also referred to as 'heritable' *renten.* In English the word 'perpetual' refers to the same sort of *renten.* In this article redeemable *renten* are considered heritable or perpetual *renten*, meaning that the payment of these *renten* could last endlessly unless the city wished to buy off the agreement.

result the city could calculate on liquidating the purchase after all nominees expired. There was no repayment of the principal, so the buyer risked the loss of his investment the moment the amount of the life annuity was invested. Consequently, buyers of life annuities profited from higher interest rates than purchasers of perpetual annuities[12]. Over the sixteenth century cities offered nominal returns ranging between 5% and 8.3% in the case of perpetual annuities. Where life annuities were concerned, buyers generally received amounts between 10% and 16.6% of the purchase price[13]. The variation of rates of the annuities issued by the States of Holland during the sixteenth and seventeenth centuries was corresponding[14].

The rate of return varied according to economic conditions and the creditworthiness of the city that issued the *renten*. In the case of life annuities the number of nominees also determined rates. Life annuities were usually based on either one or two lives, but the buyer could also nominate more than two lives[15]. The rate of return did not depend on the age of the nominees. Life annuity rates were equal for all buyers, regardless of the age of the beneficiaries. We will not elaborate on the matter, but it is worth mentioning that in Holland rate variations depending on age were not formulated until the end of the seventeenth century[16].

The issues of 1555 and 1572

Being one of the most important means of raising capital for the state, urban rent sales are a revealing source for the entwining interests of statemaking and urban politics. Flemish scholars especially have emphasised the importance of urban rent sales for investigating the effect of statemaking on late medieval and Early Modern urban finances[17]. Such an angle is particularly interesting for the Dutch case because of the evident relation between warmaking and the selling of urban *renten*. For financing their wars both the Habsburg ruler and the States-General largely depended on taxes raised by rent sales in the wealthy cities of Holland. For the purposes of this article, such interesting connections between statemaking and urban financing are limited to the case of Dordrecht.

In the sixteenth century the Habsburg Empire very much needed the money of the wealthy cities of the Netherlands to fund its ongoing wars against France and her allies (1542-1544 and 1552-1559). Being the first and favoured city of Holland, Dordrecht traditionally supported the sovereign's political and cash demand, while demanding trade privileges and protection against rival towns in exchange[18]. Until the Dutch Revolt against Spain in 1572 Dordrecht had issued *renten* to be sold on its market for three reasons only, all of which were due to the war politics of the central government. Firstly, Dordrecht had to sell annuities in order to pay the tax (*Bede quota*) of the Spanish sovereign. In addition, the cities issued renten to pay the interest debts due to these sales. Finally, *renten* sales were needed to fund the costs of disturbances that were caused by various battles[19]. Both the sales of 1555

12 Marsilje, *Het financiële beleid*, pp. 281-288; J.C. Riley, "Life annuity-based loans on the Amsterdam capital market toward the end of the 18th century", in *Economisch- en Sociaal-Historisch Jaarboek*, 36 (1973), pp. 102-130.

13 These figures are based on my database on purchases of perpetual- and life annuities in the city of Dordrecht, in the county of Holland, during the period 1553-1700. Source: Municipal Archive of Dordrecht, *Urban accounts 1550-1700.*

14 D. Houtzager, *Hollands lijf- en losrenteleningen vóór 1672*, Schiedam, 1950, pp. 57-64.

15 Houtzager, *Hollands lijf- en losrenteleningen*, p. 6.

16 J.P. van Rooijen, "De Witt's Waerdye van Lyfrenten, in modern Nederlandsch overgebracht en toegelicht", in *De Levensverzekering*, 11 (1934), pp. 117-142. Also translated in French by P.J.L. De Chateleux, "Le rapport de Johan de Witt sur le calcul des rentes viagères", in *Het Verzekerings-Archief*, 18 (1937), pp. 41-85; Houtzager, *Hollands lijf- en losrenteleningen*, pp. 96-100.

17 W. Blockmans and W. Prevenier, *De Bourgondiërs. De Nederlanden op weg naar eenheid, 1384-1530*, Amsterdam, 1997, pp. 27-50, 166-177; M. Boone, *Geld en macht. De Gentse stadsfinanciën en de Bourgondische staatsvorming (1384-1453)*, Ghent, 1990.

18 W. Frijhoff, H. Nusteling and M. Spies (eds), *Geschiedenis van Dordrecht, 1572 tot 1813*, Hilversum, 1998, pp. 16-19.

19 This information was based on an earlier paper: M. van der Heijden, "Urban Rent Sales and Power Politics in 16th and 17th Century Holland" (European Social Science History Conference, Amsterdam, 5-7 March 2000).

and 1572 were primarily destined to fund the *Bede quota* and the huge debts that were caused by such *renten* sales.

Before issuing annuities, the sovereign officially granted permission to sell *renten*. Such a document of 'patent law' also included the sovereign's immediate reasons to grant such *renten* sales. In 1554 Charles V had issued a patent, in which he permitted Dordrecht to sell *renten* up to 7,000 £ in order to pay the large sum of 112,000 £, destined to fund his war against France. This example clearly shows the entwining interests of the urban community and central government when selling *renten* on the urban market. Dordrecht would only agree to financially support Charles V if he decided a conflict with the rivalling towns of Holland (among which Amsterdam and Rotterdam) over the important staple right, in favour of Dordrecht[20]. In the following years these sales caused huge interest debts, so in order to pay these interest debts the town had to raise huge sums by selling new *renten* in 1555. Starting in 1555 and ending in 1556, the *renten* sale included both life- and perpetual annuities, but in the end only one life annuity was sold for a rate of 12.5%. The perpetual annuities had a rate of return of 8.3%, all destined to reimburse former perpetual annuities of 7.1%, 6.6%, and 6.3%[21].

The buyers of the issue of 1555 thus were investing their money in the wars of Charles V, and in the long-term consequences of these wars for urban interest debt[22]. In 1572 new *renten* were again issued with the patent of the sovereign and sold for the same reason, this time to fund his wars with the sum of 20,000 £[23]. According to the governmental documents granting the issue, purchasers of these *renten* received interest rates similar to rates of sales in preceding years. The perpetual *renten* had a rate of 6.25%, 7.1%, and 8.3%, while investors in life *renten* received an interest rate of 14.2% on one person or 11% on two persons. However, during the actual sale, Dordrecht's citizens were enabled to also purchase life *renten* on more than two persons, while receiving interest rates of 14.2%. We will discuss these matters later on, but apparently higher interest rates were needed to persuade citizens to invest in urban *renten*.

An interpretation of the buyers' political motives in 1572 is much more complicated. During the first months of that year William of Orange, as leader of a League of court nobles, had started a military campaign against the Spanish king: the Dutch Revolt. In the months following, Orange managed to conquer urban areas and to get the support of many cities in the province of Holland. These features would mark the most important turning point in Dutch history, resulting in the international recognition of the Dutch Republic in 1648.

So this time, the ruler Philip II also needed funds to break the resistance of Dutch rebellions. To raise large sums, he granted perpetual- and life annuity sales on June 2, 1572. All the more interesting, Dordrecht decided to support Orange (June 25th) and his army while selling annuities for the sovereign at the same time (until January 1573). This may seem a contradiction, but this was only partly true. The defiant parts of the Netherlands claimed not to fight the king, but his bad counsellors. Officially, Philip II remained the ruler of the whole Netherlands until the northern provinces withdrew their allegiance from him in 1581. Dordrecht may not have formally considered the king an enemy, but obviously, it supported Orange and his army in every way. The town declared its choice in favour of the Revolt whole-heartedly by having the first official meeting of the rebellious cities in one of its cloisters, the *Augustijnenklooster*[24].

---

20 J.L. van Dalen, *Geschiedenis van Dordrecht*, Dordrecht, 1931, I, pp. 266, 480-481; Municipal Archive Dordrecht, *Archief I*, no. 491 (1554), fol. 7-8, and no. 142.

21 Municipal Archive Dordrecht, *Archief I. Rekening van de verkoop en betaling van los- en lijfrenten,* no. 492, fol. 1-3.

22 Boone, "Plus deuil", pp. 6-7.

23 Municipal Archive Dordrecht, *Archief I,* no. 146.

24 J. van Herwaarden, D. De Boer, F. Van Kan and G. Verhoeven, *Geschiedenis van Dordrecht tot 1572*, Hilversum, 1996, pp. 359-362.

Forced or voluntarily *renten*

Investigating purchase behaviour is meaningful only after determining whether purchasers invested their money voluntarily. The willingness to invest in urban public debt largely depended on the credit of the town, the financial reputation of its officeholders (who where obliged to pay debts in case of arrears), the existing alternatives to invest in bonds, houses or land, and the profits (political or economic) that could be gained by the investment. Often failing in securing such investments, late medieval and Early Modern European governments also employed coercive means to get rid of their loans and bonds. Burghers of Holland were obliged to invest in provincial *renten* as late as 1552, when the central government agreed to abandon the custom of forced buying. Free markets started when Holland managed to attract investors in provincial *renten* by issuing higher rates and assuring repayment[25].

Urban governments and city-states also applied means of coercion. For late medieval Florence, Molho showed that Florentine citizens were forced to invest their money, otherwise risking the denial of all political rights and the liability to all penalties imposed by the Florentine authorities. Those paying only a portion of their assessments in order to remain politically eligible and to avoid the imposition of penalties, lost the right to collect interest or to be eventually reimbursed for their payments[26].

Forced urban loans on the Florentine scale did not occur in the Netherlands, but presumably some level of coercion was used from time to time. Perhaps we should distinguish between voluntarily investments, forced investments, and investments made from a sense of urban duty. In the last case urban governors used various methods to urge wealthy citizens to invest in urban debt. Such a sale was levied on a handful of men who belonged to the local political elite or who represented governmental institutions. In Amsterdam pressure had been exerted with the short-term loans in which predominantly the burgomaster invested, or where urban institutions were involved as buyers[27]. In times of financial crisis citizens of the Flemish town Bruges were pressured to purchase urban *renten* as well[28]. Indeed, in Dordrecht too, urban officials were sometimes urged to sell *renten* in order to reduce the town's debt burden.

Because of the deplorable financial situation at the end of the seventeenth century, Dordrecht's town council (called *vroedschap* or *oudraad*) decided in 1694-1696 to raise sums of 25,000 £, 12,000 £, and 23,000 £ with selling life *renten* to its own members. The burgomasters, old-councillors and secretaries of the *vroedschap* were urged individually to purchase life annuities of ca. 300 to 3,000 pounds, until the requested amounts had been raised. In the end 60,000 pounds had been collected. The moral duty to keep the town financially healthy presumably prevailed in the decision making of the government. The town councillors did not gain extra financial profit, receiving annually 11.1% of the amount invested (on one person). The town council had originally planned to combine these private investments with increased wine taxes, higher taxes on the sales of urban property, and several new taxes, but again selling *renten* seemed to be the most effective method of collecting capital[29].

By increasing interest rates on *renten*, urban governments further stimulated the local elite to invest in urban debt. In Amsterdam the political elite invested significant sums in urban debt at the end

25 Tracy, *A Financial Revolution*, pp. 110-125, 221.
26 Molho, *Florentine Public Finances*, p. 69.
27 van der Burg and 't Hart, "Renteniers", in chapter 13.
28 Derijcke, "Purchasers of annuities", in chapter 11.
29 Municipal Archive Dordrecht, *Archief 3. Resolutions of the Oudraad 1694, 1695, 1696,* no. 62, f°.41v., 47–48r., 115-116r.; *Urban accounts, groot comptoir 1694, 1695, 1696* no. 1695, f°.43v., no. 2696, f°.54 v., no. 2697, f°.52v.

of the sixteenth century, but the elite also received higher returns for it's investments[30]. Persuading wealthy non-resident merchants to invest in urban renten in the fifteenth century, Bruges' town councils offered Italian merchants much higher interest rates. Financial and political profit, moral duty, and political pressure, are motives that may all have played an important role, but it often remains unclear which motive was the decisive factor. Derijcke suggests that in Bruges' case Italian merchants aimed at bettering their social-economical position in urban life as well[31]. Also, higher rates of return were usually obtainable only for a select group of wealthy citizens who occupied high local positions. Furthermore, by investing in urban debt, local elites could further increase their power in financial and political urban institutions.

Although on some occasions being pressured by town councils, Dordrecht's political elite and wealthy citizens usually invested its money voluntarily. This was the case in the issues of 1555 and 1572 as well. Unfortunately, resolutions of the *Oudraad* and urban accounts do not reveal whether buyers voluntarily subscribed to these issues. It is however likely, for two reasons, that in both years the urban government had not used pressure. First, there is nothing in the official documents signed by town magistrates, or in the unofficial notes of the town council – as was the case in 1694-1696 – that indicates that citizens had been pressured to invest. Second, in the sales of both 1555 and 1572, non-resident buyers were involved. Obviously, as in Siena, Dutch urban communities did not have the authority to impose forced loans on potential purchasers from outside the city[32].

Yet, it seems that in the issue of 1572 the town council had to use extra means to attract creditors. As noted before, Dordrecht's citizens received higher rates for their life annuities, regardless of how many nominees had been involved. Apparently, major investors were not inclined to invest in urban *renten* in times of crisis, such as the year of the revolt. By determining the political background of Dordrecht's purchasers, and by comparing 1555 with 1572, we will further discuss the effect of political circumstances on urban *renten* sales.

Identifying annuity buyers

A total of 122 buyers subscribed to the annuity sales of 1555 and 1572. Besides vendor and purchaser, other parties were involved as well. Life annuities included also the nominees, while both life and perpetual annuities may well have involved beneficiaries. Finally, a third party that dealt with the transaction often represented purchasers. For purposes of this paper these parties are not subject of our investigation. The city accounts recorded all of the buyers' names, and usually also their place of residence. It was possible to ascertain 58% of the names of all persons who bought *renten* in these issues. Obviously, such a high success rate is attributable to the high proportion of the urban elite among these sales, but more about that later on. Other factors hampered the identification seriously.

In his work on provincial *renten* Tracy has mentioned some of the problems we also had to deal with. Firstly, it was not always quite so easy to decide where buyers were domiciled, because the place-of-origin often served as a surname of someone long domiciled in another city[33]. Identification of individual purchasers is also complex, because surnames were relatively uncommon in sixteenth-

30 van der Burg and 't Hart, "Renteniers", in chapter 13.

31 Derijcke, "Purchasers of annuities", in chapter 11.

32 Bowsky, *The Finance of the Commune of Siena*, p. 168.

33 When deciding where buyers were domiciled, we used the practical rules of J.D. Tracy. Where a place-of-origin designation (e.g., 'van Amsterdam) served as a surname in the accounts, persons are treated as residents of Dordrecht as long as no other identifying designator was included (e.g., Sijmon Janszoon, korenmeester van Breda). The explicit indicator for place of residence is the preposition '*te*' or '*tot*'. Also: Tracy, *A Financial Revolution*, pp. 143-146.

century Holland[34]. Though surnames were more common among the people of wealth who often invested in *renten*; the identification was complicated by the fact that no standardisation existed. Sometimes patricians used different surnames (Jan Janszoon Oem [*gezeyd* Van Muijlwijck]), while the accounts mentioned only one. Since Dordrecht was still a relatively small community, the accounts often named town magistrates by their names and patronymic only. Following Tracy, it is here assumed that each repetition of a specific combination refers to a different person. Except in cases where the name and patronymic are accompanied by another identifying designator, such as a title (*Graaf* Dirck Janszoon), an occupation (Cornelis Aertszoon, *vleijshouwer*), and an office (Gerrit Michaels, *secretaris*) a surname (Adriaen Dirckszoon *Koninck*), or a place of origin. Female buyers, mostly widows, where usually named by their name and patronymic only, and often referred to as '*weduwe wijlen* (widow of the late) Willem Boucqet Blasiuszoon'.

One could enumerate many urban functions, but for our purposes it is important to select a few significant offices. By comparing the names of purchasers in the urban accounts with lists of the town's burgomasters, aldermen, and councillors, we could easily make out how many buyers occupied an urban office at least once. Thanks to the abundant information at the archive, we could also find out which investors were related to those who occupied high local offices, that is, the participation of family members in the town magistracy. The same was done for other important urban offices related to ecclesiastical functions, and charitative and military institutions. Buyers of urban *renten* will here be segregated into three different categories: members of the town council and magistracy (burgomasters, councillors, aldermen, the public prosecutor), lower urban officeholders[35], and family members of town magistrates and urban governors. The phrase 'family members' includes blood relatives and in-laws up to the fourth degree.

A profile of urban creditors

Who were actually the *renten* purchasers in 1555-1556 and 1572? Did they belong to the local political elite or were they wealthy outsiders, and to what extent did female investors contribute? Let us start with the numbers according to sex in tables I and II, with the issue of 1572 being separated in perpetual and life annuities. Since the issue of 1555-1556 included only one life annuity transaction (of 100 £), no differentiation has been made for those years.

34 R.A. Ebeling, *Voor- en familienamen in Nederland. Geschiedenis, verspreiding, vorm en gebruik*, The Hague, 1993; P.J.J. Stavenuiter, "Waren achternamen familienamen? Een functioneel achternamensysteem te Enkhuizen in de 16^{e} en 17^{e} eeuw", in *Bijdragen en Mededelingen van de commissie voor Naamkunde en Nederzettingsgeschiedenis van de Koninklijke Nederlandse Akademie van Wetenschappen te Amsterdam*, 29 (1975), pp. 19-42; J. van der Schaar, "De Hollandse naamgeving in de Middeleeuwen en haar maatschappelijke achtergronden", in *Bijdragen en Mededelingen van de commissie voor Naamkunde en Nederzettingsgeschiedenis van de Koninklijke Nederlandse Akademie van Wetenschappen te Amsterdam*, 14 (1959), pp. 29-48.

35 Included are: *tresorier, heilige geestmeester, kerkmeester, weesmeester, leproosmeester, gasthuismeester, officier van de schutterij, functionaris ten beleide van stadszaken, stadssecretraris and the stadspensionaris.*

TABLE I. **Number of buyers in 1555 according to sex**
Perpetual annuities (*losrenten*)

Male	Female	All
20 (60.6 %)	13 (39.4%)	33

N = 33
Source: city accounts Dordrecht, 1555-1556 and 1572.
Charitable institutions are counted by the sex of the person buying the annuity (1 female, 2 male).

TABLE II. **Number and percentage of buyers in 1572 according to sex**

	Male	Female	Total
Perpetual annuities	35	16	51 (57.3 %)
Life annuities	24	14	38 (42.6 %)
Total	59 (66.3%)	30 (33.7 %)	89

N = 89
Source: same as table I

In case representatives handled the procedure, the names of both buyer and representative were always mentioned. So, where women are mentioned without a representative, it means she was the buyer. In the case of joint purchase by spouses, the urban accounts named both husband and wife, and accordingly both names are here included in our list of purchasers[36].

The proportion of women subscribing to urban *renten* was quite large: 39.4% in 1555-1556 and 33.7% in 1572, which corresponds with the buyers of Union loans in 1649-1650 that have been investigated by Marjolein 't Hart. Among the individual subscribers, female purchasers accounted for 41%[37]. What was the marital status of these women? 'T Hart found that widows did not dominate the share of female purchasers of Union loans[38]. Also, married women as well as unmarried women invested in generality loans. Unfortunately, there was no further information on their backgrounds, but clearly widows invested higher amounts than unmarried women did. Those women who brought in the highest amounts of *renten* belonged to the noble families, having the title of nobility *vrouwe*. Apparently, such women belonged to the wealthiest group of female purchasers.

In the urban *renten* market of Dordecht widows did play a dominant role, with 70% accounting for the largest share of female purchasers (table III). The other 30% were equally divided between married and unmarried women. When referring to the proportionally high share of female buyers, 't Hart concludes that women in the Low Countries had a significant say in the management of their finances. Indeed, in premodern times widows especially were quite independent. Dutch widows were enabled to partially receive competences that women usually did not have. This also applied to women whose husband stayed abroad for a long period of time. Besides that, husbands could officially hand over certain competences to their wives for a certain period of time. Local notaries and aldermen handled such procedures. In such cases, thus, women enjoyed wide powers, and they were therefore allowed to contract loans and engage in various financial transactions. Consequently, it was quite

36 In contrast to J.D. Tracy who treats males as the buyer in the case of joint purchase by spouses: Tracy, *A Financial Revolution*, p. 148.
37 't Hart, "Public loans and money lenders", in chapter 13.
38 't Hart, "Public loans and money lenders", in chapter 13.

common that married women contracted urban *renten* without being assisted by guardians or representatives[39].

TABLE III. **Number and percentage of female buyers according to their marital status in 1555 and 1572**

Marital status	Number	Percentage %
Widows	30	69
Married females	3	9
Unmarried females	4	7
Missing	6	14
Total	43	100

N = 43
Source: same as previous tables.
Missing = those cases in which the marital status remained unknown.

Did female investors belong to wealthy and locally important families of Dordrecht? A very small proportion of the female purchasers in Dordrecht belonged to the group of nobles. No woman had the title of *vrouwe*, while seven women had the title of *juffrouwe*. Only one investor of the latter group brought in a higher *renten* sum, compared to the average sums that were invested by female purchasers. However, quite a large proportion of these female *renten* purchasers did belong to the local political elite: 58% of all women investing were in some way related to important local officeholders. Their (late) husbands, fathers, brothers or in-laws performed offices, such as burgomaster, alderman or councillor. However, the share of women connected to the local political elite was larger in 1572 than in 1555. Almost 70% of those females buying bonds belonged to that group in 1572, while their proportion had been almost 40% in 1555.

The proportional amount that women subscribed to urban annuities differed per year as well (tables IV and V). Those women buying in 1555 invested much smaller amounts than their male counterparts; 39.4% of all purchasers were women, but these female buyers were responsible for only 11.9% of the total amount invested. During the issue of 1555 female investors generally subscribed to smaller amounts than male buyers did. Most women invested amounts of 15 to 30 pounds, while men invested amounts up to 266 pounds. In 1572 however, the proportion of women investing (33.7%) corresponded with their proportional investment: their share was 31.6% of the total amounts subscribed. Moreover, with regard to the amounts invested, women had the largest share (64%) in the purchase of life annuities in 1572. In the same issue a female purchaser invested the largest sum in annuities (both life- and perpetual). Since the issue of 1572 differed in many ways from other issues, such a proportion was probably exceptional. I will explain this hereafter.

39 A. Schmidt, *Overleven na de dood. Weduwen in Leiden in de Gouden Eeuw*, Amsterdam, 2001; M. van der Heijden, "Women as victims of sexual and domestic violence in seventeenth-century Holland: criminal cases of rape, incest, and maltreatment in Rotterdam and Delft", in *Journal of Social History*, 33 (2000), pp. 623-644.

TABLE IV. **The total amount subscribed in 1555 by the 33 individual buyers according to sex**

	Male	Female	Total
Amount	1,741 £	236 £	1,977 £
Percentage	88 %	12 %	100 %

Source: previous tables

The amounts counted in pounds £ (pond Hollands/guilders).

TABLE V. **The total amount subscribed to perpetual- and life annuities in 1572 by the 89 buyers according to sex**

	Male	Female	Total £
Perpetual annuities	2,012 £	309 £	2,321 £ (63.7 %)
Life annuities	481 £	844 £	1,325 £ (36.3 %)
Total	2,493 £ (68.3 %)	1,153 £ (31.6 %)	3,646 £

N = 3.646 £

Source: previous tables

The amounts counted in pounds £ (*pond Hollands*/guilders).

A second issue deserves some attention: the number and proportion of buyers from outside the city. It was quite common that non-domiciled purchasers – wealthy immigrants from the Southern Netherlands especially – invested considerable sums in urban *renten*. In 1550-1650 the number of investors in Dordrecht *renten* consisted of 23% of buyers that were not domiciled in Dordrecht. Such 'outsiders' belonged to the most important investors in urban annuities, since in 1555 almost all sums larger than 100 pounds were invested by persons other than citizens from Dordrecht. But again, there are significant differences between the issue of 1555 and 1572. While 24.2% of the buyers subscribing in 1555 was not domiciled in the city, in 1572 only 4.4% were non-resident. For Dordrecht, it could easily be determined which issue deviated from the average proportion of non-residents in other sales. Table VI shows that the proportion of non-residents in all purchases counted during 1550-1650 amounted 23%. The sale of 1572 thus deviates from the mean proportion of domiciled buyers.

TABLE VI. **Number of domiciled and non-domiciled buyers, 1555 and 1572, and the mean Number of purchases counted in 1555-1560**

Year	Dordrecht	Outside Dordrecht	Total
1555	25	8	33
1572	85	4	89
1550-1650	400	90	490

Source: previous tables

It may not be surprising that the year of 1572 deviated from other years, considering the major political developments. The year of 1572 marked the decisive start of the Dutch Revolt, and also the direct involvement of Dordrecht. The question is: what do these figures suggest? Did the start of the Dutch Revolt depress the market value of urban bonds? Were investors from outside the city more reluctant to buy urban *renten* during the first years of the revolt, being afraid that cities could not reimburse their debts? After all, the urban *renten* market depended largely on the creditworthiness of the town. Perhaps, as a result, Dordrecht's *renten* issue of 1572 was short of wealthy non-resident buyers. As was noted above, non-domiciled purchasers invested larger amounts than citizens from Dordrecht did. Their share in 1555-1556 amounted to 56% of the total amount being invested during that issue. Only one citizen from Dordrecht subscribed an amount larger than 100 pounds to this sale; Jacob Cornelisz Gijselaer – three times a councillor during 1556 – invested a sum of 195 pounds.

We do not have any figures on the proportion of the sums being invested in Dordrecht *renten* by non-domiciled buyers over the years. We do know, however, that the mean proportion of the number of non-resident buyers comprised 23% of the total sum. Presumably, the proportion of the amounts invested by such outsiders generally was much higher. So, in all probability, urban *renten* sales, at least in Dordrecht, highly depended on the large financial investments of wealthy non-domiciled purchasers.

This could also explain another remarkable difference between the years of 1555 and 1572: the high proportional participation of town magistrates of 1572 in urban rent sales. Cities being desperately in need of really big investors, possibly town magistrates were urged to enlarge their share in the issue of 1572. The local government would face huge problems in case it did not manage to raise the required sum of 20,000 pounds, thereby failing to observe it's obligations to Philip II. It is in any case remarkable that in 1572 the share of Dordrecht's officeholders and their family members was considerably larger. By comparing the original lists of names of Dordrecht's officeholders in 1549-1577 with my own list of *renten* purchasers subscribing to issues during 1550-1650, I easily determined the proportion of urban purchasers among the town magistrates. Table VII shows the numbers and proportions of urban officeholders in 1549-1577 who bought *renten*, including aldermen, counsellors, and burgomasters.

TABLE VII. **Number of buyers among the urban officeholders and their family members, 1549-1577**

	Aldermen N = 269	Percentage %	Councillors N =147	Percentage %	Burgomasters N = 22	Percentage %
B	98	36.4 %	45	30.6 %	8	36.3 %
F	50	18.5 %	34	23.1 %	8	36.3 %
Total	148	55 %	79	53 %	16	72.6 %

N = 438
B = buyers among the urban officeholders
F = buyers among the family members of urban officeholders
Source: city accounts; database municipal archive Dordrecht; Matthijs Balen Janszoon, *Beschrijvinge der stad Dordrecht* (Dordrecht 1677).

According to these figures, in 1549-1577 on average 34.4% of these town magistrates themselves were active as buyers on the urban renten market. Comparing each year separately (not included in the table), I found that these figures per year did not differ substantially. Except – it may not be surprising – for the year of 1572. That year, 58.3% of the aldermen, councillors, and burgomasters, were investors in urban (Dordrecht) *renten* in the last half of the sixteenth century. The share of family members (of town magistrates) purchasing urban *renten* proved to be only a little higher in 1572. On the whole, 55.4% of the town magistrates and their family members were registered in the urban accounts as *renten* buyers during 1549-1577. In the crucial year of the revolt, 79.1 of these urban officeholders and their kin belonged to the group of investors in *renten*. Compared to other years, this is a considerably higher proportion.

Urban officeholders and their kin were thus highly involved in urban finances, being major investors in urban *renten*. However, do these figures correspond with the actual proportion of urban officeholders in the sale 1572? In other words, was their share considerably higher compared to other investors in urban bonds? The above figures have proven only that the political elite invested their money in Dordrecht *renten*, but so far we have no indication of their proportional share in 1572. For purposes of this paper, it would be too large a project to examine other buyers than those of the issues of 1555 and 1572. So, as far as the relative contribution of urban officeholders in urban *renten* is concerned, the comparison is limited to these issues. Table VIII shows the numbers of officeholders and their kin among renten purchasers of 1555 en 1572. In this, we have used the aforementioned three categories: 1. Members of the town council and magistracy (burgomasters, councillors, aldermen, public prosecutor); 2. Lower urban officeholders; 3. Family members of town magistrates and urban governors.

TABLE VIII. **Number of urban officeholders and family members of officeholders among the annuity buyers, 1555 and 1572**

	1555-1556 N = 33	1572 N = 89
Town magistrates	3	22
Other urban officeholders	8	10
Family members	5	23
Total	16	55

N = 122

Source: same as table VII.

Indeed, these figures show that, compared to 1555, the contribution of magistrates and their family members was higher in 1572. Clearly, in both issues the circle of urban officeholders played a substantial role as investors. On the whole, 58.1% of *renten* buyers was either an urban officeholder or closely related to one. In 1572 however, their share was 61.9%, while their share was 48.4% in 1555. Thus, in the year of the revolt nearly 80% of the burgomasters, aldermen, and councillors, and their kin, were investors in Dordrecht *renten*. Besides that, in that year the contribution of higher and lower officeholders and their family members was larger than in other years. In the year of the revolt their share was larger, presumably because wealthy investors from outside Dordrecht were less prepared to invest their money in times of crisis. As rich outsiders stayed away, the local political elite had to fill the financial gap. The proceeds and duration of the issues further indicate that the sales were most disappointing. According to the patent of 1572 Dordrecht was allowed to bring *renten* on the market for 20,000 pounds. However, the town council did not manage to raise such a sum. The entire proceeds were 3,646 pounds only, even while the sale of *renten* continued the next year. For that reason the city offered town officials higher rates for their life annuities on more than one person. In the end Dordrecht had only managed to raise one fifth of the amount requested. In the following years Dordrecht hardly managed to raise the sums necessary for the costs of warfare and the tax *quota's* for the States General. Now, members of the local elite were individually requested to invest large sums in urban loans[40].

40 Municipal Archive Dordrecht, *Archief 3*, no. 2445 a-b-c.

Conclusion

By selling *renten* on the urban market, purchasers of Dordrecht *renten* made substantial contributions first to the funding of the Habsburg wars, and after 1572 to the funding of the Dutch revolt against the Habsburg ruler. This article aimed at determining the background of the buyers of Dordrecht *renten* in two specific years, before and during the revolt: 1555 and 1572. To compare these two years with other years, all issues in 1550-1650, and urban *renten* investments of town officials in 1549-1577, have been included.

Comparing 1555 with 1572 proves that the start of the revolt affected the population of urban rent purchasers considerably. While wealthy outsiders usually accounted for nearly a quarter of the investments, in 1572 wealthy non-domiciled buyers withdrew their money from Dordrecht's *renten* market. Second, in 1572 female buyers invested proportionally large amounts, and they even dominated in life bonds. Nearly 60% of these female investors were related to high town officeholders. In comparison with other years in the period 1549-1577, members of the town council and their family members were more active on the urban *renten* market. This was the case with regard to the representation of *renten* buyers among burgomasters, aldermen, and councillors, and their kin, as well as to the contribution of this group to the issue of 1572. Their share was larger in the crucial year of the revolt, because wealthy investors from outside Dordrecht were less prepared to invest their money in times of crisis. Since such investors usually brought in considerable amounts, Dordrecht largely depended on rich outsiders. To fill the financial gap, the local political elite was compelled to increase its *renten* share. In exchange they received higher interest rates for their life *renten* on more than one person. Despite their increasing contribution, the town managed only to receive 20% of the entire sum required.

RENTENIERS AND THE RECOVERY OF AMSTERDAM'S CREDIT (1578-1605) [1]

Martijn van der Burg and Marjolein 't Hart
University of Amsterdam

In May 1578 the States of Overijssel requested to float a loan of 15,000 guilders in Amsterdam. In order to resist the Spaniards, the *Drost* of Vollenhove needed funds on a short term for his province. The Amsterdam burgomasters, however, declined the request. They argued that the financial situation of their town was far from blooming. Moreover, in case investors were to be found, they were in extreme want themselves for such funds[2].

Such a request for a loan issued among the Amsterdam population, be it by other towns, provinces or foreign princes, was by no means uncommon. In the earlier 16th century, the fame of Amsterdam's wealth, backed up by a powerful market position, had radiated far beyond Dutch borders. After 1609, with the establishment of the Bank of Amsterdam, the power of its financial market was even acknowledged world-wide[3].

Yet the strength of Amsterdam's finances in the last two or three decades of the 16th century is still unclear. The 1570s had been a most distressful phase in the Dutch Revolt. In restoring Amsterdam's powers, much was to depend upon the flexibility and the wealth of the base from which loans could be contracted. In that respect, one question is particularly intriguing: Who were actually the *renteniers*[4] that supported the Amsterdam government with their loans? Did they belong, predominantly, to the political elite, as in most other towns?[5] Were rich Amsterdam widows over represented among them, as is known from other studies on *renteniers*?[6] Or did the recent immigrants from the Southern Netherlands stand out in this respect?[7] This paper aims to trace the identity of the *renteniers*, using a sample from the surviving loan records. First, though, the general political situation is sketched, followed by an overview of the annuities policy and the burden of the debt.

GAA = Gemeente Archief Amsterdam

1 We thank the participants of the Ghent conference and Henk van Nierop for their comments on an earlier version of the paper.

2 J. ter Gouw, *Geschiedenis van Amsterdam*, Amsterdam, 1891, VII, p. 318. Amsterdam was governed by four burgomasters, elected annually from the Old Council. 1 pound flemish = 6 guilders; 1 pound sterling = 10 guilders.

3 J.D. Tracy, *A financial revolution in the Habsburg Netherlands. Renten and renteniers in the County of Holland, 1515-1565*, Berkeley (Cal.), 1985, p. 60; P. Dehing and M. 't Hart, "Linking the fortunes: currency and banking, 1550-1800", in M. 't Hart, J. Jonker and J.L. van Zanden, *A financial history of the Netherlands*, Cambridge, 1997, pp. 46-47; L. Neal, *The rise of financial capitalism. International capital markets in the Age of Reason*, Cambridge, 1990; J.C. Riley, *International government finance and the Amsterdam capital market, 1740-1815*, Cambridge, 1980.

4 Rentenier = person who bought a *rente* (annuity, a typical kind of long-term loan).

5 See, for example, M. Boone, "'Plus deuil que joie'. Renteverkopen door de stad Gent in de Bourgondische periode: tussen private belangen en publieke financiën", in *Gemeentekrediet*, 45 (1991/2), p. 18.

6 See also M. van der Heijden, "Renteniers and the public debt of Dordrecht (1555-1572)" in chapter 12.

7 W. Brulez, "De diaspora der Antwerpse kooplui op het einde van de 16e eeuw", *Bijdragen voor de Geschiedenis der Nederlanden*, 15 (1960), pp. 279-306.

Amsterdam in the 1570s and 1580s

In 1572, the Revolt of the Dutch provinces against their lawful overlord, Philip II of Spain, struck out on a new path. From the month of April onwards, several Holland and Zeeland towns joined the uprising. The Spanish governor Alva managed to recapture some localities (the town of Haarlem being the most important), but by the end of 1573 the chances turned, and the revolutionary States of Holland and Zeeland strengthened their territorial independence. In the northern provinces, the Spanish continued to command a couple of strongholds only.

One of these Spanish strongholds was Amsterdam. Between 1572 and 1578, this town continued to be loyal to the Spanish king[8]. In the end, Amsterdam was won over by the revolutionaries. In February 1578, the urban government signed the *Satisfactie*, which stipulated the rights of the former elite in return for surrender. Several months later, in May, the (Catholic) town government was removed by a revolutionary town council, mainly consisting of Calvinists. This is called the *Alteratie*.

Loyalty to Spain had cost the urban government dearly. First of all, Amsterdam paid 114,000 guilders for the fortifications at Flushing in 1571 and 1572, in return for not having a fortress built at Amsterdam itself. Furthermore, the burgomasters refused the stationing of a Spanish garrison and hired town soldiers instead. These companies ensured Amsterdam's autonomous position vis-à-vis Brussels, yet they were quite expensive[9]. Moreover, Alva had requested the payment and provisioning of Spanish troops operating in Holland in 1572. Also, the Amsterdam government had equipped and financed the fleet of Bossu in 1573. Most of these payments had been financed through short-term loans, to be repaid in due term by the Brussels government. Yet in October 1573 Alva snuck out of Amsterdam, in the middle of the night, leaving many bills unpaid and numerous financiers indebted[10]. In the following years the Spanish king demanded further loans[11]. In addition, the urban poor had to be supplied with grain, which constituted another costly item for the urban Treasury. As tax revenues were contracting, a major part was financed by the issuing of a massive amount of long-term annuities. In due course, these could only be sold under pressure[12].

In addition, the 1570s were a period of severe economic distress. Many religious dissident merchants fled the town following the arrival of governor Alva[13]. The number of new citizens (still 129 in 1570) dwindled to lows of only 3 to 5 in the mid-1570s[14]. House rents fell accordingly[15]. Floods and marauding soldiers eroded the earnings of the rural population in the region. Hunger and want reigned in all the Low Countries in 1573, which was a particularly low year. The *Watergeuzen* (revolutionary

8 H. van Nierop, *Het foute Amsterdam*, Amsterdam, 2000, p. 7.

9 Around 40,000 guilders per annum, for which the town government did receive some compensation from the king, amounting to around 25-30% of the costs. Calculations based upon E. Lievense-Pelser, "De Alteratie en de financiële toestand", in *Jaarboek Amstelodamum*, 71 (1979), p 53.

10 H. Brugmans, *Opkomst en bloei van Amsterdam*, Amsterdam, 1911, p. 90.

11 See GAA 5039, *Thesaurieren Ordinaris*, no. 115 III ("Staat wat Amsterdam geleend heeft") and no. 167 on loans to the Spanish king.

12 In contrast to the voluntary character of Amsterdam's previous loans. For the loans during 1576-1577, see Ter Gouw, *Geschiedenis*, pp. 158, 207, 218; in the last year, even soldiers had to be billeted upon unwilling creditors and goods were confiscated, see p. 243; in 1577 the Amsterdam government tried to float a loan of 10 to 12,000 guilders in Antwerp, yet this attempt failed completely, see p. 186.

13 Brugmans, *Opkomst en bloei*, p. 82, notes that in 1572 only 100 *vermogende* burghers were living in the town. Several of the fugitives continued their business in towns in northern Germany. A. Pettegree, *Emden and the Dutch Revolt. Exile and the development of reformed protestantism*, Oxford, 1992, pp. 167-168.

14 Lievense-Pelser, "De Alteratie", p. 44.

15 C. Lesger, *Huur en conjunctuur. De woningmarkt in Amsterdam, 1550-1850*, Amsterdam, 1986, p. 43.

privateers) blocked Amsterdam's trade routes. No vessels came through at all during the final siege, which lasted throughout the winter of 1577-1578[16].

The surrender of 1578 entailed enormous costs as well. Fortifications had to be restored. The Amsterdam troops had to be disbanded, yet this was only possible after the soldiers had received their pay, which implied the payment of all the arrears (amounting to 35,000 guilders in March 1578, roughly a quarter of the annual urban revenues)[17]. Had they been continued in their service, the burden of payment might well have been shifted to the future. Furthermore, all hopes on repayment of prior Brussels and Spanish loans vanished.

On the other hand, the *Satisfactie* promised some relief. Former Amsterdam merchants returned to the town. The urban government claimed the revenues of the Roman Catholic institutions. In contrast to other towns, Amsterdam refused to transfer these to the provincial receiver[18]. Also, Amsterdam did not have to pay for 'old debts', the debts contracted by the revolutionary States government during 1572-1578 in their war against Spain[19].

In return, all taxes of the revolutionary provincial government were to be levied in Amsterdam too. The actual implementation of these taxes was highly contested however. The town refused to levy the new export duties (*convooien*) as well as the 100th penny upon property[20]. The first would hamper the recovery of the trade; the latter, it was argued, was used to service Holland's 1572-1578 debts, for which Amsterdam carried no responsibility at all. This arrogance in financial respect annoyed the other Holland towns, not the least because of Amsterdam's disloyal attitude during the 1570s[21].

Endless discussions followed, during which the Prince of Orange proved time and again to favour Amsterdam's position to the detriment of the other towns. In the end (December 1581), a new financial arrangement emerged[22]. The other Holland towns gnashed their teeth as they saw that Amsterdam was granted a significant financial compensation (among others, most of the revenue of the 100th penny over 1578 and 1579); Amsterdam was to retain financial control over its ecclesiastical goods; and the export duties were abolished altogether. In return, however, the town council consented to take part in the responsibility for the 1572-1578 debts. For the States of Holland, this participation opened the possibility of an improved funding of their past and future liabilities[23].

In the meantime, Amsterdam's economy recuperated. As soon as the *Satisfactie* was signed, exiled merchants returned; new immigrants bought Amsterdam citizenship again[24]. Within a couple of

---

16 On the want of bread, see I.H. van Eeghen (ed.), *Dagboek van broeder Wouter Jacobsz (Gualtherus Jacobi Masius) prior van Stein: Amsterdam 1572-1578 en Montfoort 1578-1579*, Groningen, 1959-60, p. 699. See for the decline in real wages in Amsterdam during the 1570s, H. Nusteling, *Welvaart en werkgelegenheid in Amsterdam 1540-1860*, Amsterdam, 1985, p. 163.

17 Ter Gouw, *Geschiedenis*, p. 292.

18 J.F. van Beeck Kalkoen, *Onderzoek naar de rechtstoestand der geestelijke en kerkelijke goederen in Holland na de Reformatie*, Amsterdam, 1910, pp. 262-269.

19 By April 1580, Holland's unpaid debts amounted to some 1,200,000 guilders. J.D. Tracy, "Emigré and ecclesiastical property as the sheet-anchor of Holland finance, 1572-1584", in P. Benedict et al. (eds.), *Reformation, Revolt and Civil War in France and the Netherlands 1555-1585*, Amsterdam, 1999, p. 260. At an interest rate of 6.25%, the annual interest burden amounted to some 75,000 guilders p.a.

20 On this 100th penny, see also J. Tracy, "Keeping the wheels of war turning. Revenues of the province of Holland, 1572-1619", in G. Darby (ed.), *The origins and development of the Dutch revolt*, London, 2001, p. 137.

21 Amsterdam's high-handedness had a long tradition: in 1482 and 1515, Amsterdam had refused to co-operate with the other major Holland towns in the establishment of common provincial loans. It could afford this, as its credit was strongest of all, and on its own, Amsterdam did contribute more than its share; Tracy, *Financial revolution*, pp. 58-60.

22 See for a full account of the deliberations: G. Coops. *De opheffing der Satisfactie van Amsterdam*, Amsterdam, 1919.

23 Compare the difficulties encountered by the Holland towns to get a loan of 3,400 pounds subscribed in 1581; Tracy, "Emigré", p. 260.

24 In 1578 already 170, in 1579 155. Lievense-Pelser, "De Alteratie", p. 44.

years, Amsterdam regained its former prominent position in the existing trade network[25]. Yet whether the economic revival resulted in a restored financial situation remains to be seen. In the next section, the policy of the burgomasters to reconstitute Amsterdam's credit will be examined.

The *renten* policy after the Alteratie

After the *Satisfactie* of February 1578, the (arrears in) pay for the town soldiers constituted the most pressing problem[26]. Emergency money was issued, for which the silver from churches and from the militia was used. Long-term annuities were sold to a sum of 10,695 guilders. Members of the urban government (including all former and present burgomasters, town councillors, and aldermen) were confronted with a forced levy (called *taxatie*). A voluntary loan was floated against zero% interest, which yielded around 11,000 guilders. As the town had lost its credit, the personal reputation of ten burgomasters and councillors stood as a security. These measures were not sufficient as yet, and another voluntary loan was issued, now against 12% interest annually, bringing in an additional 6,210 guilders[27].

After the *Alteratie* of May, the Amsterdam government decided not to issue any long-term annuities during the remaining months of 1578. The debt service constituted a major problem indeed. Each year, Amsterdam had to pay over 34,000 guilders interest on annuities contracted during 1572-1578. In 1577 and 1578 no interest had been paid at all: actually, these arrears were to be added to the debt burden. A telling proof of the precarious situation was the fact that four Amsterdam citizens were held hostage by other towns (one in Leiden, one in Utrecht, and two in Arnhem), as a result of the fact that some inhabitants in those towns had not received their interest upon loans for which 'the body' of Amsterdam was responsible[28]. These traditional reprisals after payment defaults were extremely harmful for the Amsterdam traders elsewhere.

Both the States of Holland and the Prince of Orange offered Amsterdam the possibility to suspend payments upon long-term annuities for a period of four years[29]. Yet suspension of payment, a partial bankruptcy in fact, was a policy which the urban government wished to avoid. Indeed, such measures might well keep prospective investors away. The burgomasters determined not to halt the payment, as they pitied the faithful citizens, widows and orphans who had invested in the *renten*. The town council proposed to pay only the interest to the small *renteniers* (those receiving annually 6 guilders and under). The treasurers and the burgomasters, however, argued that such a distinction was likely to cause much unrest among the investors. As the majority of the bonds consisted of small *renten*, this measure was not that helpful either. In the end, it was decided to reduce the interest on all 1572-1578 *renten*: for the redeemable annuities (*losrenten*, contracted at 8.3, 7.1 and 6.6%) to 6.25%; for the life annuities (*lijfrenten*) on one person to 12.5% (it had originally been 16.7 and 14.3%); and for the life annuities on two persons to 10% (it had been 12.5%). The *renteniers* who did not consent to the

25 C. Lesger, *Handel in Amsterdam ten tijde van de Opstand. Kooplieden, commerciële expansie en verandering in de ruimtelijke economie van de Nederlanden ca. 1550-ca. 1630*, Hilversum, 2001, p. 104; O. Gelderblom, *Zuid-Nederlandse kooplieden en de opkomst van de Amsterdamse stapelmarkt (1578-1630)*, Hilversum, 2000, p. 113.

26 As for threats of protesting town-soldiers, see *Dagboek van broeder Wouter Jacobsz*, p. 704.

27 Ter Gouw, *Geschiedenis*, pp. 292-294. This was still insufficient to disband all soldiers, yet further payments on the soldiers remain unclear as the accounts of 1577 and 1578 were never closed: Ter Gouw, *Geschiedenis*, pp. 446-450 and p. 348 n. 3.

28 GAA 5014, *Stadsrekeningen*, Rekening 1578.

29 Suspension of payments had also been granted to other Holland towns, see M. van der Heijden, "Urban rent sales and power politics in 16th and 17th century Holland", unpublished paper, presented at the European Social Science History Conference, Amsterdam, 2000.

reduction would receive two-thirds of the original capital in return[30]. All arrears in interest payments were converted into new annuities at similar reduced rates. The savings for the town government were considerable: 34,682 guilders, which constituted 23% of the revenues of that year[31].

Nevertheless, the debt service continued to burden the Treasury heavily. In 1582, it was deemed necessary to impose an overall cut of ten% upon the interest, with the security that installments were continued in the future, albeit at lower rates[32]. Another specific measure was to limit the prospective buyers of *renten* to inhabitants of the town. This policy reduced the danger of seizures of goods and citizens elsewhere, in case of payment defaults. The concentration on a domestic credit base was unusual: most other towns allowed non-residents to buy the urban *renten*[33].

The relationship was restored with the ecclesiastical and charitable institutions, by tradition strong pillars of urban finances, among others by returning the silver that had been confiscated during 1577 and 1578[34]. By 1585, Amsterdam's finances seemed to have regained some of their former power. When the province decided to levy a *capitale impositie* (a duty on property, for the payment of the relief of Antwerp) Amsterdam agreed, but resolved to levy only a minor part of the planned quota (almost a quarter) by way of the tax and to provide for the remainder by way of loans[35]. It was the first major issue of voluntary loans since 1578. This policy surely added to the overall debt burden of Amsterdam, to which we now turn.

Analysis of the debt burden

The public debt consisted of two parts: a floating, short-term part (in 16th century terminology *leningen* or *obligaties*, with terms varying between 3 and 18 months), and the long-term debt, consisting largely of annuities (in 16th century terminology *los- en lijfrenten*, redeemable and life-annuities)[36]. The life-annuities were generally a popular investment, allowing some provision for more rainy days. These loans were traditionally administered by the three masters of the 'Great Excise', who rendered their accounts to the treasurers. The service of the debt was funded upon the revenue of the highly rewarding urban excises on beer, wine, and grain[37]. The funding implied that the proceedings of these excises were first of all reserved for servicing the *renten*.

30 GAA 5025, *Resoluties Vroedschap*, Resolutie-boek II, 13 June 1579. The interest rates for *lijfrenten* did not distinguish as to age of the nominee, contrary to, for example, Rotterdam in the later 17th century (see Martijn van der Burg, "Burgers en bestuurders. Rotterdamse stadsfinancien in de tweede helft van de zeventiende eeuw", in *Rotterdams Jaarboekje* XI (2003) no.1 (forthcoming)).

31 Lievense-Pelser, "De Alteratie", p. 53; calculation is excluding the "saldo"; GAA 5014, Rekening 1579.

32 GAA 5025, Resolutie-boek IV 216v. 28 August 1582; the States of Holland authorised the reduction of 2 *stuivers* on every guilder, for the life-annuities 1 *stuiver*. A *korting* could also be realised by not counting 10 days (see GAA 5044, *Thesaurieren Extraordinaris*, no. 80 Rekening 1584, which states at a minority of the loan payments (410 guilders in five bonds) that these did not suffer under the *korting* of 10 days). In 1595 the Amsterdam long-term renten were still sold with a reduction (*korting*); GAA 5025 Resolutie-boek VII 106f. 27-29 March 1595: for the improvement and extension of the town and its fortifications as well as for grain purchases, a scheme to sell 160,000 guilders in annuities with *korting*, to be administered by the *Thesaurieren Ordinaris*. See also Resolutie-boek IX 22 f. 20 February 1604, 140 f. 5 September 1604, 267f. 28 April 1607, 289f. 1 August 1607: the *korting* on the *renten* is allowed because of warfare conditions.

33 See for example, L. Derycke, "Purchasers of annuities issued on the Bruges domain during the 15th century", in chapter 11; Boone, "Plus deuil" p. 15.

34 Lievense-Pelser, "De Alteratie", p. 48. In the following decades, the relationship between the Amsterdam government and the *regents* of the churches and charitable institutions was to become much more intimate [S. Stijl], *Amsterdam in zijne opkomst, aanwas, geschiedenissen, voorregten [...]*, Harlingen, 1802, VII, p. 292.

35 J.G. van Dillen, *Amsterdam in 1585. Het kohier der capitale impositie van 1585*, Amsterdam, 1941, p. xxxiii.

36 See also J.C. Riley, "Life annuity-based loans on the Amsterdam capital market toward the end of the 18th century", in *Economisch en Sociaal-Historisch Jaarboek*, 36 (1973), p. 102 n. 2.

37 Excises on beer had long constituted the traditional revenue of towns: F.N. Sickenga, *Bijdrage tot de geschiedenis der belastingen in Nederland*, Leiden, 1864, p. 57; W.F.H. Oldewelt, "De boekhouding van Amsterdam", in *Jaarboek Amstelodamum*, 63 (1971), p. 13.

In the 1570s, numerous short-term loans had been contracted. In regard of the pressing financial difficulties, many bonds were renewed regularly[38]. Initially, these were administered by the treasurers themselves. In due course, some of them were consolidated into the traditional annuities. Graph I presents the development of the annuities of the Great Excise[39]. (see also Appendix I)

GRAPH I. **Renten on the Great Excise (1570-1606)**

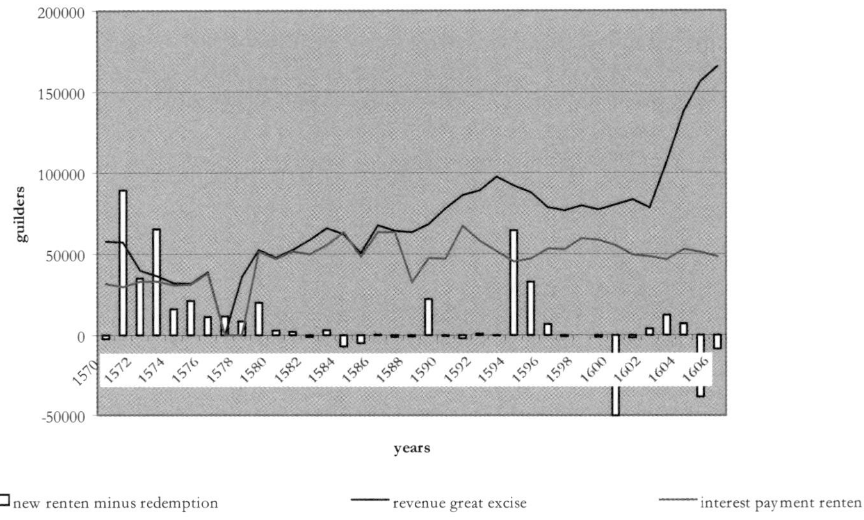

The Graph reveals the crisis situation of the 1570s. The yield of excises dropped, and for a couple of years, the office did not pay any interest at all. At the end of the 1580s, an improvement was established: the excise yield rose, partly due to the introduction of a new excise on peat and coal, partly caused by a rapid population increase[40]. At the same time, the interest burden for this office stabilised. An advantage of the numerous life-annuities was that payment halted after the death of the nominee, which implied a natural amortisation. Former *losrenten* were redeemed too. In 1609, even some 300,000 guilders were returned to the original investors[41].

Yet Graph I does not clarify the solution to the financial crisis. Almost no new burdens were added in the 1580s. Moreover, urban expenses were to rise again: 1585 was the year of the first major extension of the town, and the Fall of Antwerp caused new military and financial obligations. A new board was set up in 1584: the *Thesaurieren Extraordinaris* (thereby rendering the other Treasurers *Ordinaris*). They relieved the Ordinary Treasurers from most extraordinary financial matters of the war-

38 For example GAA 5025, Resolutie-boek IV 242f. 22 februari 1583; obligations of 1581-1582 are continued for another year.

39 These data are based on the city accounts. For an example, see H.J. Koenen, *Voorlezingen over de Geschiedenis der finantiën van Amsterdam*, Amsterdam, 1855, pp. 114-120.

40 A new tax was levied on peat and coal in 1587. Other increases/improvement of great excise taxes: wine 1589 and 1590, beer 1581, 1586, 1588, grain/milling 1570, 1582, 1584, 1604.

41 GAA 5014, *Stadsrekeningen*, 1609; GAA 5039, no. 262 Rapiamus 1609.

time situation, from most of the financial dealings with the province, and from the management of most short-term loans[42].

As such, the 1570s debt crisis was transferred to the Extraordinary Treasury. Former *renten* and short-term loans were converted into annuities. A new tax was levied with the purpose of funding this debt service: the 50th penny upon property (a house tax)[43]. New annuities were added: for the general cause (i.e. warfare of the Republic), the purchase of grain for the poor or another enlargement of the town. The traditional way of funding such expenses by way of the Great Excises Office was obviously regarded as inopportune.

Graph II provides an overview of these long-term loans (see Graph II and Appendix II).The annual interest burden was considerable: 30 to 40,000 guilders. The payments stabilised after 1587-1590.

GRAPH II. **50th penny renten 1584-1608**

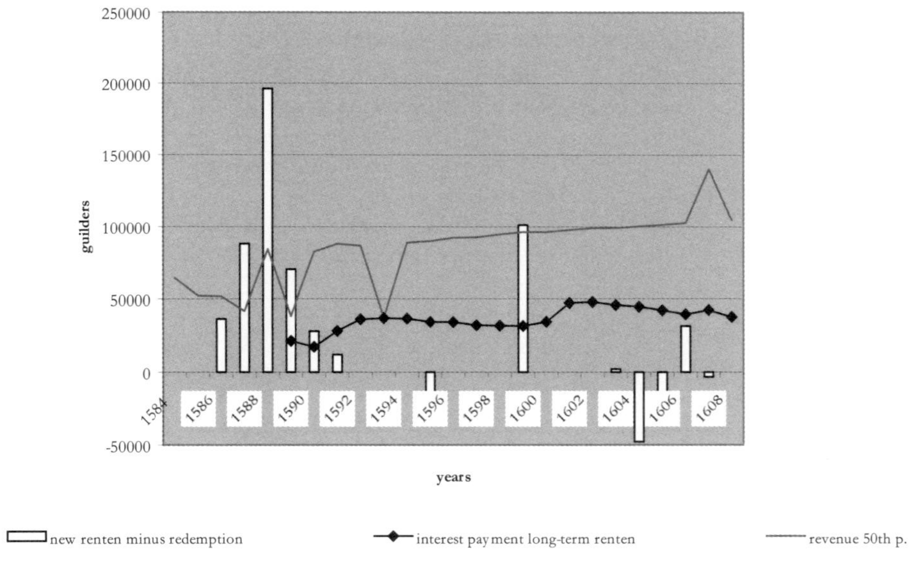

The Extraordinary Treasurers also managed the short-term loans for Amsterdam. This floating debt was hardly specified during most of the 1580s[44]. Many loans were renewed time and again,

42 *Amsterdam in zijne opkomst*, p. 390. The financial web with Holland was quite complicated indeed. Upon the request of Holland, time and again Amsterdam anticipated the revenue of the provincial taxes. For these loans interest had to be paid again. See also, for example, GAA 5025, Resolutie-boek IV 243v.: in case the States fail to provide the rentenpayment (and there should be a proper 6.25%, also for the *renten* issued since the Pacification of Ghent), Amsterdam may employ part of the Holland tax revenues. In addition, the *ordinarissen* lent funds to the *extraordinarissen* and *vice versa*. See, for example, the *renten* issued for buying grain in 1589, in which the loan was administered by one board, yet the funds were to be provided by the other board. GAA 5025, Resolutie-boek VI 265f. 26 October 1589.

43 GAA 5025, Resolutie-boek V 435f. 24 December 1586. The tax came to be levied at a double rate for most of the years since 1588, thus becoming in fact a 1/25th tax on the value of the houses.

44 This short-term debt-service proved difficult to reconstruct, as it was not always clear from the accounts whether the repayment of the capital was included in the sums or not, or how much of the sums were arrears in interest-payments, or how

pointing in all probability to some deficit finance. Around 1590 the capital sum of new short-term loans dwindled, to rise again after 1594 (see Appendix II). From then on, the reasons for new short-term loans were quite specific: for the purchase of grain, for the conversion of loans, as an anticipation of taxation for Holland, as obligations for Friesland (1600), or likewise, as short-term bonds for Emden (1599) or Delft (1604). The Extraordinary Treasury administered such loans, and received the funds the next year(s) from, respectively, the sale of grain, the *renteniers*, the States of Holland, the States of Friesland or the burgomasters of Emden or Delft. All and all, after 1590 the floating debt stood under strict control.

The *renteniers* had to come to the *Stadhuis* to receive their interest, in case of life annuities twice a year[45]. Most investors knew the way to the office themselves. Some mediation did exist: Dr. Marten Coster, one of the first burgomasters after the *Alteratie*, paid and received on behalf of numerous *renteniers*. No official fees were recorded for such insiders; neither did the treasurers receive a commission on their loans[46]. A minor sum was reserved for brokerage by persons 'from outside' the office: for example, Jan Pietersz Reaal, the Holland tax receiver for the Amsterdam district, obtained 1% upon funds mediated by him[47]. With the latter the accounts revealed a most intricate relation, in particular from 1588, when the Holland towns decided to issue loans for the province according to a quota system. Only from 1594 did Holland manage to get loans subscribed on the free market without direct mediation of its towns[48].

The revenues of the 50th penny proved quite sufficient to pay for the interest burden of the Extraordinary Treasury. A major conversion of the bonds occurred in 1586. In that year, many short-term bonds were converted into long-term ones. Arrears in interest payments were simply added to the original capital sums. In case the investors did not agree to the restructuring of their bonds, the capital invested was returned[49]. The new standard rates of interest were: for short-term obligations 8%, for *losrenten* 8.3%, for life annuities with one beneficiary 16.6 and with two beneficiaries 12.5%. This constituted, in fact, quite an elevated level; the main advantage was that the rates did not fluctuate as strongly as during the early 1580s. The rates were to decline to, respectively, 6.25, 6.25, 12.5 and 10% in 1602, which was again accompanied by a major conversion of old *renten* into new ones[50]. Only then was the interest comparable to the period before the Revolt (early 1560s), when a *losrente* had stood at 6.25%[51]. By 1625, the sums paid by the Extraordinary Treasury to the *rentenheffers sedert 1586*, as they

---

long the bonds had lasted (the terms varied between 4 and 18 months). Even within one year, the interest rates for the short-term loans varied, sometimes even from 0 to 16.6%.

45 Contrary to the proposal of the States of Holland, the Amsterdam life annuities were paid twice a year, not once; GAA 5044, Resolutie-boek V 446f. 20 January 1587.

46 GAA 5025, Resolutie-boek VI 99f. 22 September 1588. In contrast with the district receivers of Holland, who received brokerage on obligations, see M. 't Hart, "Public loans and lenders in the seventeenth-century Netherlands", in *Economic and Social History in the Netherlands*, 1 (1989), p. 121. For the grain purchases of the town in 1597, some brokerage (around 1 per mille) was paid to Pieter Stevensz, *makelaar*, and Warmen Raeffen, who had mediated for loans in 1597, yet these seem to have been rather isolated cases.

47 GAA 5044, Rekening no. 81, 1585. The Holland receiver of the Amsterdam district always held close ties to the urban government: he was appointed by the province after nomination by the town council. *Amsterdam in zijne opkomst*, 703.

48 Tracy, "Keeping the wheels", p. 144.

49 GAA 5044, Rentenboek no. 464; GAA 5025, Resolutie-boek V 478f, 17 June 1587; GAA 5044, Rentenboeken nos. 461-464. At the same time, the problematic annuities on Holland (held by Amsterdam *renteniers*), on which no interest had been received for years, were restructured and re-entered in a new register. See also Tracy, "Keeping the wheels", pp. 143-144. Henceforth the States seemed to have provided regular payment. The funds had been used, among others, for the cavalry and infantry in connection with the relief of Ghent.

50 GAA 5025, Resolutie-boek VIII 858f. 5 April 1602; GAA 5044, Rentenboek no. 469 (conversion of the obligations into *los-* and *lijfrenten*, explicitly to avoid the debt in *obligaties*: *renten* in 1603 and 1604). The debts of Holland carried comparable interest rates, see E.H.M. Dormans, *Het tekort. Staatsschuld in de tijd der Republiek*, Amsterdam, 1991, p. 26. A difference was, however, that in the early 17th century the rates declined much faster for Amsterdam. In 1623, Amsterdam's interest rates were reduced to 5%, Holland followed only in 1640.

51 Dormans, *Het tekort*, p. 26. The rate of interest on life annuities was generally twice the rate on redeemable annuities.

were labelled in the books, amounted some 29,000 guilders, declining to some 4,300 in 1655 and to 2,500 guilders in 1663[52].

Thus, in the 1580s and 1590s, numerous bonds were sold by the *Thesaurieren Extraordinaris*, on the short-term and on the long-term, to individuals and to institutions, in mediation for provinces and towns[53]. As for the loans for the Amsterdam government, we found an astonishing total of 5,795 bonds in the category 'individuals'. These were divided over short-term and long-term loans as can be seen in Table I.

TABLE I. **Amount of long-term and short-term bonds, sold by the *Thesaurieren Extraordinaris*, by destination and average amounts, 1584-1604 (in guilders)**

Destination	*Buyers*	*Term*	*Amount*	*No. of bonds*	*Average amount*
Amsterdam	Institutions only	Short*	238,993	?	?
	Individuals**	Short	858,770	4,952	173
	Individuals	Long:life-annuities	109,716	782	140
		Long: losrenten	25,391	61	461
Holland	Individuals	Short	610,218	?	?
(approx. sums)	Individuals	Long: life-annuities	155,830	?	157#
		Long: losrenten		?	434#
Emden	Individuals	Short***	119,200	80	1,490
Friesland	Individuals	Short	75,000	27	2,778

* short= 3 to12 months and under
** this category also included a minority of institutional buyers
*** renewed during 5 years
# estimation, based upon calculation of a part of these *rentenbrieven*

Source: GAA 5044, *Thesaurieren Extraordinaris*, Rapiamussen (nos. 1-13), Rekeningen (nos. 80-100), Rentenboeken (nos. 461-469).

All these bonds were sold to Amsterdam inhabitants only, and to a name, not to bearer, meaning that they were difficult to sell on the free market[54]. The overwhelming majority consisted of short-term bonds: almost 5,000, varying between 7 and 14,000 guilders. As many of such bonds were renewed, year after year, the amount is not representative for the number of investors. Yet the multitude gives an indication of the administrative task at hand. The interest had to be paid on the day stipulated in the contract: after 4, 6, 7, 8 or 12 months, at various rates of interest, with or without repayment of the capital.

The capital invested in the long-term bonds (843 *rentebrieven*) varied generally between 12,5 to 600 guilders. Life annuities predominated. According to the loan records, the investors were left the choice between a *losrente* or a *lijfrente*. Most life annuities had one beneficiary (=life annuity on one life);

52 GAA 5044, Rekeningen 1625, 1655, 1663. After 1609, major redemptions of *losrenten* occurred in 1613, and these continued on lower levels up to the early 1620s (GAA 5044, Rekeningen no. 106-113); a major conversion to lower rates of interest (5%) occurred in 1623: GAA 5044, Rentenboek no. 470.) On the development of Amsterdam's debt in the 18th century, see W. Fritschy, "Three centuries of urban and provincial public debt: Amsterdam and Holland", in chapter 6.

53 Not all accounts listed the *rentenbrieven*. The lists with names were included in the Rekeningen of the *Thesaurieren Extraordinaris* during the 1580s and 1590s; thereafter, mention was only made of the lump sum, with a notice: "blijkens kohieren", which reduces the possibility to trace the amounts of the *brieven* and the *renteniers* themselves. For the 17th century (1649-1671, inv.nos 470-490), a number of *Stadsrenten* books survived as well. They contain a small number of investors; most of them bought the bonds far before the year 1649.

54 A comparison with the urban loans in Venice is striking in this respect: there, the bonds were freely transferable on the market. On the other hand, Venice's system depended upon forced loans, whereas Amsterdam's credit market consisted predominantly of voluntary issues. L. Pezzolo, "The Venetian government debt 1350-1650" in chapter 5.

a minority (around 10% of the life annuities) was sold in bonds with two nominees. The payment of interest halted after the nominee(s) had died. The *losrenten* consisted of only 7% of all long-term bonds, yet their capital sum was higher, frequently 1.5 to 5 times larger as compared to the life annuities[55].

The loans studied here were all voluntary. More or less official pressure upon certain individuals (in particular the political elite) or institutions (churches, poor houses, orphanages) to buy bonds may have existed of course. Quite a number of loans were contracted with such institutional investors: between 1584 and 1604, approximately 20 to 25% of the capital sums in short-term bonds (238,993 guilders)[56] was bought by governors and wardens of the godly institutions[57].

One office was to stand out among all others: the *Weeskamer*. This board managed the inheritances of the orphans (*onmondige kinderen*) of Amsterdam. Their task, among others, was to take care that such funds were employed in a fruitful way, until the children had grown to maturity[58]. From 1605 the four *weesmeesters* of the Orphan Board furnished enormous sums (see also Appendix II). Their *rentenboeken* appeared separately in the accounts of the *Thesaurieren Extraordinaris*, recording interest charges on the short-term and on the long-term. Throughout most of the 17th century, the Amsterdam Orphan Chamber acted as a mediator between a mass of small investors and the urban financial regime[59]. The use of such funds was not an anomaly: in London, the very same institution was found to support the Corporation considerably in this financial respect[60].

The *renteniers* of Amsterdam

Yet without prospective investors, all policies were doomed to fail. Who, then, were the individuals operating behind the scene, who were the Amsterdam *renteniers*? The registers of Table I, with names of the buyers, proved a rich source indeed. From the loans destined for Amsterdam, a sample of one in ten was taken, resulting in 412 names[61]. The accounts stated names, amounts, dates and kind of loans. For some, the occupation was given. Women were sometimes classified as wife, widow, or daughter of [...]. In the case of life-annuities, details about family members could be got, as parents often bought a life-annuity for their children. Yet information from other sources was indispensable. In all, about 60% could be traced with some certainty in other records[62].

About one-fifth of the investors was female. This proportion is not low, yet we do know that in other towns, the proportion of female *renteniers* was higher, even one-third or half of the

55 The *losrenten* and *lijfrenten* were virtually always sold on the same date: apparently, the kind of loan was left to the preference of the investors. The composition of the loans mediated for Holland resembled those for Amsterdam. As for the sums destined for Friesland and Emden, the loans were higher, on average, as compared to the Amsterdam and Holland loans (see Table I).

56 This sum stands next to the 858,770 guilders in which predominantly individuals invested, yet among whom also institutional investors were found.

57 The *Burgerweeshuis* was always a prominent investor. See also A.E.C. McCants, *Civic charity in a Golden Age. Orphan care in early modern Amsterdam*, Urbana/Chicago, 1997, pp. 154-159.

58 H. Bontemantel, *De Regeeringe van Amsterdam, soo in 't civiel als crimineel en militaire (1653-1672)*, [G.W. Kernkamp (ed.)], The Hague, 1897, p. 119.

59 From 1623 till 1633, for example, the Extraordinary Treasurers paid between 6,569 and 169,422 guilders interest/capital on the loans mediated by the *Weeskamer* (on average 83,000 guilders p.a. during these ten years).

60 V. Harding, "The crown, the city and the orphans: the city of London and its finances, 1400-1700", in chapter 4. A difference between the arrangements of both towns was the secure funding of Amsterdam's *renten* on the excises and the 50th penny tax; in London such a system of funding did not seem to exist in the 17th century.

61 After striking out 15% double entries. Sample taken by Martijn van der Burg.

62 J.E. Elias, *De Vroedschap van Amsterdam 1578-1785*, Haarlem, 1903; Van Dillen, *Amsterdam in 1585*; J.G. van Dillen, *Het oudste aandeelhoudersregister van de Kamer Amsterdam der Oostindische Compagnie*, The Hague, 1958; Gelderblom, *Zuid-Nederlandse kooplieden*; register by Clé Lesger of Amsterdam merchants. We are extremely thankful to Gelderblom and Lesger for allowing us to use their registers; see also http://amsterdammerchants.niwi.knaw.nl

subscribers[63]. Had Amsterdam women less to say about their funds? There is no reason why this should be the case. The explanation of the difference must be sought in the large amount of short-term bonds in this sample. In most other studies, only long-term bonds were analysed. Women invested less on the short term, and – relatively speaking – more on the long term[64]. Another part of the explanation may be found in the character of some of the loans: partly, they stemmed from the 1570s when forced loans had been imposed upon the Amsterdam population, predominantly upon the (male) heads of household.

We compared, then, our sample to a direct tax record, the *capitale impositie* of 1585, levied for the relief of Antwerp, which gives an indication of the riches of the most well-to-do in Amsterdam[65]. The match was, unfortunately, not complete: of the 412 in the sample, 223 (some 54%) were found in the 1585 register. Gender was not the main explanatory factor in this regard: of the 189 persons not mentioned in the tax, only 21% were females. For a part, the non-match was explained by the difference in time: the match was 73% for those buying bonds in 1584-1586, 44% for the *renten* bought in 1587-1589, and 40% of the *renteniers* buying *rentebrieven* in the 1590s.

Still, the non-match of 27% for 1584-1586 was considerable, in particular with regard to the fact that all loans were sold to Amsterdam inhabitants only. The register might have had some deficiencies: it has been argued that several catholics were not assessed in the *capitale impositie*[66]. Another reason of the non-matching might have been recent immigration or living-in with family. Yet most likely, many *renteniers* not found in the 1585 register might simply not have owned enough property, and were excluded on that ground. The lower middle class *renteniers* may have been excluded from a property tax, yet they may well have bought a *rente*. This was not inconceivable in view of the small sums involved, or when (for instance) they had just received an inheritance[67].

Comparing the remaining 223 records from the sample, then, with the 1585 register, 5 *renteniers* were found to have become impoverished during the time of the levy itself, which was collected in two strands: they paid nothing in the second levy. Another 24 in the sample were assessed in the lowest categories of 1 to 2 guilders. In comparison with all the *capitale impositie* payers, these numbers were small indeed (see Table II).

63 M. van der Burg, "Burgers en bestuurders": 50% females; Van der Heijden, "Renteniers", in chapter 12. Investors in the provincial debt counted 41% females in the 17th century: 't Hart, "Public loans and lenders", p. 124. F. Piola Casselli, "Public debt, state revenues and town consumption in Rome (16th-18th centuries)", in chapter 7, found some 25% female investors in urban bonds in 17th century Rome.

64 Compared to male investors, the bonds bought by women were on average higher when they bought a *losrente*, lower in the case of life-annuities.The averages for females were: 170 guilders in the short-term bonds, 122 in the life-annuities, 500 in the redeemable annuities; for males: 173 guilders short-term, 164 life-annuities, 396 redeemable annuities.

65 Van Dillen, *Amsterdam in 1585*.

66 S.A.C. Dudok van Heel, "Waar waren de Amsterdamse katholieken in de zomer van 1585?", in *Jaarboek Amstelodamum*, 77 (1985), pp. 13-53. We do not agree with the suggestion of Dudok van Heel (p. 42) concerning the fact that the *capitale impositie* was voluntary – the additional term "vrijwillige contributie" had to do with the remaining part of the tax that was collected as a loan, the 1 and 1/5th levy was probably a forced duty. Also, refusals to pay were noted in the register too, which points to a forced character of the levy.

67 For comparison, lower civil servants received around 100-200 guilders in salary annually. Nusteling, *Welvaart*, p. 254. On frequent investments in provincial debt in cases of inheritances: 't Hart, "Public loans and lenders", p. 125.

TABLE II. **Distribution over seven categories of all *capitale impositie* payers (1585) compared to the *capitale impositie* paid by the buyers of bonds in our sample**

Amount paid in first levy	*Tax register*	*per cent*	*Buyers of bonds (sample)*	*per cent*
1-2 guilders	1,475	50.0	24	11.0
3-9	859	29.1	50	22.9
10-19	293	9.9	48	22.0
20-29	138	4.7	35	16.1
30-49	108	3.7	32	14.7
50-100	69	2.3	27	12.4
Over 100 guilders	7	0.2	2	0.9
Total	2,949	100.0	218	100.0

Source: Sample Amsterdam bonds; Van Dillen, *Amsterdam in 1585*.

Whereas 79% of all *capitale impositie* payers belonged to the category under 10 guilders, our sample counted a mere 34% there. Invariably, the sample was over represented in the higher categories. Obviously, about half of the buyers belonged to the wealthier group of citizens and inhabitants of Amsterdam. The person valued highest was the iron-merchant Dirck Jansz Graeff (valued at 210 guilders), one of the first burgomasters after the *Alteratie*[68]. Second came Jacob Rauwert, a catholic merchant and art-lover, who was valued at 120 guilders[69].

Not surprisingly, most of these wealthy *renteniers* – including Graeff and Rauwert – also lived in the most prosperous quarters of Amsterdam, above all in the Warmoesstraat and Kerkstraat (average *capitale impositie* there respectively 32 and 30 guilders). Although the bond-buyers in these streets comprised a fifth in our sample, they provided more than a quarter of the funds[70]. The neighbouring Oudezijds Voorburgwal counted the largest single number of *renteniers* in the sample: 34. On this canal, many artisans, smaller merchants and retailers resided (average *capitale impositie* 24 guilders). Perhaps these numbers were on the high side, as quite a number of the treasurers lived there as well[71]: their relations and knowledge of financial matters may well have stimulated neighbours and friends to buy a *rente* too.

Yet the *renteniers* also resided in the lesser quarters of Amsterdam, like the cooper Dirck Symons in the St. Annastraat or Aechte Gerrits in the Houttuinen. The Zeedijk (to the north of the Warmoesstraat) was not particularly outstanding either: the only person from the political elite who lived here was Anna Jacob Lucasdr., widow of Adriaen Pauw, one of the *Doleanten* of 1564[72]. On the 19th of February 1585 she provided the town with 50 guilders. That same day Jan Douwesz, a locksmith who lived right across the street, also lent a sum of 50 guilders.

An analysis of the occupations (known for 206 persons) might well shed some more light on the background of the *renteniers*. In Table III, the widows were included in the category to which their deceased husbands would have belonged: a widow of a burgomaster among the officeholders, a widow

---

68 Elias, *Vroedschap*, I, p. 61.

69 Van Dillen, *Amsterdam in 1585*, p. 40.

70 In the 1550s, Tracy found that many *renteniers* had lived in the Warmoesstraat as well; Tracy, *A financial revolution*, p. 172. On this street, see R. Kistemaker, *Wonen in de Warmoesstraat*, Amsterdam, 1971 (unpublished MA Thesis, University of Amsterdam, History Department). In 1557 an assessment had been made of most houses for tax purposes. The houses in Warmoesstraat and Kerkstraat were valued highest, alongside the harbour averaging 621 guilders; J.M. Verwey, "Warmoesstraat, Nieuwendijk en Damrak in het midden van de zestiende eeuw", in M. Jonker, L. Noordegraaf, M. Wagenaar (eds.), *Van stadskern tot stadsgewest. Stedebouwkundige geschiedenis van Amsterdam*, Amsterdam, 1984, pp. 64-65, 73.

71 Looking at the lists of the *Thesaurieren Ordinaris* and *Extraordinaris* between 1584 and 1597 (during which most loans were contracted), 10 out of the 55 treasurers lived on the Oude Zijds Voorburgwal (Ter Gouw, *Geschiedenis van Amsterdam*, pp. 356, 426-427; place of residence in Van Dillen, *Amsterdam in 1585*).

72 Van Dillen, *Amsterdam in 1585*, p. 56.

of a wine merchant among the merchants. A comparison was possible with the *renteniers* of a sample of James Tracy, concerning buyers of Holland's *renten* in Amsterdam during 1542-1565[73].

TABLE III. **Distribution of buyers of urban bonds over occupational categories (percentages); our sample (1584-1604) and Tracy's sample (1542-1565)**

	1584-1604		*1542-1565*	
Occupational category				
Artisans/industrial entrepreneurs	21%		20%	
(Of whom brewers)		(2%)		(7%)
Merchants	63%		47%	
(Of whom Baltic exporters)*		(8%)		(10%)
(Of whom grain dealers and millers)		(2%)		(21%)
Professionals**	7%		10%	
Officeholders, no other occupation than officeholder	5%		12%	
(Of whom with other occupations)***		(22%)		(35%)
Other occupations	4%		12%	
(Of whom skippers)		(1%)		(12%)
Total	100%		100%	
	(N=206)		(N=105)	

* Following Tracy's definition: wine and silk merchants, and other luxury traders
** Excluding 1 literary man in our sample, also belonging to category of industrial entrepreneurs
*** Including 5 from the artisans/industrial entrepreneurs, 27 from the merchants group, and 2 from the professional occupations (our sample)

Source: Sample Amsterdam bonds; Tracy, *Renten and renteniers*, pp. 169-170.

The distribution confirmed our expectation that, next to a group of wealthy and powerful investors, quite a number of the more common people had bought a *rente*. Persons in the first category of occupations included (among others) braziers, brewers, coopers, shoemakers, soap-makers, tailors and a baker. It was difficult to distinguish clear categories of (minor) artisans and (larger) entrepreneurs though: one brewer was found to pay 6 guilders in the tax records, another 80 guilders. We constructed a somewhat hybrid category of both artisans and industrial entrepreneurs, comprising around 21% of the investors.

The merchants (together a spectacular 63% of the *renteniers*) consisted of an equal varied grouping. The 10 *kramers* (retail dealers) among them varied in *capitale impositie* valuation from 2 to 15 guilders. Those under the heading of *koopman* included Gerrit van Velen (valued at 3 guilders), but also persons like the cloth merchant Jan Pietersz Coeckebacker or the merchant/soap maker Hans van Elssen (both valued at 60 guilders). Larger merchants were, in general, engaged in the luxury trades (exporting to the Baltic), the grain dealers, and the merchant/ship owners (*reders*). Jan Poppen and Hendrick Buyck were also founders of the *Compagnie Van Verre* in 1594; others (like Franchois van Hove and Geurt Dircxsz van Beuningen) were to appear among the first investors of the VOC (the Dutch East India Company) in 1602[74].

The category 'professions' (7% of the *renteniers*) included 5 chemists, 3 doctors and 3 notaries. Most famous was Dr. Marten Coster (valued at 50 guilders), also one of the 1578-post-*Alteratie* burgomasters. During his exile (1566-1576) he had been court-physician to Frederick II, king of

73 Tracy's sample, though, excluded females. The category 'occupation unknown' amounted to 49% of his sample, in our sample this percentage stood at 50%.
74 Van Dillen, *Oudste aandeelhoudersregister*. Hendrick Buyck was a nephew of the catholic burgomaster Joost Buyck who was banished during the *Alteratie*. He himself had turned reformed. Dudok van Heel, "Waar waren de Amsterdamse katholieken", p. 47; M. Sluyser and F. Thomas, *Twaalf burgemeesters, 500 jaar Amsterdam*, Amsterdam, 1939, p. 72.

Denmark and Norway[75]. In the records, he appeared recurrently as mediator for several *renteniers*, investing with or on behalf of others. Among those placed in the group 'other' (4%) were a carillonneur, two money-changers, and three skippers. The skippers were valued between 2 and 4 guilders in the *capitale impositie*.

The persons in the category officeholders belonged invariably to the political elite: burgomasters, town councillors, aldermen and some of the highest salaried officers (pensionary, treasurers)[76]. There was only a 5% in the category 'political elite' *tout court*. If we were to add the merchants, entrepreneurs, doctors and others who were burgomasters or town councillors as well (and there is no reason why we should not do so), the category would increase to 22%.

This 22% may seem high, yet from a comparative perspective the proportion is quite low, which is even more surprising in view of the financial crises of the 1570s and early 1580s. After all, when loans were difficult to get subscribed, pressure was exerted upon the local political elite to buy *renten*, in order to support the urban government and to show their fellow citizens that the investments were quite safe[77].

In comparison to the results with Tracy's sample (concerning provincial *renten* sold by Amsterdam, 1542-1565, last column Table III), the proportion of investors from the political elite had declined from 35% to 22%. Even in 1542-1565, the 35% figure of Amsterdam was quite low when compared to the other Holland towns, already pointing to a tendency among Amsterdam officeholders to leave more initiative to the burghers. In some other respects the comparison with Tracy's sample was revealing. In the 1580s, fewer grain dealers, fewer brewers and fewer skippers were found among the *renteniers*, whereas the group of merchants had increased significantly. Although part of the difference may be due to a different registration system, the 63% merchants in our sample was quite impressive indeed. The evidence points to a broadening of Amsterdam's credit base in the later 16th century, with a firm and increased role of the free market.

Naturally, not all occupational groups invested to the same amount. Comparing the *renten* with the funds paid toward the *capitale impositie*, there was a strong correlation of the tax paid and the high level of the sums invested (see Table IV).

---

75 Elias, *Vroedschap,* I, p. 20.

76 The category does not include *regenten* of the various charitable institutions who did not have a high political office. Up to 1600 or so, the *regenten* were not necessarily connected to the new regime. During the 17th century, the governors of the charitable institutions and urban officeholders were to become much more of a close-knit group. *Amsterdam in zijne opkomst*, p. 292: Burgomasters were supreme guardians of the poor and church institutions from 1598.

77 Cf. Van der Heijden, "Renteniers", in chapter 12; M. Prak, *Gezeten burgers. De elite in een Hollandse stad: Leiden 1700-1780*, The Hague, 1985, p. 120. As with all comparisons using occupation, the one concerning the political elite is the most reliable, as the details of this group are known best.

TABLE IV. **Average payment of the *capitale impositie* and capital invested (average and median) in single sums, by several categories, and average rate of interest upon the invested sums**

Category	*N*	*Capitale impositie (avg)*	*Capital sum (avg)*	*Capital sum (median)*	*Average interest (%)*
Artisans/industrial entrepreneurs	44	14	89	50	6.1
Merchants, incl. officeholders	129	27	228	70	7.0
Merchants, excl. officeholders	101	23	119	50	6.7
Professionals	14	14	42	50	5.2
Political elite/officeholders	45	41	432	100	7.6
Other occupations	8	6	83	50	3.3
Occupation unknown	206	15	73	50	5.6
Widows	22	34	98	50	5.3
Immigrants from the South	18	19	87	50	3.2
All	412	22	123	50	6.0

Source: *Sample Amsterdam bonds.*

Members of the political elite proved strong supporters for the urban finances indeed: on average they supplied 432 guilders (median: 100). They were also, on average, the wealthiest citizens according to the tax register of 1585. Indeed, in Amsterdam as elsewhere, the burgomasters furnished significant sums to the Treasury. The 12,000 guilders in short-term loans against 8.3% in 1591, for example, were bought by six (former) burgomasters, by a widow of a former burgomaster, and by the two treasurers[78]. One of the most outstanding investors was Cornelis Pietersz Hooft, burgomaster and merchant in herring, oil and grain. He was found twice to invest 14,000 guilders (with his company) in 1597 for obligations carrying 8% interest[79].

In our sample, the sum invested by the political elite constituted 38% of all funds. Merchants were a good second: on average they supplied 228 guilders (median: 70 guilders). Their investments comprised 58% of the sample sum[80]. Above all, the combination officeholder-merchant proved the strongest financial base: 34% of the sum came from them. The other occupational categories provided, both in absolute sense and in average terms, lower sums (median for all: 50 guilders).

High amounts invested, however, need not always to have corresponded with a patriotic motivation. The members of the political elite may well have provided significant sums; they also managed to obtain higher returns for their investments too. On average, their loans carried 7.6% interest. Merchants, again, were a good second: 7% was the average interest on their loans. If we were to deduct the merchants who belonged to the political elite, this rate would decline to 6.7%. Likewise, if we were to subtract the artisans and the industrial entrepreneurs who also belonged to the political elite from the category 'artisans etc.', the average interest rate would decline from 6.1% in Table IV to 5.1%. Apparently, the *renteniers* not belonging to the political elite were less informed as to the profitability of the *renten* issued.

Recent immigrants bought *renten* too. Of eighteen investors we do know that they had left recently the Southern Netherlands. Most of them came from Antwerp (thirteen). They were predominantly merchants: only one was a skipper, another a leather processor (*leerbewerker*). Their valuation in the 1585 tax record was, on average, 19 guilders; a few were assessed significantly higher,

78 GAA 5044, Rapiamus no. 2, 1591.

79 His company in herring, grain and oil encompassed, in all probability, only Cornelis and his brother Willem. H.A. Enno van Gelder, *De levensbeschouwing van Cornelis Pieterszoon Hooft, burgemeester van Amsterdam 1547-1626*, Amsterdam, 1918, pp. 5-7.

80 The opportunities to invest in other ventures were quite limited at this time: landed property and shipping companies were the most important options available. The advantage of *renten* was the secured return of interest on the investments.

as like the famous merchant Hans van Gheelen. None of them belonged to the political elite. The sums they subscribed were significant, yet not extraordinarily so: on average 87 guilders, lower than most other merchants. This may be surprising with regard to their later prominent role in financial matters, yet in the 1580s many Antwerp migrants might have been preoccupied with (re-)establishing their own business[81]. The rather low return rates (average interest: 3.16%) may also point to the circumstances of relatively new outsiders.

Another recent immigrant was Jacob Aeriaensz Block, a cloth merchant. Born in Dordrecht, he bought the *poorterschap* of Amsterdam in 1579[82]. He was one of the three Baptists in our sample. Cornelis van Tongerloo, the son of an immigrant from the Southern Netherlands and one of the leading cloth merchants later on, was a Baptist too[83]. Several Catholics were noticed in the records as well. The *Ronde Begijnhof* (a community of elderly catholic females) recurrently figured in the accounts. Two catholic *renteniers* were town councillor after the *Alteratie*: Marten Symonsz Schuytgen (compass maker) and Jacob van Campen (merchant, grandfather of the later architect by the same name). The latter was even banned from town during the tense wartime conditions of 1585. The banishment lasted only a short time, and he remained on the town council until his death in 1593[84]. One investor, Jacob Pietersz Schaap, seemed to have turned catholic in 1588 for fear of the Spanish Armada[85].

The widows in our sample all belonged to the wealthier strata, with an average tax assessment of 34 guilders. This was second only to the political elite (see Table IV). The sums provided were considerable, yet on average still below the funds supplied by the political elite and the merchants. Their rate of return was again quite average. One of the most prosperous widows was Giertgen Oomen. Her husband had been the brewer Willem Backer Zyvert Claesz, who had died in 1536. At the age of 87 years, she bought a short-term bond of 400 guilders. Her son, Willem Backer (nicknamed 'rycke Backertge') had been banned by Alva; he had died in exile, in Emden. One of her granddaughters married Hillebrant Jorisz, a herring merchant, who was also in our sample. A year later, Giertgen was recorded as paying 80 guilders in the *capitale impositie*. She was known to have left an inheritance of 48,200 guilders in 1592[86].

Giertgen Oomen was also the eldest *rentenier*. The sums provided by widows were generally higher as compared to those by the other females about whom almost no other details are known: 98 guilders against 74 guilders. The higher sums may not be surprising in view of the possible age differences. Age was a variable that was most difficult to trace though: it was ascertained for only 10% of the 412 investors. The median age at the time of buying a *rente* stood at 41 years (average 44 years). The youngest investor was only 19 years old: the dyer (*verver*) Wouter Thomasz; he became a merchant later on.

A prominent *rentenier* in our sample was Claes Fransz Oetgens[87]. He was a hard-line calvinist and eight times burgomaster between 1586-1609. In our sample, he provided the city with 200 guilders for the purchase of town-grain, at no interest, for the duration of six months. Around him a close family-network of investors could be established. His nephew Frans Hendriksz Oetgens (1558-1625) was a wealthy merchant and ten times burgomaster between 1599 and 1624. He married Alydt van Houff (see below). In our sample, Frans bought a life annuity in 1590 of 150 guilders at 16.6%. Frans' sister Aeght Hendriksdr Oetgens (1561-1639) was married to Barthelt Cromhout (1550-1624). Barthelt was a merchant and twelve times burgomaster between 1591 and 1623. In 1585 he lent the town 70 guilders for the duration of a year at 6% interest. After his death in 1624 Aeght Oetgens took over her

81 Gelderblom, *Zuid-Nederlandse kooplieden*, pp. 89, 107-8.
82 Van Dillen, *Amsterdam in 1585*, p. 106.
83 Van Dillen, *Amsterdam in 1585*, p. 66.
84 Dudok van Heel, "Waar waren de Amsterdamse katholieken", pp. 26-27.
85 Elias, *Vroedschap*, I, p. 66.
86 Elias, *Vroedschap*, I, p. 237; Van Dillen, *Amsterdam in 1585*, p. 89.
87 Elias, *Vroedschap*, I, p. 158.

husband's business, and fifteen years later, at her death, she left an inheritance of 425,000 guilders. Jan Verburch (?-1604), treasurer, burgomaster and owner of a rope-factory, was Frans Oetgens' uncle on his mother's side of the family. In 1589 he subscribed a loan of 300 guilders at an interest rate of 16.6%[88].

The family of Frans Oetgens' wife Alydt van Houff (1558-1616) was also represented in our sample. Her mother was named Machtelt Schaep (?-1588); she appears on the list of annuity buyers in February 1584. At that time her husband Anthony van Houff was still alive. She lent 100 guilders for twelve months at 10%. Baert van Houff – Alydt's sister – was married to Cornelis Pietersz Kies (1547-1606) who bought an annuity (105 guilders at 16.6% interest) in 1598[89].

Indeed, such family connections of prominent politicians and office holders were recurrent. On the other hand, we have established that relative outsiders were also in a position to buy some of the popular life annuities. For the (lower) middle classes other networks may have contributed to their investments: a neighbouring treasurer, a mediator like Dr. Martens, or institutions like the Orphan Chamber.

Conclusion

All and all, urban governments adhered to either of the two types of finance: the Florentine model, in which a narrow and closed circle furnished the necessary sums, and the Venetian model, characterised by a great number of potential lenders[90]. Amsterdam, obviously, belonged to the second sort. In accepting relatively small bonds as investments (median: 50 guilders) the burgomasters deliberatedly allowed members of the (lower) middle classes (artisans, skippers) to take part in Amsterdam's financial network[91]. As a result, many Amsterdammers could profit from the popular life annuities, storing funds temporarily away, or providing for old age, disability or sickness.

Rich widows and recent immigrants from the south provided funds too, although the restoration of urban credit did not depend on their wealth alone. With the spread of the *renten* over a large segment of the population, Amsterdam's credit system enjoyed several advanced features. The broad base from which loans could be contracted allowed flexible and steady financial policies. The role of the free market was particularly strong, among others through the significant participation by merchants.

On the other hand, Amsterdam's credit system was less advanced than that existing elsewhere in several respects. As the bonds were not sold to bearer but to one's name only, this aspect hindered their transferability on the market. With the exclusion of foreign buyers, the treasurers were restricted to contract their loans with Amsterdam inhabitants only. Also, as the life annuities made no distinction as to the age of nominee, the debt charges were on the high side, with generally twice the usual rate of interest. Actually, the interest rates of the late 16th century were quite high in comparison to a couple of decades before.

Yet all and all, Amsterdam's financial system managed well, despite these relative drawbacks. A new office, the Extraordinary Treasury, converted the burden of short-term loans and the arrears on the debt service. The new life annuities were costly, yet the death rates in most Holland towns were also high side. At the same time, the growth of the population and the extension of the trade networks resulted in higher yields of the excises.

Amsterdam's once so powerful credit, thus, was restored within two decades. Directly after the *Alteratie*, the policy of the burgomasters and the town council was aimed at restoring the relation

88 Elias, *Vroedschap*, I, pp. 120, 142, 268.
89 Elias, *Vroedschap*, I, pp. 120, 253.
90 Pezzolo, "The Venetian government debt", in chapter 5.
91 This policy of small bonds was labelled 'democratisation' of the *renten*, see Derycke, 'Purchasers of annuities', in chapter 11.

with the Amsterdam *renteniers*, by accepting small deposits and by avoiding the suspension of payments. The level of interest of the early 1560s was reached again in 1602. Well before the time of the Twelve Years' Truce (1609-1621), the financial burden of the 1570s was solved. True, because of the ongoing war, taxes were increased. Excises (the traditional way to fund *renten*) were, by and large, quite regressive indeed. Yet the new 50th penny tax was predominantly paid by the propertied. And with the restriction of prospective buyers to Amsterdam inhabitants only, many of those who paid the taxes also received some kind of interest in return. For merchants and office holders these investments carried – on average – quite advantageous rates; for many artisans and widows, these returns allowed a fair standard of living.

Much of Amsterdam's tax yields were thus pumped back into the local economy, enhancing urban strength and autonomy. This did not preclude co-operation at the provincial level, though. Along with the re-establishment of Amsterdam's financial arrangements, Holland's credit rose again. New provincial *renten* were issued from 1594. The restoration of (urban and provincial) credit and the recovery of the economy may well have stimulated one another. For many in Amsterdam (and in Holland) the secured income from urban and provincial bonds may well have levelled off the risks of war, and the risks of life in general.

APPENDIX I

Revenue of the Great Excise, payment of interest on the great-excise-annuities, sale of great-excise-annuities, and redemption of great-excise-annuities, 1570-1606 (in guilders)

Year	*Revenue*	*Interest payment*	*Sale of new renten*	*Redemption of renten*
1570	57,792	31,620	0	2,352
1571	57,162	29,772	92,508	3,192
1572	39,774	32,904	37,548	2,652
1573	36,426	33,150	71,766	6,570
1574	31,962	30,618	19,332	3,270
1575	31,716	31,044	54,768	33,642
1576	38,724[a]	38,040	36,330	25,092
1577	n.a.	n.a.	32,250	20,688
1578	35,784[b]	n.a.	10,695[c]	2,154
1579	52,326	51,528	23,340	3,300
1580	47,658	46,818	5,028	2,076
1581	52,380	51,492	2,274	234
1582	58,662	49,670	0	906
1583	65,916	55,455	5,946	2,856
1584	61,974	63,374	3,384	10,536
1585	50,340	48,224	1,848	6,738
1586	67,692	63,374	450	108
1587	64,266	63,398	426	1,596
1588	63,462	32,454	0	774
1589	68,316	47,364	22,608[d]	426
1590	77,988	47,022	0	414
1591	86,282	67,314	0	2,004
1592	89,118	58,128	3,600	2,724
1593	97,644	51,606	0	126
1594	92,167	45,258	66,743	2,204
1595	88,022	47,051	34,926	2,212
1596	78,546	53,100	8,862[e]	2,060
1597	76,722	52,775	0	768
1598	79,652	59,565	665	758
1599	77,357	58,464	0	1,099
1600	80,399	55,275	108	50,232
1601	83,507	49,441	400	2,040
1602	78,378	48,354	10,277	6,371
1603	106,711	46,435	13,742	1,395
1604	138,030	52,918	9,828	2,824
1605	156,362	50,992	0	38,785
1606	165,629	48,321	0	8,786

[a] Due to an increase in the rates; [b] Only for the year after May 1578; [c] All sold before the *Alteratie*; [d] For purchase of rye, and conversion of renten, and fortifications. GAA 5014, Rekening 1589; [e] Mainly bought by the *Leprozenhuis*: 8400 guilders .

Sources: Lievense-Pelser, 'De Alteratie en de financiële toestand', p. 42, 53-54 (for 1570-1583); GAA 5014: *Stadsrekeningen*, Rekeningen 50-73 (for 1583-1606); GAA 5039, *Thesaurieren Ordinaris*: Rapiamussen 255-291 (for 1570-1606); Koenen, *Voorlezingen*, p. 115-120 (for 1594).

APPENDIX II

Loans managed for Amsterdam by the Thesaurieren Extraordinaris: amount of short-term and long-term loans, redemption and interest payments for long-term loans, other debt charges, and the revenue of the 50th penny, 1584-1608 (in guilders)

Year	*New short-term loans*	*New long-term loans*	*Redemption long-term loans*	*Interest long-term loans*	*Interest long-term loans weeskamer*	*Other debt charges*[a]	*Interest short-term weeskamer*	*Revenue 50th penny*
1584	123,000	0	0	0	0	74,514	0	64,228
1585	176,000	0	0	0	0	51,504	0	52,147
1586	62,000	36,320	0	0	0	19,738	0	51,651
1587	71,000	88,000	0	0	0	76,514	0	41,550
1588	21,000	196,000	0	0	0	65,431	0	84,080
1589	213,000	70,250	0	21,347	0	70,449	0	38,275
1590	21,000	28,106	0	17,300	0	27,765	0	82,426
1591	0	12,000	0	28,176	0	0	0	87,945
1592	0	0	0	36,163	0	0	0	86,629
1593	0	0	0	36,942	0	0	0	36,942
1594	0	0	0	36,614	0	550	0	88,768
1595	98,000	0	23,297	34,403	0	77,500	0	89,917
1596	20,000	0	0	34,101	0	73,350	0	92,099
1597	100,000	0	0	32,015	0	41,546	0	92,436
1598	83,000	0	0	31,787	0	186,017	0	94,521
1599	122,000[b]	101,000	0	31,581	0	153,028[c]	0	96,272
1600	148,000	0	0	34,314	0	72,352	0	96,246
1601	112,000	0	0	47,080	0	96,111	0	97,688
1602	141,000	0	0	47,731	0	94,339	0	98,907
1603	111,000	2,000[d]	0	45,577	0	84,249	0	99,140
1604	58,000	0	47,703	44,486	0	51,952	0	100,097
1605	0	0	15,328	42,130	6,078	0	5,604	101,185
1606	0	41,000	9,598	39,364	9,455	0	9,598	102,435
1607	0	0	3,480	42,299	8,821	0	3,480	139,774
1608	0	0	0	37,578	8,723	0	5,131	104,493

[a] mainly interest charges on short-term loans and repayment of capital of short-term loans; up to 1590 including some interest charges on long-term loans; [b] sold for the fulfillment of the *capitale contributie*; [c] 01,262 for the *capitale contributie*; [d] partly sold in 1604.

Source: GAA 5044, *Thesaurieren Extraordinaris*, nos. 1-18 (Rapiamussen), 80-102 (Rekeningen) and 461-469 (Rentenboeken).

Glossary of terms

Bonds – IOU's, loan contracts, obligations
Leningen – short-term loans, with terms varying from 3 to 18 months
Losrenten – redeemable annuities, at generally half the interest rate of the life annuities, the interest payments halt upon repayment (redemption) of the capital sum
Lijfrenten – life annuities, generally on one or on two lives, the interest payment halting upon the death of the person(s) named in the contract
Obligations – short-term loans, mostly with terms of 6 months
Renten – annuities, loans
Renteniers – buyers of renten

Personalia

Marc BOONE (1955) is professor of Mediaeval History at the University of Ghent. His publications include *Immobiliënmarkt, fiscaliteit en sociale ongelijkheid te Gent, 1483-1503*, Kortrijk, Heule, 1981 (*Standen en Landen, LXXVIII*) (together with M. DUMON en B. REUSENS); *Geld en macht. De Gentse stadsfinanciën en de Bourgondische staatsvorming (1384-1453)*, Gent, 1990 (*Verhandelingen der maatschappij voor geschiedenis en oudheidkunde te Gent, XV*); *Gent en de Bourgondische hertogen, ca. 1384 - ca. 1455. Een sociaal-politieke studie van een staatsvormingsproces*, Brussel, 1990, (*Verhandelingen van de koninklijke academie voor wetenschappen, letteren en schone kunsten van België, Klasse der Letteren,* 52, 133 (1990)). His research focuses on urban history in the late Middle Ages, Burgundian history and financial history. He is director of an IAP (Interuniversity Attraction Pole-programme) involving research teams from the universities of Ghent (UG), Brussels (ULB), Antwerp (UFSIA), Leiden, and the Royal Library (Brussels), on the urban history of the late Middle Ages and the 16th century.

Martijn van der BURG (1980) studied Economic and Social History at the University of Amsterdam. He completed his study with an MA thesis on urban annuity sales in 17th-century Rotterdam. Currently he is a PhD candidate at the Huizinga Research Institute and Graduate School of Cultural History.

Karel DAVIDS (1952) is professor of Economic and Social History at the Vrije Universiteit Amsterdam. His publications include *Zeewezen en wetenschap. De wetenschap en de ontwikkeling van de navigatietechniek in Nederland tussen 1585 en 1815* (Ph.D. thesis, University of Leiden, 1986) and *A Miracle Mirrored. The Dutch Republic in European Perspective* (co-edited with Jan Lucassen, Cambridge UP, 1995). His research focuses on the history of entrepreneurship, technology and institutions in the early modern period and the 20th century. He is currently completing a book on the technological development of the Netherlands between c. 1350 and 1800.

Laurence DERYCKE (1975) studied history at the University of Ghent. In 1998 she obtained her degree in medieval history with a study on the socio-economic history of Ghent at the end of the Middle Ages, published as *De Sint-Michielswijk in Gent (1480-1520), een sociaal-topografische reconstructie.* Since January 1999 she has been active as a scientific researcher in the Department of Medieval History of the Ghent University. Within the framework of the international VNC-research programme *Citizens, money and town-governments. Comparative studies of the relationship between government, citizens and finances in the Low Countries, ca. 1400 - ca. 1700* she is preparing a Ph.D. on the public finances and the public debt of Bruges during the 15th century.

Wantje FRITSCHY (1949) is senior-lecturer in the department of Economic and Social history in the Faculty of Arts of the Vrije Universiteit in Amsterdam. Her thesis was on changes in Dutch public finance due to the patriot movement at the end of the 18th century. She has written several articles on the history of – mainly Dutch – public finance from the 16th to the 20th century. Under her supervision a source edition on provincial public finance in the Netherlands between 1572 and 1795 is being published in cooperation with the Institute of Dutch History in The Hague.

Hans-Jörg GILOMEN (1945) is Professor of Medieval History and Medieval Economic and Social History at Zürich University, where he has taught since 1988. He completed his thesis at Basel University in 1976. After post graduate studies at the Ecole des Hautes Etudes en Sciences Sociales in Paris, he has taught Medieval History at Basel University since 1984. He has published several books and articles on medieval credit and on a variety of other topics.

Vanessa HARDING (1951) is Reader in London History at Birkbeck, University of London. Her research focuses on the medieval and early modern periods, and especially on the interaction of government, society, and physical environment (for example, *London Journal* 26 (2001); *Journal of Interdisciplinary History* 32.4 (2002). She has recently been working on the problems of burial in the medieval and early modern city and published *The dead and the living in Paris and London, 1500-1670* in 2002. She is currently writing a short textbook study of early modern London, and working on a larger project on the metropolitan family.

Marjolein 't HART (1955) lectures in Economic and Social History at the University of Amsterdam. She has published several articles on the early modern history of the Netherlands. Her major publications include *The Making of a Bourgeois State. War, Politics and Finance during the Dutch Revolt* (1993) and *A Financial History of the Netherlands* (1997, co-editors Jan Luiten van Zanden and Joost Jonker). She is currently engaged in two major research projects: "War and Society in the Netherlands (c.1570-c.1680)" and "Amsterdam and Antwerp, Metropolis and State (c.1530-c.1830)".

Manon van der HEIJDEN (1966) received a degree in history at the Erasmus Universiteit Rotterdam. She obtained a Ph.D. in History with a thesis on *Marriage in Holland. Secular and ecclesiastical control, 1550-1700* in 1998. Between 1993 and 1998 she worked in the Faculty of History and Art Sciences at the Erasmus Universiteit Rotterdam. She has been working as a researcher in the Faculty of Arts at the Vrije Universiteit Amsterdam since 1999. She is presently engaged in research on early modern urban finances in the Netherlands.

Paul JANSSENS (1943) studied history and philosophy at the Katholieke Universiteit Leuven. He is professor of Modern History at the Europese Hogeschool Brussel (EHSAL), director of the Research Center of Public Finance and member of the History Department of the Katholieke Universiteit Brussel. In addition to numerous studies on the history of the Belgian nobility, his publications include *Drie eeuwen Belgische belastingen* (with H. Verboven and A. Tiberghien, Brussels, 1990), *Fiscaal Recht Geboekstaafd* (as editor and co-author, Brussels, 1995), *Tweehonderd jaar Frimairewet. De registratie-en successierechten in Vlaanderen, België en Europa* (as co-editor with R. Deblauwe, Ghent 1999).

Denis MORSA (1947) studied history at the *Facultés Notre-Dame de la Paix* in Namur and at the *Université catholique de Louvain* (UCL). He was assistant at the *Université catholique de Louvain* from 1972 to 1979 and then assistant at the *Crédit communal de Belgique* (which became *Dexia Banque*) from 1981 to 2003. His research focuses on urban history and the economic and social history of the Low Countries and the principality of Liège during the Early Modern period.

Luciano PEZZOLO (1959) is researcher in Economic History at the Department of Economics of the University of Venice – Ca' Foscari. He is author of a book on the Venetian fiscal system in the Renaissance (*L'oro dello Stato*, Venice, 1990) and of studies on the military and economic history of the Republic of Venice. He is currently preparing a monograph on state finance and taxation in early modern Italy.

Fausto PIOLA CASELLI (1940), professor of Economic History and Dean of the University of Cassino, Italy. Member of the national board of the Italian economic history society (1996-2000). He published several studies concerning the economic history of the Church-State in the 14th century (*La costruzione del palazzo dei papi di Avignone*; *Un cantiere navale del Trecento)*, and has recently been dealing with the history of public finances in the early modern age (*Il buon governo. Storia della finanza pubblica nell'Europa preindustriale*). As a member of a team studying the history of guilds and mutualism, he was co-editor of *Guilds, Market and work Regulations in Italy, 16th-19th Centuries* (Ashgate, 1998).

Manuel SÁNCHEZ MARTÍNEZ (1944) is Scientific Researcher at the *Consejo Superior de Investigaciones Científicas* (*Institución Milá y Fontanals*, Barcelona). After having been interested in the history of Moslem Spain and the relations of the crown of Aragon with the Nasrid kingdom of Granada during the 14th century, he is currently director of a research team dedicated to the study of royal and municipal fiscality in Cataluña during the late Middle Ages. His principal publications include: *El naixement de la fiscalitat d'Estat a Catalunya (segles XII-XIV)* (Eumo, Universitat de Girona- Estudis Universitaris de Vic, 1995); (as editor) *Estudios sobre renta, fiscalidad y finanzas en la Cataluña bajomedieval* (C.S.I.C., Barcelona, 1993) and *Fiscalidad real y finanzas urbanas en la Cataluña bajomedieval* (C.S.I.C., Barcelona, 1999); (as coordinator with D. Menjot) *La fiscalité des villes au Moyen Âge (France méridionale, Catalogne et Castille) 1. Étude des sources, 2. Les systèmes fiscaux* and *3. La redistribution de l'impôt* (Editions Privat, Toulouse, 1996, 1999 and 2002).

Remi van SCHAÏK (1950) studied history at the Catholic University of Nijmegen and the University of Ghent. He was employed at the Universities of Nijmegen, Rotterdam and Groningen and is presently (since 1995) lecturer in Medieval History at the University of Groningen. He has published on financial, economic and social history, and on socio-religious history, especially of the northern and eastern parts of the Low Countries in the late Middle Ages and early Modern Times.

James D. TRACY (1938, Ph.D. from Princeton University 1967) has been a member of the History Department at the University of Minnesota since 1966. His publications include *Erasmus: The Growth of a Mind* (Geneva, 1972), *The Politics of Erasmus* (Berkeley, 1978), *A Financial Revolution in the Habsburg Netherlands* (Berkeley, 1985), *Holland under Habsburg Rule* (Berkeley, 1990), *Reformation Europe, 1450/1640* (Lanham, Maryland, 1999), and *Emperor Charles V, Impresario of War* (Cambridge /New York, 2002).